Seaforth WORLD NAVAL REVIEW 2015

A173

Seaforth

WORLD NAVAL REVIEW

2015

Editor
CONRAD WATERS

Seaforth
PUBLISHING

Frontispiece: A panoramic image of the British Royal Navy Antarctic Patrol Ship, *Protector*, in the waters off the Ukrainian Vernadsky research base in December 2013. Although the Ukraine and its navy has suffered much from Russian assertiveness over the last year, Antarctica and the Southern Ocean remain a haven of calm from tensions impacting many of the world's seas. *(Crown Copyright)*

The editor welcomes correspondence and suggestions from readers.
Please contact him via Seaforth at **info@seaforthpublishing.com**.
All correspondence should be marked **FAO: Conrad Waters**.

First published in Great Britain in 2014 by
Seaforth Publishing
An imprint of Pen & Sword Books Ltd
47 Church Street, Barnsley
S Yorkshire S70 2AS

www.seaforthpublishing.com
Email info@seaforthpublishing.com

British Library Cataloguing in Publication Data
A CIP data record for this book is available from the British Library

ISBN 978-1-84832-220-2

Typeset and designed by Stephen Dent
Printed in China through Printworks Global Ltd.

CONTENTS

Section 1: Overview

Section 2: World Fleet Reviews

Section 3: Significant Ships

Section 4: Technological Reviews

Note on Tables: Tables are provided to give a broad indication of fleet sizes and other key information but should be regarded only as a general guide. For example, many published sources differ significantly on the principal particulars of ships, whilst even governmental information can be subject to contradiction. In general terms, the data contained in these tables is based on official information updated as of June 2014, supplemented by reference to a wide range of secondary and corporate sources, such as shipbuilder websites.

1 OVERVIEW

INTRODUCTION

'The strong do what they can, and the weak suffer what they must' wrote the Athenian general, historian and philosopher Thucydides in his *History of the Peloponnesian War*, regarded as one of the earliest surviving works of history. A stern reminder of this enduring lesson of 'realpolitik' was provided in March 2014 when Russian forces seized control of the Crimean peninsula from the Ukraine in an almost bloodless operation. Russia's military action, a response to the February 2014 revolution in Ukraine that had seen the installation of a pro-European government in Kiev, has been subject to considerable international criticism and the imposition of limited sanctions by the European Union and the United States. However, as was the case with respect to its invasion of Georgia in 2008, Russia's willingness to flex its military muscle has allowed it to achieve its key objectives, in this case the security of its Black Sea Fleet's main naval base at Sevastopol and the protection of Crimea's ethnic Russian population.

The inability of the United States – and of its European allies – to respond decisively to Russia's actions in the Ukraine has come at a time when the limitations of its global influence have started to become more apparent. For example, the Obama administration's failure to act on its previous 'red line' and undertake action against the Syrian chemical weapons attacks on regime opponents has significantly weakened its regional credibility at a time when key regional allies such as Saudi Arabia have become disconcerted about a possible rapprochement with Iran. There has inevitably been much criticism of the administration's lack of action from political opponents, as well as from some more independent commentators.[1] However, its stance arguably reflects the reality of limited public support for further overseas military adventures after the long wars in Afghanistan and Iraq, as well as the need to prioritise defence resources in an era of lower military budgets. Against this backdrop, the United States' hard-headed focus on protecting its Asia-Pacific interests through the 'Pivot to the Pacific' is undoubtedly correct.[2]

One consequence of the uncertainty over the ability – and willingness – of the United States to maintain its role of global policeman has been a reappraisal of defence plans by a number of its international partners. This has been particularly evident where the perceived threat from emergent powers is at its greatest. Whilst the United States has recently gone out of its way to stress its commitment to its military alliance with Japan, it is clear that the latter has become increasingly concerned about China's increasingly assertive stance in the East China Sea and is starting to look to its own devices. This changed emphasis was evident in a first-time *National Security Strategy* and associated new *National Defense Program Guidelines for FY2014 and beyond* approved on 17 December 2013 that will be supported by a five per cent increase in Japan's military budget over the next five years.[3] Although stressing the importance of the American alliance, the plans allow for a significant expansion in maritime and surveillance assets, as well as the development of an amphibious rapid reaction force. Fear of Chinese intentions is also driving up defence spending elsewhere in the region, most notably in the Philippines and Vietnam. Much of this is being directed towards enhanced maritime capabilities.

Table 1.0.1, outlining trends in global defence expenditure over the decade to 2013, is inevitably unable to reflect all these recent themes. However, it

Table 1.0.1: COUNTRIES WITH HIGH NATIONAL DEFENCE EXPENDITURES – 2013

RANK	COUNTRY	TOTAL: US$	SHARE OF GDP: %	CHANGE 2004–13
1 (1)	United States	640.2bn	3.8%	12%
2 (2)	China	188.0bn	2.0%	170%
3 (3)	Russian Federation	87.8bn	4.1%	108%
4 (7)	Saudi Arabia	67.0bn	9.3%	118%
5 (4)	France	61.2bn	2.2%	-6.4%
6 (6)	United Kingdom	57.9bn	2.3%	-2.5%
7 (9)	Germany	48.8bn	1.4%	3.0%
8 (5)	Japan	48.6bn	1.0%	-2.9%
9 (8)	India	47.4bn	2.5%	45%
10 (12)	South Korea	33.9bn	2.8%	42%
	World	**1,747bn**	**2.4%**	**26%**

Information from the Stockholm International Peace Research Institute (SIPRI) – http://milexdata.sipri.org
The SIPRI Military Expenditure Database contains data on 172 countries over the period 1988–2013.

Notes:
1 Spending figures are at current prices and market exchange rates.
2 Figures for China and the Russian Federation are estimates.
3 Data on military expenditure as a share of GDP (Gross Domestic Product) relates to GDP estimates from the IMF World Economic Outlook, October 2013.
4 Change is real terms change, i.e. adjusted for local inflation.
5 Figures in brackets reflect rank in 2012, revised for latest information.

does confirm the relative decline in the spending power of the United States and its traditional European allies. This reflects the rapid growth of the developing economies, as well as the negative impacts of the 2011 Budget Control Act and the Eurozone's financial crisis. American defence expenditures, particularly, have fallen significantly – approaching fifteen per cent in real terms – over the past two years. As a share of GDP, these are now below those of Russia for the first time since 2003. It is, though, important to put these changes in context, particularly as the United States continues to account for more than a third of overall global defence spending.

Perhaps more noteworthy, therefore, is the steady emergence of a number of new regional military powers, as indicated by the presence of Saudi Arabia, India and South Korea in the table of high spenders; the latter for the first time. Even here, however, the figures need to be viewed with caution. Economic growth is often accompanied by significant defence inflation; India's experience being a case in point. The country is struggling to fund much-needed modernisation against a backdrop of higher operating costs and pressure to divert funds towards social programmes. A series of high-profile accidents, most notably the destruction by fire of the Project 877EKM 'Kilo' class submarine *Sindhurakshak* with the loss of eighteen crew members whilst she was berthed at Mumbai's naval dockyard, served to highlight some of the pressures the Indian Navy is facing. Nevertheless, many of these countries have been able to fund substantial naval procurement programmes that are supported by an increasingly sophisticated indigenous manufacturing infrastructure. These advances have the potential to shift the balance of maritime influence away from the established naval powers and further towards the leading regional fleets in the years ahead.

FLEET REVIEWS

Table 1.0.2 contains the usual estimates of major fleet strengths provided by *Seaforth World Naval Review*. In contrast with previous editions, however, comparative data is that for 2009, when the first book in this series was first published. This five-year comparative period permits a more useful study of major trends, which forms the basis of the following observations:

- Whilst the table clearly illustrates the continuing theme of the shift in the balance of naval power

As part of Russia's virtually bloodless annexation of the Crimea in March 2014, a large number of Ukrainian warships were seized to neutralise any potential opposition. The most significant of these was the veteran Project 641 'Foxtrot' class submarine *Zaporizhzhya*, which hoisted the Russian flag on 22 March 2014 after an operation reportedly overseen by Russian Special Forces. The presence of large numbers of ethnic Russians in Ukrainian naval service undoubtedly helped the successful achievement of Russia's occupation, which ensures the security of its principal Black Sea Fleet base at Sevastopol. *(Anton Blinov)*

The French *Marine Nationale*'s air-defence destroyer *Jean Bart* seen operating in company with the US Navy's Aegis cruiser *Philippine Sea* (CG-55) in the Arabian Sea in April 2014. The two fleets remain amongst only a handful in the world possessing the balance of capabilities to project 'blue water' naval power on a global basis. *(US Navy)*

from the developed to the emergent fleets, it is noteworthy that very few navies have actually been able to increase overall fleet size. This is, at least partly, a consequence of high levels of defence inflation and an associated shift to smaller quantities of more sophisticated equipment.

- It also remains evident that, to date, only a very few navies have been able to afford and develop the balanced force of aircraft carriers, nuclear-powered attack submarines and amphibious shipping (as well as associated naval auxiliaries) that is required to project 'blue water' naval power on a global basis. Outside of the United States, France, particularly, stands out in this regard. The *Marine Nationale*'s disciplined approach to ensuring it remains capable of exerting such influence with restricted resources is examined in Jean Moulin's comprehensive fleet review. This has been ably translated from the French by John Jordan.
- The data also provides some tentative indications of the relative popularity of different categories of naval vessel. For example, most fleets are seeing a steady but disproportionate decline in total numbers of mine-countermeasures vessels. As well as reflecting the greater emphasis many fleets are placing on oceanic naval capabilities, this is also an indication of a shift in mine warfare technology towards systems that do not necessarily require deployment from specialist vessels. There is also a continued fall in the numbers of smaller patrol escorts. Previously associated with a decline in numbers of specialised anti-submarine frigates following the end of the Cold War, another influence is the development of specialised patrol vessels to conduct constabulary duties previously conducted by ships with a greater orientation towards front-line warfighting.[4]
- The last-mentioned point also demonstrates that there are a number of factors that such a 'high-level' table cannot adequately show. As well as the increased importance of specialised warships – such as purpose-built constabulary assets – a particularly important trend is the expanding relative significance of many of the second-tier

Table 1.0.2: MAJOR FLEET STRENGTHS 2009-2014

COUNTRY	USA		UK		FRANCE		ITALY		SPAIN		RUSSIA[2]		INDIA		CHINA[2]		JAPAN		S KOREA	
Year[1]	2009	2014	2009	2014	2009	2014	2009	2014	2009	2014	2009	2014	2009	2014	2009	2014	2009	2014	2009	2014
Aircraft Carrier (CVN/CV)	11	10	–	–	1	1	–	–	–	–	1	1	–	–	–	1	–	–	–	–
Support Carrier (CVS/CVH)	–	–	3	1	1	–	2	2	1	–	–	–	1	2	–	–	1	2	–	–
Strategic Missile Sub (SSBN)	14	14	4	4	3	4	–	–	–	–	16	13	–	–	3	4	–	–	–	–
Attack Submarine (SSGN/SSN)	57	58	8	6	6	6	–	–	–	–	20	20	–	1	5	6	–	–	–	–
Patrol Submarine (SSK)	–	–	–	–	–	–	6	6	4	3	20	20	16	12	55	50	16	16	11	12
Battleships/Battlecruisers (BB/BC)	–	–	–	–	–	–	–	–	–	–	1	1	–	–	–	–	–	–	–	–
Fleet Escort (CGN/CG/DDG/FFG)	107	95	24	19	18	15	16	17	10	11	35	25	20	23	45	60	43	39	19	22
Patrol Escort (DD/FFG/FSG/FS)	1	4	–	–	15	15	8	5	–	–	55	45	8	8	30	25	8	6	28	21
Missile Attack Craft (PGG/PTG)	–	–	–	–	–	–	–	–	–	–	50	35	12	12	65	75	6	6	1	15
Mine Countermeasures (MCMV)	14	13	16	15	16	14	12	10	6	6	45	40	10	7	20	25	29	30	9	9
Major Amph (LHD/LPD/LPH/LSD)	31	32	7	6	4	4	3	3	2	3	1	–	1	1	1	3	3	3	1	1

Notes:

1 Data refers to fleet strengths as of mid-year 2009 and 2014.

2 Figures for Russia and China are approximate.

navies. As identified in previous editions of *Seaforth World Naval Review*, some – such as Brazil and Turkey – are close to achieving major fleet status. However, there are large numbers of previous 'green water' coastal fleets that are now acquiring meaningful sea-going capabilities. Mrityunjoy Mazumdar's informative review of the neighbouring navies of Bangladesh and Myanmar provides an excellent illustration of this theme.

SIGNIFICANT SHIPS

This year's relatively diverse selection of new warship classes for detailed review has been made with the aim of providing further evidence of some of these trends. Two of these have been contributed by the editor. Italy's new FREMM (*Fregate Europee Multi-Missione*) frigates of the *Carlo Bergamini* and *Virgino Fasan* sub-types demonstrate the significant increase in sophistication and power provided by new generations of surface ships. Equipped with advanced area air-defence systems, guns capable of firing the next generation of guided munitions and a comprehensive range of stealth features, they provide a quantum leap in capability over the thirty-year-old ships of the *Maestrale* class they are intended to replace. Meanwhile, Ireland has recent taken delivery of *Samuel Beckett*, the first of a new class of offshore patrol vessel designed to police the country's economic interests in the often harsh weather conditions of the North Atlantic Ocean. Typical of a new breed of constabulary vessels built largely to commercial standards and shipping a relatively light armament, she is equipped with sophisticated propulsion and communications systems to facilitate effective oceanic patrol missions.

Another aspect of innovation is represented by Guy Toremans' latest contribution to *Seaforth World Naval Review*. This describes the Royal Norwegian Navy's *Skjold* class littoral corvettes. Specifically designed for anti-surface warfare in coastal areas, they are based on an air-cushion catamaran hull form that facilitates speedy and stable operation in the often shallow waters of the littoral. As such, they

The new Irish offshore patrol vessel *Samuel Beckett* was commissioned in 2014. She is typical of a new breed of sophisticated constabulary vessels built to commercial standards that are much more effective than the obsolescent front-line warships often previously assigned to such roles. *(Irish Defence Forces)*

The Royal Norwegian Navy's *Skjold* class fast attack craft/littoral corvettes provide an effective anti-surface warship capability to defend Norway's long coastline at a time when tensions with neighbouring Russia have increased. This photograph shows the lead ship operating off the Norwegian coast in January 2014. *(Torgeir Haugaard/ Norwegian Armed Forces)*

An expansion of Chinese naval capabilities against a backdrop of competing territorial claims has spurred increased investment by other regional naval powers. Amongst the most prominent new warships being acquired is Japan's helicopter carrier *Izumo* (DDH-183), which was launched on 6 August 2013. *(JMSDF)*

Another country in the Asia-Pacific region expanding naval aviation capabilities is Australia, which is shortly due to take delivery of *Canberra*, the first of two new *Juan Carlos I* type amphibious assault ships. In May 2014, Australia's new prime and defence ministers both revealed that the F-35B variant of the Joint Strike Fighter might be acquired to operate from the ships. *(Royal Australian Navy)*

are particularly well-suited to protecting Norway's lengthy coastline at a time when the post-Cold War thaw in relations with neighbouring Russia is becoming somewhat less temperate. All six ships of the class are now in service after a lengthy development and commissioning process; with a maximum speed in excess of 60 knots they are claimed to be the fastest sea-going warships in the world.

Meanwhile, the use of a commercial design to meet a military requirement is further illustrated by Scott Truver's review of the US Navy's new mobile landing platform, *Montford Point* (MLP-1). The US Navy has become increasingly innovative in adapting commercial concepts for military applications in recent years, most notably with respect to its Littoral Combat Ships and Joint High-Speed Vessels. However, *Montford Point* takes this approach to an entirely new level. An adaptation of a United States oil tanker design, she is intended to act as a giant floating offshore platform to assist the transhipment of troops and equipment from supply ships to landing craft and other vessels in support of amphibious operations. A modified variant currently under construction will act as a floating base for personnel, helicopters and small boats conducting special operations or mine-countermeasures missions. The approach allows purpose-built warships to be released for other missions, whilst the ships themselves cost a fraction of a warship of equivalent size.

TECHNOLOGICAL DEVELOPMENTS

The concluding section commences, as usual, with David Hobbs' wide-ranging overview of developments in the world of naval aviation. The significance of the Asia-Pacific region to global maritime developments is, again, brought to the forefront, both by the launch of Japan's carrier-type helicopter carrying destroyer *Izumo* (DDH-183) on 6 August 2013 and the commencement of sea trials by the Royal Australian Navy's new amphibious assault ship *Canberra* in the following March. Both ships would be capable of operating the new F-35B STOVL (short take-off and vertical landing) variant of the Lightning II Joint Strike Fighter and, in a notable development, Australia's new defence minister, David Johnston, revealed in May 2014 that acquisition of the type was under consideration.[5] A positive decision would result in Australia being able to operate fast jets at sea for the first time since the carrier *Melbourne* was decommissioned in 1982.

Meanwhile, Norman Friedman continues his series of technological reviews with a detailed examination of recent developments in the area of mine countermeasures. Mine warfare continues to exert a significant influence on naval operations and forms a key part of anti-access/aerial-denial (A2/AD) strategies adopted by potential United States' adversaries such as Iran. A key limitation on traditional mine-countermeasures operations has been the difficulty associated with the speedy deployment of relevant assets to where they are needed. The US Navy, particularly, has been investing significant sums in developing special mine-countermeasures modules that can be swiftly shipped by a range of vessels to the area of operations.

The final chapter, produced by distinguished naval academic and writer Ian Buxton in a first-time contribution to *Seaforth World Naval Review*, looks

The Indian 'Kilo' class submarine *Sindhurakshak* was destroyed by fire on 14 August 2013 in one of a series of serious accidents impacting the Indian Navy over the last year that demonstrates the path towards building effective naval capabilities can be lengthy and costly. This photograph was taken on 20 February 2013 at Portsmouth, United Kingdom when the submarine made a port call whilst returning to India from refurbishment in Russia. *(Conrad Waters)*

at the disposal of warships after final decommissioning. There is an ongoing need to recycle warships at the end of their service lives but heightened environmental awareness means that disposal techniques have changed significantly since the mass scrapping programmes for First and Second World War warships. Nevertheless, the aim remains to achieve the maximum recovery possible of re-useable materials; over ninety-five per cent of a ship's final displacement is usually recycled.

SUMMARY

In summing up, it is evident that the last twelve months have seen some interesting and unexpected developments with respect to the world's navies. True, the overall emphasis on the Asia-Pacific region continues, with ongoing sabre-rattling between China and a number of its neighbours continuing to spur investment in naval and other military capabilities. However, Russian actions in the Ukraine have strengthened perceptions of its resurgent influence and suggest that previous assumptions that European waters will remain tranquil cannot be taken for granted. Elsewhere, India's *annus horriblis* has provided a timely reminder that the path towards building effective naval capabilities is likely to be lengthy and costly, even when economic fundamentals are favourable.

ACKNOWLEDGEMENTS

The continued success of *Seaforth World Naval Review* as it enters its sixth year of publication is dependent on a large, if informal, team. The support of publishing editor Robert Gardiner and designer Steve Dent is always critical. The contribution of John Jordan, this year joined by Ian Johnston, in supplying high-quality line drawings is also worthy of particular note. The evident quality of an evolving list of expert writers needs no further commendation to regular readers but the willingness of Anton Blinov, Derek Fox, Bruno Huriet, Jim Lennie, Bernard Prézelin and Devrim Yaylali to supplement defence and industry sources in providing comprehensive photographic coverage merits special mention. Amongst the latter, Gillian Churchill of BAE Systems, Emmanuel Guadez of DCNS, Captain Keizo Kitagawa of the JMSDF, Esther Benito Lope of Navantia, Edward Szeto of VT Systems and Frank van de Wiel of Thales Nederland have gone out of their way to be helpful. Finally, my wife Susan's support in completing all initial proof-reading deserves continued acknowledgement.

Comments and criticisms from readers are always appreciated; please direct them for my attention to info@seaforthpublishing.com

Conrad Waters, Editor
30 June 2014

Notes

1. Much of the criticism appears to have been directed not so much at the failure to take action as at President Obama's seemingly unscripted initial 'red line' observation in August 2012, which inferred that US military action would follow substantial use of chemical weapons by the Syrian regime. This, the argument goes, put United States' credibility on the line when chemical weapons were actually used. A good summary of this contention was contained in an article by Peter Baker, Mark Landler, David E Sanger and Anne Bernard entitled 'Off-the-Cuff Obama Line Put U.S. in Bind on Syria', *The New York Times* – 4 May 2013 (New York, *The New York Times*, 2013).

2. It is worth noting that the development of shale gas reserves in the United States, potentially returning the country to energy self-sufficiency within the next ten to twenty years, will inevitably have a significant impact on future American foreign policy. Most notably, it is likely to leave it far less reliant on energy imported from the Middle East, making maintenance of US influence in the region less important than hitherto. This scenario adds further impetus to the logic of shifting limited United States' military assets to protecting key economic interests in the Asia Pacific region.

3. For further reading see *National Security Strategy December 17, 2013* and *National Defense Program Guidelines for FY2014 and beyond* (both: Tokyo, Government of Japan, 2013). English translations of both can be found on the President of Japan and His Cabinet's website at http://japan.kantei.go.jp/96_abe/documents/2013/index.html

4. The development of modern patrol vessels was contained in the editor's 'Modern European Offshore Patrol Vessels', *Warship 2013* (London, Conway, 2013), pp.78–93.

5. The news was first revealed in an article by Nick Butterly entitled 'Jump jets on Defence radar' published in *The West Australian* – 17 May 2014 (Perth, West Australian Newspapers Ltd, 2014).

2.1 REGIONAL REVIEW

Author:
Conrad Waters

NORTH AND SOUTH AMERICA

INTRODUCTION

As always, any review of naval developments in the Americas needs to be set against the backdrop of the complex and ever-evolving political debate over the United States defence budget. Overall US defence expenditure reached a peak of just over US$690bn in FY2010. Of this amount, some US$528bn related to core defence spending, with most of the balance allocated to overseas contingency operations (OCO), essentially the cost of conducting wars in Afghanistan, Iraq and elsewhere as part of the 'war against terror'. The total has since been falling steeply, reaching a seven-year low (even before adjusting for the effects of inflation) of US$578bn in FY2013. US$496bn of this related to the core budget. Much of this decline can be attributed to a natural reduction in OCO allocations as active overseas missions have wound down. However, the core defence budget has also been impacted by the large deficit between overall US government spending and income, resulting in the process known as sequestration under the 2011 Budget Control Act.[1] The impact of this process has been severe; the proposed FY2013 Presidential Budget Request for defence was US$614bn but sequestration reduced this amount by US$36bn. The equivalent impact on the US Navy was a fall in planned spending from US$174bn to an actual amount of US$163bn; a cut of a little over six per cent. Failure to plan for the reduction meant that its impact was particularly heavily felt on operational deployments, as well as training and support activities.

Indeed, an unusual feature of the sequestration debate has been the US defence establishment's apparent unwillingness to accept that budget controls would actually be implemented. This was reflected in the FY2014 budget request, submitted in April 2013, which effectively sought to restore spending to levels proposed in the previous year. A lengthy and politically fraught debate was eventually resolved by enactment of the 2013 Bipartisan Budget Act in December 2013. This provided some short-term relief to sequestration in FY2014 and FY2015 in return for a lengthier period of savings.[2] The compromise left the core defence budget of US$496bn little changed from FY2013. This compared with an original proposal of US$527bn but a cap under the previous scheme of c.US$475bn. It also allowed the submission of a FY2015 budget – requesting further flat base spending of US$496bn – that was finally aligned with the (revised) sequestration provisions. The budget was released contemporaneously with the 2014 Quadrennial Defense Review. This embodied the shift from land forces sized for prolonged stabilisation operations towards aviation and naval capabilities required to support the rebalancing to Asia-Pacific set out in the previous 2012 Presidential Strategic Guidance.[3] As such, investment in areas such as shipbuilding and strategic aviation assets have been prioritised over, for example, troop numbers and tactical aircraft.

Unfortunately, the military is still not fully aligned with the Budget Control Act provisions. Realisation of its objectives still involves expenditure in the following four years (FY2016 to FY2019) of the medium-term budget plan that is some US$115bn over the level allowed for by sequestration. As such, failure to agree further relaxation would result in a further curtailment of US military forces, including a reduction from forty-four to thirty-six ships in the five-year shipbuilding programme. There is particular uncertainty over the future of the aircraft carrier *George Washington* (CVN-73), which is shortly to enter a costly mid-life refuelling and overhaul. Failure to authorise the refit, which will now be determined in FY2016, would permanently reduce the US Navy's carrier force to ten ships.[4]

The budget backdrop has given additional prominence to a US Navy decision to change the way it counts ships in its front-line battle force for the first time since 1981. The change, which allows non-combatant ships required by forward commanders and smaller ships that are forward deployed to be included in the count, will increase battle force numbers by a net ten ships in FY2015. It has also been suggested the changes might allow some ships that are maintained in a high level of reserve to remain in the battle force. As observed by Ronald O'Rourke, the Congressional Research Service's naval analyst, 'Skeptics might … argue that these changes are being proposed at a time that the Navy is proposing to remove ships from service as a cost-saving measure, and that the changes, if implemented, would have the effect of obscuring the resulting reduction in the size of the Navy.'[5]

A close-up view of the US Navy aircraft carrier *George Washington* (CVN-73) taken in November 2013 during exercises in the Philippine Sea. The US military's 'Pivot to the Pacific' should result in an increased naval presence in the region. However, *George Washington*'s future is in doubt because funding for her mid-life refuelling and refit may not be available. *(US Navy)*

Table 2.1.1: FLEET STRENGTHS IN THE AMERICAS – LARGER NAVIES (MID 2014)

COUNTRY	ARGENTINA	BRAZIL	CANADA	CHILE	ECUADOR	PERU	USA	VENEZUELA
Aircraft Carrier (CVN/CV)	–	1	–	–	–	–	10	–
Strategic Missile Submarine (SSBN)	–	–	–	–	–	–	14	–
Attack Submarine (SSN/SSGN)	–	–	–	–	–	–	58	–
Patrol Submarine (SSK)	3	5	4	4	2	6	–	2
Fleet Escort (CG/DDG/FFG)	4	9	15	8	2	8	95	4
Patrol Escort/Corvette (FFG/FSG/FS)	9	5	–	–	6	–	4	–
Missile Armed Attack Craft (PGG/PTG)	2	–	–	5	3	6	–	6
Mine Countermeasures Vessel (MCMV)	–	6	12	–	–	–	13	–
Major Amphibious Units (LHD/LPD/LPH/LSD)	–	1	–	1	–	–	32	–

A Canadian CH-124 Sea King crew member prepares to make a mail drop to the Canadian submarine *Victoria*, the former British Royal Navy *Unseen*, during exercises off the coast of British Columbia in May 2013. Whilst an improved maintenance regime is starting to produce improvements, *Victoria* was the only one of Canada's four submarines to be fully operational as of mid-2014. *(Canadian Forces)*

MAJOR N. AMERICAN NAVIES – CANADA

The last year has seen the Royal Canadian Navy struggle to maintain the operational effectiveness of significant numbers of increasingly elderly ships and aircraft pending implementation of long-delayed replacement programmes. Whilst there has been no change to equipment numbers set out in Table 2.1.2, the headlines arguably mask an increasingly critical situation caused by a combination of accidents and obsolescence. Canada's National Shipbuilding Procurement Strategy (NSPS), first announced in June 2010 and under which lead yards were selected in October 2011, offers the prospect of a long-term solution to the navy's problems within the framework of a strategic vision for the country's maritime sector. However, overall progress with the strategy is proceeding at a relatively pedestrian rate in spite of the short-term problems that this creates.

The most critical requirement is probably the replacement of Canada's two *Protecteur* class replenishment oilers by new JSS joint support ships, which has been under discussion since 2004. In June 2013, it was announced that ThyssenKrupp Marine System's Type 702 *Berlin* class design had been selected for local construction, which will be carried out by Seaspan Marine Corporation's Vancouver Shipyards in line with the NSPS. They will be named *Queenstown* and *Chateauguay* in commemoration of victories against the United States in the War of 1812. In spite of being given priority over a polar icebreaker that has also been allocated to the yard, fabrication of the lead ship will not begin until late 2016. This suggests delivery from around 2019; at least two years after the *Protecteur* class were due to be retired. Unfortunately, the 45-year-old *Protecteur* suffered a major engine room fire whilst operating in the Pacific in February 2014. It may well not be economic to repair the damage. This will leave the navy increasingly reliant on logistical support from allied fleets until the new ships arrive.

The front-line surface fleet is also under considerable pressure. The twelve *Halifax* class frigates are in the middle of the combined *Halifax* Class Modernisation/Frigate Life Extension (HCM/FELEX) programme, reducing available numbers. The three remaining *Iroquois* class destroyers are all well over forty years old, with *Iroquois* herself reportedly docked for structural assessment in May 2014 after corrosion was detected in her machinery spaces.[6] Both classes will eventually be replaced by a single-class surface combatant comprising fifteen units that will be allocated to Halifax-based Irving Shipbuilding. It is hoped that orders will be placed in time for the first ship to be delivered by 2023. In the meantime, the yard is working on the detailed design of a new class of Arctic patrol vessels that should start construction in 2015. The JSS and

The Military Sealift Command's ocean-going tug *Sioux* (T-AFT-171) pictured towing the disabled Canadian replenishment oiler *Protecteur* into Pearl Harbor on 6 March 2014. The veteran Canadian ship suffered an engine room fire whilst operating in the Pacific in February 2014 and it may not prove economic to repair her, highlighting the need for swift delivery of the replacement *Queenstown* class. *(US Navy)*

Table 2.1.2: CANADIAN NAVY: PRINCIPAL UNITS AS AT MID 2014

TYPE	CLASS	NUMBER	TONNAGE	DIMENSIONS	PROPULSION	CREW	DATE
Principal Surface Escorts							
Destroyer – DDG	**IROQUOIS**	3	5,100 tons	130m x 15m x 5m	COGOG, 29 knots	280	1972
Frigate – FFG	**HALIFAX**	12	4,800 tons	134m x 16m x 5m	CODOG, 29 knots	225	1992
Submarines							
Submarine – SSK	**VICTORIA** (UPHOLDER)	4	2,500 tons	70m x 8m x 6m	Diesel-electric, 20+ knots	50	1990

Arctic patrol vessel programmes have both been criticised for their high costs compared with similar international projects.[7]

The need to maintain elderly equipment in service extends to the navy's helicopter fleet, where ongoing delays to the CH-148 Cyclone project mean that 1960s vintage CH-124 Sea Kings continue to operate. The Canadian government reportedly came close to cancelling the whole troubled project in 2013 but finally announced it would press on with the acquisition in January 2014. A revised plan should see interim specification Cyclones start replacing the Sea Kings in 2015 prior to the delivery of fully-capable helicopters in 2018.

News flow with respect to the navy's *Victoria* (former British Royal Navy *Upholder*) class submarines has been more mixed. On the positive side, maintenance arrangements for the boats now appear to be working satisfactorily and a five-year extension option for the *Victoria* In-Service Support Contract was exercised with Babcock Canada in June 2013. As of mid-2014, *Chicoutimi* (the former *Upholder*) was close to concluding an extended docking work period at Victoria Shipyards after returning to the water on 26 November 2013. Completion will mark the boat's return to the fleet for the first time she suffered a fatal fire on her delivery voyage from the United Kingdom in October 2004. *Corner Brook* will be the next submarine to undergo a scheduled docking period, during which time damage caused by an underwater grounding in June 2011 will be repaired. Less positively, *Windsor* has also recently commenced work in Halifax for replacement of a defective generator that was discovered only shortly after her own extended docking period was completed in 2012 and will not return to sea until the end of 2014. This leaves the Pacific-based *Victoria* as the only member of the class that is currently fully operational.

MAJOR N. AMERICAN NAVIES – USA

Overall US Navy fleet strength continues to be guided by the Navy Combatant Force Structure Requirement that was released in 2013.[8] Based on the 2012 Presidential Strategic Guidance, this establishes a target of 306 front-line combatants; a slight reduction on previous plans. As always, the actual situation is significantly behind the target, with 288 ship battle forces reported as being in service as of mid-2014. This figure itself benefits from the addition of a net ten ships under the revised counting guidance issued on 7 March 2014 referenced in the introduction that allows a number of additional small surface combatants and support ships to be included within the total. The number of ships in service is, however, scheduled to grow strongly over the next few years after reaching a low point in FY2015. This reflects previous Congressional refusal to permit early retirement of older cruisers and amphibious ships as well as the impact of series-production of the new Littoral Combat Ships. As such, as demonstrated by Table 2.1.3, the navy will achieve the targeted force level by FY2019. The headline figures do, however, arguably reflect something of a 'smoke and mirrors' approach to overall accounting. In addition to benefitting from the changed counting rules, the totals include eleven *Ticonderoga* (CG-47) class cruisers that will be held in reserve pending planned modernisation. Inevitably, the changes have resulted in questions as to whether the battle force numbers have the same quality as before. More fundamentally, perhaps,

Table 2.1.3: REVISIONS TO PROJECTED US NAVY BATTLE FORCE LEVELS: FY2015 PLAN COMPARED TO FY2014 PLAN

SHIP TYPE	PLAN[1]	FY2015		FY2016		FY2017		FY2018		FY2019		FY2020	
FY2014 Plan/**FY2015 PLAN**[2]		2014	**2015**[3]	2014	**2015**	2014	**2015**	2014	**2015**	2014	**2015**	2014	**2015**
Aircraft Carrier (CVN)	11 (11)	10	**10**	11	**11**	11	**11**	11	**11**	11	**11**	11	**11**
Strategic Submarine (SSBN)	12 (12)	14	**14**	14	**14**	14	**14**	14	**14**	14	**14**	14	**14**
Attack Submarine (SSGN/SSN)	48 (52)	59	**58**	57	**57**	54	**54**	56	**56**	56	**55**	53	**53**
Fleet Escort (CG/DDG)	88 (94)	78	**85**	82	**88**	83	**90**	84	**92 (91)**	86	**93**	87	**95**
Patrol Escort/MCMV (FFG/LCS/MCMV)	52 (55)	23	**19** (26)	27	**23** (30)	29	**27** (34)	33	**31** (38)	38	**35** (40)	37	**36** (37)
Amphibious Vessel (LHA/LHD/LPD/LSD)	33 (33)	28	**30**	29	**31**	30	**32**	31	**33**	31	**33**	31	**33**
Other – Logistics & Support Ships	62 (56)	58	**58** (61)	60	**56** (59)	62	**58** (61)	62	**58** (61)	64	**60** (63)	62	**62** (65)
TOTAL	306 (313)	270	274 (284)	280	280 (290)	283	286 (296)	291	295 (304)	300	301 (309)	295	304 (308)

Notes:

1 Plan figures relate to the Force Structure Requirement released in January 2013. The plan figures in brackets relates to the 313 ship requirement identified in the 2005 Force Structure Assessment and revalidated in 2010.

2 These figures are derived from the Long Range Plan for Construction of Naval Vessels produced for FY2014 and FY2015, the latter obtained from secondary sources.

3 Figures in brackets are based on new ship battle force accounting rules introduced in March 2014 (SECNAV Instruction 5030.8B).

plans are still being made on the assumption that current budget caps will eventually be rolled back.

One undoubtedly positive feature is the continued high priority being given to shipbuilding, which remains in line with the c. eight to nine ships p.a. required average to maintain a 306-ship fleet on the basis of an assumed ship life of some thirty-five years. The five-year shipbuilding plan contained in the FY2015 budget and set out in Table 2.1.4 shows little overall change from that proposed in FY2014. There is a maintained 'drumbeat' of two units each year for both *Arleigh Burke* (DDG-51) class destroyers and *Virginia* (SSN-774) class submarines in line with multi-year procurement contracts. A reduced Littoral Combat Ship 'buy' in FY2015 is more than counterbalanced by high numbers in later years. The success of the mobile landing platform concept is reflected in the order for an additional afloat forward staging base variant in FY2017 but the LSD-X replacement amphibious ship has been deferred for the third consecutive year. Greater detail of developments with respect to specific ship categories is provided below.

Table 2.1.4: USN FY2015 FIVE YEAR SHIPBUILDING PLAN (FY2015-FY2019)

SHIP TYPE	FY2014: ACTUAL	FY2015: REQUEST	FY2016: PLAN	FY2017: PLAN	FY2018: PLAN	FY2019: PLAN
Aircraft Carrier (CVN-78)	Nil (Nil)	Nil (Nil)	Nil (Nil)	Nil (Nil)	1 (1)	Nil (Nil)
Attack Submarine (SSN-774)	2	2 (2)	2 (2)	2 (2)	2 (2)	2 (2)
Destroyer (DDG-51)	1	2 (2)	2 (2)	2 (2)	2 (2)	2 (2)
Littoral Combat Ship (LCS-1/2)	4	3 (4)	3 (2)	3 (2)	3 (2)	2 (3)
Amphibious Assault Ship (LHA-6)	Nil	Nil (Nil)	Nil (Nil)	1 (1)	Nil (Nil)	Nil (Nil)
Dock Landing Ship (LSD-X)	Nil	Nil (Nil)	Nil (Nil)	Nil (Nil)	Nil (Nil)	Nil (1)
Mobile Landing Platform (MLP-1)	1	Nil (Nil)	Nil (Nil)	1 (Nil)	Nil (Nil)	Nil (Nil)
Replenishment Oiler (TAO(X))	Nil	Nil (Nil)	1 (1)	Nil (Nil)	1 (1)	1 (1)
Fleet Tug (TAFT)	Nil	Nil (Nil)	Nil (Nil)	2 (2)	1 (1)	1 (1))
Total	**8**	**7 (8)**	**8 (7)**	**11 (9)**	**10 (9)**	**8 (10)**

Notes:
1 Figures in brackets relate to previous FY2014 Budget Request and Shipbuilding Plan.
2 Figures relate to Ship Battle Forces – other ships are not included.
3 The FY2014 and FY2017 MLP mobile landing platform ships will be built as afloat forward staging base (AFSB) variants.

Aircraft Carriers: The first of the US Navy's new generation of aircraft carriers, *Gerald R Ford* (CVN-78), was christened at Huntington Ingalls Industries' (HHI's) Newport News shipyard on 9 November 2013 following flood-out of her building dock in the previous month. Around seventy per cent complete at launch, she was subsequently towed down the James River to her fitting-out berth for further work and testing prior to her planned delivery to the US Navy in the first half of 2016. Concerns remain about the technical maturity of the significant amount of new equipment incorporated into the design, with only seven of the thirteen critical technologies used by the ship regarded as fully mature by March 2014. More positively, there has been little further upward movement in projected total procurement costs of some US$12.9bn over the last year, of which around US$3.3bn related to design and development expenses for the entire class. Work is also ramping up on second-of-class *John F Kennedy* (CVN-79) in advance of award of a formal construction contract – delayed to incorporate process

Two images of Raytheon's new AMDR Air and Missile Defence Radar, which will be fitted to the Flight III *Arleigh Burke* (DDG-51) destroyers in lieu of the existing SPY-1D arrays. However, the initial ships will only have the lower S band arrays, with the higher X band panels used to provide precision tracking, guidance and illumination functions replaced by a system based on the existing rotating SPQ-9B until later in the programme. *(Raytheon)*

improvements into assembly plans – now anticipated towards the end of 2014. Third of class *Enterprise* (CVN-80) is due to be authorised in FY2018; work on defueling her predecessor CVN-65 is already well advanced following allocation of a US$745m inactivation contract to HHI in June 2013.

A reshuffling of US Navy carrier homeports will see *Ronald Reagan* (CVN-76) deploy to Japan in 2015 to replace *George Washington,* which has been based at Yokosuka since 2008. *Theodore Roosevelt* (CVN-71) will replace *Ronald Reagan* in San Diego, whilst *George Washington* will head for Newport News for mid-life defueling or inactivation, dependent on the budgetary situation. The decision is arguably the most significant one the US Navy faces in the run-up to the FY2016 budget, as it has the potential to determine carrier force levels for the next twenty-five years.

Surface Combatants: The mainstay of both the current and future US Navy large surface combatant force remains the *Arleigh Burke* (DDG-51) class destroyer. Production of the type restarted in 2013. Two pairs of initial continuation Flight IIA variants (DDG-113 to DDG-117) are currently under construction by HHI's Ingalls Shipbuilding division and General Dynamics' Bath Iron Works. A multi-year procurement agreement in June 2013 covered orders for a further nine ships and one option, shared between the two yards. The option was subsequently exercised in March 2014. It is envisaged that the last three units of the batch – to be procured in FY2016 and FY2017 – will be Flight III ships equipped with the new AMDR Air and Missile Defence Radar and associated power and cooling upgrades. Combining a new E/F band (US Navy S band) active phased array with an existing I/J band (X band) radar, AMDR essentially replaces the SPY-1D arrays associated with the Aegis combat system. In October 2013, Raytheon was selected over Lockheed Martin and Northrop Grumman to provide the new S-band arrays and associated radar suite controller that form the core of the new system.[9]

The three DDG-1000 land attack destroyers ordered before reversion to the DDG-51 design look set to be something of a dead-end in US Navy destroyer design. However, they are still impressive ships. The lead ship, *Zumwalt* (DDG-1000), was floated out by Bath Iron Works on 28 October 2013. She is scheduled for delivery late in 2014 prior to commencing the extensive tests and trials required to reach initial operating capability in 2016. Work is also well-advanced on the second ship, *Michael Monsoor* (DDG-1001), which will be launched during the next twelve months. In spite of displacing over 15,000 tons, the 186m-long, ultra-stealthy ships can be operated by a core crew of just 130 personnel. They encompass a wave-piercing, tumblehome hull form and a Rolls-Royce gas turbine-powered integrated electrical propulsion system designed to produce speeds in excess of 30 knots. Armament includes two 155mm advanced gun systems optimised for long-range bombardment, as well as twenty quadruple Mk57 vertical launch systems and a helicopter/UAV operating capability.

Turning to smaller combatants, the controversial Littoral Combat Ship programme continues to make headway. The type is being built to two different designs by Lockheed Martin, using Fincantieri's Marinette Marine yard, and Austal USA. Two pairs of prototype units (LCS-1 through

It was 'out with the old and in with the new' at Huntington Ingalls Industries' Newport News shipyard in 2013. The yard was awarded a contract to carry out the defueling of the first US Navy nuclear-powered aircraft carrier *Enterprise* (CVN-65), seen here making her final arrival at the shipyard in a rather battered condition in June 2013 after being stripped of re-usable equipment by the US Navy. Meanwhile the first of the new generation of carriers, *Gerald R Ford* (CVN-78), was christened on 9 November 2013, subsequently being towed into the James River and to her fitting-out berth on the 17th of the month. *(Huntington Ingalls Industries)*

Table 2.1.5: UNITED STATES NAVY: PRINCIPAL UNITS AS AT MID 2014

TYPE	CLASS	NUMBER	TONNAGE	DIMENSIONS	PROPULSION	CREW	DATE
Aircraft Carriers							
Aircraft Carrier – CVN	**NIMITZ** (CVN-68)	10	101,000 tons	340m x 41/78m x 12m	Nuclear, 30+ knots	5,700	1975
Principal Surface Escorts							
Cruiser – CG	**TICONDEROGA** (CG-47)	22	9,900 tons	173m x 17m x 7m	COGAG, 30+ knots	365	1983
Destroyer – DDG	**ARLEIGH BURKE** (DDG-51) – Flight II-A	34	9,200 tons	155m x 20m x 7m	COGAG, 30 knots	380	2000
Destroyer – DDG	**ARLEIGH BURKE** (DDG-51) – Flights I/II	28	8,800 tons	154m x 20m x 7m	COGAG, 30+ knots	340	1991
Frigate – FFG	**OLIVER HAZARD PERRY** (FFG-7)	11	4,100 tons	143m x 14m x 5m	COGAG, 30 knots	215	1977
Littoral Combat Ship – FS	**FREEDOM** (LCS-1)	2	3,100 tons	115m x 17m x 4m	CODAG, 45+ knots	<50[1]	2008
Littoral Combat Ship – FS	**INDEPENDENCE** (LCS-2)	2	2,800 tons	127m x 32m x 5m	CODAG, 45+ knots	<50[1]	2010
Submarines							
Submarine – SSBN	**OHIO** (SSBN-726)	14	18,800 tons	171m x 13m x 12m	Nuclear, 20+ knots	155	1981
Submarine – SSGN	**OHIO** (SSGN-726)	4	18,800 tons	171m x 13m x 12m	Nuclear, 20+ knots	160	1981
Submarine – SSN	**VIRGINIA** (SSN-774)	10	8,000 tons	115m x 10m x 9m	Nuclear, 25+ knots	135	2004
Submarine – SSN	**SEAWOLF** (SSN-21)	3[2]	9,000 tons	108m x 12m x 11m	Nuclear, 25+ knots	140	1997
Submarine – SSN	**LOS ANGELES** (SSN-688)	41	7,000 tons	110m x 10m x 9m	Nuclear, 25+ knots	145	1976
Major Amphibious Units							
Amph. Assault Ship – LHD	**AMERICA** (LHA-6)	1	45,000 tons	257m x 32/42m x 9m	COGAG, 20+ knots	1,050	2014
Amph Assault Ship – LHD	**WASP** (LHD-1)	8[3]	41,000 tons	253m x 32/42m x 9m	Steam, 20+ knots	1,100	1989
Amph Assault Ship – LHD	**TARAWA** (LHA-1)	1	40,000 tons	250m x 32/38m x 8m	Steam, 24 knots	975	1976
Landing Platform Dock – LPD	**SAN ANTONIO** (LPD-17)	9	25,000 tons	209m x 32m x 7m	Diesel, 22+ knots	360	2005
Landing Platform Dock – LPD	**AUSTIN** (LPD-4)	1	17,000 tons	171m x 25m x 7m	Steam, 21 knots	420	1965
Landing Ship Dock – LSD	**WHIDBEY ISLAND** (LSD-41)	12[4]	16,000 tons	186m x 26m x 6m	Diesel, 20 knots	420	1985

Notes:

1 Plus mission-related crew.
2 Third of class, SSN-23 is longer and heavier.
3 LHD-8 has many differences.
4 Includes four LSD-49 HARPERS FERRY variants.

The lead *Zumwalt* (DDG-1000) class destroyer was floated out at General Dynamics' Bath Iron Works shipyard in October 2013. Optimised for land-attack duties, the class has proved too expensive for series production, leading to a return to the veteran *Arleigh Burke* (DDG-51) design. *(General Dynamics Bath Iron Works)*

to LCS-4) were ordered from each company. A multi-year procurement programme for a further twenty ships (LCS-5 to LCS-24), split equally between the yards, followed. The final prototype vessel, the *Independence* (LCS-2) variant *Coronado* (LCS-4), completed acceptance trials at Austal in August 2013. Delivered the following month, she commissioned in April 2014. Her sister *Jackson* (LCS-6), the first of Austal's multi-year ships, was launched in December 2013. She was followed into the water a few days later by the first Lockheed Martin production-series *Freedom* (LCS-1) class variant, *Milwaukee* (LCS-5). Formal contracts for LCS-17 through to LCS-20, of which only *Indianapolis* (LCS-17) has yet been allocated a name, were placed in March 2014. The current block-buy covers procurement until FY2015/16. Further orders are expected through to FY2018 to achieve a total of thirty-two units. On 24 February 2014, US Secretary of Defense Chuck Hagel announced that no new contracts beyond this number wound be placed. Instead, the navy would submit, '… alternative proposals to procure a capable and lethal small surface combatant, generally consistent with the capabilities of a frigate'. A number of companies have submitted proposals to a task force established to examine possible alternatives. These include modifications of the existing Littoral Combat Ship designs and an adaptation of HHI's WMSL-750 national security cutter.[10]

Pending the arrival of new Littoral Combat Ships, numbers of existing small surface combatants are reducing rapidly. Withdrawals of the remaining handful of *Oliver Hazard Perry* (FFG-7) frigates are being accelerated as one of the budgetary trade-offs. Just eleven ships remained in commission in mid-2014 after seven deletions over the past year. It is likely that most of the remainder will have gone by the end of 2015. The writing is also on the wall for the *Avenger* (MCM-1) class mine-countermeasures ships, with the lead ship the first slated for scheduled withdrawal in August 2014.

Both prototype units of the *Independence* (LCS-2) variant of the Littoral Combat Ship are now in service following commissioning of *Coronado* (LCS-4) in April 2014. Meanwhile *Milwaukee* (LCS-5) was launched from Mariette Marine's shipyard in Wisconsin on 18 December 2013. *(US Navy / Lockheed Martin)*

Amphibious Shipping: Amphibious force numbers are improving both quantitatively and qualitatively. The most significant arrival in the last twelve months was the ninth *San Antonio* (LPD-17) class amphibious transport dock, *Somerset* (LPD-25), which was commissioned on 1 March 2014. Two further ships are under construction, with the keel of the eleventh and final member of the class, *Portland* (LPD-27), laid by HHI's Ingalls Shipbuilding at Pascagoula in August 2013. HHI has also delivered the lead *America* (LHA-6) class amphibious assault ship, which was accepted in April 2014 prior to her planned commissioning in October. These more than compensate for the scheduled withdrawal of the final *Austen* (LPD-4) class transport dock, *Denver* (LPD-9), still serving in her original role. Previous plans to mothball some of the *Whidbey Island* (LSD-41) class dock landing ships have been deferred in the face of Congressional opposition.

An interesting recent feature of US Navy amphibious fleet development has been the acquisition of derivatives of commercial designs to supplement – and reduce the pressure on – the front-line fleet. This value-for-money approach appears to be paying dividends. The ten new *Spearhead* (JHSV-1) high-speed transports are starting to enter service, with *Millinocket* (JHSV-3) delivered in March 2014 and *Fall River* (JHSV-4) launched two months previously. *Spearhead* herself carried out a highly successful maiden deployment to the Mediterranean, Africa and the Caribbean in the first half of 2014, demonstrating the type's flexibility. At the other end of the scale, the new giant mobile landing platforms of the *Montford Point* (MLP-1) class are also close to entering active service, with the lead ship scheduled to complete developmental and operational testing in the second half of 2014.

Submarines: Current US Navy submarine construction remains focused on the *Virginia* (SSN-774) class. Ten of the class are now in service following commissioning of the sixth and final Block II boat, *Minnesota* (SSN-783), in September 2013. She effectively replaces the *Los Angeles* (SSN-688) class submarine *Miami* (SSN-755), which was damaged by an arson attack whilst under refit in May 2012. In August 2013, the navy announced the US$450m needed to repair the vessel was not cost-effective in the light of budget cuts and she formally decommissioned in March 2014. *Dallas* (SSN-700) was also due to leave service in 2014. However, a change in plans will see *Norfolk* (SSN-714) commence inactivation in FY2015 and *Dallas* serve for a further three years.

The *Virginia* class programme has earned a rare and enviable reputation for on-time, on-budget delivery. However, commissioning of the first of eight new Block III submarines, *North Dakota* (SSN-784), which features a redesigned bow section with a new sonar and revised vertical launch system arrangement, has been delayed due to problems with the quality of components supplied by a subcontractor and the need to make design modifications. Nevertheless, the Navy remains happy with the overall design and a US$16.7bn multi-year procurement award was made to General Dynamics Electric Boat for ten Block IV units on 28 April 2014 in what was claimed to be the largest single shipbuilding contract in the US Navy's history. As previously, assembly will be split with HHI's Newport News shipyard, with the award covering construction of two submarines p.a. (one at each yard) from FY2014 to FY2018. The Block IV boats will incorporate further improvements on the Block III design, most notably changes designed to reduce major docking periods from four to three over the life of each boat. This will allow each Block IV submarine to conduct fifteen deployments over its lifetime compared with fourteen for the boats built to earlier configurations.

Looking further ahead, work continues on the SSBN(X) replacement for the *Ohio* (SSBN-726) class. Focus on completing design work is the top priority, with the new boat's length now set at 560ft (171m), the same length as the predecessor class. The first of twelve new strategic submarines will need to commence build in 2021 to meet a requirement to conduct a first operational patrol some ten years later.[11]

Operationally, the US Navy's activities continue to recover from the disruption caused by the unexpected implementation of sequestration, which has put a particularly severe strain on service personnel. A key response is the Optimized Fleet Response Plan (O-FRP) announced by Commander, US Fleet Forces Command, Admiral Bill Gortney on 15 January 2014. Starting with the carrier strike groups but ultimately designed for all US Navy surface and submarine assets, the plan envisages a standardised thirty-six month training and deployment cycle, of which only eight months will be allocated to scheduled deployment. The result will be a reduction in deployed carrier groups from between three and four to just two but with the benefit of greater predictability and home-time for serving personnel, as well as greater resilience to respond to emergencies. The plan is accompanied by a range of other measures to improve operational readiness, including increased availability of spare parts and enhanced training and inspection arrangements.

Strategically, the emphasis remains on the 'Pivot to the Pacific' response to China's increasing regional assertiveness. A string of announcements have been

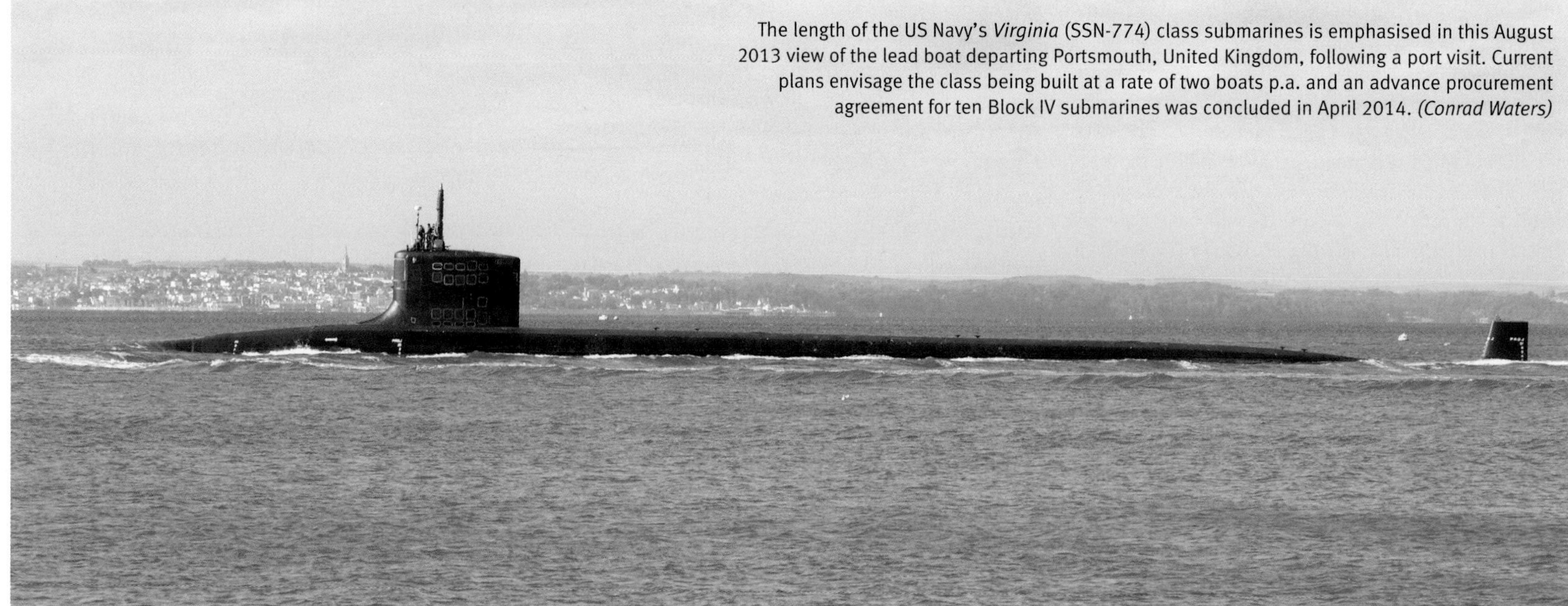

The length of the US Navy's *Virginia* (SSN-774) class submarines is emphasised in this August 2013 view of the lead boat departing Portsmouth, United Kingdom, following a port visit. Current plans envisage the class being built at a rate of two boats p.a. and an advance procurement agreement for ten Block IV submarines was concluded in April 2014. *(Conrad Waters)*

made on deployment of more modern ships to bases such as Yokosuka in Japan, whilst a new agreement to allow US forces to rotate through Philippines bases was signed on 28 April 2014. The US Defense Department is also looking at ways to strengthen and disperse existing bases in the Pacific against a backdrop of increased concern over the potential threat posed by Chinese ballistic and cruise missile capabilities. The response could include 'hardening' of structures at bases such as Guam, as well as further dispersal of forces to locations in allied countries such as Australia and Singapore.[12]

Elsewhere, the US Navy's commitment to European ballistic missile defence has taken tangible form with the arrival of *Donald Cook* (DDG-75), the first of four missile defence-capable Aegis destroyers to be based permanently at Rota in Spain, on 11 February 2014. A second destroyer, *Ross* (DDG-71), arrived in June. The crisis in the Ukraine has resulted in an increased presence in the Black Sea, where *Donald Cook* was involved in a Cold War-type stand-off in April when a Russian SU-34 'Fencer' made several low-level passes over the ship in April. Meanwhile, The US Marine Corps is seeing increased activity in the war against terror away from the recent focal points of Iraq and Afghanistan. An increased presence in Africa was highlighted in December 2013 when four personnel were wounded after MV-22 Osprey tilt rotors involved in evacuating American civilians from Sudan were hit by ground fire. The aircraft are believed to be part of a Special Purpose Marine Air-Ground Task Force (SP-MAGTF) established in Spain for crisis response after the attack on the US Embassy in Benghazi, Libya in 2012. Additional SP-MAGTF units will be established to cover Latin America and Central Asia before the end of the decade.[13]

The US Coast Guard is continuing modernisation efforts. An order for a seventh *Bertholf* (WMSL-750) national security cutter, *Kimball* (WMSL-756), was placed on 31 March 2014. In addition, both *Hamilton* (WMSL-753) and *James* (WMSL-754) have been launched over the past twelve months prior to entering service in 2014/15. Nine of the much smaller, Damen Stan Patrol 4708-based *Bernard C Webber* (WPC-1101) fast response cutters have also now been delivered. Fifteen additional members of the class have been ordered from Bollinger Shipyards and a draft request for proposals for bids to construct a second batch of up to twenty-six ships was issued in May 2014. Fifty-eight vessels are ultimately planned. Meanwhile, construction of the intermediate-sized offshore patrol cutter has moved closer with the award of preliminary design contracts to Bollinger, Eastern Shipbuilding and Bath Iron Works in February 2014. One of the designs will be selected by FY2016, when a contract will be awarded for construction of a prototype ship. The award will contain options for ten more ships out of a planned class of up to twenty-five.

OTHER NORTH AND CENTRAL AMERICAN NAVIES

Significant developments amongst the other North and Central American navies continue to be focused on the *Armada de Mexico.* **Mexico's** frontline force of obsolescent US-built surface escorts remains in pressing need of modernisation but the potential transfer of more modern FFG-7 type frigates has yet to be confirmed. Local press reports suggest that the destroyer *Netzahualcóyotl*, the former *Gearing* (DD-710) class destroyer *Steinaker* (DD-863) that was first commissioned as long ago as 1945, is not considered capable of further life-extension and will be retired before the end of 2014.[14] The even older *Edsall* (DE-129) class destroyer escort *Manuel Azueta*, formerly *Hurst* (DE-250), will also be withdrawn soon.

Images of Bath Iron Works' and Eastern Shipbuilding's concept designs for the proposed US Coast Guard offshore patrol cutter. The former's concept has been influenced by recent Navantia-built offshore patrol vessels, whilst Eastern Shipbuilding's design has been provided by the STX Marine naval architectural consultancy. Bollinger Shipyard has also been short-listed to propose a design for the project. *(General Dynamics Bath Iron Works / Eastern Shipbuilding)*

The main priority, however, remains the navy's constabulary mission. Investment is therefore concentrated on this task. Licensed construction of Damen Stan Patrol 4207 patrol vessels, known locally as the *Tenochtitlan* class, is a key priority. Six of these ships have now been ordered from the ASTIMAR 1 yard in Tampico and more are planned. Other priorities include local build of more Swedish 'Polaris' CB-90 type interceptors that are used to counter the narcotics trade and further *Montes Azules* LST-like logistic support ships. A new class of hydrographic research ships and two auxiliary oilers are also being considered.[15] Meanwhile, the navy remains heavily involved in the internal war against the country's drug barons, taking a lead role in the capture of the head of the Zetas cartel, Miguel Angel Trevino, in July 2013. However, this success has left navy personnel open to attack, as evidenced by the murder of senior naval officer Vice Admiral Carlos Miguel Salazar in an ambush by the rival Knights Templar organisation in the same month.

Elsewhere in Central America, other countries have been looking to bolster constabulary assets and a number have also ordered Damen Stan Patrol designs, including those of the **Bahamas** and **Honduras.** The latter has recently taken delivery of two Stan Patrol 4207 class vessels named *Lempira* and *Morazan* as part of a deal signed in 2012 that included six smaller Damen interceptors.

MAJOR S. AMERICAN NAVIES – ARGENTINA

The summary of Argentine fleet strength in Table 2.1.6 continues to show no major changes to the navy's principal units. However, a major improvement in fleet operational availability has been achieved by the long-delayed return to service by the TR-1700 type submarine *San Juan* following a lengthy refit at the CINAR Argentine Industrial Naval Complex. She was returned to the water in February 2014 and was redelivered to the navy on 23 May. Completion of the refit, which saw the boat cut in half for its diesel engines and batteries to be

Table 2.1.6: ARGENTINE NAVY: PRINCIPAL UNITS AS AT MID 2014[1]

TYPE	CLASS	NUMBER	TONNAGE	DIMENSIONS	PROPULSION	CREW	DATE
Principal Surface Escorts							
Destroyer – DDG	**ALMIRANTE BROWN** (MEKO 360)	4	3,600 tons	126m x 14m x 4m	COGOG, 30 knots	200	1983
Frigate – FSG	**ESPORA** (MEKO 140)	6	1,800 tons	91m x 11m x 3m	Diesel, 27 knots	100	1985
Corvette – FSG	**DRUMMOND** (A-69)	3	1,200 tons	80m x 10m x 3m	Diesel, 24 knots	95	1978
Submarines							
Submarine – SSK	**SANTA CRUZ** (TR 1700)	2	2,300 tons	65m x 7m x 7m	Diesel-electric, 25 knots	30	1984
Submarine – SSK	**SALTA** (Type 209)	1	1,200 tons	54m x 6m x 6m	Diesel-electric, 22 knots	30	1974

Note: 1. A number of units have doubtful serviceability.

replaced, demonstrates Argentina's ability to maintain its submarine fleet and will allow similar work on sister boat *Santa Cruz* to commence. Slow progress also continues to be made on repairing the fire-damaged icebreaker *Almirante Irizar*, which is now scheduled to be returned to the fleet in time for the 2015/16 Antarctic patrol season. Refits for the MEKO 360 destroyers and MEKO 140 corvettes are also planned, although funding may be an issue. Lack of money is also delaying acquisition of new offshore patrol boats but the replacement of a number of tugs and other auxiliaries is likely to proceed.

MAJOR S. AMERICAN NAVIES – BRAZIL

The current fleet strength of the *Marina do Brasil* is summarised in Table 2.1.7. Whilst there have been no changes year-on-year, the navy has longstanding modernisation plans that include a renewal of its submarine and surface forces, as well as – ultimately – the indigenous construction of new aircraft carriers.[16] Of these plans, the modernisation of the submarine being carried out in conjunction with France's DCNS under the PROSUB (*Programa de Desenvolvimento de Submarinos*) project is by far the most advanced. Involving the creation of a new submarine manufacturing facility and an adjacent shipyard and operating base at Itaguaí, south of Rio de Janeiro, the project is intended to deliver four 'Scorpène' type patrol submarines and a nuclear powered variant incorporating a Brazilian developed power plant over a 2015–25 timescale. DCNS and its local partner, the Brazilian conglomerate Odebrecht, handed over the manufacturing facility – the first phase of the project – in March 2013. As of mid-2014, local press reports suggested the first conventional submarine was approaching fifty per cent completion, whilst building work on the shipyard and base facilities were also well advanced.

Unfortunately, the very substantial investment being made in PROSUB set against a backdrop of recent reductions in the Brazilian defence budget and the need to fund new jet fighters for the Brazilian Air Force means that there is limited money available for other naval modernisation projects. In particular, the ambitious PROSUPER (*Programa de Obtenção de Meios de Superfície*) to renew the surface fleet appears to have stalled and there have been reports that the acquisition of second hand frigates is being considered to replace existing vessels that are close to forty years old. Local construction of a modernised version of the country's *Barroso* corvette design is also being pursued, with Fincantieri-owned VARD Niterói contracted to draw up a preliminary design for the new ships that will displace around 2,500 tons. A contract for up to four ships is likely to be placed before the end of 2014 at a total cost of around US$1.7bn. In the meantime, there have been reports that maintenance of existing ships is proving problematic, with all four *Inháuma* corvettes reportedly laid up under lengthy maintenance periods in early 2014.

There is slightly better news to report with respect to patrol vessels. The third and final *Amazonas* class offshore patrol vessel, *Araguari*, departed Portsmouth, United Kingdom on 3 August 2013 on

Table 2.1.7: BRAZILIAN NAVY: PRINCIPAL UNITS AS AT MID 2014

TYPE	CLASS	NUMBER	TONNAGE	DIMENSIONS	PROPULSION	CREW	DATE
Aircraft Carriers							
Aircraft Carrier – CV	**SÃO PAULO** (FOCH)	1	33,500 tons	265m x 32/51m x 9m	Steam, 30 knots	1,700	1963
Principal Surface Escorts							
Frigate – FFG	**GREENHALGH** (Batch I Type 22)	3	4,700 tons	131m x 15m x 4m	COGOG, 30 knots	270	1979
Frigate – FFG	**NITERÓI**	6	3,700 tons	129m x 14m x 4m	CODOG, 30 knots	220	1976
Corvette – FSG	**INHAÚMA**	4	2,100 tons	96m x 11m x 4m	CODOG, 27 knots	120	1989
Corvette – FSG	**BARROSO**	1	2,400 tons	103m x 11m x 4m	CODOG, 30 knots	145	2008
Submarines							
Submarine – SSK	**TIKUNA** (Type 209 – modified)	1	1,600 tons	62m x 6m x 6m	Diesel-electric, 22 knots	40	2005
Submarine – SSK	**TUPI** (Type 209)	4	1,500 tons	61m x 6m x 6m	Diesel-electric, 22+ knots	30	1989
Major Amphibious Units							
Landing Ship Dock – LSD	**CEARÁ** (LSD-28)	1	12,000 tons	156m x 26m x 6m	Steam, 22 knots	345	1956

Heavy investment in the PROSUB submarine programme means that the Brazilian Navy has little cash to spare on surface craft. The three *Amazonas* class offshore patrol vessels, originally ordered for Trinidad as the *Port of Spain* class, have therefore provided a significant boost to fleet strength. This picture shows the final ship, *Araguari*, departing Portsmouth, United Kingdom, on its delivery voyage on 3 August 2013. *(Conrad Waters)*

her delivery voyage. The second batch of five smaller licensed-built CMN 'Vigilante 400' *Macaé* class vessels are also starting to be delivered, with both *Maracanã* and *Maragogipe* expected to join their two earlier sisters in service by the end of 2014. Construction of further vessels of this type remains a priority and possible procurement under long-term leases remains under consideration.

MAJOR S. AMERICAN NAVIES – CHILE

As the *Armada de Chile* operates one of the region's most modern fleets, continued upgrades of existing assets are taking precedence over acquisitions of new ships. The most important exception to this rule is the construction of Fassmer OPV80 offshore patrol vessels at the ASMAR yard at Talcahuano, from where the third of the series *Comandante Marinero Fuentealba* was launched on 6 April 2014. Delivery is scheduled for the end of 2014 and another two are planned. The class may be seen as partial replacements for the country's ageing fast attack craft, which are steadily being withdrawn from service. Another of the northern-based former German Type 148 vessels, *Teniente Uribe,* was decommissioned on 31 March 2014, leaving just two of the class operational.

Another priority is replacement of the veteran ice-breaker *Almirante Óscar Viel,* which is now some forty-five years old.[17] She will remain in service until 2020, when a new ship will have been completed. Replacement is likely to be entrusted to ASMAR, which has been extensively refurbished since the 2010 tsunami. The navy has also been reported as having an interest in acquiring France's *Siroco* to join her sister *Sargento Aldea* (the former *Foudre*). Meanwhile, a summary of current fleet units is provided in Table 2.1.8.

MAJOR S. AMERICAN NAVIES – PERU

After a considerable period maintaining a relatively stable fleet, the *Marina de Guerra de Perú* is in the course of a major modernisation programme based on the local construction of logistic support, training and patrol vessels by local shipbuilding group SIMA-Peru. The most significant element of the programme is focused on two licence-built amphibious transport docks derived from Indonesia's *Makassar* class. Displacing around 7,500 tons in full load condition, the 122m-long vessels will incorporate a flight deck for two helicopters and a dock capable of supporting two utility landing craft. Designed to transport up to 450 marines, they feature a diesel propulsion arrangement that provides a maximum speed of 16 knots. The keel of the first ship, *Paita,* was laid in July 2013 and a second, *Piso*, will follow. SIMA has also been delivering a number of small coastal patrol ships for the coast guard and is building a new sail training ship, *Unión*, that is scheduled for delivery in 2015. A class of larger, 500-ton patrol ships built to a Korean STX design and intended for coast guard service has also been contracted.

Another major development is the purchase of the Dutch fleet replenishment ship *Amsterdam,* announced in June 2014. Her arrival, scheduled for early 2015, will significantly strengthen the navy's

Table 2.1.8: CHILEAN NAVY: PRINCIPAL UNITS AS AT MID 2014

TYPE	CLASS	NUMBER	TONNAGE	DIMENSIONS	PROPULSION	CREW	DATE
Principal Surface Escorts							
Frigate – FFG	**ALMIRANTE WILLIAMS** (Batch II Type 22)	1	5,500 tons	148m x 14m x 5m	COGOG, 30+ knots	260	1988
Frigate – FFG	**ALMIRANTE COCHRANE** (Type 23)	3	4,800 tons	133m x 16m x 5m	CODLAG, 28 knots	185	1990
Frigate – FFG	**CAPITÁN PRAT** (L class)	2	3,800 tons	131m x 15m x 4m	COGOG, 30 knots	200	1986
Frigate – FFG	**ALMIRANTE RIVEROS** (M class)	2	3,300 tons	122m x 14m x 4m	CODOG, 30 knots	160	1992
Submarines							
Submarine – SSK	**O'HIGGINS** ('Scorpène')	2	1,700 tons	66m x 6m x 6m	Diesel-electric, 22 knots	30	2005
Submarine – SSK	**THOMSON** (Type 209)	2	1,400 tons	60m x 6m x 6m	Diesel-electric, 22 knots	35	1984
Major Amphibious Units							
Landing Platform Dock – LPD	**SARGENTO ALDEA** (FOUDRE)	1	12,000 tons	168m x 24m x 5m	Diesel, 20 knots	225	1990

Peru's Navy is starting to see significant investment in amphibious and support ships but its fleet of front-line surface ships is elderly. This image shows the *Lupo* class frigate *Villavisencio,* one of seven of the type remaining in navy service, on exercise with US and allied forces in September 2013. *(US Navy)*

deployment capabilities. However, the surface fleet is ageing rapidly. The country's first *Lupo* class frigate, *Carvajal*, was decommissioned in December 2013 prior to transfer to the coast guard as the offshore patrol ship *Guardiamarina San Martin*. More of the unmodernised ships may follow shortly. Her withdrawal is reflected in Table 2.1.9 of principal Peruvian Navy warships.

OTHER SOUTH AMERICAN NAVIES

Elsewhere in Latin America, **Colombia's** navy has one of the most active procurement programmes, encompassing new construction, overseas acquisitions and modernisation of existing units. Assembly and modernisation activities are focused on local shipbuilding group COTECMAR, which is involved in a number of projects. As for Chile, licensed assembly of Fassmer OPV80 offshore patrol vessels is the most important local programme. The second of a planned series of six vessels, *7 de Agosto*, was launched in September 2013. She was delivered to the navy on 1 April 2014, when construction of a third ship was confirmed. COTECMAR is also working on a series of smaller CPV46 coastal patrol vessels built under licence from Korea's STX that would seem to be similar to but slightly smaller than Peru's equivalents. The group also delivered a LST-type logistics support ship, *Golfo de Tribugá*, in the first half of 2014. Other activities have included the modernisation of the four *Almirante Padilla* class frigates and two Type 209 submarines which, along with the two smaller former German Navy Type 206 boats acquired in 2012, form the core of the navy's warfighting potential.

Venezuela's oceanic patrol vessel *Warao* suffered heavy damage after running aground during exercises with the Brazilian Navy in 2012. She is pictured laid up in Rio de Janeiro in a rather sorry state in January 2014 prior to signature of a contract with builder Navantia to provide a new propulsion plant. *(Bruno Huriet)*

Table 2.1.9: PERUVIAN NAVY: PRINCIPAL UNITS AS AT MID 2014

TYPE	CLASS	NUMBER	TONNAGE	DIMENSIONS	PROPULSION	CREW	DATE
Principal Surface Escorts							
Cruiser – CL	**ALMIRANTE GRAU** (DE RUYTER)	1[1]	12,200 tons	187m x 17m x 7m	Steam, 32 knots	950	1953
Frigate – FFG	**CARVAJAL** (LUPO)	7	2,500 tons	112m x 12m x 4m	CODOG, 35 knots	185	1977
Submarines							
Submarine – SSK	**ANGAMOS** (Type 209)	6[2]	1,200 tons	54m x 6m x 6m	Diesel-electric, 22 knots	30	1980

Notes:

1 *Almirante Grau* remained in commission as of mid-2014 but is understood to be no longer sea-going.

2 Peru operates both T209/1100 and T209/1200 submarines. Details refer to the Type 209/1100 variant

Neighbouring **Venezuela** also has a significant navy and coast guard, which have recently made significant acquisitions from Spain's Navantia. The fourth and final 'BVL' type littoral patrol vessel *Tamanaco* – the only class member to be assembled locally – was launched in June 2014 from blocks constructed in Spain. Navantia has also been contracted to help repairs in Rio de Janeiro to the larger 'POVZEE' type oceanic patrol vessel *Warao*, which suffered extensive damage in a grounding accident off the coast of Brazil in 2012 and requires a new propulsion system. The class may subsequently be upgraded with surface-to-air missiles in partial replacement of unmodernised members of the existing *Mariscal Sucre* (*Lupo*) frigate class, which are starting to be retired. The country is one of many in Latin America that also plans to take delivery of Damen Stan Patrol and Interceptor type constabulary assets, which will be built by group shipyards in Cuba and Vietnam.

Uruguay is another country looking at new patrol ships, which will replace the existing *João Belo* class. France's *L'Adroit* type has been reported as being in competition with British and Portuguese designs but no contract had been awarded as of mid-2014.

Notes

1. The ongoing debate on how to tackle the US government's deficit between revenues and spending, most notably whether it should be dealt with by budget reductions or higher taxes, remains beyond this book's scope. The 2011 Budget Control Act attempted to solve the issue by agreeing immediate reductions to previously-planned increases in spending and setting out a mechanism for further automatic reductions through budget caps – sequestration – through to FY2021 if alternative measures could not be agreed. The US military's planned spending was reduced by a little under US$500bn over a ten-year period by the immediate reductions and looks set to be reduced by a similar amount if sequestration, implemented in March 2013, remains in force.

2. The 2013 Bipartisan Budget Act was a successful attempt by US Democrat and Republican politicians to reach a degree of short-term consensus on the spending debate. Its main provisions were to relax the impact of sequestration in US FY2014 and FY2015 in return for an extended period of budget caps (through to FY2023) and implementation of a number of other deficit reduction measures. The relaxation, split equally between defence and non-defence discretionary spending, permitted c. US$20bn of additional military spending in FY2014 and a little under US$10bn in FY2015.

3. The strategic guidance was set out in *Sustaining US Global Leadership: Priorities for 21st Century Defense* (Washington DC, Department of Defense, 2012).

4. The requirement for the US Navy to retain a set number of operational aircraft carriers was established by the FY2006 National Defense Authorization Act, which set the requirement at twelve ships. The number was subsequently reduced to eleven carriers. In addition, the FY2010 National Defense Authorization Act permitted a temporary reduction to ten ships between the decommissioning of *Enterprise* (CVN-65) and the delivery of *Gerald R Ford* (CVN-78).

5. Mr O'Rourke's observations were contained in *Navy Force Structure and Shipbuilding Plans: Background and Issues for Congress – April 2014* (Washington DC, Congressional Research Service, 2014), pp.16–17. Ronald O'Rourke – the CRS' Specialist in Naval Affairs – prepares a regularly updated series of reports on US Navy programmes. Although not made directly available to the public, many are hosted by the Federation of American Scientists as a public service at http://www.fas.org/sgp/crs/

6. The story was reported by Alison Auld of the Canadian Press news agency in an article entitled 'HMCS *Iroquois* indefinitely sidelined after rust found in warship's hull' that was carried by several media outlets on 7 May 2014.

7. An interesting comparison between the C$2.6bn (US$2.3bn) estimated cost of the two Canadian JSS vessels and the four larger 'Tide' class fleet tankers being built in South Korea for Britain's Royal Navy at a total cost of £600m (US$1.0bn) was posted on the UTC *Defense Industry Daily* website on 11 October 2013. Ordered in 2012, the 'Tide' class vessels will start entering service from 2016, only slightly later than commencement of fabrication on the first Canadian ship.

8. See further *Report to Congress: Navy Combatant Vessel Force Structure Requirement – January 2013* (Washington DC, US Navy, 2013). The US Navy also produces a yearly *Report to Congress on the Annual Long-Range Plan for Construction of Naval Vessels* but the report for 2015 was not publicly available as of mid-2014. Reference has therefore been made to secondary sources for recent changes identified in this plan.

9. The AMDR programme is intended to give US Navy improved defences against air and ballistic missile attacks. However, use of the existing DDG-51 design has resulted in some limitations on the system's capabilities, notably the use of 14ft diameter AMDR S-band arrays compared with much larger arrays originally envisaged. In addition, a new X-band radar intended for use as part of the system will not be integrated into the system until the thirteenth AMDR has been produced.

10. An excellent review of the LCS programme is contained in Ronald O'Rourke's *Navy Littoral Combat Ship Program: Background and Issues for Congress* (Washington DC, Congressional Research Service, 2014). A review of proposals for the follow-on programme is contained in Christopher P Cavas's 'Ideas Pour into Navy's Small Ship Task Force', *Defense News* – 23 May 2014 (Springfield VA, Gannett Government Media Corporation, 2014).

11. Further information on the status of the *Ohio* replacement programme is contained in Lee Willett's 'US Navy sets out priorities for Ohio replacement', *Jane's Defence Weekly* – 16 April 2014 (Coulsdon, IHS Jane's, 2014), p.6.

12. A more detailed description of the dispersal policy currently under consideration is contained in Marcus Weisgerber's 'Pentagon Debates Policy to Strengthen, Disperse Bases', *Defense News* – 13 April 2014 (Springfield VA, Gannett Government Media Corporation, 2014).

13. The plan to expand the SP-MAGTF concept was first revealed by Grace Jean in 'USMC to increase responsiveness in Latin America', *Jane's Defence Weekly* – 16 April 2014 (Coulsdon, IHS Jane's, 2014), p.6.

14. The story was covered in Spanish by Arturo Angel of the Mexican *24 Horas* news site on 11 December 2013 under the heading 'The most powerful Mexican ship will retire'. The article can currently be found at: http://www.24-horas.mx/el-buque-mas-poderoso-de-mexico-se-jubilara/

15. Additional information on the Mexican Navy's procurement plans were contained in 'Mexican Navy moves forward with Ship Procurement Projects' – *Seapower International* – November 2013 (Arlington VA, The Navy League of the United States, 2013).

16. The Portuguese-language Poder Naval website at www.naval.com.br continues to remain an excellent source of information on Brazilian Navy developments.

17. This story was reported by Juan Carlos Arancibia's *Chile's Defence & Military* blog at http://chiledefense.blogspot.co.uk/. The Spanish *defensa.com* website also remains a good source of reports on the Latin American military.

2.2 REGIONAL REVIEW

Author:
Conrad Waters

ASIA AND THE PACIFIC

INTRODUCTION

Naval developments in the Asia-Pacific region continue to be dominated by China's increasingly forceful stance to disputed maritime boundaries. Whilst these disputes have a lengthy history, the last twelve months have seen a series of actions that have ratcheted tension levels. Most international attention has been focused on friction between China and Japan in the East China Sea. Here a dispute over competing claims to the Japanese-administered Senkaku Islands (Diaoyutai to China) has produced frequent confrontations between the two countries' coast guards. On 23 November 2013, China significantly raised the stakes by unilaterally declaring an Air Defence Identification Zone (ADIZ) that covered the islands. It also overlapped with existing zones established by Japan, South Korea and Taiwan.[1]

The move brought predictably negative comments of varying severity from the various countries affected. They were also undoubtedly an influence on widely reported remarks by Japan's Prime Minister Shinzo Abe in January 2014 at the World Economic Forum in Davos, when he explicitly compared tensions between Tokyo and Beijing to animosity between the European powers prior to the First World War.[2] Japan's revised defence plans place particular emphasis on the capabilities required to defend its southern islands against a backdrop of some regional unease as to the extent to which United States' support could be counted on in a crisis. For its part, however, the United States has taken a firm stance, dispatching its own aircraft into the zone to challenge China's intentions. In April 2014 President Obama reiterated previous American statements that, as the Senkaku Islands were administered by Japan, they fell under Article 5 of the US-Japan security treaty. This obliges the United States to defend Japanese territory.

The pattern of Chinese assertion has also been evident further south. Here its 'nine-dash line' claim bulges out from its natural coastline to encompass a significant part of the South China Sea, providing a potential source of conflict with a number of neighbouring countries. In May 2014, *Jane's Defence Weekly* publicised Philippine government reports that China was involved in a major land reclamation exercise to build an island on the disputed Johnson South Reef in the Spratly Islands.[3] There have also been reports of construction of an airstrip and port on Fiery Cross Reef, also in the island chain. As well as strengthening China's territorial and economic claims, the bases could serve to bolster China's Anti-Access/Area Denial (A2/AD) strategy of limiting US Navy operations in the country's 'near seas'.

Whilst there is no evidence that any of the region's countries desire an all-out conflict that would destabilise their substantial trading interests, the fear of an accidental clash is growing. Particularly severe clashes occurred between Chinese and Vietnamese vessels in May 2014. Chinese Coast Guard vessels used water cannon and reportedly rammed several Vietnamese ships attempting to counter Chinese drilling operations close to the Parcel Islands and within Vietnam's Exclusive Economic Zone (EEZ). The resulting tensions spread to the Vietnamese mainland, where nationalist riots saw several foreign-owned factories go up in flames and at least one Chinese worker killed. Vietnam's lack of regional alliances, particularly with the United States, means that it is perceived as being particularly vulnerable to Chinese pressure. Perhaps unsurprisingly, it is spending significant sums ramping up maritime and air-defence capabilities.

Given this background, the endorsement of a new Code for Unplanned Encounters at Sea (CUES) by the main Pacific navies at the April 2014 meeting of the Western Pacific Naval Symposium in Qingdao, China has been seen as a positive, if modest, step to avoid potentially damaging miscalculations. First mooted as long ago as 2000, the agreement is intended to provide a framework for participating navies to evolve standardised protocols of safety, manoeuvring and communications procedures when warships meet in international waters. It therefore has some similarities with the more specific protocols agreed between the United States and its NATO allies on the one hand and the Soviet Union on the other at the time of the Cold War. However, the non-legally binding code does not extend to other government agencies, such as coast guards, that have been at the forefront of many of the region's maritime confrontations. Similarly, CUES' focus on international waters means that it is uncertain to what extent it will influence behaviours in waters subject to competing territorial claims.[4]

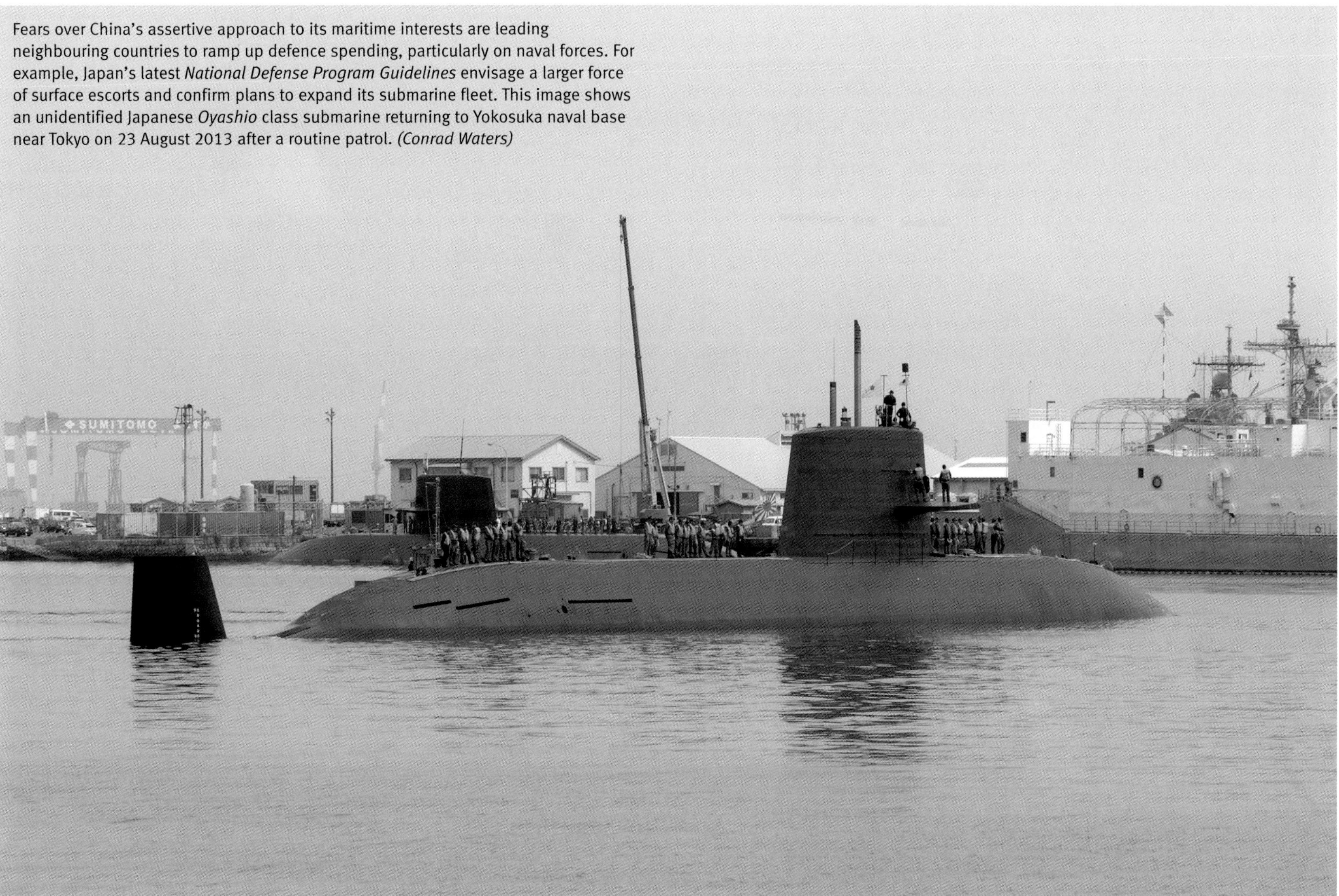

Fears over China's assertive approach to its maritime interests are leading neighbouring countries to ramp up defence spending, particularly on naval forces. For example, Japan's latest *National Defense Program Guidelines* envisage a larger force of surface escorts and confirm plans to expand its submarine fleet. This image shows an unidentified Japanese *Oyashio* class submarine returning to Yokosuka naval base near Tokyo on 23 August 2013 after a routine patrol. *(Conrad Waters)*

Table 2.2.1: FLEET STRENGTHS IN ASIA AND THE PACIFIC – LARGER NAVIES (MID 2014)

COUNTRY	AUSTRALIA	CHINA	INDONESIA	JAPAN	S KOREA	SINGAPORE	TAIWAN	THAILAND
Aircraft Carrier (CV)	–	1	–	–	–	–	–	–
Support/Helicopter Carrier (CVS/CVH)	–	–	–	2	–	–	–	1
Strategic Missile Submarine (SSBN)	–	4	–	–	–	–	–	–
Attack Submarine (SSN)	–	6	–	–	–	–	–	–
Patrol Submarine (SSK/SS)	6	50	2	16	12	6	4	–
Fleet Escort (DDG/FFG)	12	60	6	39	22	6	26	8
Patrol Escort/Corvette (FFG/FSG/FS)	–	25	24	6	21	6	–	11
Missile Armed Attack Craft (PGG/PTG)	–	75	13	6	15	–	c.30	6
Mine Countermeasures Vessel (MCMV)	6	25	11	30	9	4	10	6
Major Amphibious Units (LHD/LPD/LSD)	1	3	5	3	1	4	1	1

Notes: Chinese numbers approximate; Some additional Indonesian patrol gunboats are able to ship missiles; Taiwan's submarines are reported to have limited operational availability.

MAJOR REGIONAL POWERS – AUSTRALIA

An overview of current Royal Australian Navy strength set out in Table 2.2.2 shows no change year-on-year. However, 2015/16 will herald major changes as the remaining FFG-7 type *Adelaide* frigates start to be replaced by the new *Hobart* class AWD air-warfare destroyers and the *Canberra* class LHD-type amphibious assault ships join the fleet. The fact that the need for these ships was first heralded by Australia's 2000 Defence White Paper is an interesting lesson on the length of time it can take to turn strategic concepts into reality.

Of the two programmes, construction of the *Canberra* class is most advanced. Built to Spain's *Juan Carlos I* design, the ships' hulls were fabricated by Navantia at Ferrol in Spain prior to being transported by heavy lift vessel to Williamstown near Melbourne for installation of their island structure and final fitting out by BAE Systems. The lead ship commenced sea trials in March 2014. It should be delivered towards the end of the year when a series of minor defects have been rectified and further tests concluded. The hull of the second ship, *Adelaide*, arrived in Australia in February 2014 and is likely to enter service during 2016. Recent statements by Australian politicians suggest F-35B Lightning II

No overview of the last year would be complete without reference to Australia's International Fleet Review, which took place in October 2013 to commemorate the centenary of the first Royal Australian Navy fleet entering Sydney Harbour. This image shows Royal Australian Air Force jets overflying some of the warships that assembled from around the globe; from left to right the view shows the Royal Thai Navy's *Krabi*, the French *Marine Nationale*'s *Vendémiaire*, the Royal Malaysian Navy's *Jebat*, the British Royal Navy's *Daring* and the US Navy's *Chosin* (CG-65). *(Royal Australian Navy)*

jets may be purchased to operate from the two ships to provide an increased power projection capability.

Progress with the destroyers, which are based on Spain's F-100 frigate, has been somewhat slower. Three ships are being assembled by ASC in Adelaide under the auspices of the AWD Alliance from blocks constructed by a number of Australian shipyards and Navantia. It is expected that *Hobart* will be launched towards the end of 2014. The keel of *Brisbane*, the second of three ships, was laid on 3 February 2014 and a third, *Sydney*, will follow. Following a project rescheduling in 2012, deliveries are anticipated between March 2016 and March 2019, between fifteen and twenty-one months later than the initial plan. There are also concerns that the programme's A$8.5bn (c.US$8bn) budget will be significantly exceeded. Accordingly, after a review by former US Navy Secretary Donald Winter and industrialist John White, the programme was put on the government's projects of concern list at the start of June 2014. A series of emergency steps will be taken, including the insertion of additional managerial expertise, in the hope of bringing construction back on track.

Focus on the AWD programme comes at a time when there are significant concerns about the long-term future of Australia's shipbuilding industry. Indeed, the government has explicitly tied improvements in AWD project performance to decisions on where the eight future frigates envisaged under the SEA 5000 programme will be built. On 6 June 2014, A$78m was committed for design and engineering work to see whether the destroyer's hull could be used as the basis for a new frigate that would also feature the domestically-produced CEAFAR phased-array radar and Saab combat-management system. The decision will come as a disappointment to the UK, which had previously discussed shared development of the Type 26 Global Combat Ship to meet the Australian requirement.

Although concerns are being expressed about cost and time overruns relating to the Royal Australian Navy's Air Warfare Destroyer programme, physical assembly of the lead ship, *Hobart*, is well advanced, as this April 2014 view shows. She will be launched in the second half of 2014. *(AWD Alliance)*

The same announcement, which was made in the context of the development of a new strategic naval plan by the new Australian government headed by Tony Abbott that was elected in September 2013, included confirmation that replacements for Australia's two existing replenishment ships would be sourced from outside the country. A variant of Navantia's *Cantabria* design will compete with a version of BMT's Aegir series already selected by the United Kingdom and Norway, which would be built by Daewoo Shipbuilding & Marine Engineering (DSME) in Korea. *Cantabria* operated with the Royal Australian Navy for an extended period during 2013 and the Spanish company is therefore generally considered as favourite to win the contest. Some consolation for domestic industry, facing a gap in workload termed the 'valley of death' by some commentators, was provided with the news that orders for a new class of more than twenty small patrol boats would be accelerated. These will be replacements for the existing 'Pacific' class patrol boats donated by Australia to a host of small countries in the South Pacific, such as Fiji and Papua New Guinea, to assist the maintenance of regional

Table 2.2.2: ROYAL AUSTRALIAN NAVY: PRINCIPAL UNITS AS AT MID 2014

TYPE	CLASS	NUMBER	TONNAGE	DIMENSIONS	PROPULSION	CREW	DATE
Principal Surface Escorts							
Frigate – FFG	**ADELAIDE** (FFG-7)	4	4,200 tons	138m x 14m x 5m	COGAG, 30 knots	210	1980
Frigate – FFG	**ANZAC**	8	3,600 tons	118m x 15m x 4m	CODOG, 28 knots	175	1996
Submarines							
Submarine – SSK	**COLLINS**	6	3,400 tons	78m x 8m x 7m	Diesel-electric, 20 knots	45	1996
Major Amphibious Units							
Landing Ship Dock – LSD	**CHOULES** ('Bay')	1	16,200 tons	176m x 26m x 6m	Diesel-electric, 18 knots	60	2006

stability. The A$2bn programme was subsequently formally announced on 17 June 2014; it will cover all twelve original participants and a new member, Timor-Leste.

Further decisions on naval strategy will be made in a new Australian Defence White Paper to be released in 2015, only two years after the last such document. This will benefit from a c. six per cent rise in defence spending for 2014/15, with further growth to come. A key decision will be the direction of the *Collins* class submarine replacement under Project SEA 1000. This envisages the purchase of twelve new boats. There have been numerous reports that Australia is interested in acquiring a variant of Japan's *Soryu* design and an agreement to jointly develop stealth submarine technology has already been signed.[5] The relatively large size of the *Soryu* class submarine compared with other diesel-electric designs makes it well suited for Australia's oceanic requirements. However, commitment to a broader alliance in submarine construction would be a very significant step for both parties.

MAJOR REGIONAL POWERS – CHINA

Much of the recent news flow relating to the progressive development of China's naval capabilities has been focused on maritime boundary disputes close to home. However, the last year has also seen ongoing demonstration of the People's Liberation Army's Navy's (PLAN's) growing global reach. In October 2013 a task force headed by the Type 052C destroyer *Lanzhou* sailed through the Magellan Strait, completing the navy's first ever transit between the South Pacific and South Atlantic. The deployment, which saw exercises with a number of Latin American fleets, forms part of a pattern of voyages designed to bolster Chinese political and economic influence. Elsewhere, the PLAN has extended its virtually permanent Indian Ocean presence to encompass regular missions to the Mediterranean. The last year has also seen increasing interfaces with the Russian Navy, including exercises as far apart as the Mediterranean and the East China Sea. Russia's willingness to expand its military links with China in such politically sensitive waters is a particularly interesting development. It occurred contemporaneously with Russian President Vladimir Putin's presence in Shanghai to sign a strategically significant energy deal with his Chinese counterpart, Xi Jinping.[6] The embryonic partnership between China and Russia is certainly an unwelcome development for the United States, which is struggling to counter what it perceives as an expansionary policy agenda adopted by both coun-

Table 2.2.3: PEOPLE'S LIBERATION ARMY NAVY: PRINCIPAL UNITS AS AT MID 2014

TYPE	CLASS	NUMBER	TONNAGE	DIMENSIONS	PROPULSION	CREW	DATE
Aircraft Carriers							
Aircraft Carrier – CV	Project 1143.5/6 **LIAONING** (Kuznetsov)	1	60,000 tons	306m x 35/73m x 10m	Steam, 32 knots	Unknown	2012
Principal Surface Escorts							
Destroyer – DDG	Type 052D **KUNMING** ('Luyang III')	1	7,500 tons	156m x 17m x 6m	CODOG, 28 knots	280	2014
Destroyer – DDG	Type 051C **SHENYANG** ('Luzhou')	2	7,100 tons	155m x 17m x 6m	Steam, 29 knots	Unknown	2006
Destroyer – DDG	Type 052C **LANZHOU** ('Luyang II')	5	7,000 tons	154m x 17m x 6m	CODOG, 28 knots	280	2004
Destroyer – DDG	Type 052B **GUANGZHOU** ('Luyang I')	2	6,500 tons	154m x 17m x 6m	CODOG, 29 knots	280	2004
Destroyer – DDG	Project 956E/EM **HANGZHOU** (Sovremenny)	4	8,000 tons	156m x 17m x 6m	Steam, 32 knots	300	1999
Destroyer – DDG	Type 051B **SHENZHEN** ('Luhai')	1	6,000 tons	154m x 16m x 6m	Steam, 31 knots	250	1998
Destroyer – DDG	Type 052 **HARBIN** ('Luhu')	2	4,800 tons	143m x 15m x 5m	CODOG, 31 knots	260	1994
Plus c. 5–10 additional obsolescent destroyers of Type 051 **JINAN** ('Luda') class							
Frigate – FFG	Type 054A **XUZHOU** ('Jiangkai II')	17	4,100 tons	132m x 15m x 5m	CODAD, 28 knots	190	2008
Frigate – FFG	Type 054 **MA'ANSHAN** ('Jiangkai I')	2	4,000 tons	132m x 15m x 5m	CODAD, 28 knots	190	2005
Frigate – FFG	Type 053 H2G/H3 **ANQING** ('Jiangwei I/II')	14	2,500 tons	112m x 12m x 5m	CODAD, 27 knots	170	1992
Frigate – FSG	Type 056 **BENGBU** ('Jiangdao')	15	1,500 tons	89m x 12m x 4m	CODAD, 28 knots	60	2013
Plus c.10 additional obsolescent frigates of Type 053 H/H1/H1G/H2 **XIAMEN** ('Jianghu') classes							
Submarines							
Submarine – SSBN	Type 094 ('Jin')	3+	9,000 tons	133m x 11m x 8m	Nuclear, 20+ knots	Unknown	2008
Submarine – SSBN	Type 092 ('Xia')	1	6,500 tons	120m x 10m x 8m	Nuclear, 22 knots	140	1987
Submarine – SSN	Type 093 ('Shang')	3+	6,000 tons	107m x 11m x 8m	Nuclear, 30 knots	100	2006
Submarine – SSN	Type 091 ('Han')	3	5,500 tons	106m x 10m x 7m	Nuclear, 25 knots	75	1974
Submarine – SSK	Type 039A/039B (Type 041 'Yuan')	12+	2,500 tons	75m x 8m x 5m	AIP, 20+ knots	Unknown	2006
Submarine – SSK	Type 039/039G ('Song')	13	2,300 tons	75m x 8m x 5m	Diesel-electric, 22 knots	60	1999
Submarine – SSK	Project 877 EKM/636 ('Kilo')	12	3,000 tons	73m x 10m x 7m	Diesel-electric, 20 knots	55	1995
Plus c.15 obsolescent patrol submarines of the Type 035 ('Ming' class). A Type 032 'Qing' trials submarine has also been commissioned.							
Major Amphibious Units							
Landing Platform Dock	Type 071 **KULUN SHAN** ('Yuzhao')	3	18,000 tons	210m x 27m x 7m	CODAD, 20 knots	Unknown	2007

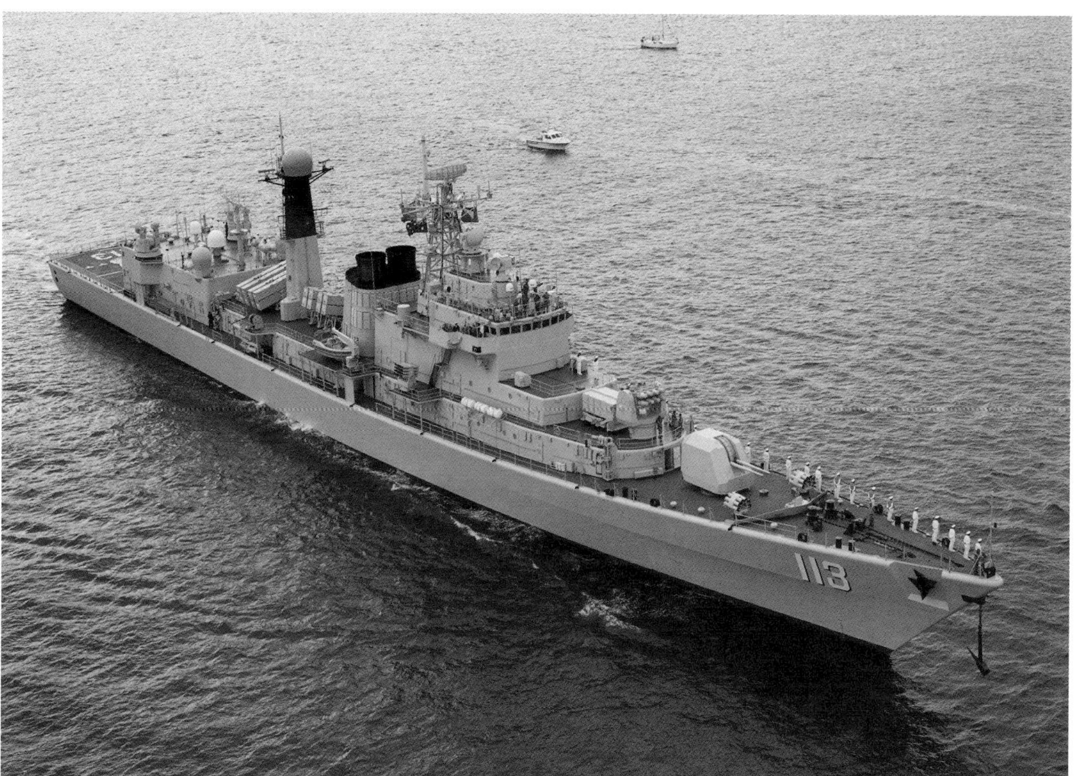

An image of the Chinese Type 052 'Luhu' class destroyer *Qingdao* in Australian waters in October 2013. China's 'blue water' naval expansion means that the People's Liberation Army Navy's warships are becoming an increasingly common sight across the world's oceans. *(Royal Australian Navy)*

tries. However, China also appears to be open to a level of cooperation with the United States Navy. For example, it will participate in the US-hosted biennial RIMPAC exercises off Hawaii for the first time in mid-2014.

Meanwhile, the PLAN is steadily expanding the overall quality of its naval forces, as described in detail under the various ship categories listed below. A summary of overall fleet strength is also provided in Table 2.2.3.[7]

Aircraft Carriers: The first Chinese aircraft carrier *Liaoning*, the former Russian Project 1143.5/6 *Varyag*, has continued a series of trials and exercises over the past twelve months as the PLAN steadily learns the art of fixed-wing naval aviation. In April 2014, US Secretary of Defense Chuck Hagel became the first foreign dignitary to tour the ship after a request to visit the ship was accepted by the Chinese authorities. Various reports suggest that China ultimately wants to deploy a force of at least four carriers, which will be built in the Dalian Shipyard where *Liaoning* was refurbished. In spite of local media claims that the first of these indigenously-built ships will enter service before the end of the decade, no tangible evidence has yet emerged of construction underway.

Major Surface Combatants: The PLAN's rapid modernisation of its surface fleet remains focused on three major design streams. The most powerful ships are the latest variants of the Type 052 'Luyang' series of destroyers. Initially comprising two pairs of Type 052B and Type 052C ships completed in 2004–5; renewed production of these air-defence orientated ships resumed towards the end of the decade. Three ships out of this second batch of four destroyers have now been delivered. The last ship is due to be commissioned by the end of 2014. Construction has now turned to the follow-on type 052D 'Luyang III' variant, with lead ship *Kunming* commissioned on 21 March 2014. Commentators suggest twelve members of the class will eventually be delivered to provide a front-line force of around twenty-six modern destroyers. As details of the programme

The Type 052C 'Luyang II' class destroyer *Haikou* seen in the Indian Ocean in April 2014. One of an original pair of ships delivered in 2005, they have been followed by a quartet of additional vessels that are currently in the course of delivery. The 'Luyang' hull is also being used for an improved Type 052D 'Luyang III' class that may extend to as many as twelve ships. *(Royal Australian Navy)*

The frigate *Linyi* is the thirteenth member of China's Type 054A class and was commissioned in December 2012. In September 2013 she was one of a flotilla of Chinese ships that paid a goodwill visit to the US Navy's base at Pearl Harbor. *(US Navy)*

have emerged it has become clear the new ships have adopted the same basic hull and propulsion plant of the earlier destroyers. However, they feature improved multi-function radars and a new vertical launch system (VLS) that can support a range of anti-air, anti-submarine and anti-surface missiles, thereby giving the ships a more general-purpose orientation.

Looking further ahead, design work has also been reported on a much larger Type 055 cruiser-sized vessel, which may displace around 10,000 tons. A mock-up of the ship has been built at the China Ship Design and Research Centre at Wuhan, where a replica of *Liaoning* was previously constructed. This suggests the new ship will be approximately 175m long and over 21m in width with space for 128 VLS cells. Some commentators suggest that the first vessel will commence construction in Shanghai before the end of 2014.

Frigate construction continues to be focused on the proven Type 054A 'Jiangkai II' class, with seventeen of a likely production-run of twenty in service as of mid-2014. There have been reports of plans for a follow-on Type 054B variant, focused on anti-submarine duties and incorporating an integrated electric propulsion system.

Meanwhile, rapid production of the Type 056 'Jiangdao' littoral-warfare corvettes has seen around fifteen delivered as of mid-2014, with perhaps as many again under construction. It appears that the class may be built to different configurations, with some of the more recent units adapted to ship a large variable-depth sonar. The successful introduction of the class appears to be spelling the end of the older Type 053 'Jianghu' class, which is disappearing rapidly from front-line service.

Submarines: After a hiatus of several years, Chinese submarine production appears to be back in full swing. The last year has seen news of the launch both a modified Type 094 'Jin' nuclear-powered strategic submarine and an improved Type 093B 'Shang' nuclear-powered attack submarine. The latter is reportedly the first of four additional upgraded variants. Whilst firm information is difficult to come by, a number of commentators suggest that initial members of the two classes suffered high noise levels, with the pause in construction necessary to allow better noise insulation to be developed. The new variants are likely to be interim designs featuring limited enhancements before series production of the much-rumoured Type 095 and Type 096 submarines commences. US intelligence reports suggest that the JL-2 ballistic missile that forms the 'Jin' class's principal armament has now completed development trials and is ready for operational deployment.[8]

Conventional submarine production has migrated to a Type 039C variant of the Type 039/41 'Yuan' series. The first boat was launched in December 2013 from Wuhan Shipyard and appears slightly larger than previous members of the class with a revised sail arrangement. The PLAN is believed to maintain two submarine flotillas, each comprising eight patrol submarines, in its three fleets. Whilst the majority of these are now comprised of modern 'Song', 'Yuan' and Russian 'Kilo' designs, further construction is necessary to replace remaining legacy 'Ming' types that have limited operational utility.

Other Warships: Away from the front line, increasing the number of available replenishment ships remains a high priority. At present, lack of these ships remains a major limitation on international operations but construction of the existing Type 903 'Fuchi' class has been stepped up to fill the gap. Two additional Type 903A variants *Taihu* and *Chaohu* joined the fleet in 2013 and a fifth ship was launched in May 2014. There has been little firm news of further amphibious ship construction but mine-countermeasures capabilities are being steadily upgraded.

MAJOR REGIONAL POWERS – JAPAN

The *National Security Strategy* and associated new *National Defense Program Guidelines for FY2014 and beyond* approved by the Japanese government in December 2013 mark a further shift in Japan's military strategy towards the defence of its southwest islands.[9] Replacing the previous 2011–15 Japanese Mid-Term Defence Programme, the revised plan focuses on acquiring surveillance, amphibious and associated aviation and maritime assets that will enable a more effective and rapid response to any actualisation of a perceived Chinese threat to the Nansei island chain. Although set in the context of ongoing reliance on the Japan-US alliance, the strategy clearly aims to provide Japan with a greater ability to act independently in defence of its own interests.[10] The need to counter North Korea's nuclear and missile development programmes remains another important consideration.

From a maritime perspective, the revised strategy's most important outcome is a decision to increase the Japan Maritime Self Defence Force's destroyer force from the current forty-seven vessels to fifty-four ships. The increase will be implemented through life-extensions of older vessels. It will allow an additional, sixth, local escort division to be formed to supplement the four two-division escort flotillas that comprise the heart of the surface fleet. The guidelines also provide for the acquisition of two additional Aegis-equipped air-defence destroyers to increase the number of Aegis ships within the overall total number of escorts to eight. These will presumably replace the two existing *Hatakaze* (DDG-171) class vessels that were commissioned between 1986 and 1988. Submarine numbers were already scheduled to grow from sixteen to twenty-two in the previous programme. The new guidelines confirm this increase, which is likely to start to take effect on an incremental basis from 2015. A key question is the extent to which sufficient crews can be found to man this larger fleet given that there are seemingly no plans to increase personnel beyond current numbers.

The FY2014 defence budget reflects the new defence strategy's emphasis on trying to do a lot more with only a limited increase in resources.[11] As

Japan's new mid-term defence plan envisages the acquisition of two new Aegis-equipped destroyers, which will provide a total of eight ships. The new vessels will replace the aging *Hatakaze* class destroyers; the lead ship of the pair is pictured at Yokosuka in August 2013. *(Conrad Waters)*

The two final members of the Japan Maritime Self Defence Force's *Akizuki* class were delivered in March 2014, replacing two older *Hatsuyuki* class destroyers. This image shows *Suzutsuki* (DD-117) soon after delivery in April 2014. *(JMSDF)*

for FY2013, new construction is based on one new destroyer, one new submarine and one new minesweeper, although there is also provision for a replacement 5,600-ton submarine rescue ship at a cost of 51bn Japanese yen (US$510m). The submarine will be the tenth member of the AIP-equipped *Soryu* class, whilst the destroyer and minesweeper are the second members of the new 25DD and 25MSO types. Around US$100m is allocated for the modernisation of no fewer than eleven destroyers and two submarines. Preparatory work will also begin for a large-scale modernisation of the *Osumi* (LST-4001) dock landing ships as part of moves to strengthen amphibious capabilities.

The last year has seen only modest changes in the overall fleet composition set out in Table 2.2.4. The main development has seen the third and fourth *Akizuki* (DD-115) class destroyers replace two older *Hatsuyuki* (DD-122) types. However, next year will see the arrival of the first new carrier-like *Izumo*

Table 2.2.4: JAPAN MARITIME SELF-DEFENCE FORCE: PRINCIPAL UNITS AS AT MID 2014

TYPE	CLASS	NUMBER	TONNAGE	DIMENSIONS	PROPULSION	CREW	DATE
Support and Helicopter Carriers							
Helicopter Carrier – DDH	**HYUGA** (DDH-181)	2	18,000 tons	197m x 33m x 7m	COGAG, 30 knots	340	2009
Principal Surface Escorts							
Helicopter Destroyer – DDH	**SHIRANE** (DDH-143)	2	7,500 tons	159m x 18m x 5m	Steam, 32 knots	350	1980
Destroyer – DDG	**ATAGO** (DDG-177)	2	10,000 tons	165m x 21m x 6m	COGAG, 30 knots	300	2007
Destroyer – DDG	**KONGOU** (DDG-173)	4	9,500 tons	161m x 21m x 6m	COGAG, 30 knots	300	1993
Destroyer – DDG	**HATAKAZE** (DDG-171)	2	6,300 tons	150m x 16m x 5m	COGAG, 30 knots	260	1986
Destroyer – DD	**AKIZUKI** (DD-115)	4	6,800 tons	151m x 18m x 5m	COGAG, 30 Knots	200	2012
Destroyer – DDG	**TAKANAMI** (DD-110)	5	5,300 tons	151m x 17m x 5m	COGAG, 30 knots	175	2003
Destroyer – DDG	**MURASAME** (DD-101)	9	5,200 tons	151m x 17m x 5m	COGAG, 30 knots	165	1996
Destroyer – DDG	**ASAGIRI** (DD-151)	8	4,300 tons	137m x 15m x 5m	COGAG, 30 knots	220	1988
Destroyer – DDG	**HATSUYUKI** (DD-122)	3 (3)	3,800 tons	130m x 14m x 4m	COGOG, 30 knots	200	1982
Frigate – FFG	**ABUKUMA** (DE-229)	6	2,500 tons	109m x 13m x 4m	CODOG, 27 knots	120	1989
Submarines							
Submarine – SSK	**SORYU** (SS-501)	5	4,200 tons	84m x 9m x 8m	AIP, 20 knots+	65	2009
Submarine – SSK	**OYASHIO** (SS-590)	11	4,000 tons	82m x 9m x 8m	Diesel-electric, 20 knots+	70	1998
Submarine – SSK	**HARUSHIO** (SS-583)	0 (2)	3,300 tons	77m x 10m x 8m	Diesel-electric, 20 knots+	75	1990
Major Amphibious Units							
Landing Platform Dock – LPD	**OSUMI** (LST-4001)	3	14,000 tons	178m x 26m x 6m	Diesel, 22 knots	135	1998

Note: Figures in brackets refer to trials or training ships.

The new helicopter-carrying destroyer *Izumo* (DDH-183) will be delivered in the spring of 2015. Larger than the preceding *Hyuga* class with a full-load displacement in excess of 24,000 tons, she is one of a number of light carrier type vessels entering service with the larger Asian fleets. *(JMSDF)*

(DDH-183) class helicopter-carrying destroyer, which was launched in August 2013. A significantly enlarged derivative of the existing *Hyuga* (DDH-181) class, she is the first of two ships intended to replace the existing *Shirane* (DDH-143) destroyers. Although orientated towards anti-submarine missions, she has the potential to be adapted for amphibious or even short take-off and vertical landing (STOVL) fixed-wing operations at some future date.

MAJOR REGIONAL POWERS – SOUTH KOREA

Although Table 2.2.5 shows no change in the composition of the Republic of Korea Navy's major units over the past twelve months, a large number of programmes are underway that will start to deliver additional vessels in the years ahead. In the short term, the second and third FFX patrol frigates of the *Incheon* class, *Gyeonggi* and *Jeonbuk*, have now been launched by Hyundai Heavy Industries and are expected to enter service before the end of 2014. More details of the improved Batch II variant to be built by rival DSME are also starting to emerge. They will incorporate an all-electric propulsion system in place of the Batch I design's combined diesel or gas (CODOG) arrangement, as well as a vertical launch system for anti-submarine and anti-surface missiles and an improved, medium-range air-defence system. Both types are able to operate the Lynx and upgraded Lynx Wildcat helicopters that form the mainstay of the navy's helicopter fleet. The new ships are optimised for littoral operations and will operate in conjunction with the PKX missile-armed fast attack craft, of which fifteen are now in service. The existing *Ulsan* and *Po Hang* class light frigates are considered increasingly vulnerable in the context of improvements to North Korean submarine and missile armouries and their replacement is therefore a high priority.[12]

The second South Korean *Incheon* class frigate *Gyeonggi* pictured on her naming day on 18 July 2013. Third of class *Jeonbuk* is seen behind. Both ships will be delivered in the second half of 2014. *(Hyundai Heavy Industries)*

Table 2.2.5: REPUBLIC OF KOREA NAVY: PRINCIPAL UNITS AS AT MID 2014

TYPE	CLASS	NUMBER	TONNAGE	DIMENSIONS	PROPULSION	CREW	DATE
Principal Surface Escorts							
Destroyer – DDG	KDX-III **SEJONGDAEWANG-HAM**	3	10,000 tons	166m x 21m x 6m	COGAG, 30 knots	300	2008
Destroyer – DDG	KDX-II **CHUNGMUGONG YI SUN-SHIN**	6	5,500 tons	150m x 17m x 5m	CODOG, 30 knots	200	2003
Destroyer – DDG	KDX-I **GWANGGAETO-DAEWANG**	3	3,900 tons	135m x 14m x 4m	CODOG, 30 knots	170	1998
Frigate – FFG	FFX **INCHEON**	1	3,000 tons	114m x 14m x 4m	CODOG, 30 knots	140	2013
Frigate – FFG	**ULSAN**	9	2,300 tons	102m x 12m x 4m	CODOG, 35 knots	150	1981
Corvette – FSG	**PO HANG**	21	1,200 tons	88m x 10m x 3m	CODOG, 32 knots	95	1984
Submarines							
Submarine – SSK	KSS-2 **SON WON-IL** (Type 214)	3	1,800 tons	65m x 6m x 6m	AIP, 20+ knots	30	2007
Submarine – SSK	KSS-1 **CHANG BOGO** (Type 209)	9	1,300 tons	56m x 6m x 6m	Diesel-electric, 22 knots	35	1993
Major Amphibious Units							
Amph Assault Ship – LHD	LPX **DOKDO**	1	18,900 tons	200m x 32m x 7m	Diesel, 22 knots	425	2007

In the longer term, there is still a strong desire to develop a powerful 'blue water' maritime capability that is, perhaps, influenced by historic rivalry with neighbouring Japan. The Korean Joint Chiefs of Staff approved a navy plan to double the fleet of Aegis-equipped destroyers to six over the 2023–7 timeframe at the end of 2013. A smaller KDX-IIA destroyer, also equipped with Aegis, has also been previously discussed. Another high priority for the surface fleet is construction of a sister, tentatively named *Marado*, for the existing amphibious assault ship, *Dokdo*, before the end of the current decade. In the meantime, the first of a class of new 4,500-ton tank landing ships, *Cheonwangbon*, was launched by Hanjin Heavy Industries & Construction in September 2013.

The Republic of Korea Navy's amphibious assault ship *Dokdo* is seen with her larger US Navy counterpart *Bonhomme Richard* (LHD-6) in March 2014. South Korea hopes to commission a second member of the class before the end of the decade. *(US Navy)*

Underneath the waves, *Kim Jwa-Jin*, the first of Korea's second batch of Type 214 AIP-equipped submarines was launched by DSME on 13 August 2013. She will enter service in the autumn of 2014. A further five boats are in various stages of construction. Attention will then turn to delivery of the new indigenously designed KS-III type, the first two of which were ordered from DSME in December 2012.

OTHER REGIONAL FLEETS

Brunei: The Royal Brunei Navy has added to its fleet of three *Darussalam* class offshore patrol vessels with the delivery of an additional unit, *Daruttaqwa*, from Germany's Lürssen on 9 May 2014. The new ship commenced construction in 2012 and, in common with her sisters, is fitted with a 57mm gun and a large flight deck for helicopter operations. The navy operates four smaller *Itjihad* coastal patrol vessels, also built by Lürssen.

Indonesia: As the world's fourth most populous country, as well as one of the twenty largest economies, Indonesia has the potential to become one of Asia's major regional naval powers. However, the massive challenge involved in policing the vast Indonesian archipelago, undue reliance placed on a historically inefficient domestic shipbuilding industry, and limited defence budgets have all served to limit the country's maritime influence. More posi-

An image of the Royal Brunei Navy's offshore patrol vessel *Darulehsan* on exercise with the US Navy in November 2012. The navy has recently taken delivery of *Daruttaqwa*, a fourth member of the class. *(US Navy)*

tively, a recent improvement in funding is spurring significant investment and a multitude of indigenous and international procurement programmes are underway.

The core of the country's somewhat limited front-line fleet is comprised of six elderly Dutch *Van Speijk* class frigates bought second-hand in the late 1980s and the four modern 'Sigma' type *Diponegoro* corvettes completed by Damen between 2007 and 2009. Two larger 'Sigma' type PKR 10514 frigates were ordered from Damen in 2012/13; they will be assembled by PT PAL in Surabaya from modules constructed in both Europe and Indonesia. Fabrication of the first ship commenced with simultaneous steel-cutting ceremonies on sections at Damen Schelde Naval Shipbuilding in the Netherlands and PT PAL on 15 January 2014. The fleet is being further strengthened by mid-life modernisation of the three *Fatahillah* corvettes under a programme being coordinated by Britain's Ultra Electronics. Acquisition of the three former *Nakhoda Ragam* corvettes originally built for Brunei by BAE Systems has also been confirmed. To be renamed the *Bung Tomo* class in Indonesian service, the three ships have been maintained and prepared for sailing in a project involving, amongst others, James Fisher Marine Services of Barrow-in-Furness and will be handed over from mid-2014 onwards. The lead ship was reportedly undergoing trials in Scottish waters in the spring of 2014. Completion of all these programmes will provide Indonesia with a fleet of eighteen, reasonably modern surface escorts. Sixteen *Kapitan Pattimura* (Project 1331 'Parchim I') corvettes and the sole *Ki Hajar Dewantara* training frigate also remain in service to form a second-line escort force.

There remains considerable focus on indigenous construction of missile-armed fast attack craft, which are well-suited for littoral defence of the arch-

The Indonesian Navy is steadily expanding its fleet of modern corvettes and light frigates. These images show the Dutch-built 'Sigma' type corvette *Sultan Iskandar Muda* delivered in 2008 and the British-built *John Lie*, the lead ship of three *Nakhoda Ragam* class vessels ordered by Brunei in the mid-1990s and finally bought by Indonesia in 2012. *(Royal Australian Navy) (Rob van der Wurff)*

ipelago's extensive territorial waters. A fleet of around forty of these vessels appears to be the final objective. An initial order for four of the 250-ton KCR-40 type has now been completed, whilst the first of three larger, 450-ton KCR-60 vessels, *Sampari*, was commissioned on 27 May 2014. It also appears that the navy has decided to proceed with the 63m-long KCR trimaran design built by PT Lundin in spite of the prototype's destruction by fire soon after delivery. Construction of a replacement reportedly commenced in early 2014 and will incorporate a Saab combat-management system, radar and surface-to-surface missile system. Modernisation of the older *Mandau* and *Todak* classes is also being contemplated.

Indonesia has an ultimate requirement for a fleet of ten to twelve submarines; a significant increase from the two Type 209/1300 *Cakra* boats currently in commission. DSME of Korea was contracted to build a further three Type 209 submarines of Korea's *Chang Bogo* variant in December 2011, of which the last will be built by PT PAL in Surabaya. Additional funding of US$250m has been advanced to PT PAL for the construction of new shipyard facilities, technical expertise and personnel training in the hope of establishing a domestic submarine industry.[13] It also seems that Russia has been approached to ascertain the cost of new or second-hand 'Kilo' class boats, although funding could be a problem.

The two *Lekiu* class frigates form the core of the Royal Malaysian Navy's surface combat capability and are very active. This April 2014 view shows the lead ship leaving Australia's Fleet Base West near Perth during the search for missing Malaysia Airlines Flight 370. *(Royal Australian Navy)*

Malaysia: The Royal Malaysian Navy's most important acquisition project remains the 'Kedah 2' corvette programme. Often referred to as the littoral combat ship project, this involves the construction of six French-designed 'Gowind' type corvettes by local shipyard Boustead Naval Shipyard. The new ships will be larger and much better armed than the six initial *Kedah* class corvettes based on the German MEKO 100 design that were commissioned between 2006 and 2010. Current plans envisage fabrication of the first ship commencing by early 2015 prior to entry into operational service in 2018. Meanwhile, the existing *Kedah* class ships are to be upgraded with an improved radar system and surface-to-surface missiles to give them greater combat potential.

The most important ships remain the two BAE Systems-built *Lekiu* class frigates. Both are very active, with *Lekiu* being one of a number of ships despatched to search the Indian Ocean for the wreckage of Malaysia Airlines Flight 370 that disappeared on 7 March 2014. The two older German *Kasturi* class frigates are close to completing a mid-life upgrade that includes installation of a Thales Tacticos combat-management system. Both should have returned to operational service by the end of 2014.

Malaysia is one of a number of countries in the region impacted by China's territorial ambitions in the South China Sea and is taking steps to respond to the challenge. The main operating base for the navy's two 'Scorpène' type submarines is already located in Sabah in East Malaysia and a new amphibious base is being established in neighbouring Sarawak, close to the disputed James Shoal. A major constraint on Malaysia's plans is the lack of meaningful amphibious shipping following the destruction of the *Newport* class landing ship *Sri Inderapura* by fire in 2009. The US Navy has offered the 'hot transfer' of the amphibious transport dock *Denver* (LPD-9) once she decommissions in the autumn of 2014. However, it is believed that Malaysia would prefer to acquire a more modern vessel.

New Zealand: The last year has seen the Royal New Zealand Navy make progress with two important modernisation programmes. Most significantly, the upgrade of the country's two *Anzac* class frigates has been agreed with the award of a C$180m (US$165m) contract to Lockheed Martin to upgrade the two ship's combat-management systems along similar lines to the Royal Canadian Navy's *Halifax* class mid-life upgrade. The ships will also be equipped with the new MBDA Sea Ceptor surface-to-air missile that has previously been ordered for the British Royal Navy's Type 23 frigate modernisation programme. Meanwhile, the first of eight new Kaman SH-2G(I) Super Seasprite helicopters (plus two spare airframes) ordered in 2013 began flight testing in April 2014 prior to delivery before the end of the year. All the helicopters should be in New Zealand by 2015, with the fleet scheduled to become fully operational during 2016.

Looking further forwards, an announcement on the multi-purpose support vessel designed to replace the existing fleet replenishment tanker *Endeavour* was scheduled to be announced in mid-2014. There have also been reports that the New Zealand government is considering an order for a third offshore patrol vessel to help release the two frigates for other operations.

The Philippines: The Philippines are, perhaps, the country most impacted by China's 'nine-dash line' claim in the South China Sea and were widely regarded as having come off worse in a spat over the disputed Scarborough Shoal in 2012. Having previously devoted much of the country's limited resources to countering long-standing communist and Islamist insurgencies, much greater focus is now being placed on external defence. The navy is, accordingly, benefiting from much greater resources than hitherto as it works towards achieving a 'Philippine Fleet Desired Force Mix' revealed in 2012. This includes six frigates, twelve corvettes, eighteen offshore patrol vessels, various amphibious, logistics and support assets, as well as – most ambitiously – three submarines.

Even with improved funding, it is clear that the desired fleet structure is not going to be achieved overnight. Nevertheless, a start has been made. Two former US Coast Guard *Hamilton* (WHEC-715) class high-endurance cutters have already been delivered and it is hoped to acquire up to two more. The ships have been re-categorised as patrol frigates in Philippine Navy service and will be upgraded with new sensors and weapon systems. The desired frigate force of six ships will be completed by acquisition of two new-build ships at an estimated cost of c. US$420m, for which a derivative of South Korea's *Incheon* design appears to be a strong contender. Korea will reportedly donate one of its existing *Po Hang* class corvettes to the Philippine Navy in the second half of 2014 to support its bid. South Korea will be retiring large numbers of this class over the next few years and further transfers would help meet the desired force mix for corvettes. The navy is also acquiring five AgustaWestland AW109E Power helicopters to operate from its frigates and plans to buy two additional anti-submarine rotorcraft. AgustaWestland's AW159 Wildcat is considered the likely winner of this contract.

Amphibious support will be enhanced through a c. US$85m contact concluded in August 2013 with

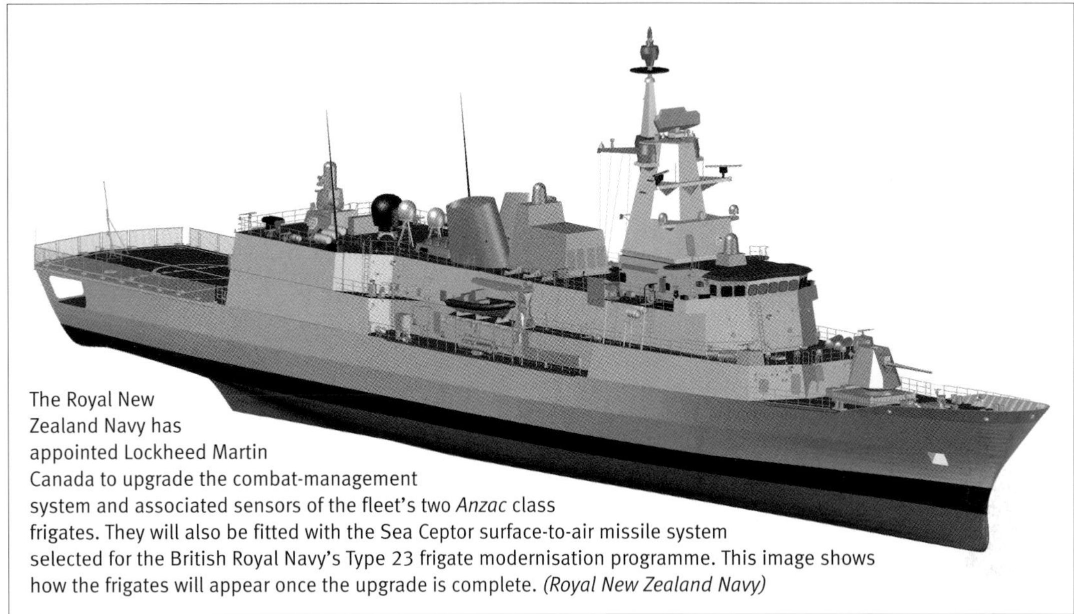

The Royal New Zealand Navy has appointed Lockheed Martin Canada to upgrade the combat-management system and associated sensors of the fleet's two *Anzac* class frigates. They will also be fitted with the Sea Ceptor surface-to-air missile system selected for the British Royal Navy's Type 23 frigate modernisation programme. This image shows how the frigates will appear once the upgrade is complete. *(Royal New Zealand Navy)*

The Royal New Zealand Navy is happy with the cost-effectiveness of the new offshore patrol vessels acquired under Project Protector and are contemplating acquisition of a third ship. This image shows the second member of the class, *Otago*, in home waters in October 2013. *(Royal New Zealand Navy)*

The Royal Thai Navy's modified *Port of Spain* class offshore patrol vessel *Krabi* was completed in 2013 and represented Thailand at Australia's International Fleet Review. She is more heavily armed than the three ships BAE Systems sold to Brazil after they were rejected by Trinidad and Tobago and incorporates a combat-management system and sensors provided by Thales Nederland. *(Royal Australian Navy)*

Indonesia's PT PAL for two amphibious transport docks similar to the Indonesian Navy's *Makassar* class. The two ships will be delivered from 2016 onwards and the navy hopes for another two. Logistic support will be improved by the transfer of three tankers from the Philippine National Oil Corporation.

Singapore: One of the most modern and effective of the Asian navies, the Republic of Singapore Navy is committed to a rolling programme of fleet renewal to maintain a considerable technological edge over its neighbours' typically larger fleets. The most significant development over the past year was an announcement on 2 December 2013 that the navy would acquire two new submarines from ThyssenKrupp Marine Systems (TKMS). The new submarines are being designated as Type 218SG boats and are understood to be derived from the German company's successful air-independent propulsion (AIP) equipped Type 214 class. Together with the pair of second-hand Swedish *Archer* class submarines re-commissioned in 2011 and 2013, they will replace the older quartet of *Challenger* class boats. TKMS' decision to bid the Type 218 design over Sweden's proposed A-26 submarine, which has been designed by TKMS' subsidiary Kockums, has been a significant factor behind a major falling-out between the German firm and the Swedish government. As a result, future Swedish submarine production is likely to be transferred to local company Saab.

Looking further forward, the navy is reportedly considering larger amphibious ships when the current *Endurance* class dock landing ships reach the end of their current lives in a move that could be associated with the acquisition of F-35B STOVL jets.[14] In the meantime, the most important surface programme is construction of eight replacement ships for the existing *Fearless* class patrol vessels under a contract allocated to Singapore-based ST Engineering in January 2013.

Taiwan: The Republic of China Navy is continuing a process of fleet renewal that comprises both indigenous production and overseas acquisitions. However, this is being conducted at a pedestrian pace compared with the rival PLAN's rapid build-up. The lack of urgency is particularly surprising given statements in Taiwan's latest *National Defense Report 2013*, published in October 2013, stating that mainland China would be capable of mounting an invasion of the main island by 2020.[15]

There is currently a pressing need to replace the eight obsolescent *Knox* (FF-1052) class patrol frigates that comprise nearly a third of the country's front-line fleet of twenty-six surface escorts. However, only two of four surplus FFG-7 type frigates offered by the United States are likely to be purchased, largely on cost grounds. Greater priority is being placed on the new catamaran-type 'Hsun Hai' stealth corvettes. The prototype *Tuo River*, was launched on 14 March 2014 and is likely to enter service in 2015. Up to twelve ships are eventually planned.

The long-running saga that marks Taiwan's quest for new submarines has taken a new twist with reports that the pressure hull of one of the country's existing 'Guppy II' submarines currently used for training will be replaced. The project could provide an important step towards developing the skills necessary to commence an indigenous submarine construction programme. Meanwhile, anti-submarine capabilities are starting to be bolstered by the arrival of modernised P-3C 'Orion' maritime patrol aircraft from the United States. A total of twelve aircraft will be delivered before the end of 2015.

Thailand: The Royal Thai Navy's most important current construction programme is that for a DW03000H class frigate awarded to DSME of South Korea under a contract reportedly valued at around US$450m. More details of the 3,700-ton ship, which is said to be derived from Korea's KDX-1 destroyer design, are steadily becoming available. It will feature a Saab combat-management system, a Mk 41 VLS for Evolved Sea Sparrow surface-to-air missiles, Harpoon surface-to-surface missiles, Atlas Elektronik sonar systems and an integrated mast. A second ship is planned but not yet contracted. The navy also looks likely to receive two second-hand FFG-7 type frigates under the same legislation that will see members of the class transferred to Taiwan.

Krabi, the locally-built offshore patrol ship based on the BAE Systems' *Port of Spain* class design, has now entered service, representing Thailand at Australia's 2013 centennial international fleet review. Plans for a second ship look set to be confirmed and a further pair may follow.

Purchase of submarines remains on Thailand's 'wish list'. Indeed, a submarine squadron headquarters and training centre has already been completed in anticipation that authorisation for a flotilla of at least three submarines will be forthcoming.[16]

Vietnam: The Vietnam People's Navy is yet another South East Asian navy that is receiving significant investment in response to fears of Chinese maritime expansion. The most important programme is the order for six Project 636 'Kilo' class submarines from Russia that was signed in 2009. Two of these submarines have now been delivered to Vietnam, whilst the sixth and final boat was laid down at the Admiralty Shipyard in St Petersburg at the end of May 2014. All the class will be in service by 2016, giving Vietnam its first underwater flotilla.

Russia is also Vietnam's principal supplier of surface warships. Larger ships such as the Project 1161.1E 'Gepard' class frigates are typically produced in Russia but there is increasing licensed construction of smaller corvettes and fast attack craft. In line with this approach, the keels of a second pair of 'Gepard' class ships were laid at the Zelenodolsky Plant Gorky in Tatarstan in September 2013. Compared with the first two vessels that are now in service, they will have enhanced anti-air and anti-submarine systems. Vietnam is also looking to European sources for some new equipment, having ordered a pair of Dutch 'Sigma' 9814 corvettes from Damen Schelde Naval Shipbuilding. The new ships will be fitted with combat management and radar systems from Thales Nederland and will be equipped with Mica surface-to-air and Exocet surface-to-surface missiles.

Notes

1. An Air Defence Identification Zone (ADIZ) is an area of airspace where a country requires the identification, location and control of aircraft in the interests of its national security. There are no international treaties covering ADIZs, which were first developed by the United States in the early Cold War period. Japan and South Korea both have long-established ADIZs, which partly overlap the new zone created by China. Whilst, therefore, there is a history of such measures, China's action has been regarded as confrontational in that it is the first to cover territory that is under dispute at the time of its creation.

2. Prime Minister Abe's remarks were interesting in that he noted that the significant trade links between the European powers, reflective of economic ties in Asia today, did not prevent them being drawn into conflict. Amongst extensive coverage of Mr Abe's remarks was Ben Chu's 'Japanese premier Shinzo Abe compares tension between Tokyo and Beijing to that in Europe before First World War', *The Independent* – 22 January 2014 (London, Independent Print Ltd, 2014).

3. For further detail see James Hardy's 'China building island in South China Sea', *Jane's Defence Weekly* – 21 May 2014 (Coulsdon, IHS Jane's, 2014), p.5.

4. Amongst extensive coverage of the agreement, a good overview of the strengths and weaknesses of the code was provided by Rear Admiral (rtd) James Goldrick in 'Cue co-operation? Pacific naval code aims to improve collaboration at sea', *Jane's Defence Weekly* – 21 May 2014 (Coulsdon, IHS Jane's, 2014), pp.24–5.

5. The potential implications of the widely reported deal were assessed in an informative article by Paul Kallender-Umezu and Nigel Pittaway entitled 'Japan, Australia Deal Poses Tech Issues', *Defense News* – 15 June 2014 (Spring-field VA, Gannett Government Media Corporation, 2014).

6. A local perspective on the naval exercises was provided by Minnie Chan in 'China, Russia start joint naval exercise', *South China Morning Post* – 20 May 2014 (Hong Kong, South China Morning Post Publishers Ltd, 2014). The article was accompanied by pictures of the Chinese and Russian premiers meeting participating personnel, adding to the political significance of the event.

7. As always, accurate information on the PLAN is difficult to obtain and the table needs to be regarded with particular caution. Much of the information provided in this section is derived from web-based sources. The *China Air and Naval Power* blog at http://china-pla.blogspot.co.uk/ and the *China Defense Blog* at http://china-defense.blogspot.co.uk/ remain particularly useful.

8. The US Department of Defense is obliged to update Congress annually on its assessment of Chinese military capabilities. The most recent update was published at the start of June 2014. See *Annual Report to Congress: Military and Security Developments Involving the People's Republic of China 2014* (Washington DC, US Department of Defense, 2014). A web-based version can be found at: athttp://www.defense.gov/pubs/2014_DoD_China_Report.pdf

9. *National Security Strategy December 17, 2013* and *National Defense Program Guidelines for FY2014 and beyond*, op cit.

10. In this regard, the strategy is in line with the current Japanese administration's desire to have greater freedom of action in its use of the Japanese Self Defence Forces, as evidenced by an ongoing debate on revisions to Article 9 of the Japanese Constitution that outlaws the country's recourse to war as a means of settling disputes. Japan's President Abe is regarded as having right-wing, nationalistic leanings by critics who see him as attempting to revise away Japan's responsibilities for war crimes in the Second World War. His visit to the Yasukuni Shrine, which venerates a small number of war criminals amongst some 2.5 million people who died in the service of Japan, on 26 December 2013, brought severe criticism from China and South Korea, as well as an expression of disappointment from the United States.

11. A copy of the annual Japanese defence budget, the *Defense Programs and Budget of Japan: Overview of FY2014 Budget* (Tokyo, Japanese Ministry of Defence, 2014) can be found at: http://www.mod.go.jp/e/d_budget/pdf/260130.pdf

12. North Korea's acquisition of sophisticated Russian Kh-35 surface-to-surface missiles is one particular area of concern for the South. See 'New N. Korean Anti-Ship Missiles Threaten Older Patrol Boats', *The Chosun Ilbo* – 9 June 2014 (Seoul, Chosun Media Group, 2014).

13. The news was reported in an article entitled 'PT PAL gets $250m to build submarines', *The Jakarta Post* – 18 February 2014 (Jakarta, PT Bina Media Tenggara, 2014). The article suggested that the project to construct the third submarine of the class locally was already badly delayed, with only thirteen of more than 200 technicians requiring training by DSME sent to Korea so far.

14. The possibility of Singapore acquiring aircraft carriers was considered by Wendell Minnick in 'Is a Light Carrier in Singapore's Future?', *Defense News* – 1 March 2014 (Spring-field VA, Gannett Government Media Corporation, 2014).

15. *National Defense Report 2013* (Taipei, Ministry of National Defense, 2013). A copy can currently be found at: http://report.mnd.gov.tw/

16. The story was first reported by Wassana Nanuam under the title 'Submarine base nears completion' in the *Bangkok Post* – 12 October 2013 (Bangkok, The Post Publishing PCL, 2013). The headquarters were authorised as part of a plan to acquire former German Type 206A submarines which ultimately failed to gain government approval. A copy of the article was published on the *Defense Studies* website – http://defense-studies.blogspot.co.uk/ – which is an excellent source of new stories on Asian military developments.

2.3 REGIONAL REVIEW

Author:
Conrad Waters

THE INDIAN OCEAN AND AFRICA

INTRODUCTION

Events in August 2013 vividly demonstrated the progress India has made towards becoming a regional naval power; but also the limited extent of its achievement. On Friday 10 August, engineers at the Ship Building Centre at Visakhapatnam in Andhra Pradesh activated the nuclear reactor of the indigenously-constructed strategic submarine *Arihant*. The event marked a major step in India's ambition to become the first country outside of the five permanent members of the UN Security Council to build a strategic missile-armed submarine. Two days later, in the southwest coast city of Kochi, India's first domestically-built aircraft carrier, *Vikrant*, was launched amidst considerable ceremony by Elizabeth Antony, wife of the then minister of defence, A K Antony. Champion of a 'Buy and Make Indian' defence procurement policy, Antony lauded the event as a '… remarkable milestone …' in India's technological and military development.

On 14 August the aura of hubris that surrounded these two undoubtedly significant developments evaporated after the newly refitted Project 877EKM 'Kilo' class submarine *Sindhurakshak* exploded and sank in Mumbai's naval dockyard. The disaster, which claimed eighteen lives, was just one of a series of accidents and mishaps that culminated in the resignation of India's Chief of Naval Staff, Admiral D K Joshi, on 26 February 2014. His departure took place amongst growing frustration in Indian defence circles over shrinking capital expenditure, stalled procurement projects and the inability of industry to deliver new equipment in a timely fashion. One *cause célèbre* has been a failure to order torpedoes for the new 'Scorpène' submarines, themselves considerably delayed, which will start to enter service from 2016.[1]

India's problems, whilst partly self-inflicted, provide a broader lesson on the challenges the emergent regional powers face in converting their economic success into effective regional military – including maritime – power. Shifts in economic performance, political interference and vacillation, competing social priorities, a limited domestic industrial infrastructure and simple lack of competence can all serve to undermine the best-laid modernisation plans. A particularly interesting aspect of the Indian situation is the squeeze on the overall defence budget caused by rapidly increasing personnel costs. These have grown from twenty-five per cent to thirty-seven per cent of total spending in just the six years between 2008 and 2014.[2] Spending on basic but essential items such as spares and maintenance has shrunk in consequence. It seems much has still to be learned about the need to counter the acceleration in defence inflation that accompanies economic growth. For example, India's latest Project 17 *Shivalik* class frigates require a crew of some 260 personnel. The equivalent figure for France's comparable *Aquitaine* is just 110.

The Indian Navy's troubles come at a time when significant changes are impacting the balance of power in the Indian Ocean and, particularly, the neighbouring Middle East. There is a growing perception that US interest in the region is waning as it becomes less reliant on Saudi Arabian oil supplies and pivots to the Pacific. The 2012 Presidential Strategic Guidance, subsequently reinforced by the 2014 Quadrennial Defence Review, stressed a focus on maintaining stability in the Middle East.[3] However, there are considerable fears amongst America's regional partners about the strength of this commitment, placing increased emphasis on the rivalry between Sunni Islam-dominated Saudi Arabia and the Shia-based theocracy of Iran. The two regional powers are using proxy organisations in a battle for influence across the Middle East, with the civil wars in Syria, Iraq and elsewhere one aspect of this struggle. Saudi Arabia, particularly, is concerned about the United States' growing rapprochement with Iran, as well as its failure to assist the rebels fighting Iran's major regional ally, Syria.

The naval consequences of these developments are many and varied. Positively, there seems to be a lower likelihood of conflict in the Persian Gulf, particularly if an agreement on Iran's nuclear weapons programme can be reached. However, the level of naval activity across the region remains high, be it counter-piracy operations off the coast of Somalia or deployments in support of the disposal of Syria's chemical weapons stockpile. As elsewhere, the increased presence of China's PLAN is a noteworthy feature. Another is the growing willingness – and ability – of many of the Middle East's larger countries to assume greater responsibility for their own maritime security. This is particularly evidenced by a progressive increase in the number of major naval acquisition programmes underway.

The first indigenously-constructed Indian aircraft carrier *Vikrant* was floated out from the Cochin Shipyard in the southwest city of Kochi on 12 August 2013. Although largely structurally complete, considerable outfitting remains to be undertaken before she is ready for service. The celebrations surrounding her launch were short-lived as a result of the destruction of the 'Kilo' class submarine *Sindhurakshak* by explosion and fire with considerable loss of life at Mumbai naval dockyard just two days later. *(Indian Navy)*

Table 2.3.1: FLEET STRENGTHS IN THE INDIAN OCEAN, AFRICA AND THE MIDDLE EAST – LARGER NAVIES (MID 2014)

COUNTRY	ALGERIA	EGYPT	INDIA	IRAN	ISRAEL	PAKISTAN	SAUDI ARABIA	SOUTH AFRICA
Support/Helicopter Carrier (CVS/CVH)	–	–	2	–	–	–	–	–
Attack Submarine (SSN/SSGN)	–	–	1	–	–	–	–	–
Patrol Submarine (SSK/SS)	4	4	12	3	5	5	–	3
Fleet Escort (DDG/FFG)	–	6	23	–	–	10	7	4
Patrol Escort/Corvette (FFG/FSG/FS)	6	4	8	7	3	–	4	–
Missile Armed Attack Craft (PGG/PTG)	12	30	12	24	8	8	9	4
Mine Countermeasures Vessel (MCMV)	–	14	7	–	–	3	7	4
Major Amphibious (LPD)	–	–	1	–	–	–	–	–

Notes:

1 Egyptian fast attack craft numbers approximate.

2 The South African attack craft and mine-countermeasures vessels serve in patrol vessel roles.

INDIAN OCEAN NAVIES

Bangladesh: A detailed review of the Bangladesh Navy's historical development and current status is set out in Chapter 2.3A. A particularly notable recent event for British readers has been the decommissioning of the former Royal Navy 1950s-era Type 41 frigates *Abu Bakr* (the former *Lynx*) and *Ali Haider* (the former *Jaguar*) at a ceremony in Chittagong on 22 January 2014.[4] They have been replaced by two former Chinese Type 053H2 'Jianghu III' class vessels. The similar-vintage Type 81 frigate *Umar Farooq* (formerly *Llandaff*) still remains in service as a training ship.

India: As noted in the Introduction, the last twelve months have seen mixed fortunes for the Indian Navy. In addition to the destruction of *Sindhurakshak*, two officers were killed in a fire on her sister boat, *Sindhuratna*, in February 2014 and there was a further casualty after a gas leak on the new destroyer *Kolkata* in March during pre-delivery trials. A dockyard worker also lost his life in the same month in an accident on one of the new strategic submarines being built at Visakhapatnam. However, the long-delayed arrival of the refurbished Russian carrier *Vikramaditya* (the former *Admiral Gorshkov*) has provided a major boost to Indian naval air power, whilst a number of important domestic construction projects moved further forward. Table 2.3.2 provides an overview of current fleet composition, whilst further details on major ship categories are provided below.

Aircraft Carriers: The refitted *Vikramaditya* was finally commissioned into the Indian Navy at the Sevmash yard in Severodvinsk on 16 November 2013 following rectification of boiler problems identified during her 2012 sea trials. In spite of reports of further glitches during her delivery voyage, she arrived safely in Indian waters in January 2014. She has subsequently been involved in aviation trials with the MiG-29K jets of 303 Naval Air Squadron that form the core of her air wing and was reported as being operational by May 2014. However, further work is already planned to provide her with enhanced surface-to-air and close-in missile defence systems.

Vikramditya's arrival allows the Indian Navy to operate two aircraft carriers simultaneously for the first time since the former *Vikrant* was retired in January 1997.[5] The current plan is to decommission the second carrier, *Viraat* (the former British Royal Navy *Hermes*), when the new *Vikrant* is completed but hopes that the latter will commence sea trials before the end of 2016 seem to be overly optimistic. In June 2014, *Jane's Defence Weekly* reported that work had largely come to a standstill due to lack of funding in the months after her August 2013 launch, with over US$2.5bn being requested from the new Indian government to complete construction.[6]

Major Surface Combatants: The first Project 15A destroyer *Kolkata* was close to delivery in mid-2014, reportedly completing test firing of its BrahMos surface-to-surface missile system at the start of June. Laid down in 2003 and launched as long ago as March 2006, she will have taken even longer to complete than the lead ship of the preceding Project 15 *Delhi* class. Two further members of the class are reportedly at an advanced stage of construction by builders Mazagon Dock Ltd of Mumbai. The yard has been extensively rebuilt in recent years and hopes to achieve considerably shorter building times for the follow-on Project 15B class. Four units of this type were authorised in 2011 and the keel of the first, Yard No. 12704, was laid on 12 October 2013. Mazagon Dock is also involved in the programme to construct seven Project 17A frigates in partnership with Kolkata's Garden Reach Shipbuilders & Engineers Ltd (GRSE). The first of the new destroyers is scheduled to enter service in 2018, with the first frigate following in 2020.

Although indigenous Indian Navy construction programmes have been impacted by considerable delays, a number are now close to fruition. This photograph shows the new Project 15A destroyer *Kolkata* in September 2013; she was close to completing sea trials in mid-2014, when her delivery was said to be imminent. *(Indian Navy)*

GRSE's current major project is the completion of four Project 28 *Kamorta* class anti-submarine corvettes, which are also badly delayed. Laid down in late 2006 and launched in April 2010, the lead ship was in the course of carrying out sea trials in the first half of 2014 and is expected to be delivered in the summer of the same year. Displacing around 3,400 tons in full load condition, she incorporates a raft-mounted combined diesel and diesel (CODAD) propulsion system to minimise acoustic signature and is equipped with an indigenous, bow-mounted sonar. Armament includes anti-submarine rocket launchers and torpedo tubes, as well as facilities to operate and support a medium-sized helicopter. A further three ships of the class are in various stages of construction. India also plans to construct a class of smaller anti-submarine patrol vessels for operations in coastal waters. A tender for up to sixteen of the new ships was issued to both public and private yards in June 2014.

Submarines: The explosion and fire that destroyed the Project 877EKM 'Kilo' class submarine *Sindhurakshak* has been a major setback to an underwater flotilla that had already been experiencing declining numbers due to delays in commissioning replacements. The submarine had only recently completed a midlife upgrade in Russia and was fully armed in preparation for an extended patrol when the initial explosion occurred shortly after midnight on 14 August 2013. Whilst the cause of the submarine's loss has yet to be definitively ascertained, it seems that a hydrogen gas leak from the submarine's batteries or a mishap relating to the boat's weapons are the most likely possibilities. The submarine was recovered by the local subsidiary of US salvage company Resolve Marine in June 2014 but it seems highly unlikely that repair will be practical. There is also scepticism over whether it will be possible to complete the mismanaged refit of sister boat *Sindhukirti*, which has been in dockyard hands since 2006. This leaves a flotilla of just twelve conventional submarines until the new Project 75 'Scorpène' class start to be delivered by Mazagon Dock. These were originally scheduled for delivery from December 2012 but this date has progressively been pushed back to September 2016. A long-awaited tender for six follow-on Project 75-I class submarines, of which two will be built abroad by the successful overseas partner, has yet to be launched.

More positively, the lease of the Project 971 'Akula II' class nuclear-powered attack submarine *Chakra* is proving to be a success. There have been reports a second boat may also be acquired from Russia on loan. Meanwhile, the first indigenous *Arihant* class strategic missile submarine has continued harbour trials throughout the first half of 2014 and is scheduled to head for the sea before the end of 2014.

Other Warships: Construction of second-line, constabulary-orientated patrol vessels appears to be progressing more smoothly than the introduction of front-line warships. Three of the new Goa Shipyard-built *Saryu* class offshore patrol vessels are now in service, with second ship *Sunayna* being delivered in October 2013 and *Sumedha* following on 7 March 2014. The latter vessel was the 200th ship delivered by the yard. Six similar vessels have been ordered for the Indian Coast Guard, which is undergoing a massive expansion after the 2008 Mumbai terrorist attacks revealed weaknesses in India's coastal security. Indian yards are also using patrol-vessel designs for a tentative exploration of export markets. *Barracuda*, a 1,300-ton offshore patrol vessel being built for the Mauritian Coast Guard under India's first major warship export contract, was launched by GRSE in August 2013.

The refurbished Russian aircraft carrier *Admiral Gorshkov*, now renamed *Vikramaditya*, was commissioned into the Indian Navy in November 2013 prior to embarking on the long delivery voyage to India. She was met by an Indian naval task force headed by the existing aircraft carrier *Vikrant*, the former British *Hermes*, in January 2014 prior to arriving at her new home base. This image shows the two carriers sailing together for the first time. *(Indian Navy)*

Table 2.3.2: INDIAN NAVY: PRINCIPAL UNITS AS AT MID 2014

TYPE	CLASS	NUMBER	TONNAGE	DIMENSIONS	PROPULSION	CREW	DATE
Aircraft Carriers							
Aircraft Carrier (CV)	Project 1143.4 **VIKRAMADITYA** (KIEV)	1	45,000 tons	283m x 31/60m x 10m	Steam, 30 knots	1,600	1987
Aircraft Carrier (CV)	**VIRAAT** (HERMES)	1	29,000 tons	227m x 27/49m x 9m	Steam, 28 knots	1,350	1959
Principal Surface Escorts							
Destroyer – DDG	Project 15 **DELHI**	3	6,700 tons	163m x 17m x 7m	COGAG, 32 knots	350	1997
Destroyer – DDG	Project 61 ME **RAJPUT** ('Kashin')	5	5,000 tons	147m x 16m x 5m	COGAG, 35 knots	320	1980
Frigate – FFG	Project 17 **SHIVALIK**	3	6,200 tons	143m x 17m x 5m	CODOG, 30 knots	265	2010
Frigate – FFG	Project 1135.6 **TALWAR**	6	4,000 tons	125m x 15m x 5m	COGAG, 30 knots	180	2003
Frigate – FFG	Project 16A **BRAHMAPUTRA**	3	4,000 tons	127m x 15m x 5m	Steam, 30 knots	350	2000
Frigate – FFG	Project 16 **GODAVARI**	3	3,850 tons	127m x 15m x 5m	Steam, 30 knots	315	1983
Corvette – FSG	Project 25A **KORA**	4	1,400 tons	91m x 11m x 5m	Diesel, 25 knots	125	1998
Corvette – FSG	Project 25 **KHUKRI**	4	1,400 tons	91m x 11m x 5m	Diesel, 25 knots	110	1989
Submarines							
Submarine – SSN	Project 971 **CHAKRA** ('Akula II')	1	9,500+ tons	110m x 14m x 10m	Nuclear, 30+ knots	100	2012
Submarine – SSK	Project 877 EKM **SINDHUGHOSH** ('Kilo')	8	3,000 tons	73m x 10m x 7m	Diesel-electric, 17 knots	55	1986
Submarine – SSK	**SHISHUMAR** (Type 209)	4	1,900 tons	64m x 7m x 6m	Diesel-electric, 22 knots	40	1986
Major Amphibious Units							
Landing Platform Dock – LPD	**JALASHWA** (AUSTIN)	1	17,000 tons	173m x 26/30m x 7m	Steam, 21 knots	405	1971

Table 2.3.3: PAKISTAN NAVY: PRINCIPAL UNITS AS AT MID 2014

TYPE	CLASS	NUMBER	TONNAGE	DIMENSIONS	PROPULSION	CREW	DATE
Principal Surface Escorts							
Frigate – FFG	**ZULFIQAR** (F22P)	4	3,000 tons	118m x 13m x 5m	CODAD, 29 knots	185	2009
Frigate – FFG	**ALAMGIR** (FFG-7)	1	4,100 tons	138m x 14m x 5m	COGAG, 30 knots	215	1977
Frigate – FFG	**TARIQ** (Type 21)	5	3,600 tons	117m x 13m x 5m	COGOG, 32 knots	180	1974
Submarines							
Submarine – SSK	**HAMZA** (AGOSTA 90B/AIP)	1	2,100 tons	76m x 7m x 6m	AIP, 20 knots	40	2008
Submarine – SSK	**KHALID** (AGOSTA 90B)	2	1,800 tons	68m x 7m x 6m	Diesel-electric, 20 knots	40	1999
Submarine – SSK	**HASHMAT** (AGOSTA)	2	1,800 tons	68m x 7m x 6m	Diesel-electric, 20 knots	55	1979

Myanmar: A review of the Union of Myanmar Navy is set out alongside that of Bangladesh in Chapter 2.3A. The most significant event over the last year has been the delivery of the fleet's second indigenously-built frigate, *Kyansitthar*, which features substantial improvements over first of class, *King Aung Zeya*. A third member of the class, *Sin Phyu Shin*, was launched on 29 March 2014.

Pakistan: Table 2.3.3, outlining key Pakistan Navy units, reflects a small but significant reduction in surface forces following the decommissioning of *Badr* (the former British *Alacrity*), the first of six elderly Type 21 frigates to be withdrawn. The Pakistan Navy has a pressing need to acquire more modern frigates and submarines to replace existing obsolescent ships but political and economic factors are making this difficult. Whilst defence funding is seeing nominal increases, the army and air force have priority in defence allocations. Meanwhile, hoped-for transfers of former US Navy equipment are being blocked by the continued political fall-out from Osama bin Laden's discovery and assassination in Abbotabad in the country's north east.

There are continuing reports that further equipment will be sourced from China to make good the shortfall. Additional submarines are seen as the highest priority, with an export variant of China's Type 039A/Type 41 'Yuan' class seen by many as the most likely way forward. The origin and nature of new surface vessels is less apparent, although further licensed construction of Chinese designs by Karachi Shipyard and Engineering Works (KRSE) seems to be a possibility. The yard delivered *Dehshat*, the second Chinese-designed *Azmat* class missile-armed fast attack craft, in June 2014 and has previously assembled a F-22P *Zulfiqar* class frigate. The former have a heavy armament of eight, C-802 surface-to-surface missiles and a top speed in excess of 30 knots. However, their relatively light, c. 500-tons, displacement and short, 63m hull make them unsuitable as replacements for fully-fledged frigates.

AFRICAN NAVIES

The scourge of piracy, which has previously had a major impact off both the east and west coasts of Africa, now appears to be in decline.[7] Nevertheless, its legacy – bolstered by a growing awareness of the need to protect offshore economic assets – is being felt in the delivery of increasingly capable constabulary assets across the continent's navies. A particularly significant process of fleet renewal is taking place in **Nigeria**, where Chinese help has been enlisted to redevelop the naval shipyard at Port Harcourt into a facility capable of building and supporting ships of offshore patrol vessel size and above.[8] The facility will be used to support the assembly of the second of two P-18N offshore patrol vessels ordered from China in April 2012. The first of these, which are reportedly derived from the PLAN's Type 056 corvette design, was launched at Wuchang Shipyard in Wuhan on 27 January 2014. Delivery is expected to be during the second half of the year. The navy has also acquired a second former United States Coast Guard *Hamilton* (WHEC-715) class cutter to bolster *Thunder*, the former *Chase* (WHEC-718), that was acquired in 2011. *Gallatin* (WHEC-721) was handed over on 7 May 2014, taking the name *Okpabana*. Additional investment is being made in modernising older ships and buying smaller vessels, whilst improvement of coastal surveillance systems is another high priority.

Although most of Africa's other west coast navies have more modest aspirations than Nigeria, many are also enjoying substantial expansion.[9] For example, the **Ivory Coast**, **Senegal** and **Togo** are all in the course of taking delivery of new coastal patrol vessels from France's Radico, **Cameroon** has obtained new ships from Spain's Grup Aresa and **Mauritania** has plans for a fleet of new offshore and coastal patrol vessels. Investment on Africa's east coast has been more restrained, although **Mozambique** announced a major contract with France's CMN in September 2013. The US$200m deal encompassed both naval and commercial vessels; the former comprising three patrol vessels and three fast interceptors. The patrol vessels will be built to the company's innovative 43m Ocean Eagle trimaran design, which incorporate a small helipad for UAV operations and a stern ramp to support fast boat operations.

South Africa remains the only navy of more than local consequence south of the Sahara. Its future trajectory has been given a little more clarity with the cabinet's approval of the South African Defence Review 2014, which builds on previous drafts published in 2012.[10] The first South African defence review since 1998, the new document sets out key defence goals and establishes four milestones to arrest what is described as a '... critical state of decline ...' and build a force capable of meeting the government's ambitions to promote regional peace and stability. The various milestones cover the period from 2015 to 2028 and each is associated with a stated percentage of GDP that would allow the goal to be met. The key immediate naval priorities are the strengthening of surveillance and offshore patrol capabilities, whilst the acquisition of heavy sealift vessels and additional combat support ships is anticipated in the medium term. It is also acknowledged that the existing frigates and submarines will need to be renewed in time. The defence review has been broadly welcomed as a starting point for rebuilding South African defence capabilities. However, the key question is whether sufficient funding will be made available to achieve its objectives.

In line with the review's objectives, the long-delayed Project Biro to replace the existing four

'Warrior' class fast attack craft with purpose-built offshore patrol vessels has been given formal approval. A tender process is expected to start before the end of 2014 and a number of potential foreign bidders are likely to team with local builders to meet the requirement. A new hydrographic ship is another high priority. The new patrol vessels will be based at the re-established facility at Durban, which is currently being refurbished. Meanwhile, a lengthy refit of the navy's first Type 209 submarine, *Manthatisi*, is almost complete following her return to the water in May 2014.

In northern Africa, **Morocco** has taken delivery of its sole FREMM type frigate *Mohammed VI*, which was handed over by DCNS on 30 January 2014. In contrast to her French sisters, she is only equipped with two, eight-cell Sylver A43 modules for Aster 15 surface-to-air missiles, lacking the longer Sylver A70 launchers for SCALP naval cruise missiles. She joins three smaller 'Sigma' type corvettes/light frigates delivered by Damen during 2011–12 and forms part of a trend of significant naval investment along the Mediterranean's southern shores.

Neighbouring **Algeria** appears to be the main driver of this wave of expenditure, with new projects including two MEKO A-200 frigates under construction in Germany, three Chinese light frigates that are reportedly similar to Pakistan's F-22P class and a new amphibious transport dock based on the Italian *San Giorgio* design. The latter ship was launched at Fincantieri's Riva Trigoso yard in January 2014, taking the name *Kalaat Beni-Abbes.* Displacing nearly 9,000 tons in full load condition, she is powered by a CODAD diesel plant that will provide speeds in excess of 20 knots. The new ship is unusual in that her primary amphibious role is supplemented by an area air-defence system built around an EMPAR phased-array radar and Sylver A50 launchers capable of supporting the medium-range Aster 30 missile. As such, she will arguably be the most potent warship on the African continent when she is delivered in the second half of 2014. Algeria is also sourcing additional equipment from Russia, which is reportedly constructing two new corvettes based on the *Steregushchy* class for delivery in 2015 and has also been modernising some of Algeria's older, Soviet-era ships. In addition, an order for an additional two 'Kilo' class submarines was confirmed in June 2014, increasing Algeria's underwater flotilla to six boats.

Egypt is not being left out of this process of naval regional re-armament. It ordered two Type 209 submarines from Germany's ThyssenKrupp Marine Systems in 2011 and has recently been reported as exercising an option for two additional boats. In addition, France's *La Tribune* news group announced in early June 2014 that DCNS had obtained a c.€1bn (US$1.35bn) contract to supply four 2,400-ton corvettes based on its 'Gowind' series, of which three would be constructed locally in Egypt.[11] Meanwhile, the first two of four 'Ambassador IV' fast attack craft built by VT Halter Marine in the United States were loaded onto a heavy-lift ship in Pensacola Bay, Florida in May 2014 to commence their long journey to the Mediterranean.

MIDDLE EASTERN NAVIES

Although tensions in the Persian Gulf have been somewhat reduced by Iran's seeming willingness to negotiate about its nuclear programme, the region remains a focal point of activity by both regional and international naval forces. Previous construction programmes are now starting to bear fruit, with **Oman** taking delivery of all three of its *Al Shamikh* class corvettes from Britain's BAE Systems over the

Morocco is one of a number of navies along the Mediterranean's southern coast bolstering their naval forces in what seems to be a largely fruitless regional arms race. This view shows the new FREMM class frigate *Mohammed VI* on sea trials in the middle of 2013; she was delivered by DCNS on 30 January 2014. *(DCNS)*

Egypt is finally taking delivery of four 'Ambassador IV' fast attack craft built by US yard VT Halter Marine under a c. US$1.3bn contract funded by the American government. The agreement became controversial in view of the military overthrow of Egypt's democratically-elected government in July 2013 but the first two vessels were shipped to Egypt in mid-2014. This image shows lead ship *S Ezzat* undergoing trials. *(VT Halter Marine)*

Britain's BAE Systems has delivered all three *Al Shamikh* class corvettes to Oman in the last twelve months, with the third and final ship, *Al Rasikh*, being handed over at HM Naval Base Portsmouth on 28 May 2014. She will be the last complete ship built at BAE System's shipyard in the base. This image shows the lead ship in British waters in August 2013. *(Conrad Waters)*

Iraq has reached agreement with Italy's Fincantieri to refurbish two 'Assad' class corvettes built during the 1980s and laid up at La Spezia since the 1990 invasion of Kuwait. This 31 March 2014 picture shows *Mussa Ben Massair*; her sister *Tariq Ibn Ziad* is behind. *(Conrad Waters)*

course of the last twelve months. The neighbouring **United Arab Emirates'** long-standing *Baynunah* programme is also drawing to a close with the delivery of the sixth and final ship, *Al Hili*, by Abu Dhabi Ship Building in February 2014. The two navies have additional construction programmes for surface warships underway whilst both the UAE and **Saudi Arabia** are said to be considering the acquisition of submarines. In the meantime, the latter has agreed a major contract with DCNS for the refurbishment of its four *Madina* class frigates and two *Boraida* replenishment ships that were originally delivered in the mid-1980s.

Iran continues to be focused on maintaining a strong balance of forces capable of asymmetrical warfare as part of its A2/AD anti-access/area denial strategy. However, it is steadily developing an ability to produce more technologically-advanced warships to serve in both the Persian Gulf and Caspian Sea. A number of news reports during early 2014 refer to the construction of a new type of 600-ton submarine, known as the 'Fateh' class, at both Bostanu Shipyard near the Straits of Hormuz and Bandar Anzali on the Caspian Sea. The boats provide a considerable leap in capability over Iran's previous indigenous 'Ghadir' midget submarines, around twenty of which have been built to date. Construction of further 'Moudge' class frigates is also underway. Meanwhile **Iraq** has received the last of twelve 35m fast coastal patrol ships from US-builder Swiftships, which – along with two larger 60m offshore support ships and four 53m Italian-built *Saettia* Mk4 offshore patrol vessels – form the core of its fleet. An agreement has also been reached with Italy's Fincantieri for refurbishment of the two 'Assad' class corvettes that have been laid up in La Spezia since the start of the Gulf War. Whether this deal survives Iraq's descent into civil conflict remains to be seen.

Elsewhere in the Middle East, the largely land-

Israel's Navy has a pressing need to replace older surface ships, with some of the older fast attack craft dating back to the early 1980s. This image shows an unidentified member of the 'Sa'ar 4.5' class on exercise with the Hellenic Navy in 2012. *(Israel Defence Forces)*

based civil conflict in Syria has descended into stalemate. Significant preparations were made by the US Navy and other American forces for potential strikes on selected Syrian targets in September 2013 following the regime's use of chemical weapons. The deteriorating political situation also saw the British Royal Navy's destroyer *Dragon* deployed to the Eastern Mediterranean to augment Royal Air Force Typhoon fighter jets in the protection of the Sovereign Base Areas in Cyprus from potential Syrian retaliation. In the event, the agreement for Syria to eliminate its chemical weapon stockpile codified under United Nations Security Council Resolution 2118 meant that external military intervention was avoided. Attention then turned to the shipment of chemicals out of Syria for destruction under a process lead by Norway and Denmark and supported by a number of other of the leading naval powers. The last shipment was made in June 2014, with the most hazardous chemicals scheduled to be transhipped to the US Navy auxiliary *Cape Ray* (T-AKR-9679) for neutralisation in international waters.

The British frigate *Montrose* escorting the Norwegian freighter *Taiko* during operations to dispose of Syria's chemical weapons in February 2014. The failure of the United States to act on its pledge to take action against Syrian chemical weapons' abuses during that country's civil war has weakened its regional credibility. *(Crown Copyright 2014)*

Destruction of Syria's chemical arsenal will be a considerable relief to neighbouring **Israel**, which is rumoured to have used one of its own *Dolphin* class submarines to strike at Russian-supplied anti-ship missiles stored in the Syrian port of Latakia. Three of the class are in operational service and another two, delivered in 2012 and 2013, are expected to become operational before the end of 2014. A sixth boat is under construction. The most pressing future need is therefore for replacement surface vessels, with the navy's current fleet of fast attack craft becoming increasingly old. The two remaining 'Sa'ar 4' class boats, *Nitzachon* and *Atzmaut* have recently been decommissioned and the older 'Sa'ar 4.5' class vessels are also long in the tooth. A number of international designs have been considered; South Korea's *Incheon* class is one of the likely frontrunners.

Notes

1. See Ajai Shulka's 'Scorpène subs to join fleet without torpedoes', *Business Standard* – 15 May 2014 (New Delhi, Business Standard Ltd, 2014).

2. The pressures on India's defence budget are described in more detail in an article entitled 'What is Choking the Indian Defence Budget?' published by The Institute for Defence Study and Analysis (New Delhi, IDSA, 2014).

3. *Sustaining US Global Leadership: Priorities for 21st Century Defense* (Washington DC, Department of Defense, 2012). An alternative narrative to that of decreasing US commitment to the region is set out by Anthony H Cordesman in *The FY2015 US Defense Budget, the New Quadrennial Defense Review and the U.S. Commitment to the Middle East and Asia* (Washington, DC, Center for Strategic & International Studies, 2014).

4. The ships' decommissioning was reported by Tarek Mahmud in an article entitled, 'BNS *Abu Bakar*, BNS *Ali Haider* de-commissioned', *Dhaka Tribune* – 22 January 2014 (Dhaka, Dhaka Tribune, 2014).

5. Launched as the British Royal Navy's *Hercules* in 1945, the first *Vikrant* was earmarked as a museum after her withdrawal but efforts to find a commercial partner to take the project forward failed. In May 2014 she was towed from Mumbai's naval dockyard in preparation for scrapping.

6. For more detailed information see Rahul Bedi's 'IN requests funds for next phase of indigenous carrier', *Jane's Defence Weekly* – 11 June 2014 (Coulsdon, IHS Jane's, 2014), p.10.

7. A news release by the International Maritime Bureau, part of the International Chamber of Commerce's Commercial Crime Arm, on 24 April 2014 reported that maritime piracy had dropped to its lowest level since 2007. The Gulf of Guinea, particularly Nigeria, remained the focal point of African piracy following the successful curtailment of lawlessness off Somalia. For further detail see, 'Lowest first quarter figures since 2007 but no room for complacency, reports IMB' at http://icc-ccs.org/

8. Nigeria's ambitious naval development plans have been described in several articles on the navy's website at http://www.navy.mil.ng/ and analysed by a number of main defence media groups, including HIS Jane's. A particularly detailed analysis of the Port Harcourt development was provided by Mrityunjoy Mazumdar's 'Details of Nigerian naval shipbuilding plans revealed', *Jane's Defence Weekly* – 20 October 2013 (Coulsdon, IHS Jane's, 2013), p.17.

9. An invaluable resource for news of developments amongst the smaller African navies is the South African *defenceWeb* news portal that can be found at http://www.defenceweb.co.za/

10. The *South African Defence Review 2014* (Pretoria, Republic of South Africa, 2014) can be accessed online at http://www.gov.za/documents/detail.php?cid=402524. A good overall summary of this rather weighty volume is provided by Jakkie Cilliers in the Institute for Security Studies' *Policy Brief 56: The 2014 South African Defence Review* (Pretoria, ISS, 2014) at http://www.issafrica.org/uploads/PolBrief56.pdf

11. The news was reported by Michel Caribol under the title, 'Armement: DCNS décroche un contract de 1 milliard d'euros en Egypte', *La Tribune* – 3 June 2014 (Paris, La Tribune, 2014).

2.3A Fleet Review

Author:
Mrityunjoy Mazumdar

BANGLADESH AND MYANMAR

Resurgent Navies in the Bay of Bengal: Friendly Rivalry or Something More?

Bangladesh (formerly East Pakistan) and Myanmar (formerly Burma) are neighbouring countries with shared land and maritime borders, the latter including overlapping continental and maritime zone claims in the Bay of Bengal. Whereas Bangladesh is a relatively stable democracy, Myanmar is only now emerging from almost five decades of isolation and re-engaging with the international community as it gradually transitions from a military-run state into a quasi-democracy, albeit one where the generals remain very influential. Besides rich fish stocks, very substantial offshore oil and gas deposits exist in the maritime zones of both countries. Both face very similar maritime security threats to the maintenance of good order at sea.

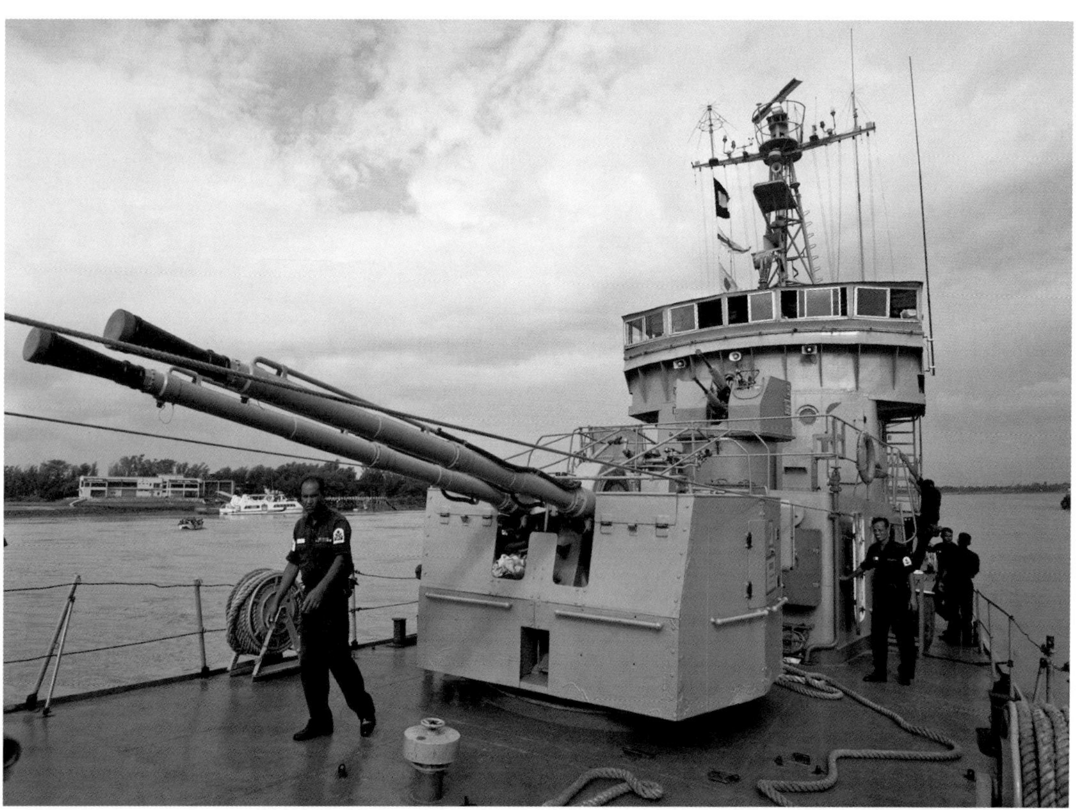

The Bangladesh Navy's Type 037 'Hainan' class large patrol craft *Nirbhoy* prepares to get underway in September 2012. Whilst popular perceptions of both the Bangladesh and Myanmar fleets are dominated by images of largely 'green water' coastal forces operating obsolescent equipment, both navies are rapidly developing a much broader spectrum of capabilities. *(US Navy)*

Bangladesh and Myanmar have experienced a long-standing offshore territorial dispute, while Myanmar has also had some disagreements over illegal fishing with Thailand. The maritime dispute between Bangladesh and Myanmar reached its peak in October-November 2008. A naval standoff occurred over exploratory drilling operations by Myanmar in waters claimed by Bangladesh but a clash was avoided when Myanmar backed down. The matter was subsequently taken to an international tribunal for adjudication at the end of 2009 after attempts to find a bilateral solution failed. In a precedent-setting case, the boundary issue was resolved in 2012 when both countries accepted the rulings of an International Law of the Sea Tribunal (ITLOS) in Hamburg. Both parties agreed to accept a compromise solution in spite of the potentially negative consequences for each. 'There were serious economic and political consequences for both states in the event of an adverse decision; yet, both states consented to the jurisdiction of the ITLOS to decide their overlapping maritime boundaries' said Mark E Rosen, Vice President and Deputy General Counsel at the United States based Center for Naval Analyses.[1] It remains to be seen if this adjudication will serve as the template for the resolution of similar disputes elsewhere like the lingering India-Bangladesh maritime boundary dispute.

More broadly, the discovery of substantial offshore mineral resources in the Bay of Bengal has been crucial to changing perceptions with respect to both the Bangladesh and Myanmar fleets by their respective governments. Having largely neglected their navies, realisation has set in that fleets are needed to protect the two countries' Exclusive Economic Zones (EEZs) and assist energy security. This has been especially true in Myanmar's case, where decades of army-dominated military rule, isolationist and xenophobic policies, insurgencies, economic sanctions and associated commercial malaise had hobbled the navy's growth, largely reducing it to a riverine force in support of army counter-insurgency operations, with limited coastal defence and offshore patrolling capabilities.

Consequently, both navies are now in the midst of major fleet modernisation programmes. Whilst these will these provide significant gains in combat power, they will also start to transform them more fundamentally; from 'green water' coastal forces into navies with respectable sea denial and limited sea control 'blue water' capabilities. This change is underscored by the acquisition of larger seagoing platforms, and, crucially, undersea and naval aviation capabilities.

A picture of the Bangladesh Navy's Type 053H1 'Jianghu II' frigate *Osman* taken whilst she was performing United Nations' duties. The Bangladesh Navy's willingness to participate in support of UN peacekeeping missions, most notably with respect to the UNIFIL operation off the Lebanon, has helped portray the country in a positive light in spite of its international image as a relatively poor nation. *(Brazilian Navy)*

SIMILAR YET DIFFERENT

There are a number of interesting parallels between the Bangladesh Navy (BN) and the Union of Myanmar Navy (UMN). Historically, both have roots in the British Royal Navy (RN), albeit via the Pakistan Navy in the case of Bangladesh. Both have operated and grown in the face of an unfavourable funding situation for protracted periods. Both have operated under army-dominated juntas, interspersed with periods of civilian rule. Both face common maritime security threats and have also suffered losses from natural disasters, largely the effects of tropical cyclones.

Another historical similarity is the fact that both fleets have been largely equipped with near-identical platforms and weapons systems of Chinese provenance. Indeed, China continues to play a significant role in both navies. One often-overlooked aspect of being a recipient of Chinese arms, especially technologically-intensive platforms like warships, is the difficulty in obtaining correctly translated technical documentation for the effective operational exploitation of these systems. This has resulted in a longer than expected dependence on Chinese technical expertise for the effective utilisation of weapons systems, along with frustration at poor product support.[2] Consequently, both have ongoing domestic warship construction programmes in a drive for self-sufficiency.

Turning to the present, both navies play key diplomatic roles. Despite Bangladesh's image as a poor nation, the BN has successfully portrayed a positive image with port calls, training deployments, participation in international fleet reviews and United Nations (UN) peacekeeping missions, notably the deployment of two vessels – a frigate and a large patrol vessel – on a continuing basis with the United Nation Interim Force in Lebanon (UNIFIL) since May 2010. In Myanmar's case, the navy has been instrumental in re-engaging with other navies at a time when the ruling junta was proscribed, initially through its participation in the Indian MILAN exercises from 2006 onwards.[3] These interactions doubtless played a role in Myanmar's ongoing movement towards a quasi-democratic state since the turn of the decade. Engagements by the navies of the key regional and extra-regional players are on the rise, with flag visits by foreign warships becoming the norm in Yangon (formerly Rangoon). Since 2012, the pace of international engagement has picked up, with visits to Bangladesh, Malaysia, Thailand and Vietnam, as well as continued interface with the Indian Navy (IN), most notably the first India-Myanmar coordinated patrol (CORPAT).

Yet there are some important differences between the two navies. After decades of isolation, the UMN cannot be said to be on a par with other regional navies in terms of currency of exposure to prevailing doctrinal and operational thinking. There are also difficulties in communicating with other navies, since English is not yet widely spoken. Devoting resources to running the country as part of the military regime has also created operational problems and impacted the technical proficiency of its personnel. The BN, on the other hand, has a much richer and varied exposure to current operational doctrines through its regular interaction with many leading fleets. For the time being, it is the better-trained fleet.

Conversely, in terms of warship design and construction capabilities, the UMN is well ahead of the BN due to its history of self-reliance. However, Bangladesh's shipbuilding industry on the whole is much more diverse, exporting considerable numbers of merchant ships in consonance with Bangladesh's much more diverse economy. The BN also currently has an advantage in its overall breadth of technological capability as it moves towards a 'three-dimensional' force structure. The UMN has the greater number of significant deficiencies, for example with respect to modern air defences.

Another crucial difference is the way in which India, the dominant regional maritime power, is perceived by these countries and, by extension, their navies. For a number of reasons, Bangladesh sees India as a potential adversary. The strength of this view waxes and wanes dependent on the leanings of the heads of state – Bangladesh's leadership is currently pro-Indian – but this, of itself, hinders a strategic government-to-government relationship. There is consequently a bureaucratic tendency to make navy-to-navy staff talks a 'hostage to transient political vicissitudes' according to Vice Admiral Pradeep Chauhan, former head of the Indian Navy's Directorate of Foreign Cooperation, Intelligence and Transformation.[4] He adds, 'this is counterproductive in the extreme and effectively prevents the forum from acting as a bridge or channel through which the two sides can continue to constructively engage each other even in times of transient political difficulties'. Consequently, it has been difficult to establish meaningful navy-to-navy interaction. On the other hand, Myanmar sees India as a welcome counterbalance to Chinese influence on its economic and military spheres. This potentially works to India's advantage as it seeks to counter China's growing regional influence with its Look East policy, in which the Indian Navy plays a vital role. However, to the frustration of Myanmar, the Indian response has been much less than expected, probably reflecting bureaucratic inertia and disconnect in the key Indian ministries. Whilst navy-to-navy interactions – as well as transfers of weapons systems, sensors, platforms and training – are ongoing, the comparative disadvantage with China this causes is also of considerable frustration to the IN.

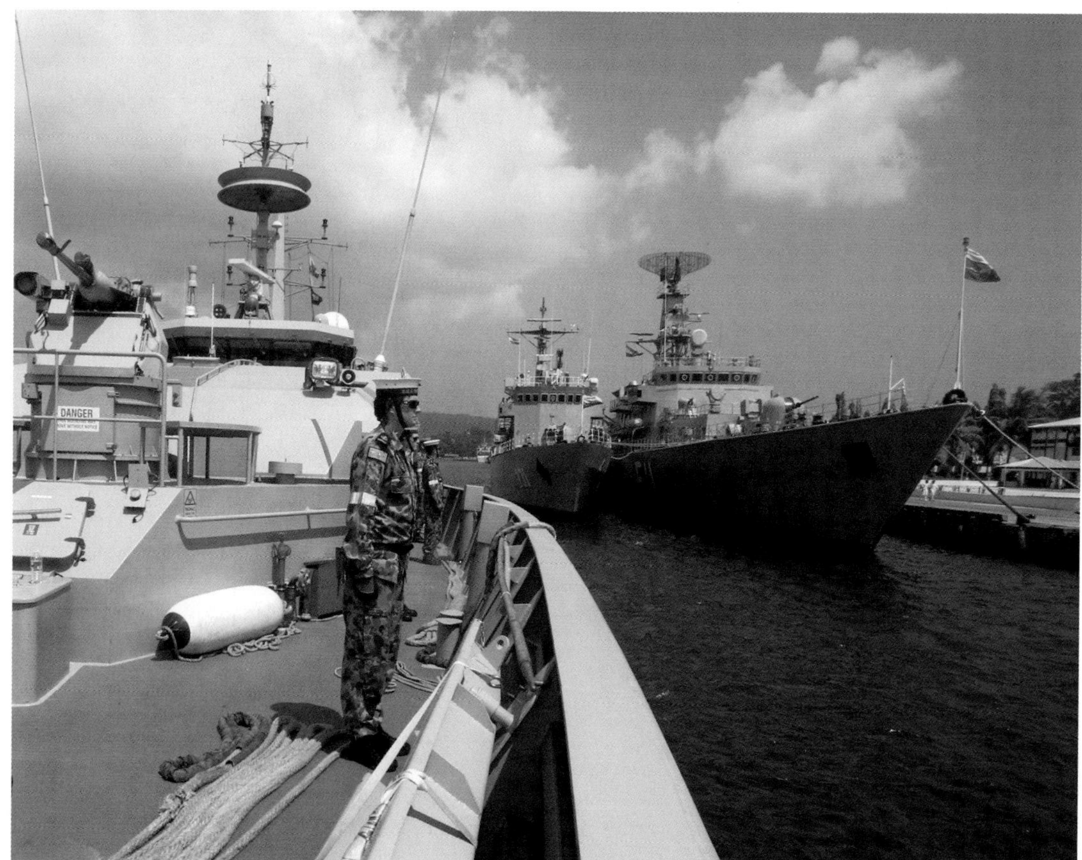

The Royal Australian Navy patrol vessel *Childers* berthing next to the Union of Myanmar Navy's indigenously-built frigate *King Aung Zeya* and corvette *Anawrahta* during an Indian-sponsored training exercise in the Andaman Islands. Myanmar sees India as a welcome counterweight to Chinese regional influence. *(Royal Australian Navy)*

BANGLADESH NAVY (BANGLADESH NAU BAHINI)

The BN, numbering about 15,000 uniformed personnel and 4,000 civilians, is headed by a Chief of Naval Staff (CNS); currently Vice Admiral Muhammad Farid Habib. As of June 2014, there are around eighty commissioned vessels and at least sixty minor craft.

History: The BN formally came into being on 7 April 1972 with 180 men, although it was not until June/July 1972 that two riverine gunboats were acquired.[5] The navy was built around a nucleus of repatriated Bengali sailors and officers (mostly submariners and technicians) from the Pakistan Navy, as well as a small group of Indian-trained *Mukti Bahini* (freedom fighter) frogmen who were active during the 1971 India-Pakistan War that resulted in the creation of Bangladesh out of East Pakistan in December 1971.

The fledgling navy operated just a handful of riverine craft until a pair of Indian-supplied seaward defence boats, renamed *Padma* and *Surma*, arrived in 1973 and 1974, followed by a pair of ex-Yugoslav 'Kraljevica' class submarine chasers in 1975. A converted trawler, *Shaheed Ruhul Amin*, briefly operated as flagship until its first major warship, a Type 61 *Salisbury* class frigate *Umar Farooq* (the former Royal Navy *Llandaff*) arrived in December 1976. She was followed by two Type 41 *Leopard* class frigates; *Ali Haider* (the former HMS *Jaguar*) in 1978 and *Abu Bakr* (ex HMS *Lynx*) in 1982. These frigates marked a turning point for the BN as it began its transition away from a purely coastal navy into one with a modest offshore capability.

Although India provided much of the early training and support to the BN, souring relations

The Bangladesh Navy's Type 61 class frigate *Umar Farooq*, the former British Royal Navy *Llandaff*, entering the Indian Navy base at Visakhapatnam in December 2010. The first major warship in the Bangladesh Navy when she was transferred in 1976, she remains in operational service on patrol and training duties. Two half-sisters of the Type 41 *Leopard* class that were also in Bangladesh Navy service have now been replaced by more modern Chinese frigates. *(Indian Navy)*

between the two nations over a number of border issues coupled with a military takeover meant that by the late 1970s China became the primary source for weapons and platforms – offering reasonably state-of-the-art platforms and weapons systems at terms the financially-strapped service could not refuse. This was yet another turning point. It allowed the BN to grow its force levels and acquire a modest deterrent capability, directed largely at the Indian Navy given rising perceptions of India as a regional hegemon that could destabilise Bangladesh at will (even though there were maritime boundary issues with Burma at the time). By the early 1990s there were also regular interactions with US Navy. However, significant transfers from the United States did not materialise until the current decade, when large numbers of small craft for use by BN Special Forces were delivered. More recently, these have been followed by the first of at least two planned transfers of decommissioned US Coast Guard *Hamilton* (WHEC-715) class cutters. *Jarvis* (WHEC-725) was handed over on 23 May 2013, being commissioned as *Somudra Joy* at Chittagong on 23 December of the same year.

Organisation and Force Structure: Given its roots in the Pakistan Navy, the BN is organised much along the same lines. Aside from the Naval Headquarters (NHQ) and the Naval Administrative Authority Dhaka (Admin Dhaka) in the capital city of Dhaka, the main operational Commands are Commodore Commanding BN Flotilla (COMBAN); Commodore Naval Aviation (COMNAV); and Special Warfare and Diving and Salvage Command (SWADSCOM).

Area Commands responsible for both ships and shore establishments include Commodore Commanding Chittagong (COMCHIT). This is responsible for supporting the bulk of the naval fleet (BN Flotilla) at Chittagong. Ships are organised into several squadrons, including 2FF Squadron, 10FSG Squadron, 81 (811 and 812) FAC Squadron, 82 Torpedo Boat Squadron, 9 MCM Squadron, 26 Patrol Craft Squadron and 101 Patrol Squadron. Commodore Commanding Khulna (COMKHUL) at Khulna is responsible for supporting about twenty-five ships of the Khulna Flotilla. This is organised into Offshore Patrol Vessels ('Island' class), 41 Patrol Craft Squadron, 31 Patrol Craft Squadron and an auxiliary squadron. Maintenance of afloat assets falls under Commodore Superintendent Dockyard (CSD).

Table 2.3A.1 provides an overview of the BN's principal warships. Major surface combatants

The largest front-line warship in the Bangladesh Navy is the recently-commissioned *Somudra Joy*, the former US Coast Guard *Hamilton* class high-endurance cutter *Jarvis* (WHEC-725). Capable of operating at long ranges into the Bay of Bengal, she is also able to support helicopter operations and gives Bangladesh its first experience of operating a gas-turbine propelled warship. Further acquisitions of the type are planned. *(US Navy)*

Table 2.3A.1: BANGLADESH NAVY – PRINCIPAL UNITS AS AT MID 2014

TYPE	CLASS	NO.	YEAR	TONNAGE	DIMENSIONS	SPEED	ARMAMENT
Principal Surface Escorts (10)							
Frigate – FFG(H)	**BANGABANDHU** (ULSAN)	1	2001	2,300 tons	104m x 12m x 4m	25 knots	4 x Otomat SSM, 8 x HQ-7 SAM, 1 x 76mm, 2 x CIWS, 6 x TT
Frigate – FFG	Type 053H2 ('Jianghu III')	2	1986 (2013)	2,000 tons	103m x 11m x 3m	26 knots	8 x C-802 SSM, 2 x twin 100mm, 4 x twin 37mm, 2 x A/S launchers
Frigate – FFG	Type 053H1 ('Jianghu II')	1	1982 (1989)	1,900 tons	103m x 11m x 3m	26 knots	8 x C-802 SSM, 2 x twin 100mm, 4 x twin 37mm, 2 x A/S launchers
Frigate – FF(H)	WHEC-715 **HAMILTON**	1	1967 (2013)	3,100 tons	115m x 13m x 4m	29 knots	1 x 76mm [To gain SSM in due course]
Frigate – FF	Type 61 **SALISBURY**	1	1957 (1976)	2,400 tons	104m x 12m x 5m	24 knots	1 x twin 114mm, 1 x twin 40mm
Corvette – FS(H)	**LEEDS CASTLE**	2	1981 (2010)	1,400 tons	81m x 12m x 4m	20 knots	4 x C-704 SSM, 1 x 76mm
Patrol Ship – FS	**DURJOY**	2	2013	700 tons	64m x 9m x 3m	28 knots	4 x C-704 SSM, 1 x 76mm, 2 x CIWS, 2 x A/S launchers.
Additional transfers of WHEC-715 type cutters are planned from the US Coast Guard, whilst further *Durjoy* type patrol ships are reportedly under construction in Bangladesh. Two new corvettes based on the Chinese PLAN's Type 056 design are being constructed in China.							
Missile-Armed Fast Attack Craft (7)							
FAC – PTG	Type 021 'Huangfen'	4	1985 (1988)	210 tons	39m x 8m x 3m	35+ knots	4 x C-704 SSM, 2 x CIWS
FAC – PTG	Type 024 'Hegu'	5	1983 (1968)	80 tons	27m x 6m x 1m	35+ knots	4 x C-704 SSM, 1 x twin 25mm
Missile-armed fast attack craft are supplemented by around sixteen torpedo and gun-armed fast attack vessels.							

Notes:

1 Front-line units are supplemented by considerable numbers of offshore and coastal patrol craft, including five former British Royal Navy 'Island' class OPVs (a sixth is used for training) and five of the new indigenously-constructed 50.5m, 350-ton *Padma* class that are used for coastal patrols. Mine countermeasures capabilities are provided by a solitary Chinese-built Type 010 ocean minesweeper and four former British Royal Navy 'River' class minesweepers, all largely used as patrol ships.

2 Acquisition of at least two former Chinese Type 035'Ming' class submarines is scheduled for completion before the end of 2015 to provide an embryonic underwater capability.

3 Year relates to year lead ship of the class was completed, with year in brackets the date of first transfer to Bangladesh.

comprise six frigates (four armed with missiles), two missile-armed corvettes, and two missile-armed large patrol ships. Four of these ten ships are helicopter-capable.

The most modern and capable warship is the Korean-built DW2000H *Bangabandhu*. She is also the only warship currently equipped with an organic surface-to-air missile (SAM) system. The three Chinese-built Type 053H1/H2 'Jianghus', although obsolete, possess reasonably good anti-surface and short-range anti-submarine capabilities but lack modern air defences save man-portable systems such as the Chinese QW-2. The largest warship is the *Hamilton* class cutter, *Somudra Joy*, which is helicopter-capable and slated to receive missiles in due course. She provides a persistent offshore patrol capability by virtue of her endurance and range. Finally, the elderly frigate *Umar Farooq* is essentially a large gunboat cum training ship, not to mention a veritable floating museum of 1950s British naval technology.

The six frigates are supplemented by the four missile-armed corvettes and large patrol craft. Two of these are elderly former Royal Navy 'Castle' class offshore patrol vessels that were upgraded with a larger gun and surface-to-surface missiles after transfer. The pair of smaller but newer *Durjoy* class vessels were delivered from Wuchang Shipyard in China in 2012.

The major missile-armed ships are complemented by nine smaller missile boats that are being upgraded with C-704 missiles in place of the obsolete but powerful SY-1/2 ('Silkworm'). There are also around sixteen torpedo and gun-armed fast attack craft with considerable inshore combat potential. However, no more than fifty per cent of this fleet is likely to be operational at any given time.

The front-line combat fleet is balanced by significant constabulary assets, including both offshore/large and coastal patrol vessels. Offshore vessels include five former British Royal Navy 'Island' class patrol ships (a sixth acts as a training vessel), as well as additional ships of Chinese and South Korean origin. Coastal patrols are increasingly in the hands of the indigenous 350-ton, 50.5m long *Padma* class, which mark the country's first major indigenous construction programme. Their arrival should bring a more homogeneous look to a rather motley collection of existing vessels.

Mine warfare assets comprise a Chinese-built Type 010G ocean-going minesweeper and four former Royal Navy 'River' class minesweepers, which also double as patrol or survey vessels. There are two bespoke survey ships. Amphibious assets are limited to around ten landing craft of various sizes. Auxiliaries include two small tankers.

South Korean and American assistance was instrumental in developing counter-terrorist and maritime interdiction capabilities for the newly-formed SWADS (Special Warfare Diving and Salvage) special operations force. This force, numbering a few hundred strong, is primarily equipped with American-built small craft, including at least sixteen 25ft SAFE Boats Defender response craft and about two dozen 7.5m Impact 750 Rigid Inflatable Boats (RIBs).

Future Acquisitions: Future acquisitions are being driven by a plan, announced in 2009, to transform the BN into a modern three-dimensional force – including surface, aviation and submarine elements – by the end of the current decade. This plan includes both the recapitalisation of existing assets and acquisition of new capabilities. There is also an emphasis on building up indigenous construction capabilities.

Having built a few simple patrol craft and some auxiliary vessels, the BN has progressed to more

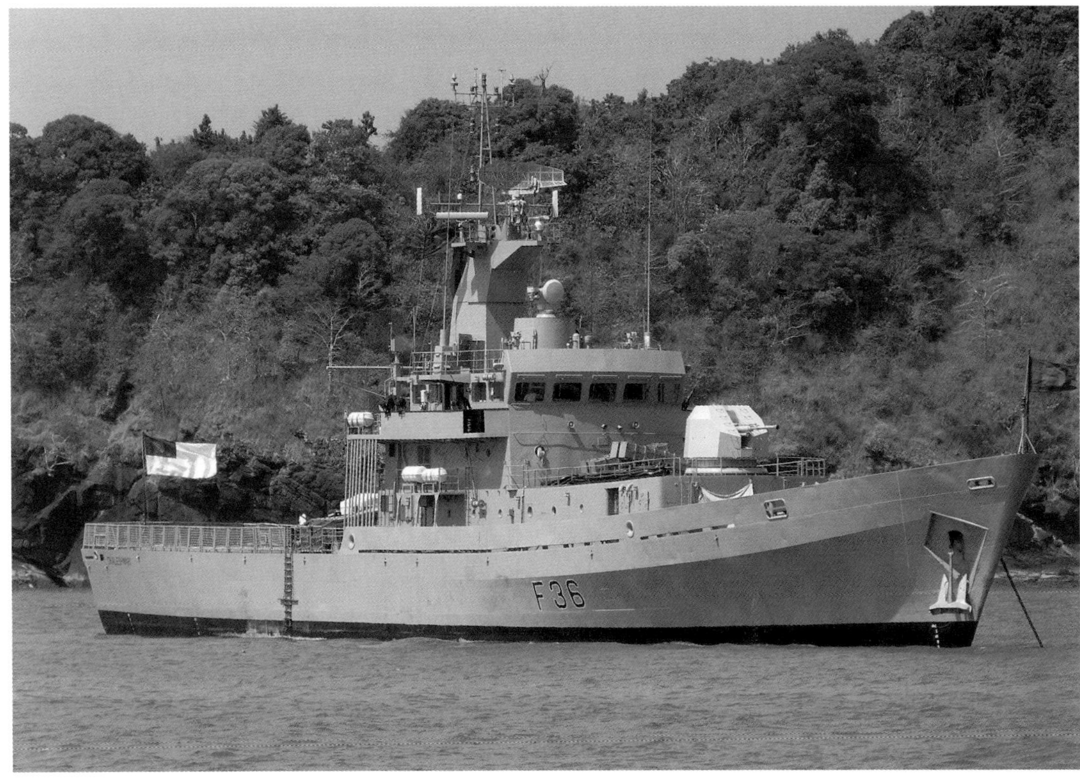

An image of the former British Royal Navy offshore patrol vessel *Leeds Castle,* which is now in service with the Bangladesh Navy as the missile-armed corvette *Dhaleshwari.* Seen here in March 2013, the photograph shows the significant increase in armament that has been implemented since transfer in 2010, most notably the installation of a 76mm gun and C-704 surface-to-surface missiles. *(Mrityunjoy Mazumdar)*

sophisticated warship-building programmes at the navy-owned shipyards; Khulna Shipyard (KSY) and Dockyard and Engineering Works Narayanganj (DEWN). Auxiliary vessels and patrol craft have also been built at Ananda Shipyard. Naval vessels being built are largely to Chinese designs using material packages from China.

KSY has delivered five *Padma* class patrol boats ahead of schedule, and is now reported to be building two large patrol craft based on the *Durjoy* design; larger corvettes are also planned from 2016 onwards. KSY is also building two 42m utility landing craft with a 415-ton cargo capacity, while DEWN is building two smaller, 25.6m landing vessels. Ananda Shipyard is believed to have delivered an 80m fleet tanker, said to be named *Khan Jahan Ali* after the ship she will replace, in July 2013, having launched the ship in March. With a fuel capacity of 2,400 tons, the tanker can replenish two ships simultaneously.

Turning to overseas construction, two 90m, 1,300-ton corvettes that are believed to be based on the Chinese Type 056 are under construction at Wuchang Shipyard in China for delivery from 2015. However, the most significant new acquisition, bringing the fleet's three-dimensional vision closer to reality, will be the arrival of submarines. Two 'off-the-shelf' boats will initially be acquired to act as training submarines – both for submariners and to provide much-needed anti-submarine experience for the surface fleet. It is very likely these boats will be former People's Liberation Army Navy Type 035 'Ming' class submarines. They may arrive as early as 2015. The BN has been building up a cadre of submariners for some time, with Turkey providing training. Up to four boats will eventually be required, with surplus Type 209 boats from Turkey or South Korea also a possibility.

Naval Aviation: The nascent naval aviation arm was formed in late 2011 with two AgustaWestland AW109 Power helicopters. These were followed by two RUAG Dornier Do-228NG maritime patrol aircraft fitted with Telephonics RDR-1700B radars in July 2013. More aircraft are planned, including nine Chinese K-8W jet trainers and additional utility and transport helicopters.

UNION OF MYANMAR NAVY (TATMADAW YAY)

As of March 2013, the UMN numbered around 22,000 personnel including some 2,000 officers. At this time it operated some 125 or so vessels.[6] These numbers are not expected to have been subject to significant change subsequently.

History: With its roots in the Burma Royal Naval Volunteer Reserve that had been created in 1940, the Union of Burma Navy (UBN) formally came into being in 1947 with 700 men. It operated almost sixty platforms supplied on independence by the British. These included the 'River' class frigate UBS *Mayu* (the former HMS *Fal*), two small motor minesweepers, four river gunboats and a myriad of smaller patrol craft.[7]

The 1950s and 1960s saw continued support and transfers from the British, as well as from the United States under the Mutual Defense Assistance Program. Burma's leading role in the non-aligned movement also saw equipment acquired from fellow non-aligned states such as Yugoslavia, whilst the beginnings of a local shipbuilding programme took the shape of the construction of river gunboats. By the end of the latter decade, the navy was mainly a riverine force (operating largely in support of army counter-insurgency operations) with just four ocean going vessels. The 1960s were also a turning point for the UBN, as the military assumed power and proceeded to create an inward-looking totalitarian state – the Burmese Road to Socialism – under which all aspects of Burmese civic society was run by the military. The xenophobic nature of the army-dominated government, an exaggerated desire for self-reliance and the need to devote resources to civic action programs would eventually create all manner of operational and doctrinal problems for the UBN. There were extensive periods when military cooperation with the 'Western' powers was suspended, leaving the navy hard pressed to meet its maritime security commitments. By the late 1980s, the renamed Myanmar had virtually become a pariah state to the major democratic powers, subject to sanctions and arms embargoes driven by the United

States and European Union countries. A pragmatic shift towards China took place despite a record of historical animosity.

Despite a worsening economy, the military (Tatmadaw) expanded. The navy, now known as the Union of Myanmar Navy (UMN), benefitted greatly through the 1990s and 2000s as a result of improved funding and Chinese largesse. No fewer than sixteen large ocean-going patrol vessels, including six armed with C-801 missiles, were procured from China, along with a few patrol boats from Yugoslavia, weapons from North Korea, and Italian Oto Melara 76mm guns (the latter through third parties to circumvent sanctions). Increasing numbers of indigenously built 45m patrol boats, including some missile-armed variants, and a couple of 77m corvettes were also obtained. Clearly, these acquisitions not only provided hitherto unseen numbers of sea-going combatants but also provided a credible deterrent force. Reportedly, there were attempts to procure North Korean submarines, although these never materialised.

However, successful integration of the relatively sophisticated, missile-armed combatants proved problematic, necessitating long-term dependence on Chinese technical support. Consequently, the UMN's overall experience with Chinese-supplied platforms and combat systems, including a lack of follow-up support, was not an entirely a happy one. This, no doubt, resulted in requests for Indian assistance given that the choices for sourcing weapons were limited because of sanctions. That said, Chinese support was instrumental in building up the navy, as well as its shipbuilding infrastructure at the naval dockyard facilities at Yangon. For example, these gained an extensive ship-lift system. This played a crucial role as construction of progressively larger surface combatants commenced.

Despite rising Chinese influence, the country maintained its independent stance and did not permit the Chinese to use its bases, contrary to reports circulating at the time. For instance, Indian fears of Chinese radar and COMINT outposts on the Great Coco Island were greatly exaggerated. In fact, it was the IN that ended up providing a surveillance capability.[8]

Organisation and Force Structure: Details of the UMN and its organisation remain sparse, although more information is gradually emerging as the country opens up. There are five regional commands at Irrawaddy, Danyawaddy, Panmawaddy, Mawyawaddy and Tanintharyi. In addition, the No. 1 Naval Training School and the Naval Dockyard Headquarters are located in the Yangon (Rangoon) area, which was the former capital of Myanmar. Fleet forces are organised into three numbered Fleets – No. 1 (at Yangon), No. 2 (at Heinzae), and No. 3 (Kyut Phyu).

Table 2.3A.2 provides an overview of the UMN's principal warships. There are around fifty or so front-line, sea-going vessels, the most significant of which are three guided-missile frigates and two guided-missile corvettes.

Completed by December 2010, the indigenously-built 108m, 3,000-ton *King Aung Zeya* is the prototype for a class of up to six new frigates. Capable of helicopter operations, she is armed with combat systems procured from a myriad of sources. Armament comprises an Oto Melara 76mm/62 main gun, four AK630 close-in weapons systems and two manually-operated Gatling-type machine guns from North Korea, eight Chinese C-602 surface-to-surface missiles, two Chinese RDC anti-submarine rocket launchers and what appears to be a man-portable air-defence missile system, along with decoy launchers. Sensors include commercial Furuno navigation radars, an Indian-origin RAWL02 2D air/surface-search radar, three gun fire-control radars, and a Chinese missile target-acquisition radar identical to those on that country's Type 022 catamarans. A sonar, possibly of Indian origin, is also installed to provide targeting information for the RDC launchers.

The two Type 053H1 'Jianghu II' frigates – *Mahar Bandoola* and *Mahar Thiha Thura* – were acquired second-hand from China in 2012. They were upgraded with eight C-802 surface-to-surface missiles, an electronic warfare system and new radars shortly after their arrival in Myanmar. The two 77m indigenously-built missile corvettes – *Anawrahta* and *Bayintnaung* – with an estimated displacement of 1,500 tons are armed with an Oto Melara 76mm/62 gun, a twin 40mm gun, two manually operated smaller-calibre gun mounts and four C-802 surface-to-surface missiles. These ships were originally gun armed but continue to receive upgrades. Most recently, they have received better sensors and what appears to be a man-portable SAM launcher atop the bridge house.

As with the BN, there are also significant numbers of missile-armed coastal fast attack craft. These include six Chinese-built Type 037/1G 'Houxin' class vessels armed with surface-to-surface missiles and, possibly, up to a dozen smaller 45m and 49m

Starting with the construction of simple riverine patrol craft in the 1950s and 1960s, Myanmar has steadily built a significant warship construction capability focused on extensive facilities at Naval Dockyard Yangon. A major step forward was the construction of two sea-going corvettes of the *Anawrahta* class at the turn of the Millennium; more sophisticated frigates have followed. This image shows the corvette *Bayintnaung*. *(Indian Navy)*

Table 2.3A.2: UNION OF MYANMAR NAVY – PRINCIPAL UNITS AS AT MID-2014

TYPE	CLASS	NO.	YEAR	TONNAGE	DIMENSIONS	SPEED	ARMAMENT
Principal Surface Escorts (5)							
Frigate – FFG(H)	**KING AUNG ZEYA**	1	2010	3,000 tons	108m x 13m x 4m	25 knots+	8 x C-602 SSM, 1 x 76mm, 4 x CIWS, 2 x A/S launchers[1]
Frigate – FFG	Type 053H1 ('Jianghu II')	2	1982 (2012)	1,900 tons	103m x 11m x 3m	26 knots	8 x C-802 SSM, 2 x twin 100mm, 4 x twin 37mm, 2 x A/S launchers
Corvette – FSG(H)	**ANAWRAHTA**	2	2001	1,500 tons	77m x 12m x 4m	25 knots+	4 x C-802 SSM, 1 x 76mm, 1 x twin 40mm, 2 x twin 25mm, 2 x A/S launchers
Additional, much-modified units of the *King Aung Zeya* class are under construction, with up to five new ships expected to become operational at roughly yearly intervals from the end of 2014 onwards. The first, *Kyansitthar,* was reportedly commissioned for trials in March 2014. A modernised class of 77m corvettes is also under consideration.							
Missile-Armed Fast Attack Craft (16+)							
FAC – PTG	Type 037/1G 'Houxin'	6	1991 (1995)	500 tons	62m x 7m x 2m	28 knots+	4 x C-801 SSM, 2 x twin 37mm
FAC – PTG	491-Class	1	2013	c.300 tons	49m x 8m x 2m	c. 30 knots	4 x C-802 SSM, 1 x CIWS
FAC – PTG	5-Series	10+	1996	c. 250 tons	45m x 7m x 2m	c. 30 knots	2/4 x C-802 SSM, 2 x CIWS
Missile-armed fast attack craft are supplemented by twenty or more gun-armed fast attack craft, including nine Chinese-built Type 037 'Hainan' class vessels and a number of gun-armed '5 series' vessels. It appears some gun-armed '5 series' vessels are receiving surface-to-surface missiles so numbers of missile- and gun-armed vessels are interchangeable to an extent.							

Notes:

1 Much of the detail on Myanmar warships is speculative and the data in this table should be considered as being no more than indicative. For example, some sources suggest *King Aung Zeya* is armed with a variant of the Russian KH-35 Uran (SS-N-25 Switchblade) surface-to-surface missile. In addition, many ships are being upgraded with more modern systems, such as CIWS and/or surface-to-air missiles on the *Anawrahta* class.

2 Front-line units are supplemented by considerable numbers of gun-armed coastal patrol vessels and river gunboats. The most significant are two helicopter-capable, 500-ton 'Osprey' patrol vessels acquired from Denmark between 1980 and 1982.

3 Year relates to year lead ship of the class was completed, with year in brackets the date of first transfer to Myanmar.

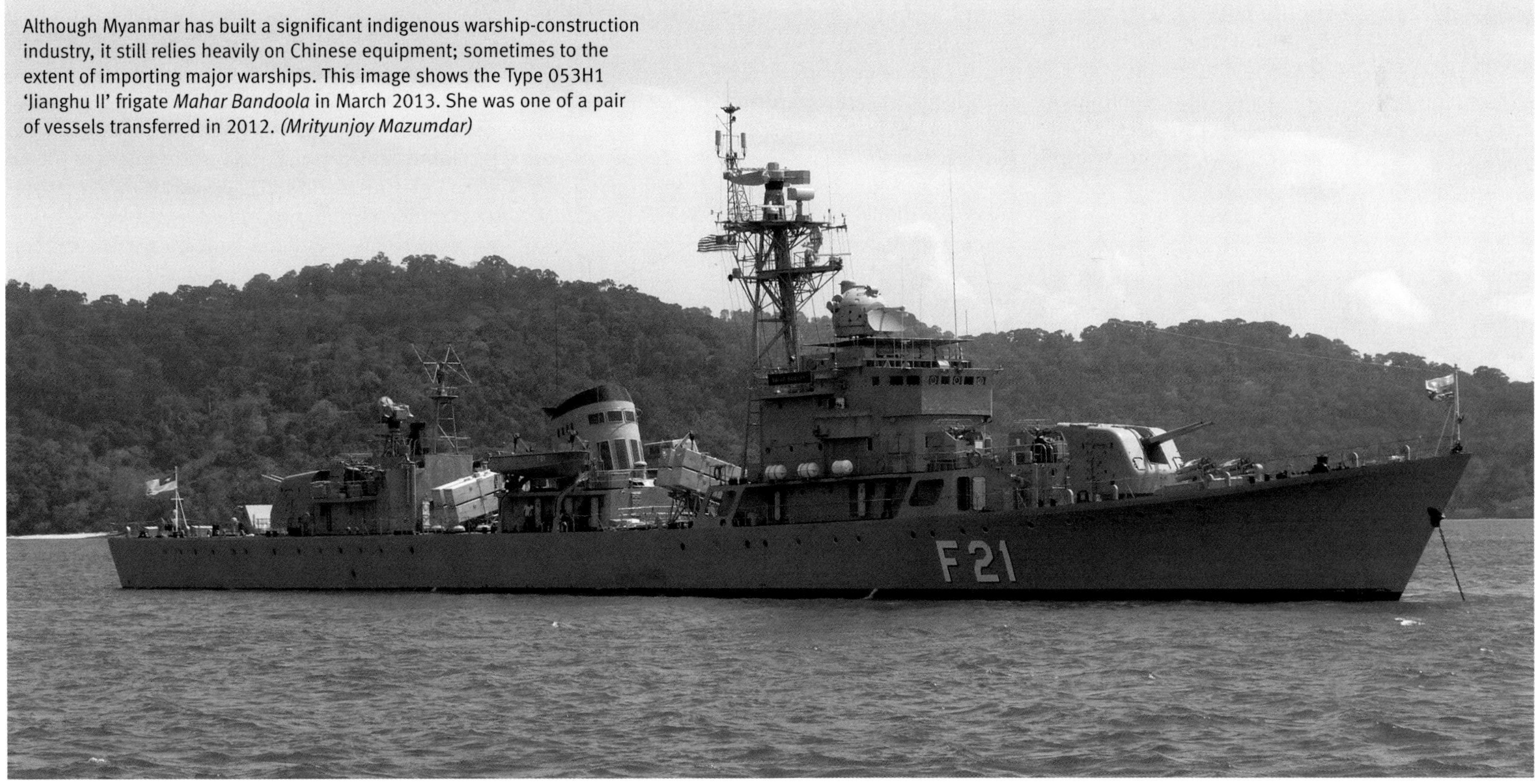

Although Myanmar has built a significant indigenous warship-construction industry, it still relies heavily on Chinese equipment; sometimes to the extent of importing major warships. This image shows the Type 053H1 'Jianghu II' frigate *Mahar Bandoola* in March 2013. She was one of a pair of vessels transferred in 2012. *(Mrityunjoy Mazumdar)*

indigenously-built missile-armed fast attack craft. A new class of stealthy, missile-armed fast attack craft is also entering service. However, not all these ships are outfitted with their full complement of launchers at all times. Another two dozen or so gun-armed fast attack craft, including nine 59m Chinese Type 037 'Hainan' class and a growing number of indigenous types, make up the balance of warfighting vessels. In similar fashion to the major surface combatants, some of the older fast attack craft have received upgrades to their combat systems, including new electronic equipment, multi-barrelled decoy launchers and man-portable SAM launchers.

Constabulary vessels include four offshore patrol ships, including two Danish-built helicopter-capable 'Osprey' class vessels delivered in the early 1980s. There are a much larger number of gun-armed patrol vessels of a variety of classes and weapon fits procured from a myriad of sources ranging from Australia to Yugoslavia. They are complemented by indeterminate numbers of small, 8–10m long riverine patrol craft. Other platforms include around two dozen auxiliary and support craft including at least three new tank landing vessels, a handful of small oilers and a large hydrographic ship with a helicopter deck. A number of tugs and a small floating dock have been recently inducted.

A naval infantry force – reportedly comprised of as many as four battalions – is thought to be deployed on counter-insurgency operations. A small Special Forces contingent also exists, whilst a naval air defence force protects naval bases. There is less evidence of a naval air capability, although the Indian Navy transferred at least five of its fleet of BN-2/BN-2T Islander maritime patrol aircraft to the Myanmar Air Force. There have also been reports that four Harbin Z-9 helicopters are to be acquired from China, with the first to arrive during 2014; Z-9s have been conducting landing trials on the *Aung Zeya*. There are similar reports of interest in Kamov Ka-28 anti-submarine helicopters. If true, it is unclear if the navy or air force would operate these aircraft.

Warship Construction: Despite many constraints, the UMN has made progressive and significant strides in its warship-building capability and capacity. Starting with small riverine craft in the 1950s, by the 1990s domestic naval shipbuilding had progressed to the extent that indigenous 77m corvettes and 45m fast attack craft were under construction. Most construction has been focused on Naval Dockyard Yangon (NDY), although the nearby Myanma Shipyard has also been involved in fast attack craft construction.

The most ambitious programme to date has been the construction of 108m frigates, of which up to six are planned. Work on the project started around 2002–3 and the first frigate, *King Aung Zeya*, was completed by the end of 2010. Thereafter, series construction of a much modified stealthy version of the design has been underway, with *Kyansitthar* being launched in September 2012 and *Sin Phyu Shin* following in late March 2014. The construction of a third hull is also progressing rapidly at the Yangon Naval Dockyard. Additional ships may feature a longer, 117m hull. These frigates are expected to feature a better combat system suite than extant ships, including relatively advanced sonars, radars and combat-management systems from India. *Kyansitthar* was reportedly delivered in March 2014 and should be operational by the end of the year. There are also reports further corvette-sized ships in the order of 77-81m are under construction.

Meanwhile, the 45m patrol boat has evolved into a 49m stealthy missile boat with the first entering service in 2013. A second is under construction and up to eight more planned. *T201*, the prototype of new class of 21m torpedo-armed fast attack craft was also launched in early May 2014 ahead of an extensive series of sea trials to validate the design and seaworthiness of the hull. Its external appearance owes something to the Israeli Super Dvora fast attack craft design.

Myanmar, therefore, has the capacity both to design and build several types of warship simultaneously. According to Indian naval officers who have visited Myanmar, the UMN employs more engineers and scientists with doctorate degrees in its naval design group than the Indian Navy. Their ability to design seaworthy hull forms without access to advanced testing facilities or material external assistance has been deemed as 'impressive'. These naval architects and engineers are the product of an ambitious programme initiated in 1989, when the Tatmadaw began sending 'hundreds and hundreds' of young officers trained by the Defence Services Academy (DSA) and Defence Services Technological Academy (DSTA) to leading universities in Russia to study for post-graduate degrees. The infrastructure at NDY is also impressive, including a ship-lift facility which was reportedly built with Chinese assistance. Indeed, construction of new infrastructure at the dockyard is an ongoing process. Of note is the rapid pace of warship building with relatively complex stealthy frigates being constructed and outfitted within four years.

Myanmar-built warships tend to use largely Chinese-sourced propulsion systems, machinery, combat systems and equipment. Recently, the Indians have made inroads; for example through the supply of systems for the frigate programme. Co-design and construction of offshore patrol vessels with India has also been mooted. The country's warships still exhibit weaknesses in significant areas, for example anti-submarine torpedoes and sophisticated surface-to-air missiles. These will doubtless be rectified through further external cooperation as international relations improve.

CONCLUSION

The BN is a good example of how a cash-strapped naval service can judiciously grow its force levels to provide a credible deterrence capability whilst maintaining good order at sea. In Bangladesh's case, the latter is not only the case in home waters, as it has also deployed small forces for sustained periods in support of UN operations overseas. As Vice Admiral Habib noted in the March 2014 issue of the US Naval Institute's *Proceedings*, the BN is committed to promoting peace and maintaining stability in the littorals of the Bay of Bengal and the Indian Ocean region in general and will continue to engage in trust and confidence-building initiatives while developing interoperability as a cornerstone for combined effort against maritime-security challenges.[9]

While the BN is in the midst of an overdue fleet recapitalisation programme, it is also successfully developing a three-dimensional capability – that is to say a naval air arm and, equally importantly, an undersea warfare capability, possibly as soon as 2015. This will allow it to '... maintain a deterrent posture across the full spectrum of conflict ...' according to the Chief of Naval Staff's vision statement. At a stroke, this alters the balance of regional power. It also profoundly changes the BN's ability to influence events and perceptions, as James Goldrick and Jack McCaffrey write in the introduction to their book *Navies of South-East Asia: A Comparative Study*.[10] 'We envisage a greater role for the Navy in the Bay of Bengal in the future' says Vice Admiral Habib.

The UMN, meanwhile, is – in a sense – emerging from the shadows. After years of isolation and many constraints, the path to modernisation and achieving interoperability with other navies will be difficult. Its past performance and current force structure may give the impression that it is a navy of attack craft and riverine craft, largely incapable of offshore deployments. However, it would be a mistake to assume that the past informs its future course. 'Contrary to the commonly held misperception of the Myanmar Navy as a mere riverine force, and despite the stifling dominance of the Myanmar Army, the Myanmar Navy is actually a very intelligent and competent maritime force, with a growing reach and combat capability' notes Vice Admiral Chauhan.

The UMN has not only managed to double its fleet in the last two decades, but is charting a deliberate course to acquire a respectable blue-water capability through a sizeable force of largely indigenously designed and built ocean-going warships. The force structure is changing rapidly; it has been projected it will have as many as fifteen large surface combatants within the decade. Clearly, it would have come a long way from just ten years ago, when it was operating two corvettes and two elderly Second World War-era patrol ships. In recent years, there have been large-scale annual combined fleet exercises involving over twenty warships, with gun and missile firings. These developments clearly demonstrate a determination to succeed against all odds.

The missile-armed corvette *Anawrahta* photographed during the Indian-sponsored MILAN exercise in 2010. Myanmar is developing a meaningful naval capability based on a force of largely indigenously-designed and built frigates and corvettes. *(Indian Navy)*

However, deciding what its navy is to be used for and then seeking the right force structure, and whether, for example, Myanmar decides to pursue an undersea capability will not be an easy task and may require objective guidance from other navies.[11] Even so, such a capital-intensive capability may still be acquired simply to counter similar developments in Bangladesh and, potentially, Thailand which is also seeking to reacquire submarines.

While Myanmar eyes naval developments in Bangladesh warily, recent navy-to-navy interactions with its neighbours signal steps towards constructive and mutually beneficial engagement in maintaining good order at sea. In any event, it will be fascinating to watch naval developments in the Bay of Bengal as they unfold.

Notes

1. Mr Rosen's comments were contained in a detailed analysis of the ITLOS adjudication published by the US federally-funded Center for Naval Analyses. See Mark E Rosen, JD, LLM *Myanmar v. Bangladesh: The Implications of the Case for the Bay of Bengal and Elsewhere* (Alexandria VA, CNA Corp., 2013) at http://www.cna.org/sites/default/files/research/Myanmar_Bangladesh.pdf

2. For further reading see James Goldrick and Jack McCaffrie, *Navies of South-East Asia: A Comparative Study (Cass Series: Naval Policy and History)* (New York, Routledge, 2012).

3. The accelerating pace of international maritime links with Myanmar was described in Tim McLaughlin's article – 'Engaging Myanmar's Navy' posted to *The Diplomat* website on 7 February 2014. A link can currently be found at: http://www.thediplomat.com/2014/02/engaging-myanmars-navy/

4. Vice Admiral Chauhan's remarks were contained in 'Importance of Myanmar', *Force* – April 2014 (Noida, Force Arrowhead Media Pvt Ltd, 2014).

5. This information is taken from a more detailed overview on the Bangladesh Navy website at http://www.bangladeshnavy.org

6. Detailed information on Myanmar's fleet remains sparse. These details were provided by Captain Aung Zaw Hlaing, Commander of Myanmar Number 1 Fleet, during an inaugural deployment to Thailand. His comments were reported in Isaac Stone Simonelli's 'Myanmar Navy makes historic visit to Phuket' in the *Phuket Gazette* – 6 March 2013 (Phuket, The Phuket Gazette Co Ltd, 2013).

7. *Navies of South-East Asia: A Comparative Study (Cass Series: Naval Policy and History)*, op. cit.

8. 'Importance of Myanmar', *Force* – April 2014, op. cit.

9. Vice Admiral Habib's full remarks are contained in 'The Commanders Respond: Bangladesh Navy', *Proceedings Magazine* – March 2014 (Annapolis, MD, US Naval Institute, 2014). See: http://www.usni.org/magazines/proceedings/ 2014-03/commanders-respond-bangladesh-navy

10. *Navies of South-East Asia: A Comparative Study (Cass Series: Naval Policy and History)*, op. cit.

11. There have been several rumours that Myanmar is considering developing an underwater capability. For example, see Andrew Selth's 'Is Burma really buying submarines?' on the Australian Lowry Institute for International Policy's 'The Interpreter' website published on 29 January 2014. See: http://www.lowyinterpreter.org/post/2014/01/29/Burmas-submarine-dream.aspx

12. In addition to sources mentioned above, a number of websites and blogs provide good sources of information on two fleets that are rarely covered in detail in the formal United States and European media.

2.4 REGIONAL REVIEW

Author:
Conrad Waters

EUROPE AND RUSSIA

INTRODUCTION

Recent naval developments in Europe have inevitably been dominated by the Crimea and wider Ukraine. Following the February 2014 Ukrainian revolution and the installation of a pro-European government in Kiev, Russia moved swiftly to support pro-Russian secessionists in the Crimea through a military operation that was as efficient as it was ruthless. Russia's existing presence on the peninsula was reinforced by both air and sea as a prelude to the seizure of Ukrainian bases.[1] At the same time, Ukrainian naval forces in Sevastopol and its Southern Naval Base at Novoozerne were subject to a blockade by Russian forces. This included the scuttling of the decommissioned Project 1134B 'Kara' class cruiser *Ochakov* and smaller units in the Donuzlav Bay as blockships to hinder any potential Ukrainian intervention.

Effective resistance to Russia's actions was negated by divided loyalties amongst Ukrainian forces, with many of its sailors being of Russian ethnicity. On 2 March 2014, the newly appointed commander of the Ukrainian Navy, Rear Admiral Denis Berezovsky, effectively switched sides by pledging loyalty to the (pro-Russian) people of the Crimea. He was subsequently appointed deputy commander of Russia's Black Sea Fleet. Efforts to eradicate the remaining Ukrainian presence in the peninsula were stepped-up following overwhelming support for joining the Russian Federation in a referendum on 16 March 2014 and subsequent formal accession. The Ukrainian Navy's headquarters in Sevastopol was seized on 19 March. All its ships in Crimean waters surrendered or were seized over the following week, most notably the elderly Project 641 'Foxtrot' class submarine *Zaporizhzhya* on 22 March. Nearly all Russia's objectives in Crimea were achieved without fatalities, although a captured Ukrainian officer, Major Stanislav Karachevsky, was one of a handful of casualties when he was shot in an incident whilst awaiting repatriation in early April 2014. A number of the seized ships have subsequently been returned by Russia. However, it appears that many former Ukrainian Navy personnel have opted to transfer to the Black Sea Fleet.

Russia's actions in Crimea and the Ukraine have effectively presented the 'Western' powers with a *fait accompli*, particularly since the Ukraine falls outside of the NATO security umbrella. However, the impact on neighbouring NATO countries, as well as on the alliance itself, has been significant. The major NATO members such as the United States, the United Kingdom and France, have rushed to reassure their allies in eastern European with increased deployments to countries such as the Baltic States and Poland. In addition, US President Barack Obama has requested additional overseas contingency operations funding in the FY2015 budget to bolster US military capabilities in Europe, including a greater naval presence in the Baltic and the Black Sea.[2] The latter intention will, however, be severely restricted by the constraints of the 1936 Montreux Convention governing the Bosphorus and Dardanelles Straits. This limits, *inter alia*, the amount of time warships from non-Black Sea countries can remain within the inland sea.[3]

Another likely outcome of Russia's actions will be increased defence spending by neighbouring countries, with Poland, Romania and Sweden amongst several seeking to bolster military budgets. Sweden's expansion plans include both the acquisition of more aircraft and increased investment in submarines. The latter intention has provided added impetus to resolving a festering dispute with Germany's ThyssenKrupp Marine Systems (TKMS), the owner of the former Kockums AB submarine manufacturer. There had been growing irritation in Sweden that TKMS had failed to support the country's planned domestic A-26 submarine programme. The German company gave preference to the Kiel-manufactured Type 218 in its successful bid to construct Singapore's new submarines and failed to agree a firm price to develop the A-26. As a result, the Swedish government started to look at local firm Saab as an alternative supplier. The dispute reached its nadir in April 2014 when the FMV, Sweden's defence procurement agency, reportedly staged an armed raid on TKMS' premises in Malmö to secure materials relating to the A-26 design and its Stirling air-independent propulsion (AIP) engine.[4] This somewhat bizarre development seems to have brought matters to a head and it was subsequently announced that TKMS was in talks with Saab to sell its interests in Swedish naval construction. The deal was concluded at what many considered to be a bargain price of SEK340m (c.US$50m) on 29 June 2014, returning control of the submarine programme to domestic industry.

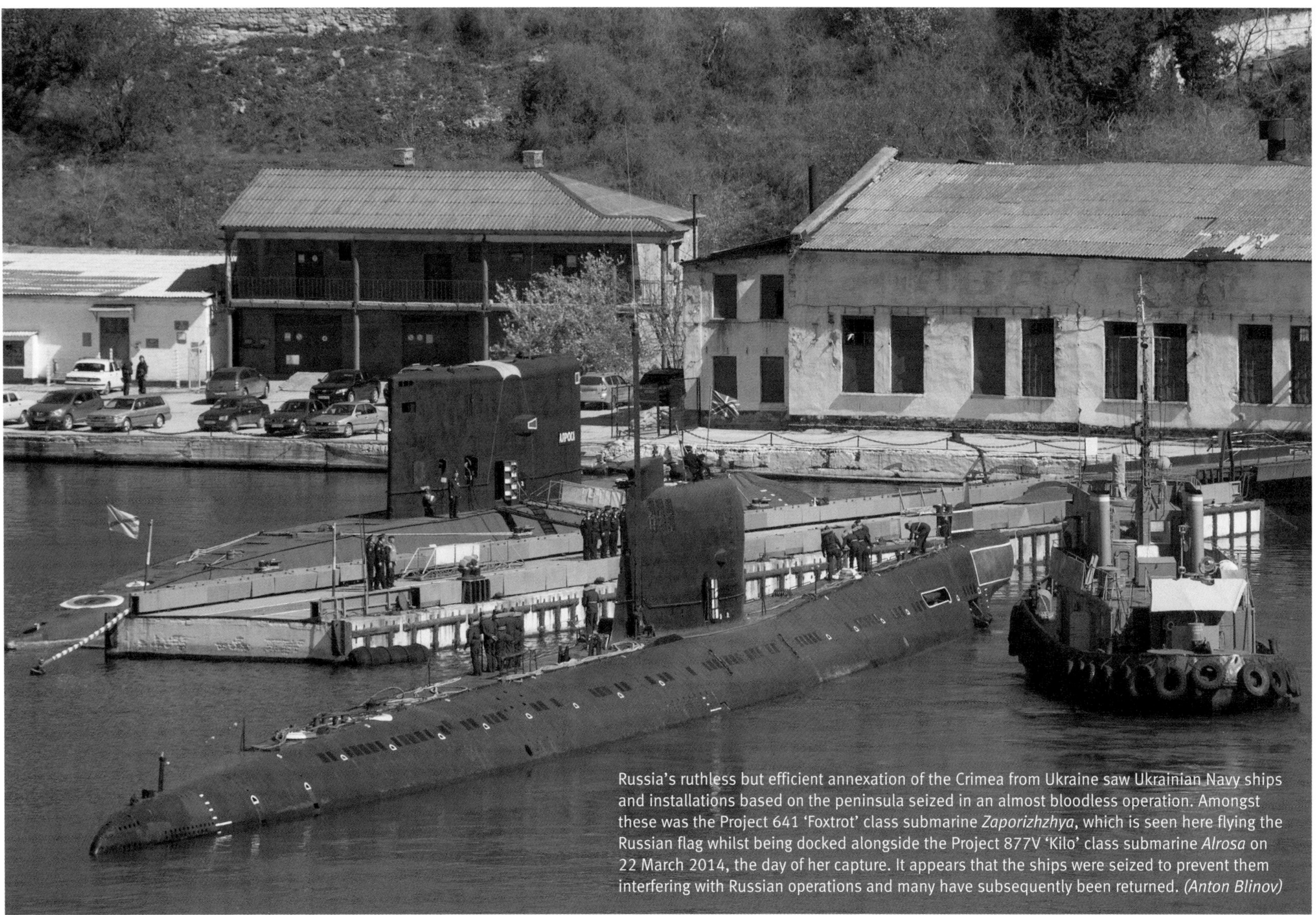

Russia's ruthless but efficient annexation of the Crimea from Ukraine saw Ukrainian Navy ships and installations based on the peninsula seized in an almost bloodless operation. Amongst these was the Project 641 'Foxtrot' class submarine *Zaporizhzhya*, which is seen here flying the Russian flag whilst being docked alongside the Project 877V 'Kilo' class submarine *Alrosa* on 22 March 2014, the day of her capture. It appears that the ships were seized to prevent them interfering with Russian operations and many have subsequently been returned. *(Anton Blinov)*

TABLE 2.4.1: FLEET STRENGTHS IN WESTERN EUROPE – LARGER NAVIES (MID 2014)

COUNTRY	FRANCE	GERMANY	GREECE	ITALY	NETHERLANDS	SPAIN	TURKEY	UK
Aircraft Carrier (CVN)	1	–	–	–	–	–	–	–
Support/Helicopter Carrier (CVS/CVH)	–	–	–	2	–	–	–	1
Strategic Missile Submarine (SSBN)	4	–	–	–	–	–	–	4
Attack Submarine (SSN)	6	–	–	–	–	–	–	6
Patrol Submarine (SSK)	–	4	8	6	4	3	14	–
Fleet Escort (DDG/FFG)	15	11	13	17	6	11	16	19
Patrol Escort/Corvette (FFG/FSG/FS)	15	5	–	5	–	–	8	–
Missile Armed Attack Craft (PGG/PTG)	–	8	16	–	–	–	23	–
Mine Countermeasures Vessel (MCMV)	14	15	4	10	6	6	20	15
Major Amphibious (LHD/LPD/LPH/LSD)	4	–	–	3	2	3	–	6

Normandie, the second FREMM-type frigate being built for France's *Marine Nationale*, spent much of the first half of 2014 on sea trials. These two images show her in March 2014. *(DCNS)*

MAJOR REGIONAL POWERS – FRANCE

A full review of the *Marine Nationale*'s recent development is set out in Chapter 2.4A, whilst Table 2.4.2 summarises current fleet strength. Frigate numbers are declining as older members of the *Georges Leygues* class start to be withdrawn from service. The lead ship was formally decommissioned in March 2014 and her sister *Dupleix* completed her last operational voyage two months later. Progress is being made with their replacements in the form of the French variant of the Franco-Italian FREMM class; the second French ship, *Normandie*, should be delivered in the second half of 2014 after completing an extensive series of sea trials. The third frigate, *Provence*, was launched on 18 September 2013 and a further three members of the class are in the course of construction. Production will then shift to two modified 'FREDA' (*frégate de défense aérienne*) air-defence type units. However, there are doubts whether three further planned class members will ever be started given the overall reduction in first-line frigates to fifteen envisaged in the 2013 defence white paper and plans for a cheaper frigate type. A final decision will be taken in 2016.

The white paper and associated 2014–19 military programme largely protected other projects. However, a number have been scaled back or had their delivery times extended. For example, only three fleet tankers will now be ordered to replace the remaining four vessels of the *Durance* type. *Meuse* will therefore be retired within the next twelve months in line with the new planned structure. In similar fashion, only three amphibious assault ships of the *Mistral* class are now envisaged and the older amphibious transport dock *Siroco* will be withdrawn soon without replacement. The rate of construction of the six 'Barracuda' type nuclear powered-attack submarines is also being slowed and only the first of class, *Suffren*, will be operational before the end of the decade.

More positively, long-awaited orders for three B2M (*Bâtiments Multi-Missions*) logistic support ships that will serve in France's overseas territories were placed at the end of 2013. Displacing c. 1,500 tons and with a length of 65m, the new ships will have a speed of 15 knots and an endurance of around thirty days without replenishment. They will be able to transport a force of up to twenty troops and two vehicles, along with weapons and ammunition. Delivery is planned for 2015–16 and an option for a fourth was included in the contract.

TABLE 2.4.2: FRENCH NAVY: PRINCIPAL UNITS AS AT MID 2014

TYPE	CLASS	NUMBER	TONNAGE	DIMENSIONS	PROPULSION	CREW	DATE
Aircraft Carriers							
Aircraft Carrier – CVN	**CHARLES DE GAULLE**	1	42,000 tons	262m x 33/64m x 9m	Nuclear, 27 knots	1,950	2001
Principal Surface Escorts							
Frigate – FFG	**AQUITAINE** (FREMM)	1	6,000 tons	142m x 20m x 5m	CODLOG, 27 knots	110	2012
Frigate – FFG	**FORBIN** ('Horizon')	2	7,000 tons	153m x 20m x 5m	CODOG, 29+ knots	195	2008
Frigate – FFG	**CASSARD** (FAA-70)	2	5,000 tons	139m x 15m x 5m	CODAD, 30 knots	250	1988
Frigate – FFG	**GEORGES LEYGUES** (FASM-70)	5	4,800 tons	139m x 15m x 5m	CODOG, 30 knots	240	1979
Frigate – FFG	**LA FAYETTE**	5	3,600 tons	125m x 15m x 5m	CODAD, 25 knots	150	1996
Frigate – FSG	**FLORÉAL**	6	3,000 tons	94m x 14m x 4m	CODAD, 20 knots	90	1992
Frigate – FS[1]	**D'ESTIENNE D'ORVES** (A-69)	9	1,300 tons	80m x 10m x 3m	Diesel, 24 knots	90	1976
Submarines							
Submarine – SSBN	**LE TRIOMPHANT**	4	14,400 tons	138m x 13m x 11m	Nuclear, 25 knots	110	1997
Submarine – SSN	**RUBIS**	6	2,700 tons	74m x 8m x 6m	Nuclear, 25+ knots	70	1983
Major Amphibious Units							
Amph Assault Ship – LHD	**MISTRAL**	3	21,500 tons	199m x 32m x 6m	Diesel-electric, 19 knots	160	2006
Landing Platform Dock – LPD	**FOUDRE**	1	12,000 tons	168m x 24m x 5m	Diesel, 20 knots	225	1990

Note:
1 Now officially reclassified as offshore patrol vessels.

MAJOR REGIONAL POWERS – ITALY

The last twelve months have been rather mixed for Italy's *Marina Militare*, with a number of positive developments being over-shadowed by longer term pressures on the defence budget. Most significantly, the Italian part of the FREMM programme is now starting to deliver ships on a rolling basis. This is reflected in the summary of overall Italian fleet strength in Table 2.4.3. The anti-submarine configured *Virginio Fasan* and *Carlo Margottini* have joined the lead general purpose type, *Carlo Bergamini*, in operational service over the course of the past year and further ships should be delivered at approximately annual intervals. In addition, whilst there were previous concerns that the original ten-ship programme would be truncated at just six ships, orders for the seventh and eighth units were placed in September 2013. Work on the first of these

Italy's *Marina Militare* attracted industry sponsorship to assist a combined sales and training deployment to the Middle East and Africa. These images show the warships that participated in the five-month mission, which was headed by the aircraft carrier *Cavour* and included the new FREMM frigate *Carlo Bergamini*. *(OCCAR)*

commenced in early June 2014. A decision on the remaining pair of ships is to be taken before the end of 2015.

Looking further forward, the navy hopes that a special €6bn (c. US$8bn) additional fund for new naval construction over the next ten years that was agreed in December 2013 will go some way to stemming the block obsolescence of much of the existing, second-line surface fleet. The core of this programme will be the new *pattugliatore d'altura multimissione* or multi-role oceanic patrol ship. This is essentially a flexible frigate-type ship capable of being configured for either low- or high-intensity operations. The special budget should fund around six of the new vessels, as well as a long-planned amphibious assault ship, a new replenishment tanker and two high-speed vessels to support Special Forces operations. However, it is by no means certain that all the allocated money will actually be delivered throughout the life of the planned programme in spite of a strong political imperative to keep Italy's shipyards busy. Meanwhile, the core defence budget remains under considerable pressure, with plans to make further cuts in the planned purchase of F-35 Joint Strike Fighter aircraft potentially reducing the numbers of the F-35B STOVL variant available for naval operations. There have also been rumours that the veteran carrier *Giuseppe Garibaldi*, now operating as an amphibious helicopter carrier, will be retired early as an economy measure. There should be greater clarity on the way forward by the end of 2014, when a new defence white paper is due for publication.

Operationally, an interesting development has been the deployment of a task group headed by the carrier *Cavour* to the Middle East and Africa on a five-month training cruise partially financed by Italian industry. The lead FREMM frigate *Carlo Bergamini*, the replenishment tanker *Etna* and the offshore patrol vessel *Comandante Borsini* comprised the remainder of the group. As well as fostering links with local navies and supporting humanitarian activities, the mission allowed Italian defence – and civilian – companies to showcase their products to a wide range of potential buyers. The perceived success of the deployment is a welcome distraction from events in the Mediterranean, where the navy and coast guard are struggling to cope with a seaborne influx of refugees in a humanitarian disaster that is claiming hundreds of lives. Additional naval vessels and reconnaissance assets are being deployed to mitigate an ongoing crisis that has been little-reported outside of the immediate region.[5] Meanwhile, the controversial case of the two San Marco Regiment marines arrested over the deaths of Indian fishermen mistaken for pirates and shot when their boat approached the tanker *Enrica Lexie* that the marines were guarding continues to progress slowly through the Indian courts.

MAJOR REGIONAL POWERS – SPAIN

Table 2.4.4, highlighting the current strength of the *Armada Española*, shows no change in fleet strength year-on-year. This is, of itself, something of a positive feature given the severe financial pressures faced by the navy over the past few years due to the Spanish government's wider financial problems. The return to something closer to stability has also been marked by government efforts to pay debts relating to previous projects. These have included the allocation of around €190m (c. US$250m) to pay sums owing to Navantia on the *Juan Carlos I* amphibious assault ship, *Cristóbal Colón* F-100 class frigate and *Cantabria* replenishment tanker that were delivered during 2010–12.

The more stable funding position has also allowed some progress with new projects, albeit this has been driven more by industrial than financial considerations. Most notably, in May 2014, Navantia was awarded a €400m (c. US$550m) contract to build two additional BAM (*buque de acción maritima*) offshore patrol ships of the *Meteoro* class. This will take total class numbers to six vessels out of an original projected total of fourteen. Construction will be split between Navantia's shipyards in the Bay of Cadiz and Ferrol, which have both been struggling

Table 2.4.3: ITALIAN NAVY: PRINCIPAL UNITS AS AT MID 2014

TYPE	CLASS	NUMBER	TONNAGE	DIMENSIONS	PROPULSION	CREW	DATE
Aircraft Carriers							
Aircraft Carrier – CV	**CAVOUR**	1	27,100 tons	244m x 30/39m x 9m	COGAG, 29 knots	800	2008
Aircraft Carrier – CVS	**GIUSEPPE GARIBALDI**[1]	1	13,900 tons	180m x 23/31m x 7m	COGAG, 30 knots	825	1985
Principal Surface Escorts							
Frigate – FFG	**CARLO BERGAMINI** (FREMM)	3	6,500 tons	144m x 20m x 5m	CODLOG, 27 knots	145	2013
Frigate – FFG	**ANDREA DORIA** ('Horizon')	2	7,100 tons	153m x 20m x 5m	CODOG, 29+ knots	190	2007
Destroyer – DDG	**DE LA PENNE**	2	5,400 tons	148m x 16m x 5m	CODOG, 31 knots	375	1993
Frigate – FFG	**MAESTRALE**	8	3,100 tons	123m x 13m x 4m	CODOG, 30+ knots	225	1982
Frigate – FFG	**ARTIGLIERE**	2	2,500 tons	114m x 12m x 4m	CODOG, 35 knots	185	1994
Frigate – FS	**MINERVA**	5	1,300 tons	87m x 11m x 3m	Diesel, 25 knots	120	1987
Submarines							
Submarine – SSK	**TODARO** (Type 212A)	2	1,800 tons	56m x 7m x 6m	AIP, 20+ knots	30	2006
Submarine – SSK	**PELOSI**	4	1,700 tons	64m x 7m x 6m	Diesel-electric, 20 knots	50	1988
Major Amphibious Units							
Landing Platform Dock – LPD	**SAN GIORGIO**	3	8,000 tons	133m x 21m x 5m	Diesel, 20 knots	165	1987

Note:
1 Now operates largely as a LPH.

Table 2.4.4: SPANISH NAVY: PRINCIPAL UNITS AS AT MID 2014

TYPE	CLASS	NUMBER	TONNAGE	DIMENSIONS	PROPULSION	CREW	DATE
Principal Surface Escorts							
Frigate – FFG	**ÁLVARO DE BAZÁN** (F-100)	5	6,300 tons	147m x 19m x 5m	CODOG, 28 knots	200	2002
Frigate – FFG	**SANTA MARIA** (FFG-7)	6	4,100 tons	138m x 14m x 5m	COGAG, 30 knots	225	1986
Submarines							
Submarine – SSK	**GALERNA** (S-70/AGOSTA)	3	1,800 tons	68m x 7m x 6m	Diesel-electric, 21 knots	60	1983
Major Amphibious Units							
Amph Assault Ship – LHD	**JUAN CARLOS I**	1	27,100 tons	231m x 32m x 7m	IEP, 21 knots	245	2010
Landing Platform Dock – LPD	**GALICIA**	2	13,000 tons	160m x 25m x 6m	Diesel, 20 knots	185	1998

to find sufficient work as previous contracts have been completed.

The news flow is not, however, entirely positive as stringent economies remain in force. The navy air arm's fleet of Harrier jump jets has been reduced by a quarter with the withdrawal of four older AV-8B versions. This will leave twelve AV-8B Harrier II Plus aircraft, as well as one trainer, in service. The lives of the remaining aircraft will be extended past 2025 given it is unlikely funding will be found to purchase F-35B STOVL Joint Strike Fighters, which are their only natural replacement.

A major ongoing concern is the troubled S-80 submarine programme, which envisages completion of four boats to replace Spain's existing underwater flotilla. Construction work has effectively been suspended until major weight and buoyancy problems identified in the first submarine, *Isaac Peral*, in May 2013 are resolved. General Dynamics Electric Boat of the US has been brought in to assist a major re-design, which will involve lengthening the submarines into a S-80 Plus configuration. Spanish press reports suggest that the second boat, *Narciso Monturiol*, will now be the first to be completed to the new specification with planned delivery before the end of 2017. The third and fourth boats will follow by 2020, after which *Isaac Peral* will be rebuilt. It also seems that there have been separate difficulties with the development of the class's new AIP system. This incorporates production of hydrogen through a new bioethanol processor supplied by a subsidiary of Spanish energy conglomerate Abengoa. It appears that the development process has not gone entirely smoothly, with local engineering group Técnicas Reunidas brought in to help.[6] The ongoing problems will not have helped Navantia's hopes to secure export orders for the new design.

MAJOR REGIONAL POWERS – UNITED KINGDOM

The last twelve months have seen a picture of broad stability for Britain's Royal Navy. This is reflected in Table 2.4.5, with the only change since mid-2013 being a temporary fall in the number of nuclear attack submarines due to the decommissioning of *Tireless* before arrival of her replacement, the third *Astute* class boat, *Artful*. The significant reductions in fleet strength and personnel that resulted from the 2010 Strategic Defence and Security Review have now largely been implemented. In addition, the introduction of an enhanced planning framework around the future equipment programme seems to be bringing benefits. Orders for new equipment are being progressed without the frequent reductions in scope and delays to timescale that previously typified defence procurement, whilst delivery of a number of incremental enhancements such as the Crowsnest airborne early-warning system are being accelerated. Developments with respect to major ship types are highlighted below.

Aircraft Carriers and Amphibious Ships: The sole remaining *Invincible* class carrier, *Illustrious*, continues to operate as a helicopter carrier following the withdrawal of the Harrier jet fleet and has now entered her final year of service. She will be replaced in the active fleet by the purpose-built amphibious helicopter carrier, *Ocean*, which will commence post-refit trials in the second half of 2014 after completion of a £65m (c. US$110m) upgrade at Devonport Dockyard that started in 2012. There are hopes that *Illustrious* will escape the scrapyard when she finally decommissions and a number of alternative uses ranging from a royal yacht to a museum and conference centre have been proposed.

Good progress has been made with the assembly

The British Royal Navy's last *Invincible* class aircraft carrier, *Illustrious*, will be withdrawn in the second half of 2014 after thirty-two years of service. It is hoped that a new use can be found for her so that she can avoid the scrapyard and ideas to achieve this aim have been sought. Amongst the most imaginative is a proposal by BMT Nigel Gee and Sigmund Yacht Design for her to be adapted as a 'Commonwealth Yacht'. The proposal includes three modern 'sails' containing bedrooms, leisure and conference facilities above the deck; below decks there would be space for a hospital and heavy equipment to support disaster relief and humanitarian activities. *(Peter Symonds)*

of the lead *Queen Elizabeth* aircraft carrier prior to her naming by HM Queen Elizabeth at Rosyth on 4 July 2014. She will be floated out of her dry dock

Table 2.4.5: BRITISH ROYAL NAVY: PRINCIPAL UNITS AS AT MID 2014

TYPE	CLASS	NUMBER	TONNAGE	DIMENSIONS	PROPULSION	CREW	DATE
Aircraft Carriers							
Aircraft Carrier – CVS	**INVINCIBLE**[1]	1	22,000 tons	210m x 31/36m x 8m	COGAG, 30 knots	1,100	1980
Principal Surface Escorts							
Destroyer – DDG	**DARING** (Type 45)	6	7,400 tons	152m x 21m x 5m	IEP, 30 knots	190	2008
Frigate – FFG	**NORFOLK** (Type 23)	13	4,900 tons	133m x 16m x 5m	CODLAG, 30 knots	185	1990
Submarines							
Submarine – SSBN	**VANGUARD**	4	16,000 tons	150m x 13m x 12m	Nuclear, 25+ knots	135	1993
Submarine – SSN	**ASTUTE**	2	7,800 tons	93m x 11m x 10m	Nuclear, 30+ knots	100	2010
Submarine – SSN	**TRAFALGAR**	4	5,200 tons	85m x 10m x 10m	Nuclear, 30+ knots	130	1983
Major Amphibious Units							
Helicopter Carrier – LPH	**OCEAN**	1	22,500 tons	203m x 35m x 7m	Diesel, 18 knots	490	1998
Landing Platform Dock – LPD	**ALBION**	2	18,500 tons	176m x 29m x 7m	IEP, 18 knots	325	2003
Landing Ship Dock – LSD (A)	**LARGS BAY**	3	16,200 tons	176m x 26m x 6m	Diesel-electric, 18 knots	60	2006

Note: 1. Now operates as a LPH

shortly afterwards to allow assembly of the second of class, *Prince of Wales*, to commence. Sea trials of *Queen Elizabeth* are now scheduled to begin in August 2016 prior to delivery in the first half of 2017. The new carrier will then carry an extensive work-up period, including at-sea trials of the F-35B Joint Strike Fighter, before entering operational service around the turn of the decade. The total cost of the programme has grown to £6.2bn (c. US$10.5bn) over the past year following confirmation in November 2013 of a further £750m 're-basing' of the value of the government's contract with the Aircraft Carrier Alliance tasked with building the new ships due to changed specifications, inflation and other adjustments. This compares with a budgeted cost of £3.5bn when the programme was authorised but is still much less than the US$12.9bn America is spending on the first US Navy *Gerald R Ford* (CVN-78) class nuclear-powered aircraft carrier.

Major Surface Combatants: The Type 45 destroyer programme has now come to an end following the commissioning of the sixth and last of class, *Duncan*, on 26 September 2013 prior to entry into operational service at the end of the year. She will reportedly be the first of four ships to be equipped with Harpoon surface-to-surface missiles recovered from withdrawn Type 22 class frigates, the others being *Daring*, *Diamond* and *Dragon*. Meanwhile, *Daring* has completed a highly successful circumnavigation of the world that included preliminary ballistic missile defence (BMD) trials with the US Navy in the Pacific, participation in Australia's centennial fleet review and initial disaster relief in the Philippines following Typhoon Haiyan prior to

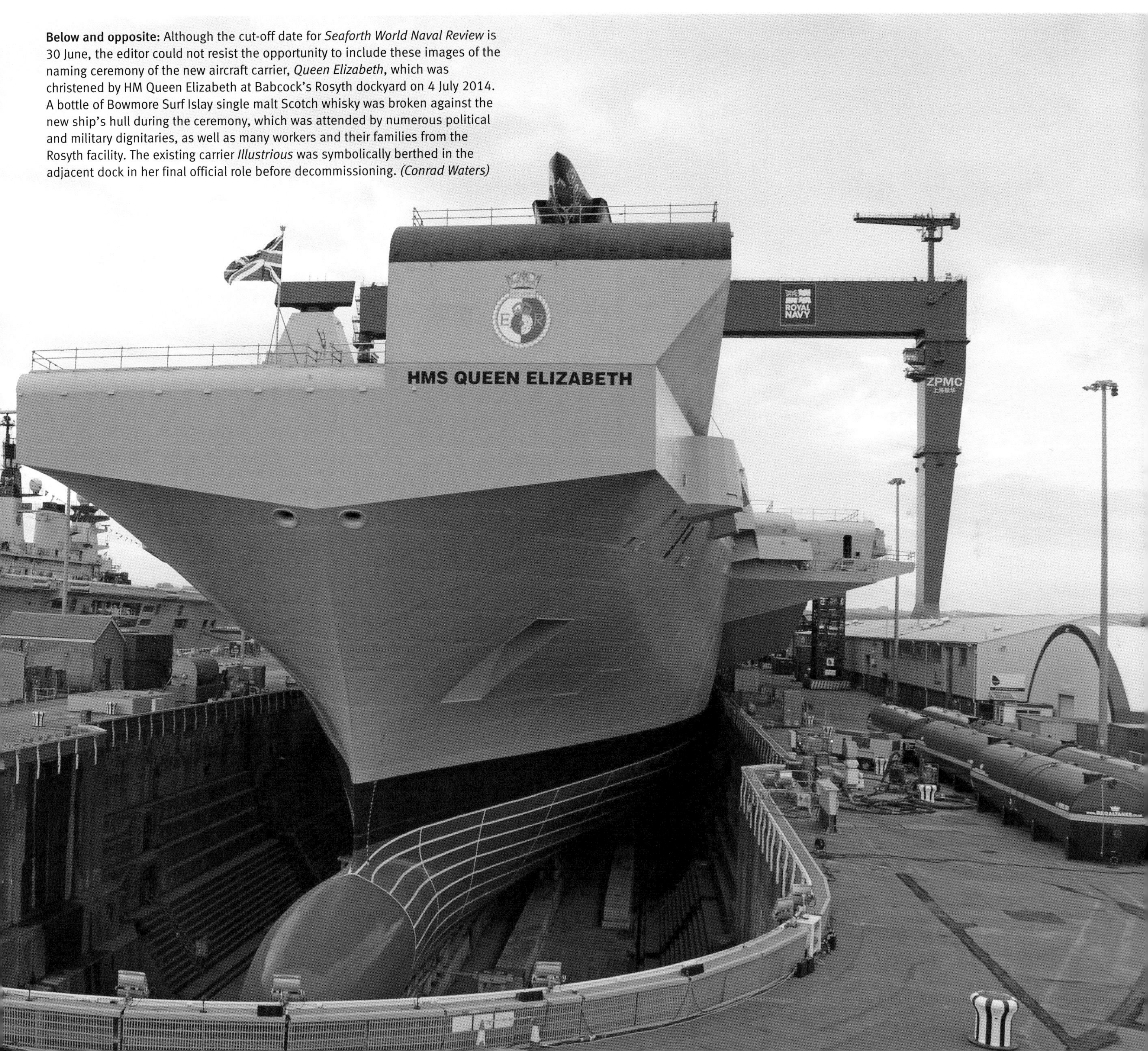

Below and opposite: Although the cut-off date for *Seaforth World Naval Review* is 30 June, the editor could not resist the opportunity to include these images of the naming ceremony of the new aircraft carrier, *Queen Elizabeth*, which was christened by HM Queen Elizabeth at Babcock's Rosyth dockyard on 4 July 2014. A bottle of Bowmore Surf Islay single malt Scotch whisky was broken against the new ship's hull during the ceremony, which was attended by numerous political and military dignitaries, as well as many workers and their families from the Rosyth facility. The existing carrier *Illustrious* was symbolically berthed in the adjacent dock in her final official role before decommissioning. *(Conrad Waters)*

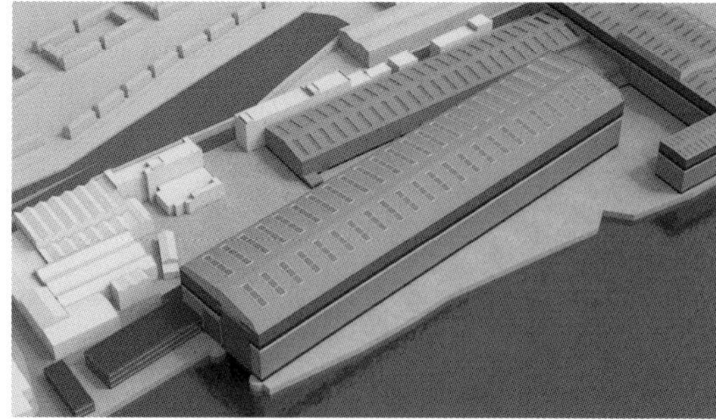

Although BAE Systems has announced the closure of its facilities in Portsmouth to new shipbuilding, large amounts will be invested in its other shipyards to support future programmes. Its preferred option for surface warships is construction of a new 'frigate factory' at Scotstoun on the Clyde incorporating a long, covered dock. However, an alternative is to modernise the existing assembly facility at Govan, with Scotstoun continuing to be used for integration and commissioning work. Further sums will be spent modernising the Devonshire Dock Hall and other facilities at Barrow-in-Furness in preparation for 'Successor' strategic submarine construction. *(BAE Systems)*

Design work and the acquisition of long lead materials continues on Britain's new 'Successor' class strategic missile submarines pending a decision on whether to proceed with the project after the 2015 general election. This graphic of the new design, dating from 2013, suggests the new class will have a relatively streamlined hull and incorporate an 'X' rudder arrangement. *(BAE Systems)*

relief by *Illustrious*. The missile defence tests, carried out in conjunction with the US Missile Defence Agency, in September 2013 demonstrated the potential of the class's Sampson radar in the BMD role and are to be followed by a second round of trials in 2015. However, significant investment would be required, not least in the class's Aster missiles, to develop a true BMD capability.

Meanwhile, detailed design work continues on the Type 26 global combat ship prior to an initial order planned for late 2014. It appears that eight ships out of a planned total of thirteen of the new frigates will be contracted in this initial batch. Construction of the first should commence by mid-2016 to allow entry into operational service by 2021. A significant revamp of BAE Systems' Clyde facilities is being planned to support the new programme following a decision announced in November 2013 to close the company's Portsmouth facility to new building and concentrate construction of surface warships in Glasgow. The preferred option is the creation of a new £200m (c. US$350m) 'frigate factory' at Scotstoun focused on a 330m-long covered dock hall that would allow all construction, integration and commissioning activities to be concentrated on a single site. A fall-back plan, costed at around £100m, would continue to see assembly and integration split between the Govan and Scotstoun facilities.[7]

Submarines: Current submarine construction remains focused on the *Astute* programme in advance of final decisions with respect to the 'Successor' class of strategic missile submarines that are expected to be taken after the 2015 general election. Third of class, *Artful*, was launched on 17 May 2014, somewhat later than previously planned, and is scheduled to start sea trials in 2015. Assembly of a further three boats is underway following the keel-laying of the sixth of class, *Agamemnon*, in July 2013. Long lead items for the final submarine, *Ajax*, have also been ordered. National Audit Office figures suggest the four final boats will cost between £1.4bn and £1.6bn, highlighting the cost of a modern nuclear-powered submarine.

Work continues to ramp up on the 'Successor' programme, which now seems almost certain to go ahead given the support of all three main political parties for a replacement for the existing *Vanguard* class.[8] Contracts for design and long lead items continue to be placed as part of a £3bn (c. US$5bn) assessment phase that is intended to ensure timely delivery of the first of class into operational service by 2028. The importance of the programme means that BAE Systems' submarine facility is another yard that is benefitting from significant investment, with around £300m earmarked to extend the existing 1980s-built Devonshire Dock Hall and modernise other parts of the site.[8] The existing *Vanguard* class continue to progress through a cycle of refits, with *Vanguard* expected to commence her final major refit in 2015. In March 2014, it was announced that the work will encompass refuelling with a new nuclear reactor core following detection of low levels of radioactivity in a prototype core of the same type that has been under test at the Naval Reactor Test Establishment at Dounreay in Scotland since 2002. The refuelling is the second time the process has been carried out since *Vanguard* entered service in 1993 and will add around £120m to the refit's cost.

Other Units: The announcement confirming the end of BAE Systems' warship-building activities in Portsmouth and the concentration of Type 26 production on the Clyde also included revelation of an unexpected plan to build three new helicopter-equipped offshore patrol vessels as replacements for the existing 'River' class. The decision appears to be largely based on a need to maintain production at Govan and Scotstoun between completion of blocks for the *Prince of Wales* and start of work on the Type 26 frigates. Whilst full details have yet to emerge, it seems that the new ships will be based on the existing *Port of Spain/Amazonas* class but include a larger flight deck and an upgraded combat system. A £20m contract to buy long lead items for the new ships was announced in March 2014 and the first should enter service during 2017. Work has also commenced on the new 'Tide' class fleet tankers being constructed by DSME in Okpo, Korea to BMT's Aegir design. Steel for the first, *Tidespring*, was cut on 27 June 2014, with delivery expected during 2016.

More broadly, the referendum on Scottish independence scheduled for 18 September 2014 continues to provide a backdrop of considerable uncertainty to Royal Navy construction and basing plans, particularly given continued United Kingdom government denials of any fall-back 'Plan B' to current arrangements in the event of a 'yes' vote. The most critical issue a vote for Scottish independence might raise would be the future of the Faslane nuclear submarine base given opposition from the Scottish National Party (SNP) to the presence of nuclear weapons on Scottish soil. Current SNP policy envisages removal of nuclear weapons by 2020 at the latest, which would pose a significant challenge to the remainder of the United Kingdom given the cost and difficulty of establishing alternative base facilities.[9]

MID-SIZED REGIONAL FLEETS

Germany: The *Deutsche Marine* continues to see the progressive retirement of older vessels pending the entry of new construction into service. The planned withdrawal of 1980s-vintage F-122 *Bremen* class frigates saw the decommissioning of *Emden* at the end of November 2013, followed by *Bremen* herself on 28 March 2014. The remaining quartet will remain in service pending delivery of the four F-125 *Baden-Württemberg* class stabilisation frigates from late 2016 onwards. The lead ship of the new class was christened at the Blohm & Voss yard in Hamburg on 12 December 2013 prior to float out in the spring of 2014. Construction of the second ship, *Nordrhein-Westfalen*, is well underway at Lürssen's yard in Bremen, whilst the keel of the third, *Sachsen-Anhalt*, was laid at Hamburg on 4 June 2014.

The main addition to the fleet in the last year has been the third and final Type 702 *Berlin* class replenishment ship, *Bonn*, which entered operational service in September 2013. The two Batch 2 Type 212A AIP-equipped submarines are also complete but had yet to be formally commissioned as of mid-2014.

Operationally, the German Navy continues to be involved in a range of European Union, NATO and United Nations-sponsored tasks – most notably Operation 'Atalanta' in the Indian Ocean and the UNIFIL stabilisation mission off Lebanon – in line with the more expeditionary focus of recent years. The new K-130 *Braunschweig* class corvettes are now starting to deploy in support of the UNIFIL opera-

The main German surface construction programme is focused on the new F-125 stabilisation frigates of the *Baden-Württemberg* class, which should be delivered at roughly annual intervals from 2016. The lead ship was floated out of her building dock at Hamburg on 28 March 2014 after being christened in December 2013. The second member of the class, *Nordrhein-Westfalen*, is being constructed by Lürssen, ThyssenKrupp Marine Systems' partner in the ARGE F-125 consortium tasked with building the ships, whilst the keel of the third ship, *Sachsen-Anhalt*, was laid at Hamburg in June 2014. *(ThyssenKrupp Marine Systems)*

tion, supplementing the Type 143A *Gepard* class fast attack craft that have formed the mainstay of Germany's contribution. The new F-125 frigates and planned MKS-180 multi-purpose corvettes are both orientated towards long-distance stabilisation missions and it will be interesting to see whether these plans change in the light of heightened perceptions of a new Russian threat.

Greece: The Hellenic Navy is another fleet from the so-called peripheral Eurozone countries that is starting to see a return to something close to stability as financial conditions in Europe stabilise. In particular, construction programmes that were effectively put 'on ice' during the worst of the crisis are now being resumed. In March 2014 it was announced that work would finally commence on commissioning the three German-designed Type 214 submarines that were constructed by Hellenic Shipyards at Skaramangas, near Athens. The intention is for them to join the Kiel-built *Papanikolis*, the only member of the class currently in service, in the operational fleet by 2016. The older Type 209/1200 submarine *Okeanos*, the only one of the class to receive an AIP hull-plug under the Neptune II programme before the project was cancelled, will also be returned to service at the same time. The largely complete submarines have been laid-up at Skaramangas for over two years and bringing them into operational service might not be easy. The long-troubled contract with Germany's ThyssenKrupp Marine Systems, which formerly controlled Hellenic Shipyards, has become something of a *cause célèbre* in Greek political circles. A former Greek defence minister has been jailed over the alleged handling of bribes from another company involved in the deal and others Greek officials are under investigation. In June 2014 it was reported that the Greek government are seeking a multi-billion euro compensation payment from TKMS and Abu Dhabi Mar, who subsequently acquired the yard, on the somewhat strange basis of the damage to Greece's reputation caused by the contract.[10]

Work has also recommenced on bringing the three remaining British-designed *Roussen* fast attack craft into operational service. Four of these small but powerful warships were put into service between 2005 and 2010 and the fifth, *Ritsos*, was almost ready for commissioning before work was suspended. It is hoped that she will now become operational before the end of 2014 but more work is required on her two sisters. The Hellenic Navy continues to have a requirement to renew its fleet of larger surface vessels but it is unlikely that funding will be available to do this in the near future. However, a mid-life modernisation of the four *Hydra* class MEKO-200HN frigates may commence soon.

The Netherlands: The Royal Netherlands Navy remains subject to significant financial pressure, with additional reductions in defence spending revealed in September 2013 threatening to see the new JSS joint support ship, *Karel Doorman*, sold before she had even entered into service. In the event, the decision was swiftly reversed and the new ship was christened on 8 March 2014 before commencing sea trials three months later. Constructed at Damen's yard in Galati, Romaina but fitted out by Damen Schelde Naval Shipbuilding in Vlissingen, the new 28,000-ton ship combines amphibious transport dock and replenishment roles. She will replace the existing tanker, *Amsterdam*, which has been sold to Peru.

Elsewhere, all four vessels of the *Holland* class are now in operational service following the commissioning of *Zeeland* on 23 August 2013 and the final ship, *Groningen*, on 29 November of the same year.

The *Deutsche Marine* continues to be active in stabilisation missions under the auspices of the United Nations, European Union and NATO. A heavy commitment has been UNIFIL peacekeeping duties off the coast of Lebanon. The Type 143A *Gepard* class fast attack craft – *Frettchen* is shown here – have been prominent in this role but they are now being supplemented by the newer and larger K-130 *Braunschweig* class corvettes. *German Navy)*

Greece's Hellenic Navy is returning to financial normality and a number of stalled programmes are being resumed. Amongst these is completion of three remaining *Roussen* class fast attack craft to join the four existing vessels. This image shows the fourth ship, *Grigoropoulos*, leading sister *Krystallides* and other units during exercises in June 2014. *(Hellenic Navy)*

The new ships are designed to operate the NFH-90 helicopter being acquired from Airbus but it was announced at the end of June 2014 that deliveries of the type are being suspended due to the discovery of excessive corrosion and wear in operational aircraft. The Dutch Ministry of Defence anticipates that the problems will mean that it will not be until 2019 that sufficient helicopters and trained personnel are available to support all required operations and various contingencies are being examined.

Turkey: The Turkish Navy has one of the most ambitious procurement programmes of all the European fleets and is steadily cementing its position as the dominant naval power in the Eastern Mediterranean, as well as a significant counter-weight to Russia in the Black Sea. The major development over the last year was the selection of a variant of Spain's *Juan Carlos I* LHD-type amphibious assault ship for the navy's amphibious transport dock requirement. Media reports suggest the new ship, which will be constructed by the Sedef Shipyard with Navantia's technical assistance, will be shorter and lighter than her Spanish equivalent. She will have the capacity to transport 700 troops with their vehicles, as well as 200 command staff. The flight deck will support simultaneous operation of at least four large helicopters and the hangar will be able to accommodate a similar number. The ship's acquisition marks the culmination of a broader plan to acquire new amphibious vessels that also encompasses two tank landing ships (LSTs) and eight smaller tank landing craft (LCTs). All of the tank landing craft are now in service, whilst work on the first LST, *Bayraktar*, commenced at the ADIK yard on 14 May 2014.

Progress with surface combatants has been less straightforward. The award of a contract to RMK Marine for construction of six follow-on 'Milgem' or 'Ada' class corvettes to the two built in Istanbul Naval Shipyard was cancelled in August 2013. National politics appear to have played a key part in this decision, with RMK Marine's parent company, Koç Holding, reportedly out of favour with Turkey's authoritarian Prime Minister Recep Erdo?an. Istanbul Naval Shipyard will now take responsibility for the third and fourth vessels of the class, with the other four being re-tendered. The keel of the third ship, *Burgazada*, was laid on 27 September 2013; the same day that the second corvette, *Büyükada*, was commissioned. The political shenanigans surrounding the programme will doubtless result in further delays to the TF-2000 air-defence frigate project, which is intended to mark a further step forward in the development of an indigenous naval sector. There is also an intention to commence a new fast attack craft programme, with existing members of the old 1960s-vintage *Kartal* class now being rapidly decommissioned.

Another high priority for Turkey is improved coastal security given the substantial problem of illegal migration and the threat of a spill-over of terrorist activity from neighbouring conflicts. Additional investment is being made in coastal surveillance radars and UAV reconnaissance capabilities are also being developed as part of a general strengthening of the coast guard. All four of the new 1,700-ton *Dost* class search and rescue patrol vessels have now entered service with the commissioning of the final ship, *Yaşam*, on 13 April 2014.

Operationally, the navy's deployments are becoming increasingly ambitious as its use as a diplomatic tool starts to be appreciated. A notable recent development was the departure of the Barbaros Turkish Maritime Task Group on a c. 100-day circumnavigation of Africa on 17 March 2014. This is expected to encompass forty port visits in twenty-eight countries. The voyage, which will mark the first time the Turkish Navy has passed the Cape of Good Hope in nearly 150 years, has been criticised by some as a distraction from the more pressing issue of the volatile security situation in the Black Sea. However, it provides another sign of Turkey's growing maritime influence beyond its immediate waters.[11]

OTHER REGIONAL FLEETS

Atlantic and North Sea: The Atlantic-facing countries of Ireland and Portugal have both suffered similar economic difficulties during the Eurozone crisis; a similarity that is, to an extent, replicated in the challenges faced by their respective fleets.

Of the two countries, **Ireland** seems to be having more success in configuring its navy to focus on this core requirement, steadily replacing its elderly patrol vessels with more modern ships that are better-suited to extended Atlantic patrols. The first of the new *Samuel Beckett* class ships entered service on 17 May 2014, replacing the lead *Emer* class patrol vessel, which was decommissioned in September 2013. The two remaining *Emer* class ships, *Aoife* and *Aisling*, will be similarly replaced over the next two years following exercise of an option for a third *Samuel Beckett* class patrol vessel in June 2014.

By contrast, **Portugal**, has successfully acquired a potent front-line naval force focused on five modern frigates and two AIP-equipped submarines but is struggling to replace a larger force of second-line corvettes and patrol vessels. A previous plan for the construction of new offshore and coastal patrol vessels by indigenous builder ENVC was reduced to just two of the larger ships. The last of these, *Figueira da Foz*, was commissioned in November

Turkey is spending heavily on naval procurement, including both navy and coast guard vessels. This image shows *Güven*, one of four *Dost* class offshore patrol vessels that have recently been delivered. *(Devrim Yaylali)*

2013 and the ENVC yard has now been privatised, reportedly focusing largely on repair work. As such, it is not clear if further patrol vessels could be built domestically, even if funding was available.

Belgium, meanwhile, is seeing good progress with construction of the two coastal patrol type 'ready duty' ships ordered from French builder Socarenam in 2013. The first of these 450-ton vessels was launched at Boulogne-sur-Mer on 14 April 2014 prior to planned delivery in July of the same year. Named *Castor*, she will be followed by her twin, *Pollux*, around the end of the year.

Black Sea: Russia's seizure of the Crimea has left **Ukraine** with little more than a shadow of its previous navy given around eighty per cent of its naval personnel and the majority of its warships were based on the peninsula. The latter were all seized in the course of Russia's occupation, although a number have subsequently been handed back. Ukraine's flagship, the Project 1135 'Krivak' class frigate *Hetman Sahaydachniy* was returning from European Union-led anti-piracy operations in the Indian Ocean when the occupation occurred. She was therefore able to return safely to Ukraine's Western Naval Base at Odessa, which is the only significant naval installation remaining in Ukrainian hands. Irrespective of the outcome of political events elsewhere in the Ukraine, the loss of the Crimean bases will inevitably cripple Ukrainian Navy operations for many years ahead.

Russian actions will also have an impact on **Bulgaria** and **Romania**, which are both NATO members. The two countries have gone some way to rebuilding their Soviet-era fleets with second-hand Western equipment, with Bulgaria acquiring three *Wielingen* class frigates and a minehunter from Belgium and Romania two Type 22 frigates from the United Kingdom. However, plans for more ambitious modernisation with new ships have largely been stalled for lack of funds. Greater uncertainty in the Black Sea, coupled with Russian plans to modernise its own Black Sea Fleet, may unblock money for some of these projects, although modernisation of existing ships is likely to be the immediate priority.

Scandinavia and the Baltic: Having steadily reconfigured their navies to be better-suited to international stabilisation missions since the end of the Cold War, the Scandinavian countries are starting to adapt their force structures to take account of the perception that Russia now poses a renewed threat. **Sweden**, particularly, is looking to bolster its military to respond to a resurgent Russia, increasing defence spending over a ten-year horizon and focusing investment on capabilities that are most necessary for homeland defence. As mentioned in the introduction, a key priority is to advance construction of the planned two new A-26 submarines, which will replace the existing modernised A-17 *Södermanland* class. These will now be built under Saab's leadership. The three existing A-19 *Gotland* class boats will also be modernised to provide a five-strong submarine flotilla. Above the waves, all five *Visby* class stealth corvettes have now been delivered to 'version V' operational standard (including surface-to-surface missiles, mine-clearance systems and full helicopter operating capabilities) and are ready for deployment. Some of the older corvettes will also have their service lives extended. Neighbouring **Finland** has already completed a mid-life modernisation of its four *Rauma* class fast attack craft which, together with the more modern quartet of *Hamina* class, form the heart of its strike capabilities. Minehunting capabilities are also being upgraded and the second of three *Katanpää* mine countermeasures vessels was delivered in September 2013. The final ship should follow before the end of 2014.

Although the majority of the Ukrainian Navy's warships were seized during Russia's annexation of the Crimea, the fleet's principal surface warship, the Project 1135 'Krivak' class frigate *Hetman Sahaydachniy*, was in the course of returning from an Indian Ocean deployment at the time and was able to divert to the Ukrainian-controlled port of Odessa. This image shows her transiting the Bosphorus during her homeward voyage on 4 March 2014. *(Devrim Yaylali)*

Denmark is, perhaps, the Scandinavian country which has shifted furthest from its defensive Cold War posture, sacrificing its submarine flotilla and Stanflex 300 multi-role patrol vessels for more deployable ships such as the *Absalon* and *Iver Huitfeldt* classes. The latter are steadily receiving their full outfit of weapons systems as part of an incremental approach to achieving full operational capability. Denmark, along with Norway, has taken leadership of the maritime operation to transport chemical warfare agents out of Syria in accordance with an Organisation for the Prohibition of Chemical Weapons plan incorporated under UN Security Council Resolution 2118 and members of both classes have been deployed as escort vessels. The Danish political agreement covering defence force structures currently lasts until 2017 but it will be interesting to see whether the changed security environment leads to an early revision. Meanwhile, **Norway** has typically taken a relatively robust approach to defence strategy, with its focus on the 'High North' adjacent to Russia meaning a wary eye has been kept on its neighbour. Re-capitalisation of the surface fleet over the past few years has seen delivery of the Spanish-built *Fridtjof Nansen* and indigenous *Skjold* class corvettes. In addition, an order for a British BMT-designed Aegir type logistics support vessel from Korea's DSME in July 2013 will provide a new replenishment capability. Similar to, but smaller than, the new British Royal Navy 'Tide' class vessels, the 28,000-ton ship will provide wet and dry stores support. The next major decision will be on whether to upgrade or replace the six existing German-built *Ula* class submarines. A preliminary decision is likely by the end of 2014.

Elsewhere in the region, **Poland** has outlined plans for a major naval recapitalisation programme that will determine fleet structure through to 2030. Three new submarines will replace the five existing boats, whilst there will also be three new corvette-type coastal patrol vessels, three larger but less heavily-armed offshore patrol vessels and three mine-hunters, alongside other specialist ships. An order for the mine countermeasures vessels was placed in the autumn of 2013, when completion of the existing MEKO A-100 corvette *Ślązak*, as an offshore patrol vessel was confirmed.

An image of Russia's *Mistral*-type amphibious assault ship, *Vladivostok*, departing Saint-Nazaire on 5 March 2014 on preliminary sea trials. In spite of American pressure, France looks set to honour her contract to deliver two ships of the class. *(Bruno Huriet)*

RUSSIA

Although Russia's intervention in the Crimea has served to strengthen perceptions of its military potential, the underlying picture is far less straightforward. The country is investing heavily in its armed forces to negate years of post-Cold War neglect. Around US$750bn (c. £444bn) has been allocated to the Russian Ministry of Defence and associated ministries over the course of the 2011–20 State Armaments Plan to make good past deficiencies by replacing some seventy per cent of existing equipment.[12] However, the moribund state of much of Russia's military-industrial complex, high rates of defence inflation and simple corruption all mean that modernisation is proceeding at a slow pace. Somewhat ironically, the take-over of the Crimea only serves to exacerbate these difficulties. It makes it more difficult for Russia to access key components from factories located in other parts of the Ukraine during the Soviet era and will hinder attempts to acquire up-to-date 'Western' technologies. Although France has – to date – decided to honour its contrac-

The Royal Norwegian Navy ordered a new logistics support vessel based on BMT's Aegir design in July 2013. This computer generated image shows her supporting a Norwegian *Ula* class submarine; a decision on the type's modernisation or replacement is expected soon. *(BMT Group)*

Poland has confirmed that it is to complete its MEKO A-100 type frigate *Ślązak*, as an offshore patrol vessel. In spite of the change in her designation, she will be fitted with a sophisticated Thales Nederland radar and combat-management system and could easily be adapted for a front-line role. *(Thales Nederland)*

TABLE 2.4.6: RUSSIAN NAVY: SELECTED PRINCIPAL UNITS AS AT MID 2014

TYPE	CLASS	NUMBER[1]	TONNAGE	DIMENSIONS	PROPULSION	CREW	DATE
Aircraft carriers							
Aircraft Carrier – CV	Project 1143.5 **KUZNETSOV**	1	60,000 tons	306m x 35/73m x 10m	Steam, 32 knots	2,600	1991
Principal Surface Escorts							
Battlecruiser – BCGN	Project 1144.2 **KIROV**	1 (1)	25,000 tons	252m x 29m x 9m	CONAS, 32 knots	740	1980
Cruiser – CG	Project 1164 **MOSKVA** ('Slava')	3	12,500 tons	186m x 21m x 8m	COGAG, 32 knots	530	1982
Destroyer – DDG	Project 956/956A **SOVREMENNY**	c.5	8,000 tons	156m x 17m x 6m	Steam, 32 knots	300	1980
Destroyer – DDG	Project 1155.1 **CHABANENKO** ('Udaloy II')	1	9,000 tons	163m x 19m x 6m	COGAG, 29 knots	250	1999
Destroyer – DDG	Project 1155 **UDALOY**	c.8	8,400 tons	163m x 19m x 6m	COGAG, 30 knots	300	1980
Frigate – FFG	Project 1154 **NEUSTRASHIMY**	2	4,400 tons	139m x 16m x 6m	COGAG, 30 knots	210	1993
Frigate – FFG	Project 1135 **BDITELNNY** ('Krivak I/II')	c.2	3,700 tons	123m x 14m x 5m	COGAG, 32 knots	180	1970
Frigate – FFG	Project 2038.0 **STEREGUSHCHY**	4	2,200 tons	105m x 11m x 4m	CODAD, 27 knots[2]	100	2008
Frigate – FFG	Project 1161.1 **TATARSTAN** ('Gepard')	2	2,000 tons	102m x 13m x 4m	CODOG, 27 knots	100	2002
Submarines							
Submarine – SSBN	Project 955 **YURY DOLGORUKY** ('Borey')	3	17,000+ tons	170m x 13m x 10m	Nuclear, 25+ knots	110	2010
Submarine – SSBN	Project 941 **DONSKOY** ('Typhoon')	1	33,000 tons	173m x 23m x 12m	Nuclear, 26 knots	150	1981
Submarine – SSBN	Project 677BDRM **VERKHOTURYE** ('Delta IV')	6	18,000 tons	167m x 12m x 9m	Nuclear, 24 knots	130	1985
Submarine – SSBN	Project 677BDR **ZVEZDA** ('Delta III')	3	12,000 tons	160m x 12m x 9m	Nuclear, 24 knots	130	1976
Submarine – SSGN	Project 855 **SEVERODVINSK** ('Yasen')	1	12,500 tons	120m x 14m x 9m	Nuclear, 30+ knots	90	2013
Submarine – SSGN	Project 949A ('Oscar II')	c.5	17,500 tons	154m x 8m x 9m	Nuclear, 30+ knots	100	1986
Submarine – SSN	Project 971 ('Akula I/II')	c.10	9,500 tons	110m x 14m x 10m	Nuclear, 30+ knots	60	1986
Submarine – SSK	Project 677 **ST PETERSBURG** ('Lada')	1	2,700 tons	72m x 7m x 7m	Diesel-electric, 21 knots	40	2010
Submarine – SSK	Project 877/636 ('Kilo')	c.20	3,000 tons	73m x 10m x 7m	Diesel-electric, 20 knots	55	1981

Notes:

1 Table only includes main types and focuses on operational units: bracketed figures are ships being refurbished or in maintained reserve.

2 Some sources state CODOG propulsion.

tual commitment to supply two *Mistral* type amphibious assault ships in the face of strong US objections, it is difficult to see a similar agreement being concluded today given the current political backdrop.

More detail on different ship categories is provided below.

Submarines: Modernisation of Russia's submarine-based strategic missile fleet remains the navy's top priority. Good progress is being made with construction of the Project 955 and modified Project 955A 'Borey' class strategic submarines, with second boat *Aleksandr Nevsky* commissioned in December 2013 and third of class *Vladimir Monomakh* currently undergoing final sea trials. A fourth submarine, *Knyaz Vladimir*, is under construction to the revised Project 955A specification and a fifth, *Knyaz Oleg*, will reportedly be laid down in July 2014. Unfortunately, the RSM-56 'Bulava' (NATO: SS-NX-30) ballistic missile that will arm the boats continues to be plagued by unreliability. A test firing from *Aleksandr Nevsky* on 6 September 2013 failed, reportedly due to a defect in its directable nozzles. Although this was the first problem since 2009, the overall failure rate is running at around forty per cent. An extensive programme of new launches, involving all three completed members of the class, is now planned through to the end of 2015 in an attempt to bring the missile into operational service.

The first Project 855 'Yasen' class nuclear-powered attack submarine, *Severodvinsk*, has now been commissioned following a formal flag-raising ceremony on 17 June 2014. She was delivered at the end of 2013 by the Sevmash yard, some twenty years after work on her first commenced. Sevmash is building two further boats to a modified Project 855M specification and will lay down a further unit at the same time as the Project 955A strategic submarine, *Knyaz Oleg*.

Construction of conventional submarines is currently focused on an improved Project 636.3 'Kilo' type following problems with the follow-on Project 677 'Lada' design. *Novorossiysk*, the first of six new boats ordered from St Petersburg's Admiralty Shipyards, commenced sea trials at the end of May 2014. The second submarine, *Rostov-on-Don*, was launched a month later on 26 June. Admiralty Shipyards have also resumed work on the two incomplete 'Lada' class units, whilst trials with the lead boat, *St Petersburg*, continue. Media reports suggest that she could be used as a test bed for a new AIP system, which will be installed in a new generation of 'Kalina' type submarines.

Aircraft Carriers and Amphibious Ships: There has inevitably been considerable focus on the two DCNS-designed *Mistral* type amphibious assault ships under construction at STX Europe in Saint-Nazaire. The first ship, *Vladivostok*, was floated out in October 2013, subsequently commencing trials on 5 March 2014. Her Russian crew arrived at Saint-Nazaire on 30 June to prepare for delivery in the second half of the year. Construction of her sister, *Sevastopol*, is well under way, with her Russian-built stern section scheduled to leave St

Petersburg at the end of June 2014 for integration with the rest of the ship in France. Meanwhile, the sole Russian aircraft carrier, *Admiral Kuznetsov*, remains active, completing a six-month deployment to the Mediterranean in company with the nuclear-powered battlecruiser *Pyotr Velikiy* and other units in the first half of 2014. Deliveries of new MiG-29K multi-role jets that will replace the existing life-expired SU-33 fighters commenced in 2013.

Surface Vessels: Russian Navy programmes for the construction of surface warships present a somewhat confusing array of separate projects, often focused on specific shipyards and intended for one of Russia's four principal fleets or Caspian Flotilla. A number of these programmes, including a new Project 2195.6 destroyer, are still in their infancy, and may never actually commence. The following is a summary of the main current projects:

Project 2235.0 Frigates: Intended to form the core of a new 'blue water' Russian surface fleet, the construction of the first of these 4,500-ton ships, *Admiral Gorshkov*, commenced in early 2006 but has been badly delayed. As of mid-2014, fitting-out continued at St Petersburg's Severnaya Verf, which is also working on three further members of the class following the keel laying of *Admiral Isakov* in November 2013. A planned total of up to twenty ships seems optimistic.

Project 1135.6 Frigates: Based on the Indian *Talwar* class, itself derived from the 'Krivak' design, these new ships were ordered from Kaliningrad's Yantar yard in two batches from 2010 onwards as a response to delays in other programmes and are intended for the Black Sea fleet. The programme has also suffered some delays but the first ship was launched in March 2014. A further four vessels were under construction with the start of work on *Admiral Istomin* in November 2013.

Project 2038.0/5 Corvettes: Designed for littoral operations, four of the original 2,200-ton Project 2038.0/1 *Steregushchy* variant had been completed by Severnaya Verf as of mid-2014 after delivery of *Stoiky* in May. All of these ships operate in the Baltic Fleet. A further two ships of the original type are under construction at the Komsomolsk yard in Amur for the Pacific Fleet, whilst Severnaya Verf has shifted production to the larger Project 2038.5 *Gremyashchy* variant. Two of the type, which also feature improved weapons systems, are currently under construction. There is a stated requirement for twenty ships.

Project 2163.0/1 Corvettes: Something of a cross between a corvette and a fast attack craft, three members of the original Project 2163.0 'Buyan' class were completed in St Petersburg between 2006 and 2012. Displacing around 500-tons standard displacement, the class is intended for service with the Caspian Sea Flotilla. Another seven improved Project 2163.1 variants are being built by the inland Zelenodolsk yard in Tatarstan, with the first pair of these likely to enter service before the end of 2014. Zelenodolsk has also previously delivered two larger Project 1161.1 'Gepard' class light frigates for Caspian Sea service and is reportedly working on the first of a new class of at least twelve Project 2216.0 patrol ships.

Delays to new construction mean that continued reliance is being placed on obsolete Soviet-era designs that are expensive to run and maintain. Some sanity, at least, seems to have prevailed with respect to the previous plan to rebuild three decommissioned *Kirov* class battlecruisers to re-join the sole remaining operational member of the class, *Pyotr Velikiy*, in the active fleet. It is now realised that the two older members of the class are beyond repair, although work on the third ship, *Admiral Nakhimov*, is now well underway.

Notes

1. The reinforcements included large numbers of special operations personnel – quickly termed as 'Little Green Men' by media sources in the face of initial Kremlin denials of military involvement – who were often disguised as members of local pro-Russian 'self-defence groups'.

2. Amongst numerous media reports on this development was Daniel Wasserbly's 'US to seek $1bn to boost US presence in Europe', *Jane's Defence Weekly* – 11 June 2014 (Coulsdon, IHS Jane's, 2014), p.5.

3. The Montreux Convention, which returned control of the Bosphorus and Dardanelles Straits to Turkey, was signed against the deterioration in international relations that ended in the Second World War and has been subject to considerable controversy. An excellent overview of its main terms was provided by Cem Devrim Yaylali's *Bosphorus Naval News* (http://turkishnavy.net) on 27 April 2014 under the title 'The Montreux Convention Regarding the Regime of the Straits: A Turkish Perspective'.

4. The so-called Malmö Raid was covered, *inter alia*, by Gerard O'Dwyer in 'Saab moves closer to Takeover of ThyssenKrupp Sub Building Operations in Sweden', *Defense News* – 14 April 2014 (Springfield VA, Gannett Government Media Corporation, 2014).

5. A notable exception was a report entitled 'Europe's African Refugee Crisis: Is the Boat Really Full?' that first appeared in Germany's *Der Spiegel* on 14 April 2014 (Hamburg, Spiegel-Verlag, 2014).

6. The story was carried on the *infodefensa.com* website on 11 June 2014 under the heading 'Defensa releva a Abengoa por Técnicas Reunidas en el diseño del AIP del S-80', citing a story carried in the *El Economista* newspaper.

7. A detailed overview of the shipyard rebuilding projects at both Glasgow and Barrow was provided by Richard Scott under the title 'Plans laid out for BAE Systems Shipyard Redevelopments', *Warship World* – May/June 2014 (Liskeard, Maritime Books, 2014), pp.2–3.

8. Following the production of a *Trident Alternatives Review* (London, HM Government, 2013), former Liberal Democrat opposition to replacement Trident submarines has now moved to adopting a 'contingency posture' requiring fewer submarines than the current 'continuous at-sea deterrence.'

9. The implications of independence for the defences of both Scotland and the 'rump UK' have been subject to considerable debate. A good review of the overall strategic considerations that still holds good was provided by Malcolm Chalmers of the Royal United Services Institute in 'Kingdom's End?', *The RUSI Journal* – June 2012 (London, Routledge Informa Ltd, 2012), pp.6–11.

10. The long saga of the Greek Neptune II modernisation and Type 214 acquisition programmes has been covered at length in previous editions of *Seaforth World Naval Review*. For further detail about the current arbitration claim, see Holly Watt's 'Greece sues for 7 billion euros over German submarines that have never sailed', *The Telegraph* – 12 June 2014 (London, Telegraph Group Media Ltd, 2014).

11. The editor is grateful for Cem Devrim Yaylali's review of this section.

12. A good overview of the Russian rearmament programme was provided by Karl Soper in 'Rearming Russia', *Jane's Defence Weekly* – 4 June 2014 (Coulsdon, IHS Jane's, 2014), pp.28–30.

2.4A Fleet Review

Author:
Jean Moulin
Translated by John Jordan

FRANCE The Marine Nationale: The Bare Minimum for the Job

The French *Marine Nationale* is, apart from the US Navy, the only navy to have a permanent presence in all the seas around the globe and to operate a true aircraft carrier equipped with catapults and arrester wires, nuclear-powered strategic missile submarines and nuclear-powered attack submarines. Encompassing around ninety combat and front-line support ships displacing c. 300,000 tons and over 200 aircraft, it is also one of the world's largest fleets. This short chapter aims to provide an overview of the *Marine Nationale*'s current missions, its organisational and operational structures, and its equipment. It also provides some insight into the challenges the navy faces in maintaining its current proficiency.

MISSIONS

The missions of the *Marine Nationale* can be divided into three categories:

- **Permanent Missions:** The most important of these is nuclear deterrence, which is maintained by having a strategic missile submarine constantly at sea; underwater deterrence is backed up by an aerial deterrent in the form of embarked aircraft armed with the ASMP-A missile. The other permanent missions are the protection of the strategic submarine force; the maintenance of an overseas presence to protect French territories and interests; the control of France's exclusive economic zone (*zone économique exclusive* or ZEE); and training. France's exclusive economic zone is the second largest in the world behind that of the USA, with an area of 11,035,000km^2.
- **External Operations (*opérations extérieures* or OPEX):** These are performed by ships pre-positioned or deployed overseas. The most recent of these were Operation 'Harmattan' (Libya) from March to October 2011 and Operation 'Serval' (Mali) in 2013. Some deployments, notably the 'Corymbe' missions since 1990 in the Gulf of Guinea and the 'Atalante' mission since November 2008 to counter piracy in the Indian Ocean, are also of a permanent nature. The French Navy's participation in Operation 'Serval' in January 2013 involved five maritime patrol aircraft and the amphibious assault ship (BPC) *Dixmude*, which disembarked 1,820 tonnes of *matériel* at Dakar, including 140 vehicles.
- **Participation in State-sponsored maritime operations under the control of the Maritime Prefects (*préfets maritimes*):** These include the fight against the illicit trafficking of goods, substances and people, combating pollution and taking part in air/sea rescue operations – although coastal rescue operations are generally the responsibility of the *Société Nationale de Sauvetage en Mer* (SNSM) or, on occasion, of the departments for Maritime Affairs, Customs and the *Gendarmerie Nationale*.

The nuclear-powered aircraft carrier *Charles de Gaulle* on 23 March 2010 with Rafale, Super Etendard-Mod. and Hawkeye aircraft arrayed on deck. The *Marine Nationale* – along with the US and Brazilian navies – is a rare example of a fleet that continues to operate a 'true' aircraft carrier equipped with catapults and arrester wires. *(Bernard Prézelin,* Flottes de Combat*)*

A coast guard organisation was set up on 8 December 2009, with the participation of the navy, the *Gendarmerie Maritime*, the *Gendarmerie Nationale*, the police, the Maritime Affairs and Customs departments and civil ships chartered for the purpose. The ships assigned to this task have their hulls painted with oblique stripes of the national colours: blue, white and red.

ORGANISATION

The head of the armed forces is the President of the Republic. Operational command is the province of the French General Staff – a joint body formed by senior officers of the three armed services. Since February 2014, this has been headed by General Pierre de Villiers. Organic control of the navy is the responsibility of the Naval General Staff. The Ministry of Defence, the General Staff, the general staffs of the French Army, Air Force and Navy, the operational centres for the armed forces, the central services of the Defence Procurement Agency (*Direction Générale de l'Armement* or DGA), and the General Secretariat for Administration (SGA) are currently scattered around Paris and its suburbs. In 2015 they will be grouped together in a new complex at Balard, on the southwest side of Paris.

A Landing Craft Medium 8 loaded with a French truck passes the now decommissioned BATRAL-type tank landing ship *Jacques Cartier*, whilst conducting a beach landing at Poum, Northern New Caledonia, during exercises with the Royal Australian Navy. The maintenance of an overseas presence to protect French territories and interests is an important influence on the *Marine Nationale*'s structure. *(Royal Australian Navy)*

OPERATIONAL COMMANDS

The *Marine Nationale*'s operational commands can be divided between those based on the French mainland ('Metropolitan France') and those that relate to its overseas areas of responsibility:

Metropolitan France:

- CECLANT: The Commander-in-Chief Atlantic and Maritime Prefect for the Atlantic, based at Brest. He is the commander for the Atlantic zone, the region and the maritime district (*arrondissement*).[1]
- CECMED: The Commander-in-Chief Mediterranean and Maritime Prefect for the Mediterranean, based at Toulon. He is the commander for the Mediterranean zone, the region and the maritime district.
- PREMAR Manche/Mer du Nord: The Maritime Prefect of the Channel and North Sea, based at Cherbourg. He is the commander (COMAR) for the zone of the Channel/North Sea maritime district.

The Maritime Prefects are the commanders within their zone of responsibility, and double as the representatives of the state at sea and as coordinators for state maritime operations such as pollution control and search and rescue.

Overseas:

- ALINDIEN: The admiral commanding the zone of the Indian Ocean. He is also commander of French bases in the United Arab Emirates (UAE).
- ALPACI: The admiral who is the senior officer for the armed forces based in French Polynesia. His command embraces the maritime zone of the Pacific Ocean and France's Pacific nuclear test centre.
- COMSUP FAA: The senior officer (rear-admiral) commanding the armed forces of the Antilles. He is also commander for the Antilles-Guyane maritime zone (ZMAG).

ORGANIC COMMANDS

The navy's operational commands are supplemented by a number of organic commands, all headquartered in Metropolitan France.

- ALFAN: The admiral commanding the *Force d'action navale* (FAN), which comprises all the surface units in active service with the exception of local harbour craft. His headquarters are located at Toulon, with branches at Brest and Cherbourg.
- ALFOST: The admiral commanding submarine forces and the strategic oceanic force (*Force océanique stratégique* or FOST); from his headquarters at Brest, ALFOST commands all submarines, including the nuclear-powered ballistic missile submarines (SNLE) based at Ile Longue (COMSNLE) and the nuclear-powered attack submarines (SNA) of the attack submarine squadron.
- ALAVIA: The admiral commanding the naval air arm (*Aéronautique navale*), which was formed on 19 June 1998 from the merging of embarked aviation and maritime patrol aviation. The formations are organised as flotillas (*flotilles*) for combat and surveillance aircraft and as squadrons (*escadrilles*) for logistics/service aircraft. The command, based at Toulon, embraces embarked fixed-wing aircraft, maritime patrol and airborne early-warning aircraft, and embarked helicopters.
- ALFUSCO: The admiral commanding the 2,500-strong force of *fusiliers marins* (Marines) and commandos, and the Special Forces (*commandement des opérations spéciales* or COS); the headquarters are at Lorient.
- The command of the Gendarmerie Maritime (COMGENDMAR), a specialised unit of the *Gendarmerie Nationale*, which is placed under the operational command of the Chief of the Naval Staff (CEMM).

EQUIPMENT: SHIPS

A list of principal units is provided in Table 2.4A.1 whilst detail on the major types is set out below:

Aircraft Carrier: The aircraft carrier *Charles de Gaulle*, powered by two nuclear reactors, was built and underwent trials and work-up between 1989 and 2001, the date of her admission into active service. France is, together with Brazil and the United States, the only nation to have at her disposal an aircraft carrier equipped with catapults and arrester wires. However, operational constraints, particularly those relating to nuclear propulsion, have imposed periods of immobilisation at crucial junctures; the training requirements of pilots for the air group and of a complement which is regularly renewed have resulted in an operational availability of just over fifty per cent. A half-life refit is planned to take place from September 2016 to February 2018. A second carrier, designated PA 2, was projected. Initially it was to have been identical to the *Charles de Gaulle*, then of a modified design, and finally a catapult/arrester wire variant of the British *Queen Elizabeth* class. It has now been indefinitely postponed.

Submarines: The underwater component of the deterrent force is made up of the four nuclear-powered ballistic missile submarines (*sous-marins nucléaires lanceurs d'engins* or SNLE) of the *Le Triomphant* class, which entered service between 1997 and 2010: *Le Triomphant*, *Le Téméraire*, *Le Vigilant* and *Le Terrible*. The latter submarine was fitted from the outset to fire the M51 three-stage missile, which has a range of 9,000km; the remaining three boats have been, or will be modernised to handle this missile between 2011 and 2015. Their base is at Ile Longue, in the Brest roads.

The six nuclear-powered attack submarines (*sous-marins nucléaires d'attaque* or SNA), all belong to the *Rubis* class upgraded to *Améthyste* standard. *Rubis*,

The *Charles de Gaulle* and US Navy destroyer *Bulkeley* (DDG-84) are pictured conducting an underway replenishment from the tanker *Arctic* (T-AOE-8) in the Gulf of Oman during December 2013. The *Charles de Gaulle* is France's sole carrier, proposed construction of a variant of the British *Queen Elizabeth* class having been indefinitely postponed. This will leave France without embarked air power when she undergoes a half-life refit between 2016 and 2018. *(US Navy)*

Table 2.4A.1: MARINE NATIONALE FLEET COMPOSITION – MID-2014

TYPE	CLASS	NUMBER	DATE[1]	NOTES
Carriers				
Aircraft Carrier – CVN	**CHARLES DE GAULLE**	1	2001	One ship, *Charles de Gaulle* (R91). Due to enter mid-life refit 2016.
Principal Surface Escorts				
Frigate – FFG	**AQUITAINE** (FREMM)	1	2012 onwards	*Aquitaine* (D650), the first of up to eleven ships for the French Navy. One sister has been delivered to the Royal Moroccan Navy. A joint project with Italy, which plans for up to ten of its own variants.
Frigate – FFG	**FORBIN** ('Horizon')	2	2008–9	*Forbin* (D620), *Chevalier Paul* (D621). Also a joint programme with Italy which saw two broadly identical ships being delivered to that country's *Marina Militare*. They are classified as destroyers by Italy.
Frigate – FFG	**CASSARD** (FAA-70)	2	1988–91	*Cassard* (D614), *Jean Bart* (D615). Significantly modified air-defence variants of FASM-70 type.
Frigate – FFG	**G LEYGUES** (FASM-70)	5	1982–90	*Montcalm* (D642), *Jean de Vienne* (D643), *Primauguet* (D644), *La Motte-Picquet* (D645), *Latouche-Tréville* (D646). The lead ship was decommissioned in 2013 and *Dupleix* followed in June 2014; others will be withdrawn as the new *Aquitaine* class frigates are delivered.
Frigate – FFG	**LA FAYETTE**	5	1995–2001	*La Fayette* (F710), *Surcouf* (F711), *Courbet* (F712), *Aconit* (F713), *Guépratte* (F714). An order for a sixth vessel was cancelled. Reclassified as front-line escorts by the 2008 defence white paper.
Frigate – FSG	**FLORÉAL**	6	1991–4	*Floréal* (F730), *Prairial* (F731), *Nivôse* (F732), *Ventôse* (F733), *Vendémiaire* (F734), *Germinal* (F735). Built to commercial standards for service in the overseas operational commands. Two similar vessels in service with the Royal Moroccan Navy.
Frigate – FS	**D'ORVES** (A-69)	9	1979–84	*LV Le Hénaff* (F789), *LV Lavallée* (F790), *Commandant L'Herminier* (F791), *PM L'Her* (F792), *Commandant Blaison* (F793), *EV Jacoubet* (F794), *Commandant Ducuing* (F795), *Commandant Birot* (F796), *Commandant Bouan* (F797). Survivors of a class of seventeen, they have officially been reclassified as offshore patrol vessels. Three sister ships in service with the Argentine Navy.
Submarines				
Submarine – SSBN	**LE TRIOMPHANT**	4	1997–2010	*Le Triomphant* (S616), *Le Téméraire* (S617), *Le Vigilant* (S618), *Le Terrible* (S619). Last boat fitted from build with the new M51 ballistic missile which is being retrofitted to the rest of the class.
Submarine – SSN	**RUBIS**	6	1983–93	*Rubis* (S601), *Saphir* (S602), *Casabianca* (S603), *Emeraude* (S604), *Améthyste* (S605) *Perle* (S606). Two further boats cancelled whilst under construction. To be replaced by 'Barracuda' class from 2017.
Amphibious Ships				
Amph Assault Ship – LHD	**MISTRAL**	3	2006–12	*Mistral* (L9013), *Tonnerre* (L9014), *Dixmude* (L9015). Two similar ships are being built for Russia.
Landing Platform Dock – LPD	**FOUDRE**	1	1998	*Siroco* (L9012). The lead ship was sold to Chile in 2011 and *Siroco* will also be sold soon.
Landing Ship – LST	**CHAMPLAIN** (BATRAL)	2	1983–7	*Dumont d'Urville* (L9032), *La Grandière* (L9034). Three other ships decommissioned.
Mine-Countermeasures Vessels				
Minehunter – MCMV	**ÉRIDAN** (Tripartite)	11	1984–96	*Eridan* (M641), *Cassiopée* (M642), *Andromède* (M643), *Pégase* (M644), *Orion* (M645), *Croix du Sud* (M646), *Aigle* (M647), *Lyre* (M648), *Sagittaire* (M650), *Céphée* (M652), *Capricorne* (M653). Joint programme with Belgium and the Netherlands. Ten French ships were originally ordered and a further three purchased from Belgium in 1997 but two ships have subsequently been decommissioned.
Minehunter – MCMV	**ANTARÈS**	3	1993–5	*Antarès* (M770), *Altaïr* (M771), *Aldébaran* (M772). Used to conduct surveillance in the approaches to the strategic submarine base at Brest.
Diving Support Vessel	**VULCAIN**	4	1986–7	*Vulcain* (M611), *Styx* (M614), *Pluton* (M622), *Achéron* (A613).
Support Vessels:				
Replenishment Vessel – AOR	**DURANCE**	4	1980–9	*Meuse* (A607), *Var* (A608), *Marne* (A630), *Somme* (A631). Lead ship sold to Argentina in 1999. A sister ship was also built locally for the Royal Australian Navy.

Notes:

1 Date refers to the delivery date(s) of ships in the class remaining in service. French warships undertake an extensive series of operational trials after delivery prior to formal commissioning, which can therefore be considerably later than the delivery date.

2 Other warships include fourteen offshore and coastal patrol vessels, four survey vessels and five research and experimentation vessels. There are also a number of sealift ships and tugs, largely chartered, as well as twelve training vessels and four sailing vessels.

The SNLE *Le Terrible* on trials on 18 March 2010; she entered service on 27 September of the same year. She is the last of the four units of the *Le Triomphant* class, and the first SNLE to embark the new M51 missile, which is being retro-fitted in the remaining three boats. Nuclear deterrence is the most important of the *Marine Nationale*'s permanent missions. *(Bernard Prézelin,* Flottes de Combat*)*

Saphir, *Casabianca*, *Emeraude*, *Améthyste* and *Perle* entered service between 1983 and 1993 and are based at Toulon; they are the smallest submarines of their type in the world. Their service life will be extended until they are replaced by the same number of submarines of the 'Barracuda' type (*Suffren* class) between 2017 and 2029.

Surface Escorts: The surface fleet is ageing, with the service life of ships often being extended beyond thirty years. The older ships are costly in terms of personnel and are difficult to maintain.

The French Navy hopes to retain four anti-air missile ships for area defence and for the control of the airspace around a naval force. Two anti-air frigates (*frégates antiaériennes* or FAA) remain in service: the *Cassard*, completed in 1988, and *Jean Bart*, completed in 1991. They are armed with the obsolescent US Standard SM-1 MR missile. A radical modernisation is out of the question and they are due to be replaced by an air-defence variant of the FREMM-type frigate (see below), designated the FREDA; the first of the latter is due to become operational around 2021. The more modern *frégates de défense aérienne* (FDA) *Forbin* and *Le Chevalier Paul* entered service in 2010 and 2011 respectively. They were constructed as part of the 'Horizon' frigate project, which was a joint programme with Italy (and initially with the United Kingdom) to deliver a large series of air-defence warships but which, in the event, has delivered only four ships (two for each country). Plans for two further units of the class to replace the FAA have been abandoned.

The first of the new general-purpose frigates (*frégates européennes multimissions* or FREMM), *Aquitaine*, was delivered in 2012 and is due to enter operational service in 2014. The initial programme, again a joint initiative with Italy, envisaged no fewer than seventeen ships for the *Marine Nationale*. This was subsequently reduced to eleven and, with construction slowed in 2013, only eight may be delivered. The last two units will now be designated FREDA (*frégates européennes de défense aérienne*) and will replace *Cassard* and *Jean Bart*. The FREMM frigates are large ships with a high degree of automation and a designed complement of only 108.

The five surviving anti-submarine frigates of the F70 ASM type were completed between 1982 and 1990; the name-ship, *Georges Leygues*, was stricken in 2013 and *Dupleix* followed in 2014. Three (*Primauguet*, *La Motte-Piquet* and *Latouche-Tréville*) are based at Brest, the others (*Montcalm* and *Jean de Vienne*) at Toulon. From 2014 they will be replaced by the new FREMM type.

The five frigates of the *La Fayette* class (FLF – *La Fayette*, *Surcouf*, *Courbet*, *Aconit* and *Guépratte*) entered service between 1996 and 2001. They were the world's first 'stealth' ships of their size, and influenced subsequent foreign construction. Based at Toulon, they are deployed for sea control missions overseas; they have no anti-submarine capability. A half-life modernisation with Aster 15 missiles and anti-submarine weapons and sonars is officially rated 'probable', but appears increasingly unlikely.

The front-line escorts are supplemented by six patrol frigates (*frégates de surveillance*) of the *Floréal* class, which entered service between 1992 and 1994. They were built at Saint-Nazaire to mercantile standards with a view to operations overseas in low-threat zones. *Floréal* and *Nivôse* are based at La Réunion, *Ventôse* and *Germinal* at Fort-de-France, *Prairial* at Papeete and *Vendémiaire* at Noumea. The

The *Rubis* class nuclear-powered attack submarine (SNA) *Perle* seen on a deployment to the US in the summer of 2010. These boats are the smallest of their type in the world, a fact reflected in the comparative size of the escorting tugboat. *(US Navy)*

ships remain on station, with refit and repair carried out by local shipyards, and their crews are rotated.

Patrol and Mine-Countermeasures Vessels: Nine large offshore patrol vessels of the A69 type survive; formerly light frigates, these ships have had their anti-submarine armament removed. Five (*LV Le Hénaff, LV Lavallée, Commandant L'Herminier, PM L'Her* and *Commandant Blaison*) are based at Brest and the remaining four (*EV Jacoubet, Commandant Ducuing, Commandant Birot* and *Commandant Bouan*) at Toulon. They are the last of a series of seventeen frigates (name-ship: *D'Estienne d'Orves*) which entered service between 1976 and 1984. They have proved robust and economical, and their service life has been extended to thirty-five years.

The navy also has in service eight smaller offshore patrol vessels, four public service patrol boats and two weapons-range safety patrol ships; the latter are based at Bayonne for use at the Landes Missile Test Centre. Particularly worthy of mention is the experimental offshore patrol vessel (*patrouilleur hauturier d'expérimentation* or PHE) *L'Adroit*, prototype for the 'Gowind' OPV concept, designed by DCNS and placed at the disposal of the navy for three years after completion in 2011. The *Gendarmerie Maritime* operates five patrol boats and twenty-six motor boats.

For mine countermeasures there are eleven minehunters of the 'Tripartite' type, built jointly with Belgium and the Netherlands and completed between 1984 and 1987, three mine route survey craft equipped with towed arrays (*Antarès* class), and four diving tenders (*Vulcain* class). Three of the last-mentioned are employed as base-ships for the three mine-disposal diving groups, based at Cherbourg, Brest and Toulon respectively (the fourth unit is used for training).

Amphibious Forces: The amphibious component of the French Navy is of recent construction, being centred on the three 'projection and command ships' (*bâtiments de projection et de commandement* or BPC) of the *Mistral* class. The first two units, *Mistral* and *Tonnerre*, entered service in 2006 and 2007 respectively. The third, *Dixmude*, built under an economic recovery plan which aimed to provide a boost to shipbuilding, followed in 2012. Plans for a fourth unit were abandoned in 2013. The BPCs are essentially a scaled-down version of the US Navy's LHD type amphibious assault ships. They have six flight

France operates a two-tier surface fleet, front-line escorts such as the 'Horizon' type air defence escort *Chevalier Paul* – pictured above with the USN aircraft carrier *John C Stennis* (CVN-74) – supplemented by six patrol frigates that were built to mercantile standards for operation overseas in low-threat zones. The bottom image shows the *Vendémiaire*, which is normally based at Noumea, New Caledonia. *(US Navy/Royal Australian Navy)*

deck spots for helicopter operations, a hangar capable of accommodating up to sixteen NH 90 helicopters, separate vehicle decks for tanks and wheeled vehicles, a 57m amphibious dock able to accommodate the new French EDAR landing craft (see below) or the US Navy's LCAC, berthing for 450 troops, a fully-equipped hospital and a large command centre for combined operations. All three are based at Toulon.

A single dock landing ship (*transport de chalands de débarquement* or TCD), the *Siroco*, remains in service. Completed in 1998, *Siroco* has an amphibious dock 122m long and can operate four helicopters; however, she is due to be withdrawn in the near future.

Landing craft include fifteen older LCM-type craft (*chalands de transport de matériel* or CTM), and four of a new fast LCU-type designated *engins de débarquement amphibie rapides* (EDAR), which entered service in 2012. The latter are catamarans equipped with fore and aft ramps and an adjustable pontoon deck which is raised in transit and lowered for the embarkation and disembarkation of troops, vehicles and stores.

Two of the medium landing ships (*bâtiments de transport léger* or BATRAL) built during the 1980s also remain in service on overseas stations. They will be replaced by the new *bâtiments multimissions* (B2M), of which three were ordered in December 2013.

Logistics and Support: The logistics fleet has been reduced to four fleet tankers of the *Durance* type (*Meuse*, *Var*, *Marne* and *Somme*), three of which are equipped as command ships (*bâtiments de commandement et de ravitaillement* or BCR). Completed between 1980 and 1990 they no longer meet contemporary maritime pollution standards for tankers, but their replacement by new fleet replenishment ships has been continually postponed.

A small fleet of miscellaneous vessels includes the missile-range tracking ship (*bâtiment d'essais et de mesure* or BEM) *Monge*, whose primary task is to carry out measurements during ballistic missile test firings, the intelligence-collection ship *Dupuy de Lôme*, a mine-countermeasures experimental ship, the *Thétis*, and four hydrographic vessels.

The French Navy also employs chartered civil vessels for assistance and support missions; of these the most noteworthy are the salvage tugs *Abeille Bourbon* and *Abeille Liberté*, based at Brest and Cherbourg respectively.

EQUIPMENT: AIRCRAFT

Carrier-based Aircraft: The air group of the carrier *Charles de Gaulle* comprises three types of fixed-wing aircaft. The Dassault Super Etendard-Mod. (SEM) is the successor to the Etendard IVM, the prototype of which first flew in 1958. The first production Super Etendards entered service in 1978, and they have been subjected to numerous upgrades, the latest being the Mod.5 dating from 2007 to 2009. As of 2014 twenty or so aircraft of this type are in Flotilla 17F, which is due to operate them until around 2015/16.

The main interceptor/attack aircraft is the Dassault Rafale M. Slightly different variants of this aircraft are also in service with the French Air Force. The first ten aircraft, completed to the F1 air superiority configuration, were delivered from 2001 onwards. Versions F2, then F3, followed and earlier aircraft are being progressively being upgraded to the F3 configuration. Just less than forty Rafale Ms had been delivered as at the start of 2014; they are in service with Flotillas 12F and 11F.[2] In addition, Flotilla 17F is due to be re-equipped with the plane from 2015.

Three American E-2C Hawkeye twin-turboprop early warning aircraft were delivered between 1998 and 2004. They equip Flotilla 4F, based at Lann-Bihoué in Brittany. Two of the three are embarked aboard the *Charles de Gaulle* when the carrier deploys.

Maritime Patrol and Surveillance: The Maritime Patrol Force (*patrouille maritime* or PATMAR) is equipped with the twin-turboprop Dassault Breguet Atlantique 2 (ATL 2). Derived from the Breguet Atlantic, which was designed primarily for anti-submarine warfare and was in service from 1965 to 1996, the Atlantique variant entered

The French Navy's amphibious component has been extensively modernised in recent years. These photographs show *Tonnerre*, second of three BPC amphibious assault ships, and one of the new EDAR catamaran fast landing craft, the latter pictured operating with a British Royal Marines Landing Craft Utility (LCU) in November 2012. *(Marine Nationale/Crown Copyright)*

A Rafale M of the *Aéronautiqe navale*. Subject to progressive upgrades since the first aircraft was delivered, around forty had been delivered by early 2014. They are currently in service with Flotillas 11F and 12F. *(Dassault Aviation – V Almansa)*

The venerable Dassault Super Etendard-Mod. (SEM), which traces its origins to the Etendard IVM that first flew in 1958, now only equips Flotilla 17F and will finally be retired from service around 2015/16. *(Jean Moulin)*

service in 1989. Twenty-eight were delivered between 1989 and 1997, of which twenty-two remain in service with Flotillas 21F and 23F at Lann-Bihoué. A contract for the modernisation of the first four of a planned total of fifteen aircraft was signed in October 2013. A single Atlantique is permanently stationed at Dakar, Senegal, and there are occasional deployments to the Antilles and to Djibouti (Indian Ocean). They are frequently employed in Africa as intelligence-gathering and command aircraft.

Local maritime surveillance and search and rescue are performed by two types of twin-engine jet aircraft modified from civil transports, the Falcon 50M and the Falcon 200 Gardian. The five Falcon 50M are with Flotilla 24F at Lann-Bihoué, where they will be joined in 2014–15 by five Falcon 50 aircraft used by other government departments. Five Falcon 200 Gardian belonging to Flotilla 25F are distributed between Tahiti and New Caledonia in the Pacific; they will be replaced in 2015 by the first Falcon 50M aircraft.

Helicopters: The Navy's helicopter force is in the process of a partial renewal. The Super Frelon, which was withdrawn from service in 2010, is being progressively replaced by the Caïman Marine (NH 90), of which the first was delivered in 2010 and the eleventh by March 2014. Transition for search and rescue at Lanvéoc is being provided by two EC 225 Super Pumas of Flotilla 32F. Orders have been placed for a total of twenty-seven Caïman, which will equip Flotillas 33F at Lanvéoc and 31F at Hyères. These two flotillas will provide emergency search and rescue (SECMAR) at Lanvéoc (alternating with Flotilla 32F), and will supply detachments to the latest frigates of the 'Horizon' and FREMM types.

The F70 ASM frigates normally have a Westland Lynx Mk 4 embarked. Approximately twenty surviving Lynx Mk 4s form Flotilla 34F at Lanvéoc. They are likely to remain in service until all the F70 class are stricken, as the hangar of the latter ships is too small to accommodate the Caïman.

The frigates of the FAA and *La Fayette* types, and two of the patrol frigates (*Nivôse* and *Ventôse*), have an AS 565 Panther embarked; the AS 565 is a navalised version of the Eurocopter Dauphin helicopter, and there are fifteen operational in Flotilla 36F based at Hyères.

The Alouette III, which entered service with the Aéronautique Navale as early as 1962, is still embarked in the other four patrol frigates (*Floréal*, *Prairial*, *Vendémiaire* and *Germinal*) and, on occasion, *Monge* and the fleet tankers. The twenty-three Alouette III currently in service are assigned to Squadron 22S at Lanvéoc, which is also responsible for the training of helicopter pilots.

Flotilla 35F at Hyères has three AS 365F Dauphin Pedro plane-guard helicopters for the *Charles de Gaulle* and eight Dauphin SP (Public Sector) helicopters for search and rescue missions; the latter aircraft are distributed between Le Touquet (near Boulogne), Cherbourg, Lanvéoc, La Rochelle, Hyères and Tahiti-Faa'a.

The BPCs and the single TCD regularly embark helicopters in service with the Army air force (*Aviation légère de l'Armée de Terre* or ALAT): the Cougar, the Puma, the Gazelle, the Tigre and the NH 90.

PERSONNEL

The *Marine Nationale* is now a completely professional force; compulsory national service ended in 2001. One unfortunate consequence of this is that the navy has lost contact with the majority of French people, who when the sea is mentioned now tend to think exclusively of the beach! The various structural reorganisations which have taken place since the 1970s have reduced the number of uniformed naval personnel from 65,000 in 1991 (of which 19,000 were conscripts) to 53,000 in 2000, 44,000 in 2008 and 41,000 in 2012.

In 2013, excluding those detached on inter-service liaison duties or in the various administrative bodies, the navy had 36,000 personnel on active service. These were divided as follows: 4,000 officers, 21,000 petty officers, 7,000 ratings, 1,000 short-service volunteers and 3,000 civilians. The volunteers sign up for a short period to acquire

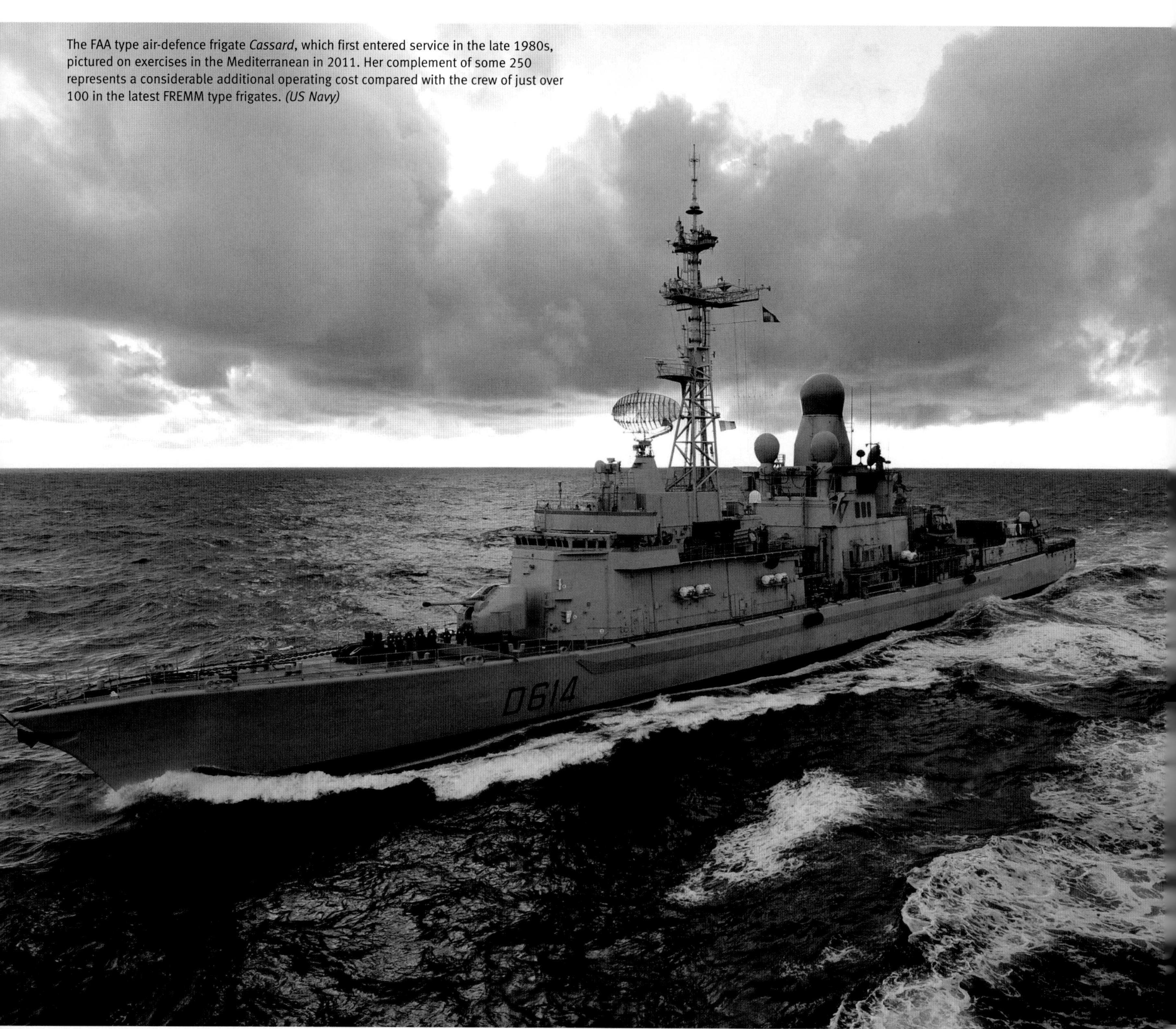

The FAA type air-defence frigate *Cassard*, which first entered service in the late 1980s, pictured on exercises in the Mediterranean in 2011. Her complement of some 250 represents a considerable additional operating cost compared with the crew of just over 100 in the latest FREMM type frigates. *(US Navy)*

formal skills training. The number of women who serve in the navy is now 13.5 per cent of the total. An operational reserve of 5,000 permits crews to be brought up to full strength in time of crisis. In 2014 a further 650 posts will be lost as part of the reduction decreed by the military programme of 2009–14.

Approximately fifty per cent of the service's officers are educated at the *Ecole Navale*, and fifty per cent sign on or have been promoted from the ranks. Most of the petty officers have undergone training at the *Ecole de Maistrance*. The French Navy favours relatively short periods of service in order to ensure the renewal of its personnel and to facilitate the subsequent adaptation to civilian life.

The new ships have much-reduced crews; the latest frigates now have a complement of a little over 100 compared to 250 or more for the older ships. This means that personnel have to be multi-skilled and particularly well trained.

INFRASTRUCTURE

The Navy has reduced its infrastructure footprint with the successive plans for savings. In Metropolitan France, the only two operational bases remaining are Brest and Toulon. These and other domestic bases are shown in the map below.

Brest is home to the surface units that provide protection for the force of strategic missile submarines. The replacement of the type F70 ASM frigates by the new units of the FREMM type has already begun. Brest is also the base for five offshore patrol vessels, eight minehunters, school ships which include the eight units of the *Léopard* class (known as the 'Menagerie'), hydrographic ships and the fleet replenishment tanker *Somme*. The four SNLEs are based at Ile Longue, on the south side of the Brest roadstead. Major refits and modernisation of the SNLEs also take place at Brest, in a specially-equipped dock.

Toulon is the base port of the aircraft carrier *Charles de Gaulle*, the four air-defence frigates, the other two F70 anti-submarine frigates, four offshore patrol vessels, three minehunters, three fleet replenishment tankers, the three BPC-type amphibious docks and the dock-landing ship *Siroco*. It is also home for the six nuclear-powered attack submarines.

The ports of Cherbourg and Lorient retain the capability to build submarines (Cherbourg) and frigates (Lorient) at the DCNS facilities located there. Cherbourg also builds public service patrol craft and is home to a number of second-line craft.

Overseas, there are bases or support installations at La Réunion (Port des Galets), New Caledonia (Nouméa), Martinique (Fort-de-France), French Guiana (Dégrad de Cannes), Polynesia (Papeete on Tahiti), Mayotte, Saint-Pierre-et-Miquelon, Senegal (Dakar), Gabon (Libreville), Djibouti and, since May 2009, at Mina Fayed, Abu Dhabi in the United Arab Emirates.

The fleet air arm in Metropolitan France is currently concentrated at four bases (*bases d'aéronautique navale* or BAN):

- Landivisiau, near Brest, with Flotillas 11F and 12F (Rafale), 17F (Super Etendard) and Squadron 57S (Falcon 10, training and liaison).
- Lanvéoc, south of the Brest roadstead, with helicopter Flotillas 32F (two EC 225 Super Puma, of which one is detached to Cherbourg), 33F (Caïman), 34F (Lynx), and Squadrons 22S

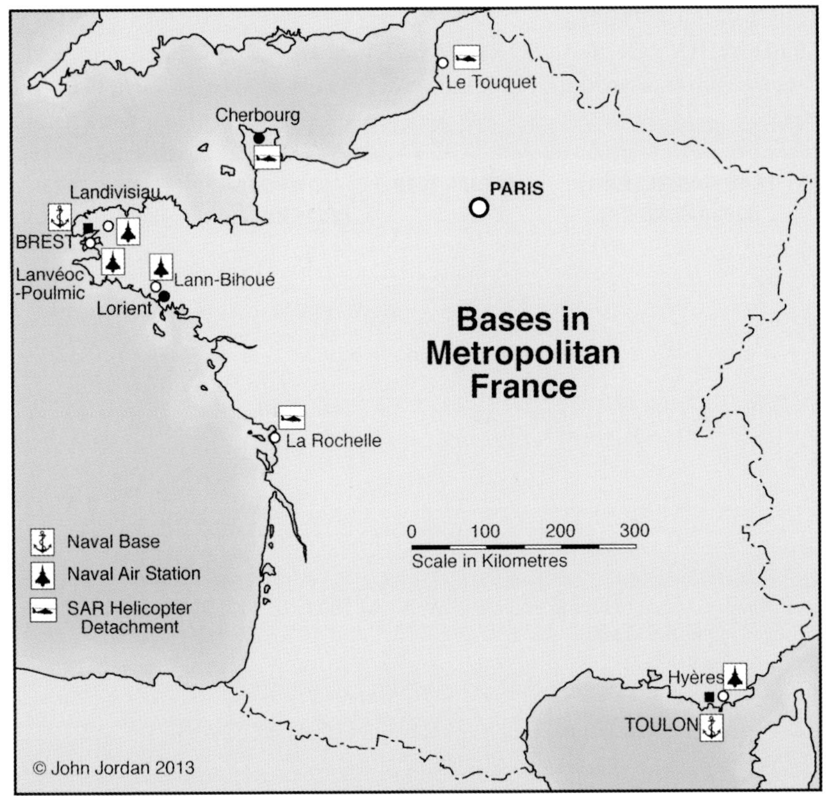

The destroyer-sized air-defence frigate *Chevalier Paul* seen fitting out at the DCNS yard in Lorient in 2008. *(Conrad Waters)*

France's 2013 white paper on defence envisages a front-line force of fifteen frigates by 2025, of which the new FREMMs will be an important constituent. It is planned that the seventh and eight members of the class will be constructed to an air-defence (FREDA) configuration, which is likely to be similar to the DCNS FREMM-ER design pictured above *(DCNS)*

There is a pressing need for new second-line warships, particularly to support naval operations in the overseas territories. The 2014–19 programme anticipates the delivery of three multi-mission ships B2M to replace retired BATRAL type tank landing ships. An order for three of these ships, together with an option for a fourth, was placed with a consortium of DCNS and Pirou in December 2013. *(DCNS)*

(Alouette III training and liaison) and 50S (selection and initial training for aircrew).

- Lann-Bihoué, near Lorient, which now has all the maritime patrol and surveillance aircraft, with Flotillas 24F (Falcon 50M), 21F and 23F (Atlantique), 4F (E-2C Hawkeye) and 28F (Xingu liaison).
- Hyères, near Toulon, with helicopter Flotillas 35F (Dauphin and Alouette III, SAR and liaison), 36F (AS 565 Panther embarked in the frigates), 33F (Caïman) and Squadron CEPA/10S (training and trials)

Overseas bases are at Faa'a in Tahiti and at La Tontouta near Nouméa (New Caledonia); the

Table 2.4A.2: MARINE NATIONALE COMPOSITION – 1970–2025[1]

SHIP TYPE	ACTUAL 1970	PLAN BLEU (1972) (1985 HORIZON)	ACTUAL 1985	PLAN MARINE (1981) (2000 HORIZON)	ACTUAL 2000	DWP 2008 (2025 HORIZON)	DWP 2013 (2025 HORIZON)
Aircraft Carrier (CV/CVN)	2	2	2	2	1	1	1
Support/Helicopter Carrier (CVS/CVH)	2	2	1	– [2]	1	–	–
Strategic Missile Submarine (SSBN)	–	5	6	6[3]	4	4	4
Attack Submarine (SSN)	–	– [4]	2	10	6	6	6
Patrol Submarine (SSK)	18	30[4]	15	4	2	–	–
Fleet Escort (DDG/FFG)	20	30	16	27	17	18	15
Patrol Escort (FFG/FSG/FS)	27	35	25	18	19	6[5]	6
Fast Attack Craft (PGG/PTG)	–	30	4	–	–	–	–
Mine Countermeasures Vessel (MMV)	85	36	25	40	16	N/A[6]	N/A[6]
Major Amphibious (LHD/LPD/LPH/LSD)	2	2	2	3	4	4	3

Notes:

1 The table aims to demonstrate the overall contraction of the *Marine Nationale* over time in spite of numerous plans to increase numbers. Whilst the 2008 and 2013 DWPs (defence white papers) looked to a 2025 timeframe, the current fleet is already close to the reduced numbers envisaged in the 2013 plan.

2 In the event, *Jeanne d'Arc* would be retained well beyond her planned service life.

3 The precise number of SSBNs was still under discussion in late 1981; six was the provisional figure.

4 The *Plan Bleu* did not distinguish between numbers of traditional patrol submarines and of the new generation of nuclear-powered attack submarines that were planned.

5 The patrol escort figure excludes nine vessels of the A69 *D'Estienne d'Orves* class that the *Marine Nationale* has re-categorised as offshore patrol vessels.

6 Neither the 2008 or 2013 defence white papers provided details of the number of mine-countermeasures vessels planned.

Falcon 200 Gardian surveillance aircraft of 25F are divided between the two. As mentioned previously, a single Atlantique maritime patrol aircraft is permanently stationed at Dakar to provide search and rescue services in the sector.

Alantique and Falcon 50M aircraft are detached on occasion to Fort-de-France (Martinique) as part of the drugs war, to French Guiana (launches from the Space Centre at Kourou), to Djibouti (Operation 'Atalante' against piracy off the Horn of Africa) and to various African airfields to counter specific threats or to support French military interventions such as Operation 'Serval' in Mali.

BUDGETS AND THE FUTURE

Since the 1960s the *Marine Nationale*, in common with the other armed services in France, has experienced several planned restructurings. These have cumulatively resulted in significant reductions in hardware and personnel. At the same time, a number of ambitious modernisation plans have failed to achieve full implementation.

For example, the *Plan Bleu* of 1972 was swiftly abandoned. It had anticipated, *inter alia*, the construction of twenty-four corvettes (subsequently frigates) of the C70 (F70) type; ultimately only nine (seven ASM plus two AA variants) would be completed. The *Plan Marine* 2000 promulgated in 1978 and 1981 would suffer a similar erosion – for the year 2000 it envisaged a fleet built around two nuclear-powered carriers, twenty-seven corvettes (frigates) and ten attack submarines.

At the end of 1992 Plan OPTIMAR 95, which aimed to restructure the navy, resulted in the closure of bases and a reorganisation of forces and the general staff. In 2008, the application of the recommendations of a white paper on defence and national security and a series of political reforms known as the *Réforme générale des politiques publiques* (RGPP) led to further reductions in planned equipment and the number of personnel. The impact of this backdrop is illustrated in Table 2.4A.2.

In the normal course of events, military programmes (*lois de programmation militaires* or LPM) covering a period of five years are voted on and executed on an annual basis following the adoption of the budget for the following financial year. In reality, each annual budget has featured a slowing down – or even the cancellation – of part of the programme due to the constant need for savings.

In May 2012, the incoming Socialist government was confronted with major financial problems. The 2009–14 programme was about to expire and a new defence white paper was published on 29 April 2013 against this backdrop of financial austerity. It determined the strategic thrust for the next fifteen years and outlined the 2014–19 defence programme, which was subsequently confirmed towards the end of the year.

The existing missions of the navy, notably nuclear deterrence, were confirmed. The *Marine Nationale* is also to contribute to a combined rapid-response force (*force interarmées de réaction immédiate* or FIRI) of 2,300 troops capable of being transported and landed at a distance of up to 3,000km from metropolitan France within seven days; it will provide a BPC, a frigate, an attack submarine and Special Forces. In the event of the need for a major 'coercive' operation, it is envisaged that the Navy will commit the carrier *Charles de Gaulle* and her air group, two BPCs, a number of frigates, an attack submarine and maritime patrol aircraft. For such an eventuality the white paper specifies a maximum response time of six months. This presents a potential problem if the only carrier happens to be undergoing refit. Zones requiring ships permanently on station, initially two/three, could be reduced to one/two.

Whilst the navy's commitments were, therefore, little modified, equipment levels were further reduced. Looking forward to the year 2025, the fleet would comprise four SNLE, six SNA, an aircraft carrier, three BPC, fifteen first-line frigates, six patrol frigates, a mine-countermeasures capability, strike fighters and maritime patrol aircraft, helicopters and light surface units, including fifteen patrol vessels for local sea control.

The 2014–19 programme anticipates the delivery of five frigates of the FREMM type, one SNA, eight of a new homogeneous class of sea-going public service vessels (*bâtiment de soutien et d'assistance hauturier* or BSAH), three multi-mission ships (B2M) to replace the BATRAL currently stationed in Polynesia, two replacement patrol vessels for the Guiana station, thirteen Caïman helicopters, Rafale fighter aircraft, the MdCN (*missile de croisière naval*) surface/submarine-launched cruise missiles, and MU90 torpedoes. Orders will be placed for new fleet replenishment vessels, the modernisation of the frigates of the *La Fayette* class, new patrol vessels (*bâtiment de surveillance et d'intervention maritime* or BATSIMAR), a new mine-countermeasures force (*système de lutte anti-mine futur* or SLAMF) to replace the 'Tripartite' MCM vessels, and modernisation of the SNLEs, the Exocet missile and the first of the Atlantiques.

CONCLUSION

The *Marine Nationale* finds itself in a difficult position, with no reduction in its commitments but fewer resources. It has to continue to perform its traditional missions on a world-wide basis with a progressively declining number of ships and personnel. The navy is still capable of confronting a major crisis (as in Operation 'Harmattan') provided the single aircraft carrier is available, but only for a limited period of time. Interoperability with other European navies, notably the British Royal Navy and the US Navy, is being developed, but effective combined operations in a conflict remain dependent on political agreements, which are not always easy to secure. However, French sailors remain faithful to their motto: *Honneur et Patrie, Valeur et Discipline.*

Notes

1. A 'zone' is a geographical sea area defined by geographical limits such as coast, a parallel or a median. A '*région*' is an administrative region whilst a 'maritime district' ('*arrondissement*') is a sub-division of a region commanded by a COMAR (*Commandant de la Marine*).

2. As of early 2014, a total of forty-eight Rafale M jets had been ordered and nearly forty delivered. Of these, ten were completed to F1 configuration and are currently non-operational pending completion of upgrade to F3 standard. A further four aircraft completed to the later configurations had been lost to accidents, leaving around twenty-five in service with the two frontline flotillas. It was originally planned to order a further ten Rafale Ms for fifty-eight aircraft overall but it is not clear how this will be impacted by decisions taken in 2013 to reduce France's overall inventory of combat aircraft and slow Rafale deliveries.

3. The original manuscript for this article was provided by Jean Moulin. John Jordan is responsible for the translation into English, and has provided some additional explanation of acronyms and French organisational structure for the benefit of our Anglo-Saxon readers. Jean Moulin wishes to extend his sincere thanks to Bernard Prézelin, Editor of *Flottes de Combat*, for checking the manuscript and, in particular, for his assistance in providing suitable photographs to illustrate the article.

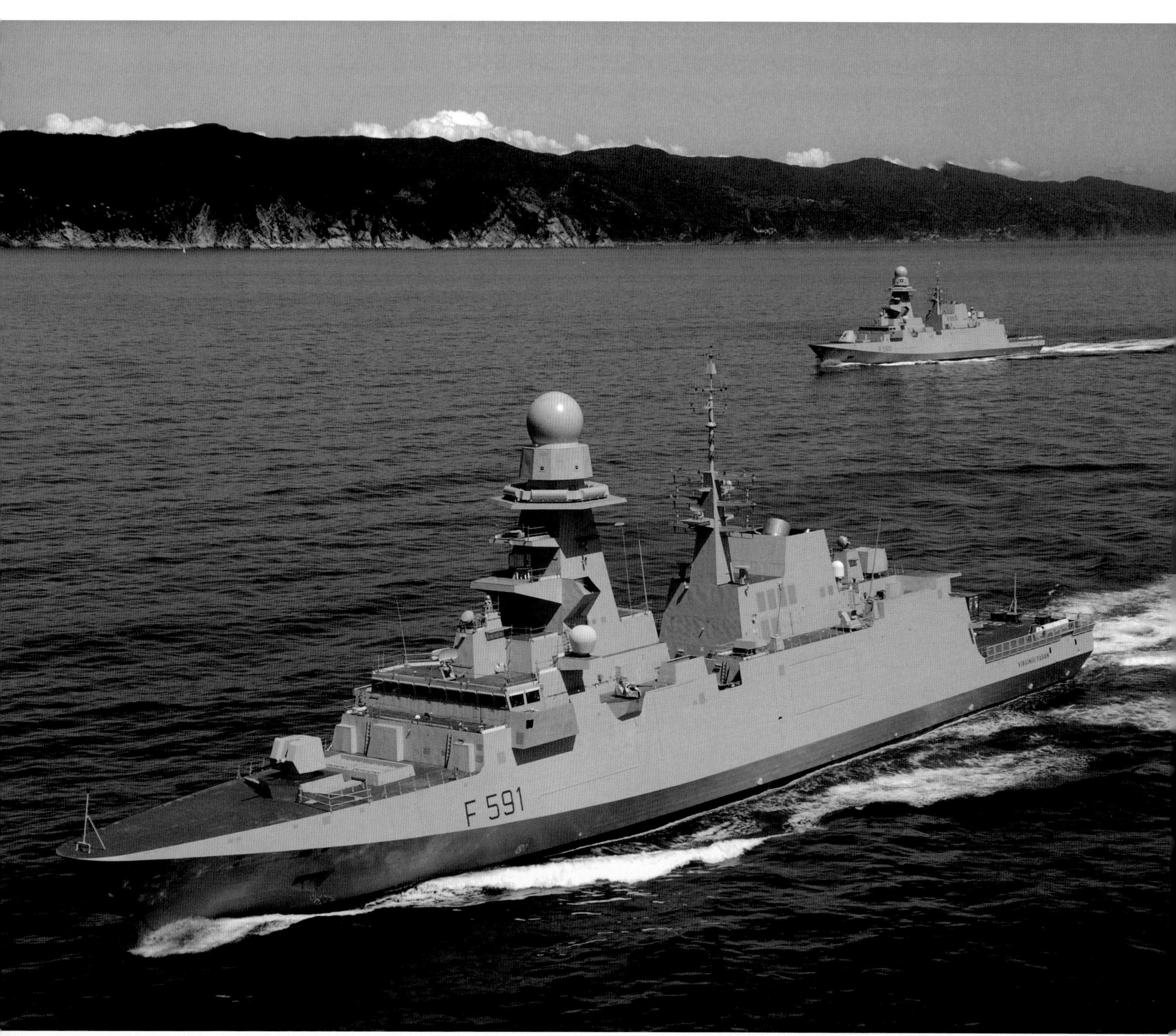
F 591

3.1 SIGNIFICANT SHIPS

Author:
Conrad Waters

ITALIAN FREMMS

Carlo Bergamini (General-Purpose) and Virginio Fasan (Anti-Submarine) Frigates

Italy's *Marina Militare* has benefitted from the delivery of some potent ships in recent years in spite of the country's financial difficulties. Warship construction is supported by a strong domestic industrial base dominated by the global shipbuilding giant Fincantieri and international defence company Finmeccanica. However, whilst the new aircraft carrier *Cavour* was entirely of indigenous design, heavy reliance has been placed on alliances with other European shipbuilders and defence groups to develop many of these new vessels. For example, recent submarine construction has been based on licence-built fabrication of German ThyssenKrupp Marine System's Type 212A design. Similarly, the new *Andrea Doria* class air-defence escorts were the product of the 'Horizon' collaboration with France's DCNS and Thales that delivered two pairs of nearly identical ships to the respective navies. This co-operative approach was also adopted with the follow-on FREMM (*Fregate Europee Multi-Missione*) programme, which envisaged the renewal of both the French and Italian surface fleets through a common, multi-role design.[1] In practice, however, the French and Italian elements of the programme have experienced significant divergence since the collaboration was first agreed. This is a reflection of the two navies' differing operational priorities, as well as both countries' desire to protect local defence equipment companies. The end result has been distinctive French and Italian variations of a shared concept that exhibit considerable differences in both appearance and capability.

A key attraction of the FREMM concept for both navies was the ability to configure a common design to different roles through limited changes to the equipment outfit. So far as Italy was concerned, its requirement was to obtain separate general-purpose and anti-submarine sub-classes and the initial order for the class in May 2006 encompassed one ship of each type. The resulting *Carlo Bergamini* (general-purpose configuration) and *Virginio Fasan* (anti-submarine configuration) were both delivered during 2013 after extensive sea trials.[2] As of mid-2014, a programme to deliver a further three units of each type was well advanced. However, funding for a further two general-purpose frigates to complete an initially planned programme of ten Italian ships (i.e. six general-purpose frigates and four anti-submarine versions) has yet to be confirmed.

Left: The Italian FREMM frigates *Carlo Bergamini* (background) and *Virginio Fasan* (foreground) sailing in company off the Ligurian coast whilst undergoing trials in June 2012. They represent the prototypes for, respectively, the Italian general-purpose and anti-submarine FREMM configurations. *(Italian Navy)*

CLASS ORIGINS

The FREMM programme was the result of a requirement that emerged during the late 1990s for both France and Italy to renew the bulk of their front-line surface escorts in the face of block obsolescence of existing vessels. For Italy, the need was to find replacements for the four *Lupo* and eight *Maestrale* class frigates that had been delivered between 1977 and 1985. The two countries initially considered how to meet their requirements through separate national programmes. However, doubtless influenced by progress with the preceding 'Horizon' project, it was decided to join forces in a further collaboration, resulting in signature of a co-operation agreement between the two partner nations in November 2002. The Italian Navy subsequently signed off its own operational requirements for the new class in January 2003, allowing a formal framework agreement to be signed in the following June and common design work to move forward. At this stage it was envisaged the programme would encompass seventeen frigates for France and ten for Italy at an aggressive targeted cost of c. €250m (c. US$250m at then current exchange rates) per unit. Delivery of the new ships was similarly optimistically planned for 2008 onwards.

The industrial structure for the new project was based on that used for the 'Horizon' air-defence destroyers. In Italy's case, delivery of the programme was entrusted to the Orizzonte Sistemi Navali (OSN) consortium of Fincantieri and Finmeccanica, working in collaboration with the similar French Armaris joint venture between DCN and Thales.[3] Overall supervision was allocated to Europe's Organisation for Joint Armament Cooperation (OCCAR). The partners faced considerable design challenges from the start of the project, having to reconcile a French preference for a relatively cheap and austerely-outfitted ship with an Italian requirement for a more capable warship. Competition between the two countries' defence industries to outfit the new ships was an additional complicating factor. The compromise that was ultimately reached

Virginio Fasan pictured on the assembly berth at the Riva Trigoso shipyard in March 2012, shortly before being loaded onto a barge for transfer to Fincantieri's 'sister' facility at Muggiano for final outfitting. The berth can support for the assembly of two ships simultaneously; the third FREMM *Carlo Margottini* can be seen under construction in the background. *(OCCAR)*

resulted in the adoption of a common hull form, broadly similar propulsion architecture and several shared equipment packages but the acceptance of considerable differences with respect to superstructure, weaponry, platform management and electronic systems. The resultant distinctive French and Italian FREMM variants can, perhaps, therefore be considered more as closely-related cousins as compared with the two pairs of sisters that emerged from the previous 'Horizon' collaboration.

The complex process of agreeing these design compromises meant that construction contracts took much longer to award than initially planned. The delay was exacerbated by the lower priority given to defence spending in Europe after the Cold War, with both France and Italy struggling to find ways to fund such a large programme. A declaration of intent to proceed was eventually made by the French and Italian governments at their 24th bilateral summit in October 2005, with this being closely followed by a detailed development contract for the new ships in November of the same year. However, whilst France was able to award production contracts for a first tranche of eight vessels at this time, further political discussions were required before finance for the Italians ships could be confirmed. As such, it was only on 9 May 2006 that orders for the first batch of two Italian frigates were finally placed.[4] The funding allocated to cover initial development costs, as well as construction and support of the two prototypes, was c. €2bn (c. US$2.5bn) spread over fifteen years. The total cost of the planned Italian ten-ship programme was reported as c. €5bn.[5]

CONTRACT AND CONSTRUCTION

The current status of the Italian FREMM programme is outlined in Table 3.1.1. The signature of the contract with the OSN consortium allowed detailed design work to commence. OSN acts as prime contractor and whole warship design authority for the Italian FREMMs, drawing on the skills of Finmeccanica's Selex ES electronic systems subsidiary in areas such as radar, communications and combat management systems whilst using Fincantieri's Naval Vessels Business Unit for production management and construction. Now the world's fourth largest shipbuilder by turnover following recent expansion, state-owned Fincantieri operates over twenty shipyards spread across four continents and has nearly 20,000 direct employees. Perhaps best-known for its high-specification cruise

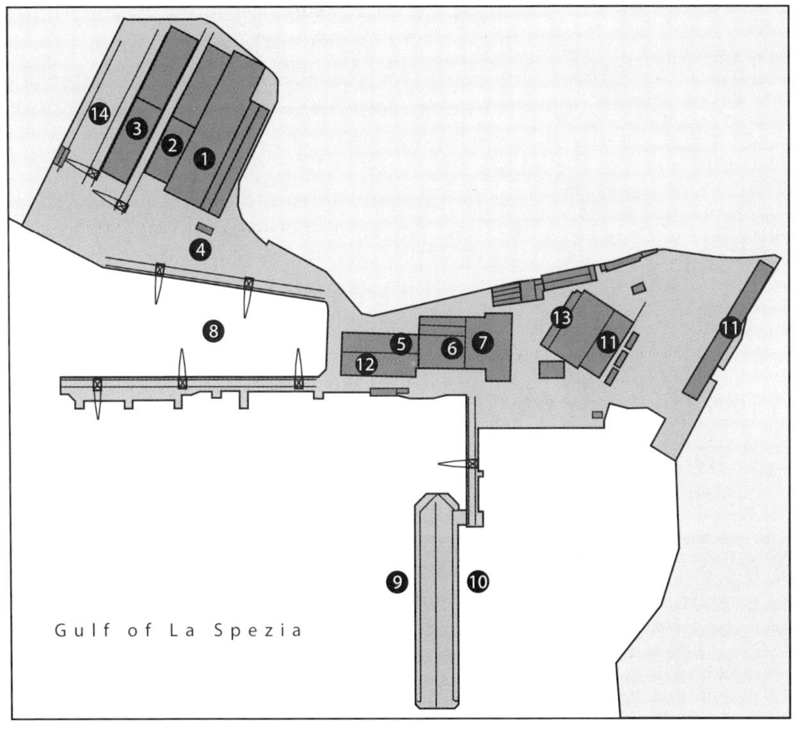

Fincantieri: Muggiano Shipyard

1. Cutting and Blending WS
2. PrefabricationWS
3. Final assembling WS
4. Sand blasting WS
5. Piping WS
6. U212 module WS
7. Submarine assembling WS
8. Outfitting piers
9. Floating dock
10. Barge (in floating dock)
11. Store
12. Yard offices
13. Italian navy offices
14. Mega yacht fairing and painting

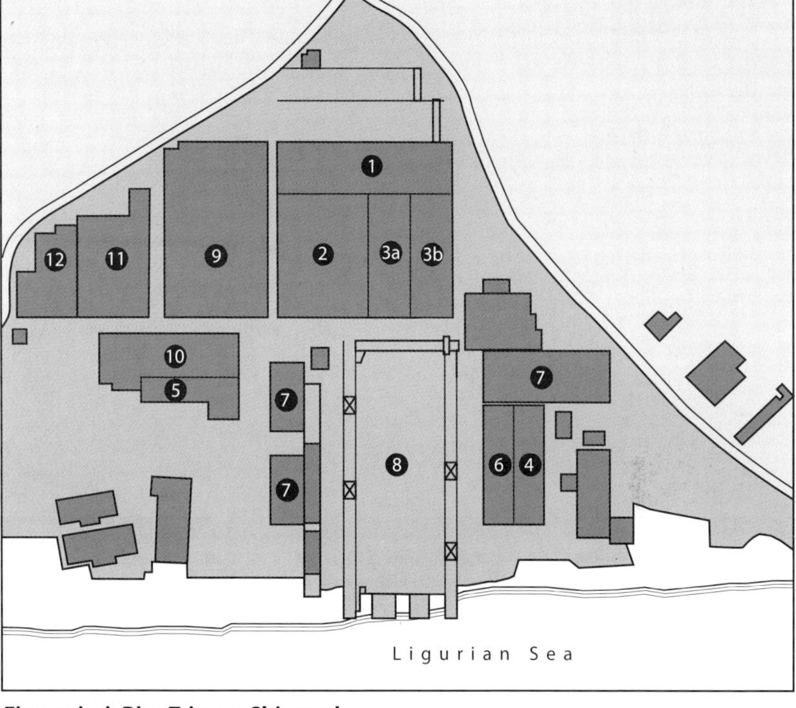

Fincantieri: Riva Trigoso Shipyard

1. Steel stockyard
2. Naval WS
3a. Panel line
3b. Curved panels WS
4. Pipes WS
5. Ducts WS
6. Modules WS
7. Units WS1. Steel stockyard
8. Slipway and assembly berth
9. Machine Tools WS
10. New flat panels / Double skin WS
11. Assembly WS
12. Test rooms

(Plans © Ian Johnston, 2014)

liners, the company also has a significant international presence in warship building through a network of subsidiaries and joint ventures.[6]

Fincantieri's domestic warship construction activities are focused on what it terms its 'integrated shipyard'. This utilises complementary facilities split between Riva Trigoso (near Genoa) and Muggiano (adjacent to La Spezia) in the Ligurian Sea. Riva Trigoso is the slightly larger of the two facilities and is principally used for the fabrication and assembly of larger naval vessels, as well as the construction of machinery and mechanical components. The site includes stockyards, workshops and a 174m x 60m assembly berth that is able to support the simultaneous completion of two frigates. Muggiano, with over 1.2km of outfitting quays, is focused on the final commissioning of the ships assembled at Riva Trigoso. It also builds smaller warships and luxury yachts. Facilities include a large floating dock that is used to help unload ships that have been barged from Riva Trigoso for completion. The combined yards provide direct employment for over 1,300 shipyard workers as well as approximately 1,700 sub-contractors, with the total workforce roughly evenly split between the two sites.

Table 3.1.1: ITALIAN FREMM TYPE FRIGATES: CLASS LIST

NAME	PENNANT	VARIANT	ORDERED	COMMENCED	LAUNCHED	DELIVERED
Carlo Bergamini	F590	General-purpose	9 May 2006	4 February 2008	16 July 2011	29 May 2013
Virginio Fasan	F591	Anti-submarine	9 May 2006	12 May 2009	31 March 2012	19 December 2013
Carlo Margottini	F592	Anti-submarine	30 January 2008	14 September 2010	29 June 2013	27 February 2014
Carabiniere	F593	Anti-submarine	30 January 2008	6 April 2011	29 March 2014	[2015]
Alpino	F594	Anti-submarine	30 January 2008	23 February 2012	[2015]	[2016]
Luigi Rizzo	F595	General-purpose	30 January 2008	5 March 2013	[2016]	[2017]
No. 7	F596	General-purpose	September 2013	4 June 2014	[2017]	[2018]
No. 8	F597	General-purpose	September 2013	[2015]	[2018]	[2019]

Notes:

1. A decision on whether or not to order a final two vessels will be taken during 2015.

2. There is some confusion between first steel-cutting and keel-laying in published sources; commencement dates must therefore be viewed with some care.

Two views of the lead Italian FREMM, the general-purpose *Carlo Bergamini*, on initial sea trials during October 2011. These images were taken before extension of her flight deck by 3.6m to facilitate operation of heavy helicopters. *(Fincantieri)*

Fabrication of the lead Italian FREMM, *Carlo Bergamini*, commenced at Riva Trigoso on 4 February 2008 when a ceremony was held to mark the cutting of the first steel for the vessel. A launch ceremony was subsequently held on 16 July 2011, when the ship was rolled onto a barge for transportation for final fitting-out at Muggiano. At this stage, the vessel was largely complete, with key equipment such as the combat management system already installed. Following further outfitting at Muggiano, the new frigate commenced the first of an extensive series of sea trials less than three months later on 6 October 2011. One major result of these tests was a decision to extend the length of the ship's flight deck to facilitate helicopter operations through installation of a 3.6m hull plug; a task that was completed during a post-trials rectification refit in early 2013.[7] The ship was finally accepted by OCCAR and delivered to the Italian Navy on 29 May 2013, some three months earlier than scheduled. The c. five-year timespan from the start of fabrication to acceptance is said to be the fastest delivery of a major new Italian warship class since the Second World War.

Construction of *Virginio Fasan* followed relatively closely behind *Carlo Bergamini*, ultimately allowing some of their trials to be carried out in concert. Fabrication started in May 2009 and a launch ceremony was held on 31 March 2012 prior to the commencement of a programme of sea trials from July 2012 onwards. Following completion of a hull extension and other modifications similar to those carried out on *Carlo Bergamini*, she was finally accepted by the *Marina Militare* on 19 December 2013.

By this time, series production of the class was already well underway following a production contract for four further frigates (three anti-submarine and one general-purpose version) in January 2008. Given the deteriorating European economic situation, rumours started to emerge from 2010 onwards that the programme would be terminated at just six ships. However, an order for a further two vessels was finally confirmed in September 2013. A decision on the remaining pair will be taken before the end of 2015.

OVERALL DESIGN

With a full-load displacement of around 6,700 tons and a length of 144m, the Italian FREMM type ships are only a little smaller than the preceding 'Horizon' class air-defence destroyers, to which they

The French-designed *Aquitaine* class FREMM variant *Mohammed VI* pictured on trials in June 2013 before delivery to the Royal Moroccan Navy. The French and Italian FREMMs share a common hull and overall layout but their equipment and superstructure exhibits significant differences. As such, the Italian FREMMs are closer in appearance to the preceding 'Horizon' class than to their French counterparts. *(DCNS)*

bear more than a passing resemblance. Unsurprisingly, given both collaboration with France and limited recent Italian experience in building large surface combatants, both classes were heavily influenced by previous French experience in warship design. For example, the *La Fayette* class 'stealth frigates' commissioned between 1996 and 2001 have been an important point of reference. The basic hull design and overall layout of both the French and Italian FREMMs is very similar.

Italian operational requirements have, however, resulted in notable differences in visual appearance – and capability – compared with the French FREMM *Aquitaine* class variant. Most notably, an Italian desire to provide their ships with an ability to conduct area air defence resulted in selection of the EMPAR multifunction radar – also fitted to the 'Horizon' class – compared with the *Aquitaine*'s arguably less capable Herakles. Similarly, the Italian FREMMs incorporate an extra foredeck to allow deeper, Sylver A50 vertical launch modules to be fitted in the forward vertical launch system (VLS) position. These can support the Aster 30 medium-range surface-to-air missile that is also used by the larger destroyers. Other major differences include the Italian ships' use of traditional exhausts to vent the forward generators compared with the French ships' use of elastically mounted ducts just above the waterline. When combined with the impact of a range of other divergences in weapon and sensor outfits, the respective superstructures of the two national variants exhibit a significant contrast.

In terms of overall structure, the Italian FREMMs have a total of fourteen deck levels when those in the masts are taken into account, with Deck 1 (the main deck) being located at flight deck level. Deck 2 is the principal deck for lateral communication and encompasses an oblong of parallel passageways in the middle of the ship with single passageways extending fore and aft. Decks 3 and 4 are the main technical decks and encompass the forward (auxiliary) and aft (main) engine rooms. Deck 01 is at forecastle level; the Combat Information Centre (CIC) and

Operations Room are also positioned at this level in the forward superstructure. The bridge is located at Deck 02 level above the CIC. A vertical communications trunk level with the forward mast provides secure access between all the principal decks.

In contrast to the significant visual difference between the French and Italian variants, the *Carlo Bergamini* general-purpose and *Virginio Fasan* anti-submarine configurations look remarkably similar and are virtually identical internally. They can be distinguished only by deviations with respect to a number of pieces of specific equipment, not all of which are readily observable. The principal particulars of both configurations are set out in Table 3.1.2 and Table 3.1.3.

WEAPONRY AND COMBAT SYSTEMS

Combat Management System: The key component of the Italian FREMMs' capability is provided by a combat management system (CMS) supplied by Finmeccanica's Selex ES subsidiary. It forms part of a scalable family, branded as Athena in export markets, that is capable of installation in a wide range of ships from patrol vessels upwards. The version in the FREMMs draws on experience gained with similar systems installed in the aircraft carrier *Cavour* and the destroyers of the 'Horizon' class, the

Table 3.1.2.

CARLO BERGAMINI PRINCIPAL PARTICULARS

Building Information:	
Fabrication Commenced:	4 February 2008
Launched:	16 July 2011
Delivered:	29 May 2013
Builders:	Fincantieri – Cantieri Navali Italiani SpA at its facilities at Riva Trigoso and Muggiano in Liguria.
Dimensions:	
Displacement:	6,700 tons full load displacement.
Overall Hull Dimensions:	144.0m x 19.7m x 5.1m (8.4m maximum). Length between perpendiculars is 132.5m.
Weapons Systems:	
Missiles:	2 x Sylver A50 8-cell VLS modules for a total of 16 Aster 15 or Aster 30 surface-to-air missiles. [Space reserved for 2 x Sylver A70 8-cell VLS modules for a total of 16 additional missiles]. 4 x twin launchers for Teseo Mk2/A surface-to-surface missiles.
Guns:	1 x 127mm Oto Melara main gun. 1 x 76mm Oto Melara Strales gun. 2 x 25mm Oto Melara KBA guns. Light machine guns.
Torpedoes:	2 x triple 324mm B515 anti-submarine torpedo tubes for Eurotorp MU-90 torpedoes.
Aircraft:	2 x NFH-90 or 1 x AW-101 and 1 x NFH-90 helicopters.
Countermeasures:	Sigen Radar (RESM) and Communications (CESM) Electronic Support Measures. Sigen Radar Electronic Countermeasures (RECM) jammers. Oto Melara SCLAR-H decoy launchers. [Space reserved for SLAT torpedo-defence system].
Principal Sensors:	1 x EMPAR (MMI/SPY-790) multifunction radar (active variant). 1 x RASS RAN-30X (MMI/SPS-791) surface-search radar. Navigation radars. Selex IFF array antenna. 2 x Selex NA-25 fire-control systems. Selex SASS Infrared Search and Track (IRST) system. 1 x Thales UMS 4110 hull-mounted sonar. 1 x WASS mine-avoidance sonar.
Combat System:	Selex Athena combat management system. Integrated communications system includes Links 11, 16 and 22.
Propulsion Systems:	
Machinery:	CODLAG. 4 x Isotta Fraschini diesel generators each rated at 2.1MW provide power to 2 x 2.2MW Jeumont electric motors, one on each shaft. 1 x GE/Avio LM2500+G4 gas turbine rated at 32MW. A 2MW retractable thruster can provide auxiliary propulsion.
Speed and Range:	Designed maximum speed 27 knots on gas turbine, 15 knots on electric motors. Range is 6,500 nautical miles at 15 knots.
Other Details:	
Complement:	The core crew is c. 130, including 20 officers. Accommodation is provided for 165, rising to 200 once space reserved for additional Sylver VLS modules (see above) but converted to additional cabin space is taken into account.
Class:	Four Italian FREMMs have been ordered in general-purpose configuration; another two are planned. There are also a further four ships in anti-submarine configuration.

latter being developed through the Eurosysnav consortium of Selex and DCNS.

Athena is similar to other modern combat management systems in linking a ship's sensors and weapons systems to a series of multi-function consoles through a local area network (LAN). The system therefore provides a complete tactical picture for the ship's command team and allows a full range of weaponry to be accessed to provide an appropriate response. The version installed in the Italian FREMMs has twenty-one separate consoles. Seventeen of these are located in the CIC, with others installed in the operations room, bridge and secondary command position. The CIC occupies almost the entire breadth of the frigate underneath the bridge and is laid out on a functional basis. As such, despite their multi-functional capabilities, the CMS consoles are normally dedicated to a specific role. For example, command functions are normally exercised from a central 'command island' with other areas of the CIC dedicated to specialisms such as anti-submarine operations, electronic countermeasures and support or helicopter control. It is possible to resort to control of specific weapons systems should the integrated network be damaged.

Command and Communications: As for the CMS,

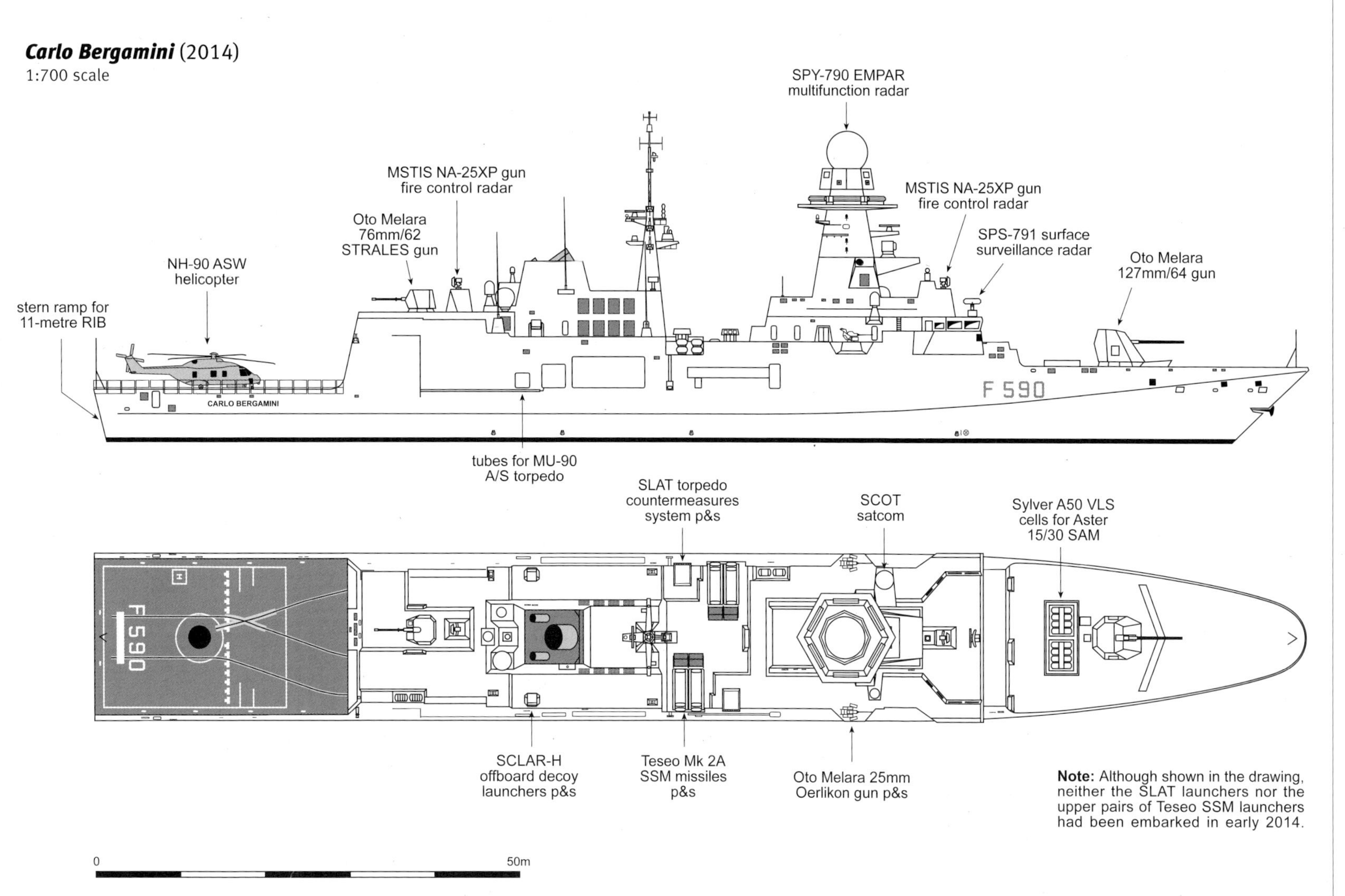

(Drawings © John Jordan, 2014)

the frigates' integrated communications system reflects experience gained by Selex and its partners with *Cavour* and the 'Horizons'. Encompassing both external and internal communications, it is focused on a secure network that can be accessed through eighty-eight communications boxes located throughout each ship. The system facilitates secure communication by satellite and across the radio frequency spectrum, supporting NATO Links 11, 16 and 22. The Italian FREMMs are designed to carry out a command role and a separate operations room equipped with extensive network access is provided for this purpose.

Anti-Air Warfare: The air-defence system capabilities of both the *Carlo Bergamini* and *Virginio Fasan* type FREMM versions are broadly similar. They are built around the SAAM-ESD combination of the new active variant of the Selex EMPAR (European Multi-function Phased-Array Radar) carried high on the foremast and MBDA's Aster 15 and 30 surface-to-air missiles.[8] The latter are housed in two, eight-cell Sylver A50 VLS modules located forward of the bridge. This configuration allows a ship equipped with the system to defend itself and other vessels operating within a c. 12 nautical mile radius from aircraft and missile attack. It was first planned to fit the Italian FREMMs with the SAAM-IT self-defence system currently used in *Cavour*, which is limited by only being able to use the shorter-range Aster 15 missile. The decision to adopt a more potent capability, taken after work on the first two ships had already commenced, effectively provides air-defence coverage that is closer to the specialised 'Horizon' class. However, the latter ships also benefit from being equipped with the longer range S-1850M three-dimensional search radar and are therefore better able to undertake an extended area defence role.

Operating in the 4,000–5,000 MHz NATO G-band (USN C-band), EMPAR is one of the new generation of software-controlled multi-function radars. These essentially allow search, target-tracking and fire-control roles to be carried out by one system. Comprising a single-faced rotating array housed within a radome, its relatively light weight compared with multi-faced systems such as Thales' APAR allow it to be installed in a more elevated position. It is reportedly able to monitor up to 300 aerial targets out to a range of 300 nautical miles. Having identified and then tracked potentially hostile targets, EMPAR can control an engagement with Aster missiles, directing them towards the target by data uplink. The missiles' own active data seekers take over this function in the final stages before the target's destruction. EMPAR is able to control multiple missiles simultaneously and the main constraint on an air-defence engagement would therefore appear to be the relatively limited complement of sixteen missiles housed in the VLS cells. Whilst space has been reserved for two additional eight-cell Sylver A70 modules, these were primarily intended to house long-range strike weapons such as MBDA's SCALP Naval. In any event, the space now been allocated for increased crew accommodation.

EMPAR's role in air-defence engagements is supported by a Selex New Generation IFF (identifi-

The 'Horizon' class destroyer *Caio Duilio* and the FREMM frigate *Virginio Fasan* berthed at La Spezia naval base. The 'Horizon' class – a product of previous Franco-Italian collaboration – had a significant impact on the design of the Italian FREMM variant. Both ships are fitted with the EMPAR multi-function radar housed within a radome on top of the foremast but the FREMM has the newer and more capable active variant. *(Conrad Waters)*

cation friend or foe) phased array antenna located in a collar on the foremast below the EMPAR radome and R-ESM (radar electronic support measures) equipment. In addition, a Selex SASS IRST (infra-red search and tracking) sensor is positioned above the bridge to identify and track the infra-red signatures of low elevation air and surface threats.

Second-line anti-aircraft and missile defence is provided by the Oto Melara 76mm/62 gun. One of these is situated above the helicopter hangar to the aft of the ship. In addition, class members in the *Virginio Fasan* anti-submarine configuration are equipped with a second mounting forwards in lieu of the 127mm/64 gun found on the general-purpose ships. Capable of being used in anti-air and anti-surface modes under the control of Selex MSTIS (multi-sensor target indicator system) NA-25 fire-control units positioned forward and aft, the gun is also fitted with the Strales guidance system to fire DART guided ammunition. Using radio frequency guidance to direct the munition towards its target in conjunction with a ship's radar, Strales can support engagements at ranges of five nautical miles and more. It provides an effective inner layer defence system against missiles and similar targets, with its longer range than traditional close-in weapons systems (CIWS) such as the US Navy's Phalanx providing greater scope for multiple engagements. All ships are also fitted with a pair of Oto Melara Oerlikon KBA 25mm/80 mounts that have a limited air-defence capability.

Anti-Surface Warfare: Italian FREMMs in the *Carlo Bergamini* general-purpose configuration are optimised for anti-surface and land attack missions and therefore have greater capabilities in these roles than

The forward mast of *Virginio Fasan*, with a radome for the single-faced, rotating EMPAR radar at its top. Although not readily apparent, this is the active MFR-A variant of EMPAR, with individually energised transceivers. Also pictured in this view are the R-ESM sensors immediately below the radome, with a collar of IFF antennae positioned slightly lower down. The prominent 'ear' halfway down the mast is one of the exhausts for the forward generators. *(Conrad Waters)*

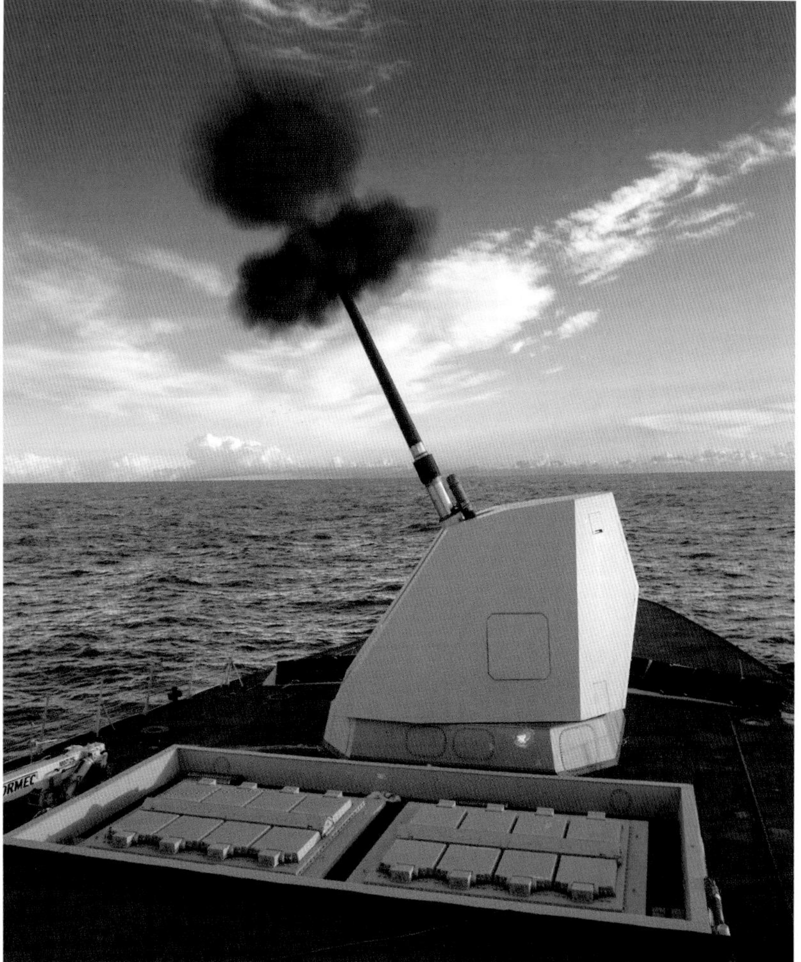

All Italian FREMMs are equipped with an Oto Melara 76mm/62 gun equipped with the Strales guidance system for use with radio-guided DART ammunition. In addition, ships in the *Carlo Bergamini* general-purpose configuration have one of Oto Melara's new lightweight 127mm/64 mountings capable of firing Vulcano extended-range munitions in place of a second 76mm/62 gun. This view shows *Carlo Bergamini* during firing trials in December 2012; the two eight-cell Sylver launchers for the ship's Aster surface-to-air missiles can also be seen. *(Oto Melara)*

the *Virginio Fasan* sub-group. A major distinction between the two types is the general purpose ships' use of the new 127mm/64 lightweight gun system in the forward position. This was first delivered to the Italian Navy for installation onboard *Carlo Bergamini* in 2011 and has also been specified for the German F125 frigate programme. An evolution of the previous 127mm/54 mount, the new gun is designed for use with the Vulcano series of extended-range ammunition as well as standard munitions. It is capable of fully automated loading.[9] Vulcano comes in non-guided BER (ballistic extended range) and GLR (guided long range) variants, the latter using GPS technology to allow targets to be engaged at ranges of up to 100km. The BER round, with a multi-function programmable fuze and pre-fragmented warhead, can also be used against air attack.

The development of Vulcano munitions provides a low-cost alternative to conventional land-attack missiles and may explain Italian hesitation to invest in this latter capability. As previously mentioned, both FREMM configurations have space reserved for strike missile-length configured A70 launch modules. However, in contrast with the French *Aquitaine*, which will be equipped with SCALP Naval, this option will not be taken up for the time being.

Both Italian FREMM types are, however, fitted

Table 3.1.3.

VIRGINIO FASAN PRINCIPAL PARTICULARS

Building Information:	
Fabrication Commenced:	12 May 2009
Launched:	31 March 2012
Delivered:	19 December 2013
Builders:	Fincantieri – Cantieri Navali Italiani SpA at its facilities at Riva Trigoso and Muggiano in Liguria.
Dimensions:	
Displacement:	6,700 tons full load displacement.
Overall Hull Dimensions:	144.0m x 19.7m x 5.1m (8.4m maximum). Length between perpendiculars is 132.5m.
Weapons Systems:	
Missiles:	2 x Sylver A50 8-cell VLS modules for a total of 16 Aster 15 or Aster 30 surface-to-air missiles. [Space reserved for 2 x Sylver A70 8-cell VLS modules for a total of 16 additional missiles]. 2 x twin launchers for Teseo Mk2/A surface-to-surface missiles. 2 x twin launchers for MILAS anti-submarine missiles.
Guns:	2 x 76mm Oto Melara Strales guns. 2 x 25mm Oto Melara KBA guns. Light machine guns.
Torpedoes:	2 x triple 324mm B515 anti-submarine torpedo tubes for Eurotorp MU-90 torpedoes.
Aircraft:	2 x NFH-90 or 1 x AW-101 and 1 x NFH-90 helicopters.
Countermeasures:	Sigen Radar (RESM) and Communications (CESM) Electronic Support Measures. Sigen Radar Electronic Countermeasures (RECM) jammers. Oto Melara SCLAR-H decoy launchers. SLAT torpedo-defence system.
Principal Sensors:	1 x EMPAR (MMI/SPY-790) multifunction radar (active variant). 1 x RASS RAN-30X (MMI/SPS-791) surface-search radar. Navigation radars. Selex IFF array antenna. 2 x Selex NA-25 fire-control systems. Selex SASS Infrared Search and Track (IRST) system. 1 x Thales UMS 4110 hull-mounted sonar. 1 x WASS mine-avoidance sonar. Thales UMS 4249 CAPTAS-4 towed-array. L-3 ELAC Seabeam 3050 panoramic echo sounder.
Combat System:	Selex Athena combat management system. Integrated communications system includes Links 11, 16 and 22.
Propulsion Systems:	
Machinery:	CODLAG. 4 x Isotta Fraschini diesel generators each rated at 2.1MW provide power to 2 x 2.2MW Jeumont electric motors, one on each shaft. 1 x GE/Avio LM2500+G4 gas turbine rated at 32MW. A 2MW retractable thruster can provide auxiliary propulsion.
Speed and Range:	Designed maximum speed 27 knots on gas turbine, 15 knots on electric motors. Range is 6,500 nautical miles at 15 knots.
Other Details:	
Complement:	The core crew is c. 130, including 20 officers. Accommodation is provided for 165 rising to 200 once space reserved for additional Sylver VLS modules (see above) but converted to additional cabin space is taken into account.
Class:	Four Italian FREMMs have been ordered in anti-submarine configuration.

with the MBDA Teseo Mk 2/A surface-to-surface missile, which can be used against both surface ships and coastal targets. It is the latest development of the Otomat family of missiles first introduced in the 1970s and is known as Otomat Mk2 Block IV for foreign sales. Capable of delivering a 210kg warhead up to 180km, it initially takes data obtained by the RASS RAN-30X surface surveillance radar or other elements of the CMS to calculate an appropriate firing solution. It then uses this or updated information provided by data link for guidance towards its target until an active homing head takes over in the final attack phase. Ships in the general purpose configuration can carry up to eight Teseo missiles, deployed from four launch positions. The *Virginio Fasan* type deploy half this outfit, using the other launch positions for MILAS anti-submarine missiles that are another iteration of the Otomat family.

Anti-Submarine Warfare: Just as the general-purpose ships are particularly capable in surface warfare scenarios, it is in the prosecution of anti-submarine warfare that frigates in the *Virginio Fasan* configuration come into their own. Both types have anti-submarine sensors provided by Thales, with the UMS 4110 bow-mounted sonar that is also found in France's *Aquitaine* common to the two configurations. A low-frequency, active and passive unit, it

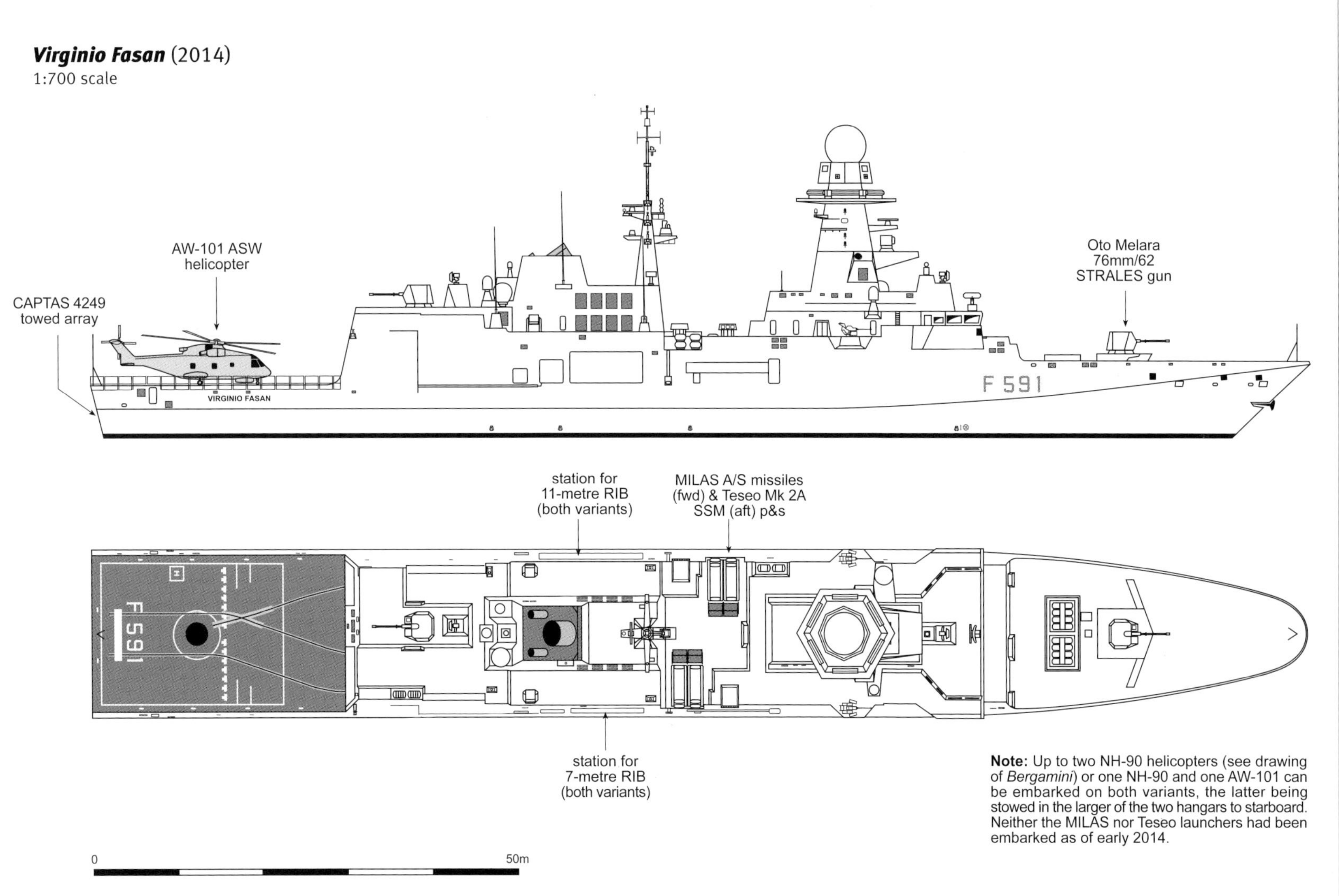

provides long-range detection above the thermal layer and has been designed to be particularly effective in Mediterranean conditions.[10] However, the anti-submarine ships are also fitted with additional equipment, most notably Thales' complementary CAPTAS-4 (UMS 4249) variable-depth sonar housed in a handling room below the flight deck. This combined active/passive towed array is more effective at detecting targets below the thermal layer, thereby providing more comprehensive anti-submarine coverage. The integrated sonar suite's capability is further supplemented by specification of a SeaBeam 3050 panoramic echo sounder from L-3 ELAC Nautik for use in littoral waters, providing additional imagery to depths of c. 3,500m. Whilst principally intended to assist submarine hunting, the system can also be used in a hydrographic role.

Once a hostile submarine has been identified, a broad selection of weapons is available to ensure its neutralisation. Prosecution of targets detected at longer ranges would normally be placed in the hands of the embarked helicopters, described in more detail below. For instant, all-weather reaction against medium-range targets, ships in the *Virginio Fasan* configuration can also make use of the MILAS anti-submarine system. Four launch canisters for this missile are shipped in the forward launch positions in lieu of the full outfit of Teseo missiles that equip the *Carlo Bergamini* type. Derived from Otomat, MILAS works in a similar fashion to the US Navy's ASROC to deliver an anti-submarine torpedo close to the area of threat. It has an operating range of between 6km and 35km and has been reported as

Virginio Fasan is optimised for anti-submarine warfare, with equipment for a CAPTAS-4 (UMS 4249) variable-depth sonar housed in a handling room immediately below the flight deck; the sonar being deployed through a hatch in the stern. The asymmetrical hangars can house up to two anti-submarine helicopters, whilst there are positions for MILAS anti-submarine missiles and shorter-range anti-submarine torpedo tubes. One of the two hexahedron-shaped launchers for the SLAT torpedo defence system can be seen to starboard on the middle of the ship, between the two masts. *(Italian Navy)*

Carlo Margottini, the third Italian FREMM, seen during post-delivery trials off La Spezia on 1 April 2014. Delivered on 27 February 2014, she is an anti-submarine variant equipped with variable-depth sonar and for MILAS launchers (not yet fitted in this view). The assembly sheds and cranes of Fincantieri's Muggiano yard can be seen in the background, where the new Algerian amphibious transport dock *Kalaat Beni-Abbes* is also berthed. *(Conrad Waters)*

being able to hit a target at maximum range within three minutes of launch. Any submarines that were identified at closer range would be engaged by the ship's triple anti-submarine torpedo tubes, located port and starboard just forward of the helicopter hangars. Both systems, as well as any anti-submarine helicopters embarked, use the MU-90 lightweight torpedo manufactured by the Franco-Italian EuroTorp consortium. The torpedo is equipped with an electric-powered pump jet to achieve speeds in excess of 50 knots and utilises a shaped-charge warhead to ensure its effectiveness against double-hulled submarines.

Helicopters and Ship's Boats: Both Italian FREMM versions can operate up to two helicopters. A normal maximum complement is either two of Airbus Helicopters' medium-sized NH90 or one NH90

An AW-101 helicopter in *Marina Militare* markings. Both Italian FREMM configurations can deploy and support one of these helicopters in addition to a smaller NH90 type. *(AgustaWestland)*

A MILAS anti-submarine missile seen during checkout after assembly. Similar to the US Navy's ASROC, this can deploy a MU-90 lightweight torpedo out to 35km within three minutes of launch. Each Italian FREMM completed in anti-submarine configuration has four MILAS launchers. *(MBDA)*

and one, heavier AgustaWestland AW-101. The frigates are equipped with two separate hangars to house these aircraft, that to the starboard being significantly larger so as to house an AW-101. The Italian Navy operates both types in anti-submarine and utility variants, with the former being equipped with dipping sonar and armed with MU-90 torpedoes and Marte air-to-surface missiles.[11] The flight deck incorporates a Curtis-Wright TC-ASIST (Twin Claw-Aircraft Ship Integrated Secure and Traverse) recovery system to assist safe handling and recovery. The flight deck extension retrofitted to the two prototype ships and fitted from build in the remainder of the class will further assist safe helicopter operation, particularly improving margins with respect to AW-101 transport type's rear ramp.

All ships have two positions for rigid inflatable boats (RIBs) located to port and starboard just forward of the main exhaust funnel. The station to port is larger so as to be able to accommodate a longer RIB for Special Forces operations. The *Carlo*

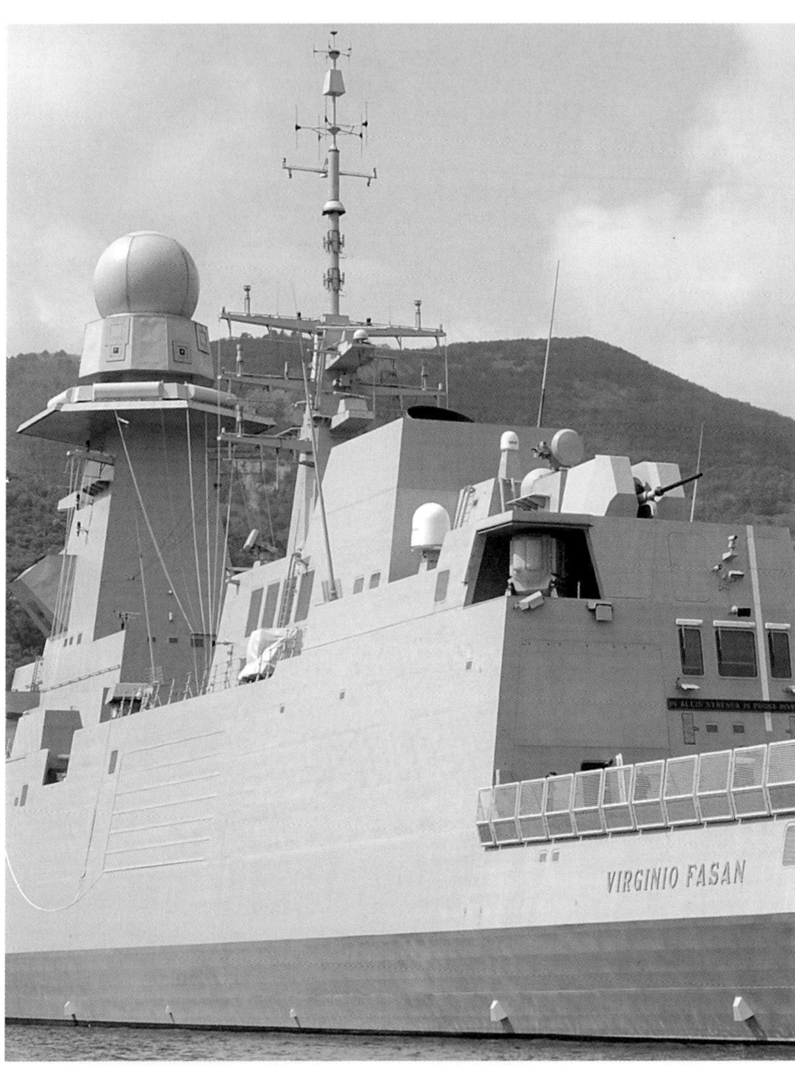

A view of *Virginio Fasan*'s superstructure, depicting some of the countermeasures equipment installed. A R-ECM JASS radar jammer is located in an enclosure above the hangar, whilst a SCLAR-H decoy launcher is hidden under a tarpaulin abreast the funnel. A SLAT launcher for torpedo defence is positioned at the same level further forward. C-ESM sensors are installed on the mainmast, with their R-ESM counterparts on the foremast immediately below the EMPAR radar. *(Conrad Waters)*

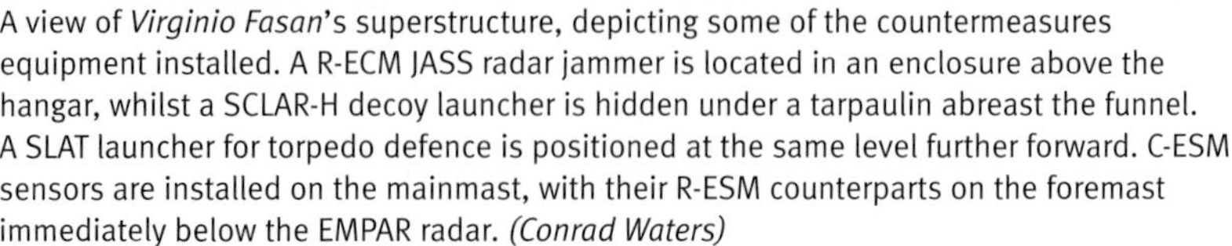

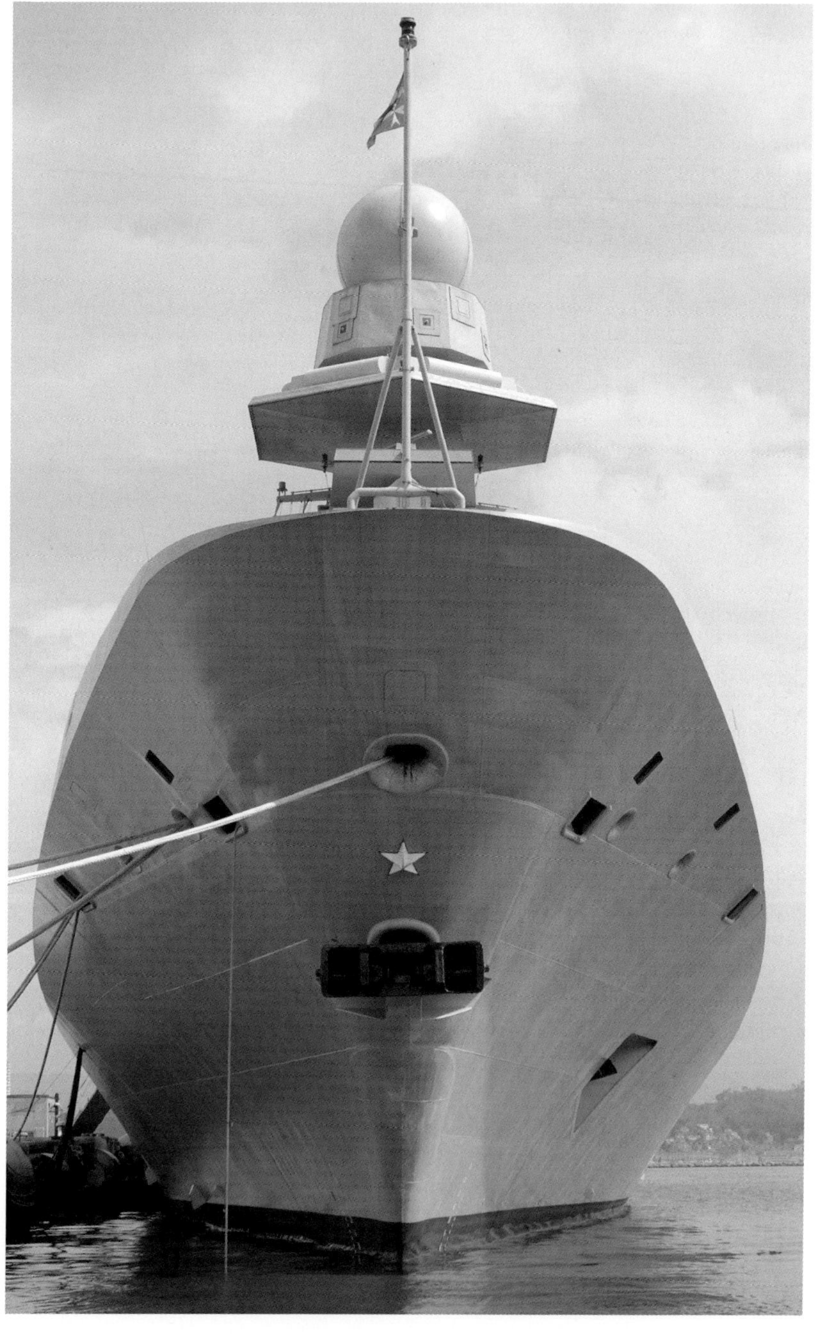

The Italian FREMMs' design reflects the attention to stealth that is apparent in all modern frontline warships. For example, the hull shape is designed to minimise radar cross-section and equipment is recessed or enclosed within hatches. *(Conrad Waters)*

Bergamini general-purpose version also has a stern ramp in lieu of the anti-submarine type's towed array for easier deployment of an additional RIB in adverse sea states.

COUNTERMEASURES AND SURVIVABILITY

As might be expected, both *Carlo Bergamini* and *Virginio Fasan* are equipped with a comprehensive range of countermeasures to supplement their weapons systems. Electronic warfare requirements are met by the Thales-Elettronica Sigen joint venture, which also provided a similar capability on the previous 'Horizon' class destroyers. The integrated suite provides both Radar Electronic Support Measures (ESM) and Communications ESM, as well as Radar Electronic Counter Measures (ECM) jammers. The R-ESM sensors are installed high on the foremast immediately below the EMPAR radar. Their C-ESM counterparts are located in a similarly elevated position on the mainmast. These systems are intended to provide early detection and warning of emissions from potential threats and to assist other sensors in providing an overall tactical picture for the CMS. The two R-ECM JASS (Jamming Antenna Sub-System) jammers are positioned on a platform to the front of the forward mast and in a sheltered housing on top of the port hangar. Their principal role is to decoy incoming missiles away from the ship.

The electronic warfare suite is supplemented by physical countermeasures, most notably two Oto Melara SCLAR-H decoy launchers abreast the funnel. The latest version of a system that first entered service in the 1970s, it reportedly incorporates interchangeable panniers supporting a range of munitions. Last-ditch defence against torpedo attack is in the hands of the SLAT torpedo defence system. The launch units associated with this system have been installed in the two anti-submarine frigates already delivered. However, they were not present on *Carlo Bergamini* during her first overseas deployment.

The close level of attention paid to the class's various countermeasures is equalled by the emphasis on stealth that is apparent in all modern warships. As well as encompassing measures to reduce the

Carabiniere, the fourth Italian FREMM frigate, pictured in the dry dock at Fincantieri's Muggiano yard on 1 April 2014. The asymmetrical arrangement of the helicopter hangars and the openings in the stern for the variable depth sonar are apparent. *(Conrad Waters)*

Two views of *Virginio Fasan* operating with her sister, *Carlo Bergamini*, at speed. The ship's CODLAG propulsion system combines a maximum speed in excess of 27 knots under gas-turbine propulsion with the ability to conduct virtually silent submarine hunting using the diesel-electric system at lower speeds. *(Italian Navy)*

frigates' radar cross-section that is apparent in the design of the hull and superstructure, this also includes infra-red and acoustic signature reduction. The latter is particularly important for the *Virginio Fasan* type's prime anti-submarine mission, where the electric element of the CODLAG (combined diesel electric and gas) propulsion system allows virtually silent operation up to speeds of around 15 knots. This is further enhanced by specification of controllable-pitch propellers, which can be less easy for submarines to detect and analyse in addition to offering greater manoeuvrability.

Ensuring survivability in the event of damage has

Carlo Margottini, the third Italian FREMM frigate, navigating the Golfo dei Poeti off Portovenere. The Italian FREMMs feature a CODLAG propulsion system in lieu of the CODLOG arrangement fond in their French equivalents. However, the aim remains to combine the economy and stealth of diesel-electric propulsion with the possibility of higher speeds offered by the gas turbine. *(Conrad Waters)*

been another key design consideration. Whilst precise details are classified, key areas such as the CIC and vertical communications trunk are protected from small arms and shrapnel damage by armour protection, whilst consoles are shock mounted.

The frigates' hulls are divided into eleven main watertight compartments and will remain stable with at least three of these flooded. There are two main, self-contained damage-control zones (Alpha and Bravo). These are, in turn, subdivided into two vertical sub-zones (viz. A1, A2, B1 and B2). The two main zones are able to operate completely independently with respect to the generation and distribution of electrical power. Each is equipped with a damage-control centre for the management of passive defence. The main damage-control position is the ship control centre at 2 Deck level in Bravo zone, with its secondary counterpart in Alpha zone located in the aft part of the bridge. There are also two local damage-control positions in the passageways of 2 Deck to support the other vertical sub zones. All positions have access to the frigates' ship management system, which includes automated detection of flooding, heat, fire and smoke. Additional portable terminals can be plugged into the system at thirty-eight points around the ship. Fire-fighting systems include fixed installations for Novec 1230 fluid, high-pressure water mist, foam and traditional sea water, all supplemented by portable equipment.

OTHER KEY DESIGN FEATURES

Propulsion and Platform Management: The Italian FREMMs are powered by a CODLAG propulsion system that is broadly similar in configuration to the CODLOG (combined diesel electric or gas) plant installed in the French FREMMs of the *Aquitaine* class. The overall aim is to combine the economy and acoustic stealth provided by diesel-electric running with the capacity for higher speed offered

by gas turbine propulsion. The ships feature twin shaft lines and controllable-pitch propellers. A rudder roll system that features twin rudders tilted at nine degrees from the vertical enhances both stability and manoeuvrability.

The main source of electrical energy for both the electric motors and shipboard 'hotel services' is supplied by four sets of 2.1MW diesel generators manufactured by Fincantieri's Isotta Fraschini subsidiary. They are located in pairs in the forward (auxiliary) and aft (main) engine rooms, thereby providing a separate source of generating capacity in the two main damage-control zones. Two 2.2MW Schneider Jeumont motors permit electric propulsion up to speeds of around 15.5 knots, with one reversible motor being wrapped around each of the twin shaft lines. There is also a 2MW electrically-powered azimuth retractable thruster located in the forward of the auxiliary engine room. This supports a 'get me home' capability at speeds of up to 7 knots.

Higher speeds require use of the single GE/Avio LM2500+ G4 gas turbine, which is rated at 32MW. The gas turbine is linked to the twin shafts through a cross connecting gearbox. It can sustain a top speed in excess of 27 knots, albeit at a significant cost to the maximum 6,500 nautical mile range available under diesel-electric propulsion. In contrast to the French FREMM design, the CODLAG arrangement allows the electric motors and gas turbines to operate in combination. This improves manoeuvrability and provides a margin against increases in ship displacement during an estimated thirty-year service life. In addition, the propulsion motors can be used as alternators to provide electrical energy when the ship is running solely in gas turbine mode.

Control of the Italian FREMMs' navigational, propulsion and other operating equipment is provided by an integrated ship management system (SMS) manufactured by Seastema, an ABB/Fincantieri joint venture. This encompasses the host of sub-systems that comprise both the integrated platform management system (IPMS) and the integrated bridge system (IBS). The SMS can be accessed through a network of nineteen fixed and six portable terminals linked by the LAN. The fixed consoles are located in the ship control, secondary ship control and local damage-control centres already mentioned, as well as in additional positions such as the bridge and the local operating positions in the two engine rooms. Safe operation of ship systems is normally focused on the primary ship control centre, where five, two-screen SMS terminals are located. Whilst multi-functional in capability, these are normally dedicated to monitoring specific IPMS-controlled equipment, such as the propulsion plant, electrical network or auxiliary machinery. The SMS also supports the damage-control functions previously described. The IBS, meanwhile, encompasses electronic chart display, automatic radar plotting and navigation sub-systems. The considerable level of automation provided allows the bridge to be operated by just two personnel.

Accommodation: The increased automation installed in the new ships has allowed a considerable decrease in numbers of personnel compared with previous frigates. For example, the crew of the previous, much smaller *Maestrale* class is c. 225 compared with the initial c. 130 (plus an up to 23-strong helicopter section) planned for the Italian FREMMs. However, in practice, it appears that the anticipated reduction in personnel has been a little overly optimistic. For example, *Virginio Fasan* has been home to around 150 personnel post-commissioning. This may ultimately increase to as many 167 on the basis of operational experience and anticipated maintenance requirements during a longer deployment. For this reason, additional accommodation space has been provided by installing more cabin units in the space currently reserved for additional VLS cells.

Accommodation already fitted is of a high standard, reflecting the pan-European focus on personnel recruitment and retention in the post-conscription era. Commissioned officers are normally allocated single cabins with their own facilities. Non-commissioned officers are housed in two-berth units, whilst ratings' cabins typically have four bunks. Another concession to social change, as well as efficiency, is the use of a central galley to provide catering to all messes. Logistical arrangements support operations at sea of up to forty-five continuous days.

Two views of *Carlo Bergamini* prior to the start of a deployment to the Middle East and Africa which had the promotion of the Italian defence industry as one of its principal objectives. The FREMM programme is a major achievement for the Italian naval shipbuilding and equipment sectors. *(OCCAR)*

CONCLUSION

The completion and entry into service of the *Carlo Bergamini* and *Virginio Fasan* represents a major achievement for the Italian naval shipbuilding sector. The alliance of Finmeccanica and Fincantieri has proved capable of delivering a pair of powerful and sophisticated prototypes for an extended class that are the equals of any other similar European warship programme. The decision to loosen the design-straightjacket that marked the previous collaboration with France on the 'Horizon' class air-defence destroyers appears to have been particularly beneficial from an industrial perspective, allowing Italy greater flexibility to showcase the technological strengths of its extensive defence equipment manufacturers. It is noteworthy that one of *Carlo Bergamini*'s first operational missions was to participate in a five-month deployment to the Middle East and Africa headed by the carrier *Cavour* that had the promotion of Italian industry as one of its principal objectives.

Given their origins in a joint project, it is inevitable that comparisons will be made between the two Italian FREMM types and their French equivalents in the form of the *Aquitaine* class. The Italian decision to emphasise capability over quantity has certainly been advantageous in the light of subsequent reductions to the overall size of the French construction programme. It is quite possible that the *Marine Nationale* may ultimately end up with the same number of (or even fewer) front-line frigates in its surface fleet than the *Marina Militare* in spite of initial cost/capability trade-offs aimed at ensuring an extended production run.

To an extent, however, many contrasts between the two projects reflect varying national priorities. As already noted, some relate to industrial considerations but other factors are also at play. For example, France's decision to build the majority of its ships in anti-submarine configuration has been influenced by the need to have sufficient numbers to protect its Atlantic-based flotilla of strategic submarines from interception by enemy underwater forces. By contrast, Italy's acquisition of just four specialised anti-submarine frigates may reflect perceptions that the threat posed by a likely limited number of hostile submarines in the Mediterranean is less important. A particularly interesting development is the steady increase in the planned complement of the Italian ships compared with the relatively lean manning in *Aquitaine*, which has a core crew of just 108. Whilst the larger crew-size will provide the Italian ships with greater flexibility, it is worth considering that personnel costs are one of the highest overheads in any of the developed nations' fleets.

In any event, *Carlo Bergamini* and *Virginio Fasan*, along with their subsequent sisters, have clearly served to reinforce Italy's long-held reputation as a leader in naval innovation. They represent a potent addition to the modern *Marina Militare*.

Notes

1. The acronym FREMM also translates into the French *Frégates Européennes Multi-Missions*. The class has also sometimes being referred to as the *Rinascimento* or 'Renaissance' class in Italian circles. The French FREMM variant was described in the editor's 'Significant Ships: France's Aquitaine', *Seaforth World Naval Review 2013* (Barnsley, Seaforth Publishing, 2012), pp.90–107.

2. *Carlo Bergamini* is named after the Italian Second World War Commander-in-Chief of the Italian Battle Fleet, Admiral Carlo Bergamini (1888–1943). He lost his life when his flagship, the battleship *Roma*, was sunk by a German Fritz-X guided bomb at the time of the Italian Armistice on 9 September 1943. *Virginio Fasan* commemorates Chief Mechanic Virginio Fasan (1914–43), an Italian war hero and posthumous holder of the Gold Medal of Military Valour (*Medaglia d'oro al Valor Militare*). He died during the same series of events as Bergamini when the destroyer *Ugolino Vivaldi* was scuttled after engagements with German-controlled coastal batteries and aircraft.

3. Armaris was essentially merged into the restructured DCNS after Thales took a 25 per cent stake in the French shipbuilder in 2007.

4. The timing of this contract was dictated by an inter-governmental memorandum of understanding between the French and Italian defence ministries committing Italy to the order no later than May 2006. The memorandum was signed on 15 November 2005, allowing the French development and production contract to be signed the next day.

5. As always, it is difficult to assess accurate costs on large and lengthy contracts such as warship design and construction, where variables such as different accounting conventions and the impact of inflation over time hinder meaningful comparisons. However, published reports suggest that Italy was responsible for around €4.5bn of an estimated total programme cost of c. €11bn at current values when the FREMM programme was confirmed in 2005. This equated to cash payments spread out over the years to 2018 and beyond of around €5.7bn.

6. In addition to its Italian shipyards at Riva Trigoso and Muggiano, Fincantieri owns the US Marinette Marine Corporation, which is responsible for building the *Freedom* (LCS-1) variant of the Littoral Combat Ship. There are also partnerships with local companies for construction of military vessels in Brazil, India, Turkey and the UAE.

7. Reports in the Italian press, denied by the *Marina Militare*, suggested that weight distribution in the lead ship had resulted in her forward part being heavier than optimal and that the hull extension was also intended to enhance trim control. An important side effect of the extension was an increase in fuel stowage, improving operating radius by 500 nautical miles.

8. It is beyond this chapter's scope to explain the development of and differences between modern multi-function radars, which are also often known as phased arrays on the basis of the software-controlled scanning technology they commonly use. In summary, however, active phased arrays use individually energised transceivers to carry out their scans whilst first generation, passive arrays have elements that are energised from a single power source. Active arrays are regarded as being more flexible than passive arrays in carrying out their various functions. They are also less vulnerable to catastrophic failure than arrays reliant on a sole source of energy. A much more detailed description of this subject is found in Norman Friedman's 'Technological Review: Naval Multifunction Radars', *Seaforth World Naval Review 2011* (Barnsley, Seaforth Publishing, 2010), pp.154–62.

9. *Carlo Bergamini*'s 127mm gun was reportedly delivered in a semi-automatic loading configuration. This will be upgraded to allow fully automatic loading during a refit that is scheduled to coincide with expiry of the builder's warranty one year after delivery.

10. Modern sonar detection is another subject covered by Norman Friedman in a previous edition of *Seaforth World Naval Review*. Please refer to 'Technological Review: Developments in Modern Sonar', *Seaforth World Naval Review 2012* (Barnsley, Seaforth Publishing, 2011), pp.166–74.

11. The Italian Navy reportedly operates twenty-two AW-101 helicopters in anti-submarine (local designation SH-101A), utility (UH-101A) and AEW (EH-101A) versions. Forty-six NFH anti-submarine (SH-90A) and ten TTH utility (UH-90A) variants of the NH90 have been ordered and are starting to enter operational service.

12. This chapter has drawn heavily on contemporary government and industry brochures, as well as other press releases, to support its preparation. The additional sources listed below provided more structured information:

Emmanuel Huberdeau. 'FREMM: L'Italie aussi ...' *Marines & Forces Navales* – No 144 (Nantes, Marines Editions, 2013) pp.38–47.

Hartmut Manseck, 'Special Ship: The FREMM Frigates', *Naval Forces* – February 2009 (Bonn, Mönch Publishing Group, 2009).

Guy Toremans, 'Common FREMM work for neighbours' frigate project', *Jane's Navy International* – October 2008 (Coulsdon, IHS Jane's, 2008) pp.18–31.

The author would also like to acknowledge the very considerable help provided by the following industry and Italian Navy personnel in facilitating the chapter's production, most notably C.F. Marco Bagni and the officers and crew of *Virginio Fasan* in hosting the author's memorable visit to their ship on 1 April 2014:

- Capitano di Fregata Marco Bagni, Commanding Officer, Nave *Virginio Fasan*
- Tenente di Vascello Umberto Bulleri, Capo Componente Artiglieria, Nave *Virginio Fasan*
- Stefano Orlando, Production Director, Muggiano Shipyard, Fincantieri
- Barbara Gaione, Project Manager, Naval Vessels Business Unit, Fincantieri
- Cristiano Musella, Press Office, Corporate, Fincantieri
- Nick MacLeod-Ash, Head of Business & Capability Development, Finmeccanica UK Ltd

P61

3.2 SIGNIFICANT SHIPS

Author:
Conrad Waters

SAMUEL BECKETT CLASS OPVs

Ireland's New Warships help Sustain English Shipbuilding Skills

The imminent closure of BAE System's shipbuilding operations within Portsmouth Dockyard has been widely reported as marking the end of English naval construction. However, there is still a part of England's West Country where warship building remains very much alive. Deep in the heart of North Devon's countryside, Babcock Marine's Appledore shipyard is busy fabricating components for the *Queen Elizabeth* class carrier, *Prince of Wales*, and is close to launching *James Joyce*, the second *Samuel Beckett* class offshore patrol vessel (OPV) ordered for the Irish Naval Service. Derived from two similar *Róisín* (PV80) class vessels also built at Appledore around the turn of the Millennium, the new ships are the result of an ambitious Irish Naval Service recapitalisation programme which was curtailed by Ireland's recent financial crisis. They will provide an important boost to an increasingly ageing fleet. This chapter aims to review the importance of the *Samuel Beckett* (PV90) class both to Ireland's future naval operations and to the last English shipyard focused on new-build surface ships.[1]

Opposite: The new Irish PV90 type OPV *Samuel Beckett* pictured off Instow in North Devon on the morning of Good Friday 18 April 2014 whilst returning to Babcock Marine's Appledore shipyard after a second series of sea trials. She is designed to sustain long-distance patrols in the potentially harsh conditions encountered in the North Atlantic areas of Ireland's Exclusive Economic Zone (EEZ). *(Jim Lennie)*

CLASS ORIGINS

The considerable expansion in national maritime rights and responsibilities that have accompanied the current United Nations Convention on the Law of the Sea (UNCLOS) III regime – most notably the adoption of the concept of an Exclusive Economic Zone (EEZ) extending 200 miles from a nation's coasts – has resulted in many countries undertaking significant investments in naval patrol capabilities. Ireland has been no exception to this trend. The country's EEZ covers an area of 132,000 square nautical miles of ocean or around 16 per cent of total European Union waters; an area which could potentially double if claims to an extended area of the continental shelf are agreed. The European Union (EU) provided Ireland with financial support to modernise its fleet to meet these responsibilities from the 1970s onwards.[2] As a result, a series of OPVs of steadily increasing capabilities were constructed at the Verolme shipyard near Cork. Additional, second-hand coastal patrol vessels were subsequently purchased from the British Royal Navy.[3] The new ships that were acquired under these programmes provided a significant uplift in the Irish Naval Service's overall proficiency. However, experience revealed that many were ill-suited for the weather conditions likely to be encountered far out into the North Atlantic.

This situation was partly rectified in December 1997 when a contract was signed with Appledore Shipbuilders, then part of the Langham Industries group, for a new oceanic patrol vessel. The agreement included an option for an additional ship. The contract for the initial vessel – excluding armament – was reportedly valued at £17m (c. US$30m at then current exchange rates). Around 65 per cent of the total cost was paid for from EU funds. The new warship was based on a concept produced by Canada's Polar Design Associates (now STX Canada Marine) that was modified from the Mauritius Coastguard's *Vigilant*, an OPV built in Chile during the mid-1990s. The resultant PV80 design lacked the earlier ship's helicopter flight deck and hangar but provided the Irish Naval Service with a unit that was much better suited to North Atlantic operations. The lead ship's name *Róisín* – literally 'Rose' – is often portrayed as a symbol for Ireland.[4]

Displacing around 1,800 tons in full load condition and with an overall length of some 79m, the PV80 class has proved capable of deployment in all weather conditions up to the most extreme Sea State 9. Propulsion is provided by twin Wärtsilä 16 V26 diesels that permit a range in excess of 6,000 nautical miles at cruising speed of 15 knots, whilst a maximum of over 23 knots was achieved during trials. Endurance is set at twenty-one days. The principal armament of a 76mm/62 Oto Melara Compact, supplemented by two 20mm Rheinmetall cannon and lighter machine guns, reflects the ship's essentially constabulary nature and there is no place for the sophisticated command and control systems found on frontline combatants. However, an extensive communications outfit and complement of as many as three rigid inflatable boats (RIBs) provides the means to carry out effective policing of Ireland's territorial waters. A high degree of automation permits the ship's operation by a crew of just forty-four, including six officers. Full technical details are provided in Table 3.2.1.

Launched in the summer of 1999, *Róisín* was formally commissioned on 15 December of the same year. Her armament was, however, only fitted after delivery in Ireland, it being considered appropriate to make separate arrangements for the installation of the 'deck protection' system given the use of EU funding for a major part of the construction cost. The new ship proved to be a success in service,

Below: Two images of the first of the Irish Naval Service's PV80 type offshore patrol ships, *Róisín*, taken whilst she was on a routine maritime policing deployment off the Irish coast in August 2013. Her primary armament of a single 76mm Oto Melara Compact gun, supplemented by lighter weapons, reflects her essentially constabulary role. Constructed at Appledore between 1998 and 1999, she was formally commissioned on 15 December 1999. A sister, *Niamh*, followed two-years later. The overall success of the PV80 design is evidenced by the fact that it formed the basis of the succeeding PV90 *Samuel Beckett* class, also ordered from the same yard, which started to be delivered some fifteen years later. *(Irish Defence Forces)*

Table 3.2.1.

RÓISÍN (PV80 CLASS) PRINCIPAL PARTICULARS

Building Information:	
Laid Down:	June 1998
Launched:	9 September 1999[1]
Delivered:	15 December 1999
Builders:	Appledore Shipbuilders, Bideford, United Kingdom.
Dimensions:	
Displacement:	1,800 tons full load displacement.
Overall Hull Dimensions:	78.8m x 14.0m x 3.8m. Length between perpendiculars is 69.0m.
Equipment:	
Armament:	1 x 76mm Oto Melara Compact. 2 x 20mm Rheinmetall Rh-202 cannon. Machine guns.
Aircraft:	No aircraft facilities.
Principal Sensors:	Kelvin Hughes surface-search and navigation radars. Radamec 1500 optronic director for main gun.
Combat System:	No combat management system. Communications package includes HF/VHF and UHF radio links plus satellite communications.
Other:	2 x 6.5m RIBs and 1 x 5.4m RIBs for boarding operations.
Propulsion Systems:	
Machinery:	Diesel. 2 x Wärtsilä 16V 26 diesels each rated at 5MW. Provide a total of 23,400shp through two shafts. Bow thruster.
Speed:	Maximum speed is 23 knots. Range is 6,000 nautical miles at 15 knots.
Other Details:	
Complement:	The core crew is 44, including 6 officers. Accommodation is provided for 47 personnel.
Class:	Two PV80 class vessels have been delivered: *Róisín* (P51) and *Niamh* (P52). The latter was commissioned on 18 September 2001.

Notes:

1 Refers to date of formal naming ceremony.

Róisín (2013)
1:500 scale

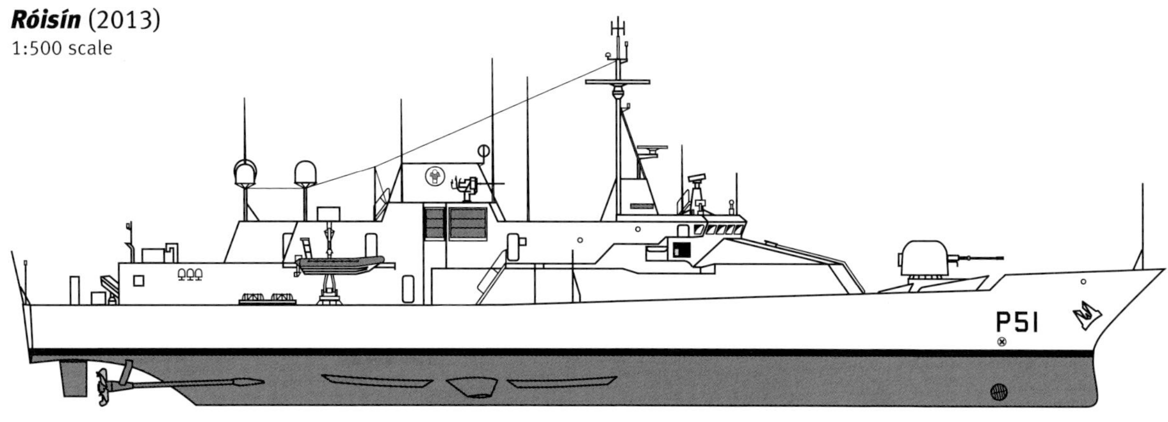

(Drawing © John Jordan, 2014)

Two further images of the Irish Naval Service's offshore patrol vessel *Róisín* taken in 2013. The new ship quickly proved to be a success in service after she was delivered in 1999, resulting in the exercise of an option to acquire a sister, *Niamh*, in 2000. This second ship replaced the prototype first-generation Irish patrol vessel, *Deirdre*. *(Irish Defence Forces)*

providing a significant boost to the navy's ability to conduct North Atlantic operations. Indeed, the Irish government's satisfaction with the vessel was confirmed when a contract to exercise the option for an additional ship was signed onboard *Róisín* on 6 April 2000. This also reflected the strategy agreed in Ireland's first-ever defence white paper, published in February 2000, which determined that the naval service would be built around a modern, eight-ship flotilla. Named *Niamh*, she was delivered in September 2001 and has subsequently represented her country both in an historic maiden deployment to Asia and an extended cruise of Latin American ports.

The arrival of *Niamh* allowed the retirement of the prototype Irish first-generation patrol vessel, *Deirdre,* at the end of her planned thirty-year service life. Attention then turned to replacing the three similar *Emer* class offshore patrol ships delivered from the late 1970s onwards and that were scheduled for decommissioning around the end of the decade. This was the period of the so-called 'Celtic Tiger' economy and the improved financial backdrop for Ireland's Department of Defence resulted in plans for an ambitious Naval Vessel Replacement Programme. This encompassed two types of new construction; additional OPVs to replace the existing ships and a class of much larger, extended patrol vessels. The latter were to be optimised for North Atlantic weather conditions and have an enhanced ability to transport personnel and equipment.[5] Initial government approval to proceed with the programme was received in July 2007. Subsequently, a tender was published on 24 August 2007 for the purchase of two OPVs, with an option for a third, as well as for one extended patrol vessel, with an option for a second.

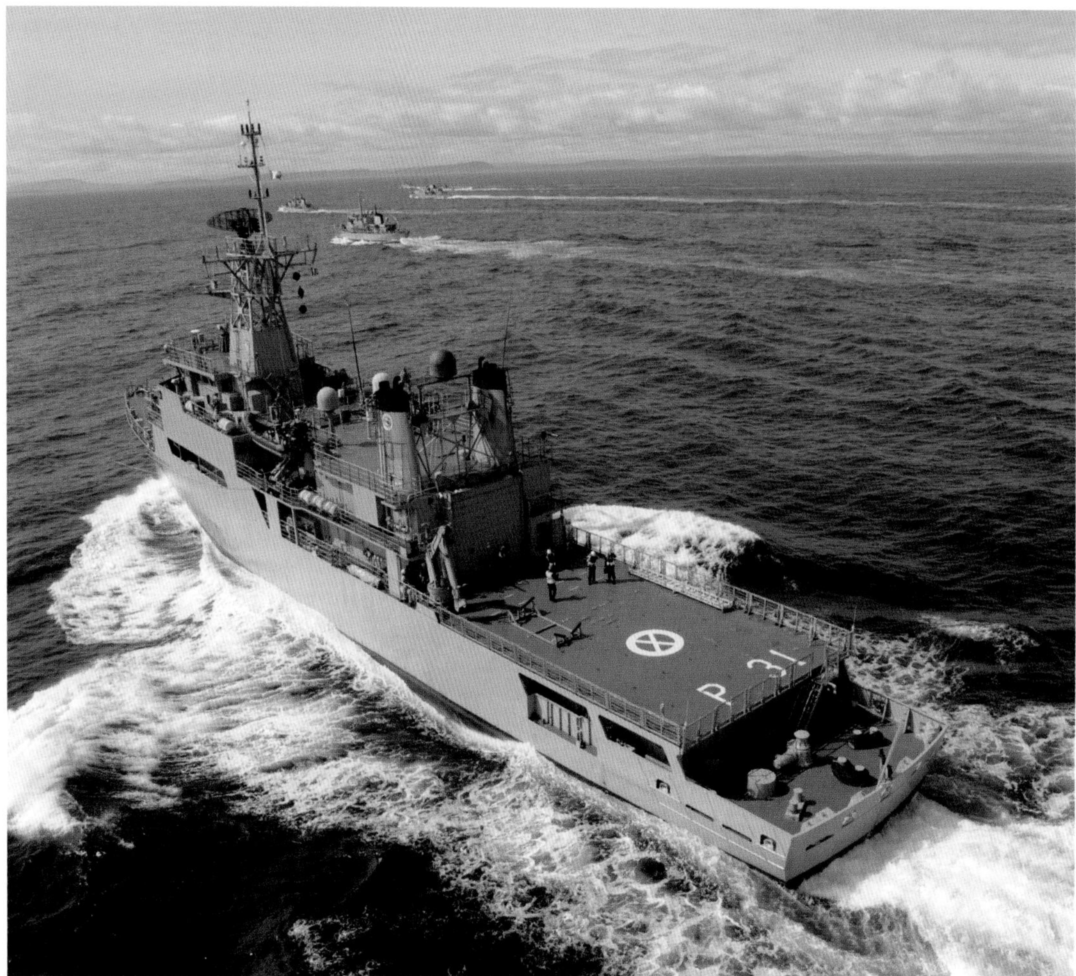

The Irish Naval Service's flagship, the helicopter patrol vessel *Eithne*, seen on exercises with other members of the fleet in June 2013. The desire to maintain a modern, eight-ship naval flotilla set out In Ireland's February 2000 defence white paper was the basis of fleet renewal plans that eventually resulted in orders for the *Samuel Beckett* class. *(Irish Defence Forces)*

Amongst the main contenders for the new contracts was the Appledore yard that had built the PV80 class but which had experienced a somewhat chequered history since *Niamh*'s delivery. A lack of work following completion of Royal Navy survey ship contracts had forced the facility into receivership in September 2003. It was subsequently rescued by DML – the firm contracted to run the Royal Navy's Devonport Dockyard in Plymouth – and a period fabricating hulls for luxury yachts followed. DML's own acquisition by Babcock International Group Plc in 2007 brought about a further change in strategy and the yard was earmarked to construct the bow sections and other constituent parts of the new *Queen Elizabeth* class aircraft carriers as part of the group's Babcock Marine business. The tender for the new Irish vessels – whilst employing fewer people overall than the *Queen Elizabeth* class work – provided an opportunity to return to the higher value-added area of new-build construction and integration. Although stiff competition was faced from yards in Europe and further afield, the final list of contenders was eventually narrowed down to Germany's ThyssenKrupp Marine Systems and Babcock Marine Appledore. Appledore was finally selected as preferred supplier of the new OPVs in early 2009.

By this time, however, Ireland had become embroiled in the global financial crisis that commenced in 2008 and significant reductions in public spending had become necessary. As such, it was no longer realistic to proceed with the original Naval Vessel Replacement Programme in its entirety. At the same time, the age of the older OPVs in the fleet – which had already exceeded their planned design lives – was becoming increasingly pressing. After protracted deliberations, approval for two new OPVs derived from the previous PV80 class was finally announced in July 2010. A formal contract with Babcock, which contained an option for a third ship, was concluded in October of the same year. The reported cost of the two firmly committed vessels was €99m (c.US$135m), with recognition of Ireland's

Right: An early computer-generated image of the PV90 design. As for the previous PV80 vessels, the concept and overall stage 1 design was provided by STX Marine Canada, with Babcock Marine being responsible for developing this into detailed production drawings. *(STX Canada Marine)*

stretched government finances being reflected in a payment schedule extending out as far as 2017. An additional €7.8m (c.US$10m) was earmarked to pay for the vessels armament, which was again acquired under separate contracts.

CONSTRUCTION AND DELIVERY

The new PV90 design that Babcock proposed to secure the contract was essentially an enlarged variant of the earlier PV80 *Róisín* class constructed a decade earlier, encompassing a range of modifications to meet the demands of the Irish tender requirement. As previously, STX Canada provided the concept and overall stage 1 design, with

Below: A photograph of the lead *Samuel Beckett* class OPV in Appledore's covered shipyard shortly prior to floating out. The 124m x 33m dry dock is capable of supporting the assembly of two ships simultaneously. *(Babcock Marine)*

Above: *Samuel Beckett* was floated out into the River Torridge on 3 November 2013. The tidal nature of the Torridge Estuary means that there are only limited windows each month when a ship can be 'launched'. *(Babcock Marine)*

Table 3.2.2.

SAMUEL BECKETT (PV90 CLASS) PRINCIPAL PARTICULARS

Building Information:	
Laid Down:	18 May 2012
Launched:	3 November 2013
Delivered:	28 April 2014
Builders:	Babcock International Group Plc's Marine & Technology Division at its Appledore yard, Bideford, United Kingdom.
Dimensions:	
Displacement:	2,250 tons full load displacement.
Overall Hull Dimensions:	89.5m x 14.0m x 3.8m. Length between perpendiculars is 81.0m.
Equipment:	
Armament:	1 x 76mm Oto Melara Compact. 2 x 20mm Rheinmetall Rh-202 cannon. Machine guns.
Principal Sensors:	Kelvin Hughes surface-search and navigation radars. GEIP fire-control director for main gun.
Combat System:	No combat management system. Communications package includes HF/VHF and UHF radio links plus satellite communications.
Other:	3 x 8m RIBs for boarding operations. Working deck can transport up to three containers with various equipment fits.
Propulsion Systems:	
Machinery:	CODOE. 2 x Wärtsilä 16V 26 diesels each rated at 5.4MW. Two PTI electric motors each rated at 0.35MW. Two shafts. Bow thruster.
Speed:	Maximum speed on main diesels is 23 knots. Range is 6,000 nautical miles at 15 knots.
Other Details:	
Complement:	The core crew is 44, including 6 officers. Accommodation is provided for 54 personnel.
Class:	Two PV90 class vessels were initially ordered: *Samuel Beckett* (P61) and *James Joyce* (P62). An option for a third vessel was exercised in June 2014.

Samuel Beckett (2014)
1:500 scale

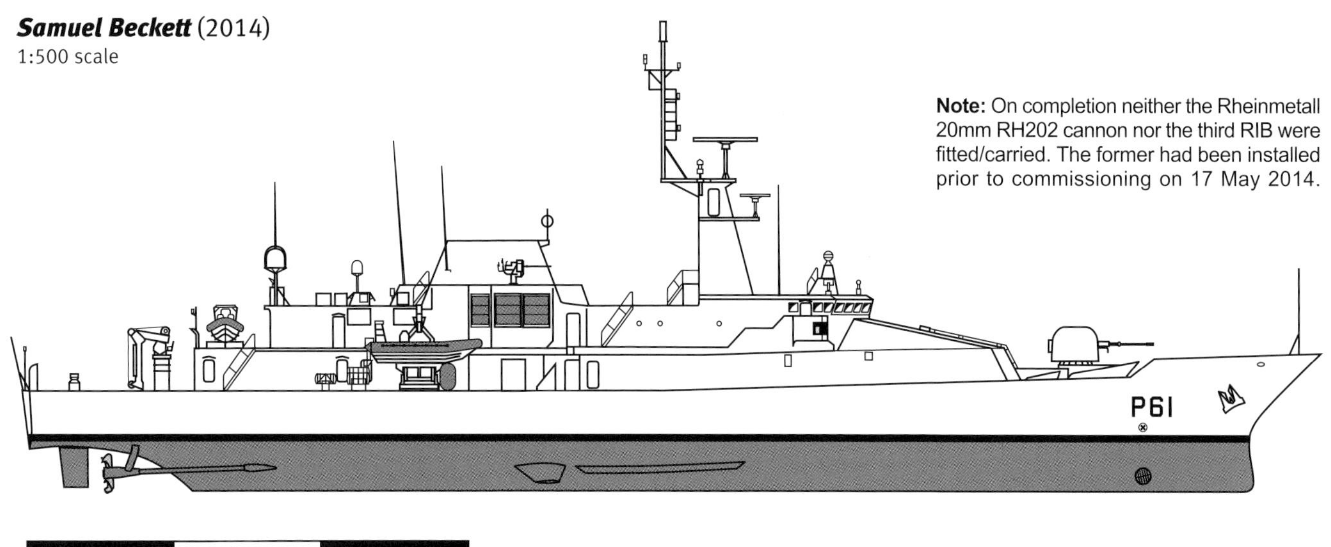

Note: On completion neither the Rheinmetall 20mm RH202 cannon nor the third RIB were fitted/carried. The former had been installed prior to commissioning on 17 May 2014.

(Drawing © John Jordan, 2014)

Appledore being responsible for stage 2 (system integration) and stage 3 (production drawing) outputs. Following completion of design work, the keel of the first vessel was laid at a traditional ceremony attended by Brian Spain, Director at the Irish Department of Defence on 18 May 2012. The significant delay between contract award and the formal start of construction reflected Babcock's desire to ensure full technical design maturity at the start of fabrication, thereby minimising the amount of re-work required and maximising cost efficiency.[6]

The new ship was laid down as programme number AS194 in Appledore's covered shipyard on the banks of the River Torridge. The huge construction hall was opened as part of a £4m green-field development spearheaded by visionary shipbuilder James Venus in 1970 and is regarded as the forefather of many similar facilities now in existence around the world.[7] It incorporates a 124m x 33m dry dock spanned by two 60-ton cranes that is capable of supporting the assembly of two vessels simultaneously. Construction progressed rapidly after fabrication commenced, aided by a 'capability/cost triangle' of co-operative working between the Irish Naval Service, Appledore and its suppliers that was regarded as crucial in ensuring completion in a timely and efficient manner. The ship was floated out at a low key ceremony on 3 November 2013, when the name *Samuel Beckett* was officially assigned. The choice of name marked a departure from the traditional Irish Naval Service practice of naming its warships after prominent women from Irish history and mythology. The change was

Two views of *Samuel Beckett* alongside Babcock Marine's fitting-out wharf on Monday 28 April 2014. This was the day of her final departure from the shipyard but last-minute alterations were still being carried out. Whilst the ship grounds at low tide, the propellers and rudders are protected by excavation of a pit in the appropriate area of the berth. *(Conrad Waters)*

explained on the basis that association with a world-renowned Irish literary figure would '... facilitate greater recognition when the ship is operation in the international maritime domain'.[8]

The tidal nature of the Torridge Estuary dictated the timing of *Samuel Beckett*'s launch, there being only limited windows each month when a ship can be floated out of the ship hall and moored at the neighbouring tidal fitting-out berth. Similarly, the bar at the mouth of the Torridge Estuary has an impact on the timing of sea trials, which were originally scheduled to commence towards the end of January 2014. Delays brought about by the extreme weather conditions experienced in the south of England from Christmas 2013 onwards and a decision to modify the ship's propulsion system to improve fuel efficiency resulted in an agreement to slightly postpone these plans. As a result, it was not until early in the morning of Saturday 29 March 2014 that *Samuel Beckett* passed out of the estuary and into the Bristol Channel for the first time.

Trials were conducted by a mixed shipyard and Irish Naval Service crew under the supervision of local Merchant Navy Captain Jerry Waller.[9] Two separate series of trials were carried out from 29 March to 3 April and from 14 April to 18 April 2014, during which all aspects of the ship's propulsion system and other equipment were tested. News reports suggest that the ship handled well up to her maximum design speed of 23 knots and even achieved 14 knots speed during an hour-long, stern first proving trial. The ship also demonstrated an overall endurance capability of between 6,000 and

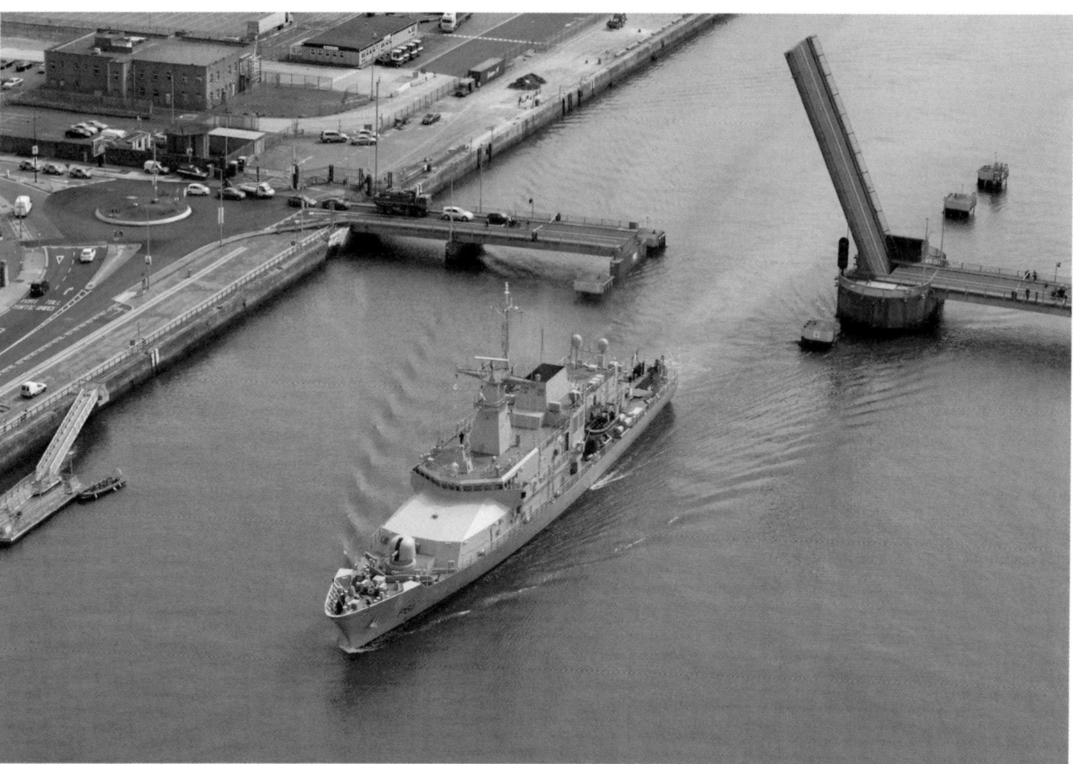

Samuel Beckett visited the Irish capital, Dublin, for her commissioning ceremony in May 2014. These images show her sailing up the River Liffey on 16 May, the day before she was commissioned. Her arrival marks something of a turnaround for the fortunes of a navy that has been struggling under the burden of Irish austerity. *(Irish Defence Forces)*

7,000 nautical miles, as well as a loiter capability of over 8 knots – in excess of the designed requirement of 6 knots – on electric propulsion.

Samuel Beckett finally departed the Torridge Estuary under the Irish flag in the early evening of Monday 28 April. She was waved off by a large crowd of onlookers gathered on Appledore Quay. She subsequently sailed for Cork Harbour the following evening after transferring Babcock technicians to an accompanying tender, arriving at Ireland's only naval base at Haulbowline Island on the morning of Wednesday 30 April. Following further familiarisation work up and the installation of secondary armament, *Samuel Beckett* was formally named by Mrs Caroline Murphy, a niece of the ship's namesake, beside the Samuel Beckett Bridge in the centre of Dublin on Saturday 17 May 2014. A commissioning ceremony, attended by a host of dignitaries and led by Mr Enda Kenny TD, the Irish Prime Minister (An Taoiseach) and Minister for Defence, followed immediately after. The new ship's commanding officer, Commander Ken Minehane, accepted the commissioning warrant.

Meanwhile, the float-out of *Samuel Beckett* allowed an immediate start to assembly of her sister ship, *James Joyce*, which took her place in Babcock's construction hall. Work on this second ship is already well-advanced, with launch expected in the autumn of 2014 prior to delivery in the early months of 2015. On 9 June 2014, the Irish Department of Defence also confirmed an €54m order for an as of yet unnamed third member of the class, which will be delivered in 2016.

OVERALL DESIGN

As previously indicated, the PV90 design is very similar in overall concept to the previous PV80 *Róisín* type. The most apparent external difference is an extension of the hull by some 11m to 90m – essentially by insertion of a 'plug' to the original design just abaft the bridge – to allow more effective operations in adverse weather far out into the North Atlantic Ocean. This has been associated with some modifications to the superstructure that have allowed an enlargement of the working area aft. The new ship's beam is unchanged from the previous class but there has been a slight increase in draft compared with the earlier vessels.

The general design comprises a five-deck monohull fabricated from fifty-four constituent blocks and displacement is a little over 2,200 tons in full load condition. The lowest deck, Deck 3, is largely taken up with the machinery spaces (amidships) and storage spaces (forwards and aft), with the machinery control room, workshop and access spaces also occupying much of the middle of Deck 2. The forward section of Deck 2 comprises crew accommodation, whilst the mess decks and galley are located further aft. Deck 1 – the weather deck – has a similar overall arrangement with respect to officers' accommodation, with the bridge, chart room and senior officers' cabins found on Deck 01. Deck 02 provides the foundation for the mast – larger and more substantial than in the PV80 type – and navigation equipment.

In common with many other modern patrol vessels, the PV90 design is built largely to commercial specifications, with construction being in line with the requirements of Lloyd's Register for

Special Service Craft.[10] The ship is designed to survive damage to two adjacent compartments but, in contrast to front-line warships, is not intended to resist shock or other action damage. The main areas of military overlay are related to the mounting and magazine arrangements for the armament, as well as installation of a military-standard communications system. Nominal design life is over twenty-five years.

ENGINEERING ASPECTS

The *Samuel Beckett* class ships are configured to have broadly similar performance characteristics to their earlier half-sisters. Their maximum speed of 23 knots and endurance of 6,000 nautical miles at 15 knots cruising speed is equivalent to that of the previous vessels. The main propulsion system comprises two Wärtsilä 16 V26 diesel engines, each rated at 5.4MW. These are installed in separate, autonomous compartments for survivability considerations. Each main engine is linked to one of two shafts that are fitted with five-bladed, controllable-pitch propellers by twin reduction gearboxes. The engine rooms are fully automated and the overall propulsion arrangement is controlled by a Wärtsilä Lipstronic engine control system.

The two main diesels are supplemented by three 630kW generators that produce electricity for hotel services. In a departure from the earlier design, these are also capable of providing low speed electric propulsion of up to eight knots through a PTI (power take in) arrangement. This involves the use of two 350kW electric motors that are connected to the gearboxes. This CODOE (combined diesel or electric) design allows a considerable reduction in fuel consumption – and therefore endurance – when the ships are engaged in routine operations, for example when loitering for an extended period in a given patrol area. Low speed manoeuvrability is assisted by a 450kW bow thruster and by twin rudders with independent movement. There is also a supplementary emergency generator rated at 300kW.

Considerable attention has been paid to ensuring crew safety and comfort in often hostile sea conditions, with a number of revisions benefitting from the experience gained in operating previous classes. For example, the fin stabilisers found in the PV80 class have been supplemented by an anti-heeling tank that helps to reduce roll at speeds below those where the stabilisers are ineffective. As well as

Irish Offshore Patrol Vessel

babcock

trusted to deliver™

Unit Breakdown

CENTRELINE PROFILE

A centreline profile of the PV90 design showing the constituent block assembly. The five deck hull is constructed from a total of fifty-four constituent blocks which are fabricated from sub-assemblies in the ship hall prior to integration in the dry dock. *(Babcock Marine)*

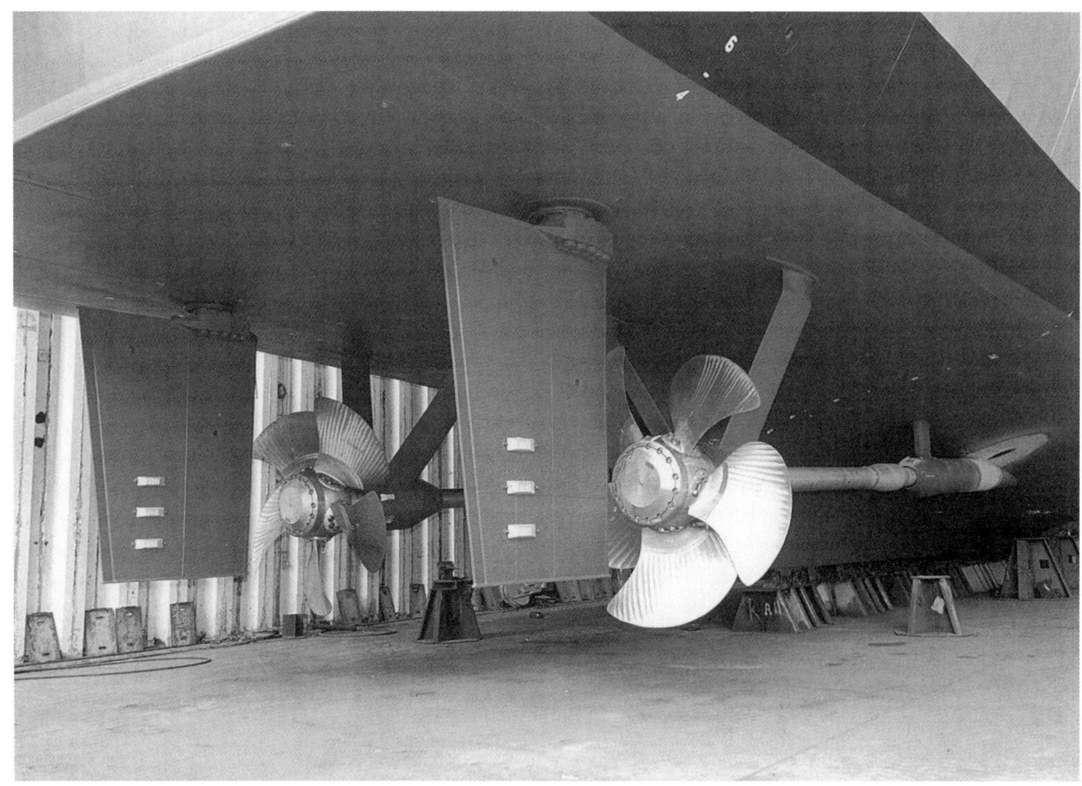

A detailed view of *Samuel Beckett's* five-bladed, controllable-pitch propellers and twin independent rudders. Combined with the bow thruster, the arrangement provides excellent manoeuvrability. *(Babcock Marine)*

Samuel Beckett departed Appledore under the Irish flag in the early evening of 28 April 2014 under the gaze of crowds of onlookers lining Appledore quay. These image show her Italian-manufactured 76mm/62 Oto Melara main gun – mounted well forward – and extensive communications outfit – including satellite communications dishes aft – to good effect. *(Conrad Waters)*

improving habitability, this assists small boat operations. Another new development is the fitting of a dynamic positioning system that assists the recovery of both manned and remotely operated craft and can also facilitate hydrographic work.

COMBAT AND COMMUNICATIONS SYSTEMS

In common with all previous Irish Naval Service patrol vessels, the *Samuel Beckett* class is not intended to be used for front-line warfighting operations. The armament outfit therefore mirrors that fitted to the *Róisín* class. It comprises an Italian-manufactured 76mm/62 Oto Melara main gun installed forward of the bridge and two 20mm Rheinmetall cannon located port and starboard abreast of the stack. These can be supplemented by heavy or light machine guns as required, whilst boarding crews can be equipped with personal weapons. The main gun can fire up to eighty-five 12.3kg shells a minute and has a maximum range of 18.4km. An electro-optical director is fitted for fire-control purposes. The lighter Rheinmetall weapon has rate of fire of 2,000 rounds a minute but its lighter 134g shells have a much shorter maximum range of around 2km. The armament is more than sufficient to deal with all constabulary tasking the class might be required to fulfil. In practice, the navy has rarely been required to use its weapons in anger.

The Irish Naval Service's primary role of protecting fishery and other resources in the EEZ does, however, require frequent boarding operations. *Samuel Beckett* and her forthcoming sisters are well fitted-out for this task. Both ships can be equipped with up to three fast-pursuit rigid inflatable boats (RIBs). Two of these are deployed from single-point davits port and starboard whilst a third can be located in a cradle aft. Supplied by Liverpool-based manufacturer MST–Marine Specialised Technology Ltd, the 8m-long RIBs are each capable of transporting ten personnel at speeds of more than 30 knots. They can be launched in up to Sea State 4 conditions whilst the host vessel is travelling at 10 knots.

The other indispensable requirement for effective performance of constabulary duties is installation of a comprehensive suite of communications equipment. The *Samuel Beckett* class's external communications system includes a full range of HF, VHF and UHF band radio links, as well as satellite connec-

tivity. The ships' internal communications network is provided by Andover-based Trilogy Communications, whilst overall supply integration of the complete navigation and communications package was assigned to Southampton-based marine systems integrator Marine Electronic Systems. The surface search and navigation radars are supplied by long-established manufacturer Kelvin Hughes.

The new ships have an extended working deck aft that provides space for up to three TEU (twenty-foot equivalent unit) containers. This large space can also be used as an operating platform and is serviced by a 4-ton deck crane that has a radius of 9.6m. The arrangement makes it easier for the patrol vessels to be appropriately configured to support specific missions; for example through ship-

Above left and right: The constabulary role assigned to *Samuel Beckett* means that an ability to effectively monitor and intercept an array of potential offenders ranging from illegal fishermen to terrorist groups is more important than pure warfighting capabilities. This series of images shows the ship's 76mm gun; one of the high-speed 8m RIBs carried to assist boarding operations; and the aft working deck – equipped with a 4-ton crane – that can handle mission-specific containers. *(Conrad Waters)*

ping of a decompression chamber to allow diving operations or to accommodate equipment for underwater search and recovery.

No provision is made for helicopter operations from the *Samuel Beckett* class, reflecting previous experience of the difficulties of operating a manned aircraft from a small ship in North Atlantic conditions gained from the previously helicopter-equipped *Eithne*. However, future use of other technologies is contemplated. For example, the Irish Maritime Energy and Research Cluster (IMERC) has been working on an initiative known as 'Sky Sails' under which a kite is used both to extend sensor range and supplement a ship's propulsion. Scheduled for initial 'at sea' testing during 2014, the system could equip the *Samuel Beckett* class if experiments prove the arrangement is feasible.

OTHER KEY DESIGN FEATURES

Lean manning arrangements remain a critical factor for a service with less than 1,000 trained personnel. Consequently, in spite of its increased size, the *Samuel Beckett* class is designed for operation by the same core crew of forty-four as the previous PV80 type. However, sufficient accommodation is provided for up to fifty-four people, with the additional berths used for crew under training or specialist personnel. Senior officers are provided with single cabins, with more junior crew members in two-berthed accommodation. Trainees normally have to share their cabins with up to three additional personnel. The ships were outfitted by Southampton-based Moss Marine under a £4.5m contract that covered both hard and soft furnishings. A mock-up of a cabin module was constructed as part of the contract to ensure an optimal arrangement. The firm had previously worked with BAE Systems on the *Al Shamikh* class corvettes for the Royal Navy of Oman and the Brazilian *Port of Spain/Amazonas* class.

Reflecting the extent of their North Atlantic patrol area, the class is designed to sustain autonomous operations for not less than twenty-one days, with fresh water and solid stores provision calculated on this basis.

Three views of *Samuel Beckett* pictured whilst on trials in the Bristol Channel in the spring of 2014. She represents the first entire ship built at Appledore since the British Royal Navy survey ship *Enterprise* and therefore demonstrates its renewed ability to construct high quality, sophisticated vessels. *(Babcock Marine)*

CONCLUSION

The successful delivery of *Samuel Beckett* marks a significant moment for the Irish Naval Service, for North Devon, and for the wider British maritime industry. At the same time, further challenges need to be overcome if this success is to be consolidated.

From an Irish Naval Service perspective, the new ship's arrival marks something of a turnaround for the fortunes of a navy that has been struggling under the burden of maintaining an increasing obsolescent fleet during a period of financial austerity. *Emer*, the ship that *Samuel Beckett* is intended to replace, was decommissioned in September 2013 and her two sister-ships are also fast reaching the end of their service lives. The three PV90 type vessels are therefore essential to maintain the eight-ship fleet set out in the 2000 white paper on defence. Moreover, the enhanced capability provided by *Samuel Beckett* and her sisters will provide a much greater capacity to patrol the extremities of Ireland's North Atlantic EEZ in a safe and efficient manner. However, further replacement orders are urgently required if the service is to build on the qualitative enhancement that the new ships bring. The forthcoming new Irish white paper on defence, due to be published before the end of 2014, will be crucial in this regard.

Turning to the programme's impact on North Devon, it is clear that the steady resurrection of the Appledore yard under the leadership of Shipbuilding Director Andy Hamilton from the financial collapse that occurred more than a decade ago has been given a major boost by *Samuel Beckett*'s completion. She represents the first entire ship built at Appledore since the Royal Navy survey ship *Enterprise* (launched in 2002) and therefore demonstrates its renewed ability to construct high quality, sophisticated vessels. Babcock Marine is significant in offering employment to a direct workforce of around seventy staff and 280 production workers, together with around 100 sub-contractors, in an area where the opportunities for skilled work are minimal.[11] The shipyard has plans to upgrade its facilities to achieve further efficiencies but this is, inevitably, contingent on securing additional orders.

Finally, Babcock Marine's ability both to win the tender for Ireland's new warships and to execute the contract in an efficient manner provides tangible evidence that the British maritime industry can still compete in international markets. The company's success therefore offers something of an antidote to the commonly-held view that indigenous shipbuilding is in an inevitable phase of terminal decline. However, there still remains a danger that the established view will become a self-fulfilling prophecy. As such, it can only be hoped that the Appledore shipyard will continue to confound the doomsayers in the years ahead.

Notes

1. Other English yards, such as Cammell Laird on Merseyside, have been involved in occasional construction projects to supplement their mainstream diet of refit and repair work. In addition, there are other facilities devoted to specialist fabrication, such as luxury yachts. However, Appledore is now unique in England in concentrating on the new-build construction of sea-going vessels.

2. A history of the recent development of the Irish Naval Service is outside the scope of this chapter. For further reading see Richard Beedall's 'The Irish Naval Service: A Model Constabulary Navy', *Seaforth World Naval Review 2013* (Barnsley, Seaforth Publishing, 2012), pp.69–78. In addition, Aidan McIvor's *A History of the Irish Naval Service* (Dublin, Irish Academic Press, 1994) provides a more historical account.

3. Domestic Irish Naval Service construction commenced in 1971 when the OPV *Deirdre* was laid down. Commissioned in 1972, she was the prototype for three modified P21 *Emer* class vessels that entered service in the 1978–80 timeframe. They were followed by the larger P31 class *Eithne* in 1984; the only helicopter-capable ship in the Irish Naval Service to date. Plans for additional members of the class were never progressed and the Verolme yard closed for lack of orders after *Eithne* was completed.

4. It should be noted, however, that there was also a real Róisín Dubh, a sixteenth-century Irish noblewoman who was one of the daughters of Red Hugh O'Neill, Earl of Tyrone. She is immortalised in the romantic poem of the same name.

5. Ireland has been an active participant in international peace-keeping and humanitarian operations under the auspices of the UN. Warships from the Irish Naval Service have occasionally been used to supply and support these missions. The specification of the planned extended patrol vessel was drawn up with this particular requirement in mind.

6. Appledore estimated that 61 per cent of an OPV's cost is accounted for by materials and sub-contracted services and a further 32 per cent by production labour. This contrasts with just 3 per cent for project management and 4 per cent for engineering services. As such, it makes sense to devote more effort to ensuring efficient engineering and design to minimise cost escalation in these more significant areas. It is also worth noting that the cost of design changes increases exponentially as construction progresses from initial fabrication through assembly until after the ship is afloat. Some studies have suggested it is over twenty times more costly to make changes post launch compared with the initial fabrication stage.

7. Born, educated and apprenticed in shipbuilding at Newcastle upon Tyne, James Venus OBE (1920–92) became chairman and managing director of both Appledore Shipbuilders and the larger Sunderland Shipbuilding Group, rebuilding both groups' yards along modern lines. His obituary can be found in the Wednesday 2 September 1992 edition of *The Independent* (London, Independent Print Ltd, 1992).

8. The explanation was provided in a commemorative booklet produced by Babcock Marine for the Irish Naval Service marking the *Float Up of LÉ Samuel Beckett* on 3 November 2013.

9. Information on the *Samuel Beckett*'s trials programme can be found on the Bideford Harbour pages of Torridge District Council's website at http://www.torridge.gov.uk. They are maintained by Captain Roger Hoad, the local Pilot and Harbour Master.

10. More specifically, the class has been designed and tested to Lloyd's Register for Special Service Craft with notations +100A1, +LMC UMS PSMR DP (CM), IWS Patrol Mono and G6 (unlimited range).

11. The importance of industrial facilities such as Babcock Marine on the local social fabric should not be underestimated. For example, Appledore's local fire engine service is based at the yard during the day as its volunteer crew work at the shipbuilder. Similarly, the yard provides several crew members for the local RNLI lifeboat, *Mollie Hunt*, and undertakes regular dockings of the boat at no cost.

12. The author would like to acknowledge with gratitude the assistance of Andy Hamilton, Shipbuilding Director and Gerald Lee, Sub-Contracts Manager, at Babcock International Group's Appledore Shipyard for providing an extensive briefing on and tour of the facilities used to construct the *Samuel Beckett* class vessels and providing much additional information.

P961

3.3 SIGNIFICANT SHIPS

Author:
Guy Toremans

SKJOLD CLASS FACs

Norway's Fighting Cats: Stealth reigns Supreme

With the re-delivery of the HNoMS *Skjold* on 29 April 2013, the Norwegian Navy finally has all six of its *Skjold* class fast attack craft in service.[1] The Royal Norwegian Navy (RNN) has a long history of operating fast patrol boats, going back as far as 1873 when the steam-powered, Thornycroft-built *Rap* was commissioned into the fleet, placing the RNN in the forefront of fast patrol boat operators. Ever since then, fast patrol boats have been an integral element in Norway's defence structure and the RNN has kept on refining the design of these vessels over time. However, they have never previously adopted a design as radical in so many ways as these latest ships.

GENESIS: EVOLUTION OF THE *SKJOLD* CLASS

The origins of the *Skjold* programme date back to the mid-1980s, when the Norwegian Defence Research Establishment (NDRE) began to study a replacement for the *Storm* and, ultimately, the *Hauk* class fast attack craft, which were, respectively, commissioned into the fleet between 1965 and 1967 and between 1977 and 1980. The emerging programme for the new units, which ultimately came to be known as Project SMP 6081, required them to be survivable, stable weapons platforms capable of operating at speeds of 45 knots in Sea State 3, to have a range of at least 800 nautical miles at 40 knots, and to be able to operate outside coastal waters in a variety of scenarios, including NATO operations. In addition, the project office undertook a wide range of studies designed to reduce the vessels' radar cross-section (RCS) and infrared (IR) signatures.

The Norwegian Navy Material Command (NAVMATCOM), together with Commander Sea Training (COMSEATRAIN), ran several analyses to balance the operational requirements with the likely available budget.[2] For the platform system, no fewer than ten different platforms concepts were initially taken into consideration. Having examined this wide range of replacement options, the study was subsequently narrowed down to a shortlist of three concepts, viz. a conventional mono-hull, a catamaran-hull and an air-cushion catamaran/surface effect ship (ACC/SES).

The studies carried out by NAVMATCOM indicated that shock levels experienced by the SES were only one-third of that of a mono-hull.[3] Similarly, the maximum displacement of structural members when subjected to shock was around half that of a comparable mono-hull. These advantages were a direct result of the SES's elevated position in the water and its low draught. In spite of this, there was some hesitation in adopting the new hull form and a SES passenger vessel was even hired to uncover operational limitations of an SES when compared with the mono-hulled *Storm* and *Hauk* classes. Additional confidence was provided through experience gained designing and constructing the *Oksøy* and *Alta* class minehunters and minesweepers, which demonstrated the stability and large deck area inherent in the SES-catamaran hull form. Ultimately, the combination of improved resistance to shock and survivability, superior sea-keeping, greater internal volume and high speed-to-power ratio that the ACC/SES provided proved decisive in its selection.

By 1994 all staff requirements were defined and, in July 1995, a Request for Proposals [RfP] was issued. Three yards ultimately submitted bids: the Norwegian shipyards Umoe Mandal and Mjellem & Karlsen and Lürssen Werft in Germany.[4] On 30 August 1996 Umoe Mandal was awarded a c. US$36m equivalent contract to build a pre-production unit, to be named *Skjold.* Following approval of construction specifications by NAVMATCOM, construction commenced in 1997. The prototype vessel was launched on 22 September 1998 and turned over to the Royal Norwegian Navy on 17 April 1999. At this stage weapons, sensors and combat management systems were not installed and 46 tons of sand ballast was subsequently provided to simulate their weight.

The pre-series vessel underwent comprehensive testing with focus on speed, sea-keeping, EMI/EMC, signatures and functionality, as well as

Opposite: The first production-series *Skjold* class fast attack craft, *Storm*, pictured off Bergen during pre-delivery gunnery trials in September 2008. A revolutionary surface effect ship, she combines the flexible air cushion of a hovercraft with the rigid twin hulls of a catamaran and is able to achieve speeds of up to 60 knots. Optimised for anti-surface warfare in littoral waters, she is capable of contributing to a much wider range in operations in both coastal and open seas. *(Torgeir Haugaard/ Norwegian Armed Forces)*

Two views of the prototype *Skjold* class fast attack craft/corvette taken during trials in May 1999, only a month after her initial delivery to the RNN. At this stage, her armament and combat management system had not been fitted. The success of her four-year trials programme resulted in an order for a five further vessels towards the end of 2003. The contract also made provision for *Skjold* herself to be upgraded to production standard. *(Torgeir Haugaard/Norwegian Armed Forces)*

the operational reliability tests – mainly in northern Norway during autumn and winter. There was also a year-long deployment to North America on loan to the US Navy. This initial trials programme had an important bearing on whether to proceed with the series production order and was to result in several changes to the production specification.

In spite of emerging doubts about the value of the programme in the post-Cold War naval environment, a new defence white paper approved by the Norwegian parliament in June 2001 envisaged the construction of five additional units. This decision was subsequently confirmed in October 2003 once terms and pricing for the programme had been provisionally agreed. Subsequently, on 28 November that year, the Material Investment Branch of Norway's Defence Logistics Organisation (NDLO) awarded the Skjold Prime Consortium (SPC) a NOK3.7bn (c.US$550m) contract to build and equip the five new ships, whilst upgrading the prototype to the same standard. The SPC was an industrial alliance that brought together three partner companies to share responsibility for the delivery of the *Skjold* platform. It comprised Umoe Mandal (responsible for detailed design, systems integration, construction, testing and integrated logistic support); the Armaris joint venture between France's DCN and Thales, now merged into DCNS (combat system design authority); and Kongsberg Defence & Aerospace (responsible for delivering and integrating the combat system in cooperation with Armaris). Umoe Mandal's share of the programme consisted of about NOK2bn; Armaris received approximately NOK1bn; whilst Kongsberg Defence & Aerospace's (KDA's) share was valued at NOK750m. The construction of the first of the five standard production units, *Storm*, began in October 2005

In spite of further challenges to the class's value and a number of project delays, commissioning of the new ships in operational configuration commenced in September 2010, with the re-delivery of the upgraded *Skjold* in April 2013 completing the programme. All units will achieve full operational capability by early 2015. It is the RNN's plan to have four units available at any time, while two undergo maintenance and further upgrades.

DESIGN DETAILS: STRUCTURE AND STEALTH

The most distinctive feature of the *Skjold* class design is undoubtedly its innovative twin ACC hull

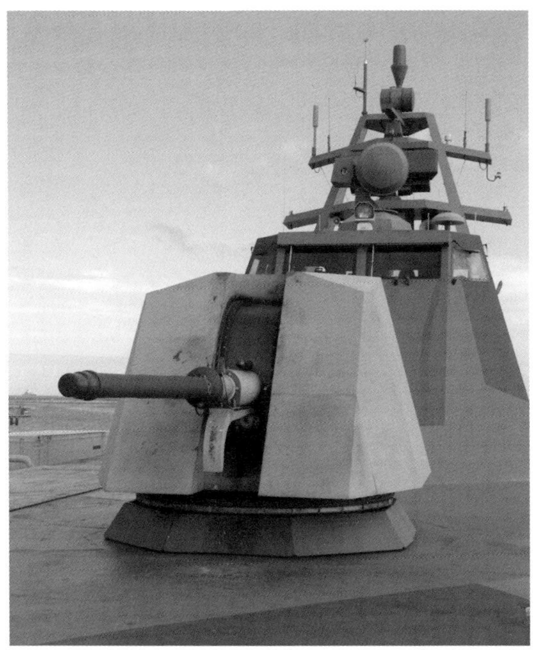

A forward view of *Skudd* in September 2011 showing the stealth mounting for the Oto Melara 76mm gun and the 9.6m high mast structure, which is constructed entirely from carbon fibre. *(Guy Toremans)*

form. The 47.5m long, catamaran SES-hull is made of a fibre reinforced plastic (FRP) sandwich construction, which reduces the overall weight of the ship. This material is capable of absorbing high levels of impact and, as such, minimising the extent of damage to the ship's structure, as well as the cost of repairs. FRP also gives the ship so much buoyancy in itself that it can hardly sink. Moreover, its use enables most types of damage – from a surface scratch in the laminate through to major damage to a panel and its underlying structure – to be repaired quickly by using specially developed techniques. Another noteworthy feature is the provision of under-deck heating to prevent build-up of ice on the deck. Umoe Mandal was licensed to use the Seemann Composites Resin Infusion Moulding Process (SCRIMP) technique in constructing the class. This consists of a resin transfer moulding process that uses a vacuum to pull liquid resin into a dry lay-up. It is used for making very high quality, repeatable composite parts with almost zero VOC (volatile organic compound) emissions.

Stealth was a major preoccupation within the project office since the programme's inception. The class has been designed to minimise all observable signatures. Controlled shaping of the ship above the waterline is evident in the absence of 90° corners and the inclination of the hull and superstructure at a small angle in order to deflect radar. The superstructure exhibits low and sleek characteristics, topside equipment is arranged to maximise concealment and there is extensive use of anechoic coatings. The air intakes to the gas turbines and lift fans are covered with a radar-absorbing mesh, the windows on the bridge incorporate a radar-absorbing material and all hatches are flush in order to reduce their RCS signatures. A similar consideration mandated the stealthy cupola provided for the Oto Melara 76mm/62 gun. The 9.6m-high main mast is constructed entirely from carbon fibre and the material is also used in beam flanges and frames.

Infra-red (IR) signature is kept to a minimum by the use of seawater cooling for the gas turbine exhausts; the water outlets are ducted into the air cushion between the two hulls and through the stern of the vessel. Similarly, the acoustic signature is decreased thanks to the fibre-reinforced plastic materials, which provide better structure-borne noise damping qualities. In addition, the water-jet propulsion generates lower hydro-acoustic signatures. The material composition in the wetted area of the twin hulls has been modified in order to produce a 'smoother' finish thus reducing hydrodynamic friction.

Operating in the littoral environment of fjords and archipelagos has also helped the Nordic navies become leaders in the application of present-day visual stealth and protective colourings. The *Skjolds* feature a camouflage scheme which is the result of the thorough study and testing of the hues and tones found in the Norwegian topography; scientists actually travelled around various areas and measured the colourings at different times of the year. The resulting paint scheme, which also incorporates high infra-red absorption properties, greatly reduces the ships' electro-optical and visual signatures. As such, the *Skjolds* are hard to detect when lurking close to the coastline and are able to engage hostile forces from close range while remaining undetected. Another important asset is the class's capability to access very shallow waters denied to other vessels. With about 75 per cent of their displacement being 'carried on air', a shallow draught of as little as 0.9m allows the ships to operate safely in shallow coastal waters whilst still maintaining excellent sea-keeping qualities.

PLATFORM MANAGEMENT SYSTEMS

The ships have been equipped with an advanced L-3 MAPPS integrated platform management system (IMPS) featuring multi-functional consoles with high-resolution colour monitors that display ergonomically designed graphical pages of the ship's machinery and systems. This highly automated system incorporates an integrated bridge system (IBS) supplied by Kongsberg; a digital gas turbine control system; an integrated battle damage-control system (IBDCS); an equipment monitoring system (inclusive of a vibration monitoring capability); and a digital CCTV system. The overall system's modular design, which combines widely distributed but intelligent and interconnected electronics, enables the crew to control, monitor and operate all platform machinery, electrical and emergency systems from several shipboard locations

The cockpit-style bridge, featuring a Kongsberg Maritime IBS, provides the pilot and navigator with full control over the bridge display consoles. It incorporates a K-Bridge autopilot, a voyage data recorder, a Kongsberg Seatex AIS 100 automatic identification system, an AGI electromagnetic log, a meteorological station, a Sagem 40 inertial navigation system, a Sperry Marine NAVIGAT 2100/SR 2100 fibre-optic gyro compass, a Trimble Navstar GPS/PPS receiver, JRC NAVTEX, a Skipper GDS 101 echo sounder and a Brudeseth optical bearing device. The bridge consoles display chart data from an Electronic Chart Display & Information System

The *Skjold* class are equipped with primary and secondary machinery control rooms, which also act as the ship's damage control stations. They provide access to the highly automated L-3 MAPPS integrated platform management system, which features a number of multi-function consoles and high-resolution colour screens, both pictured here. These allow the small crew to operate and monitor all the ship's equipment. *(Guy Toremans)*

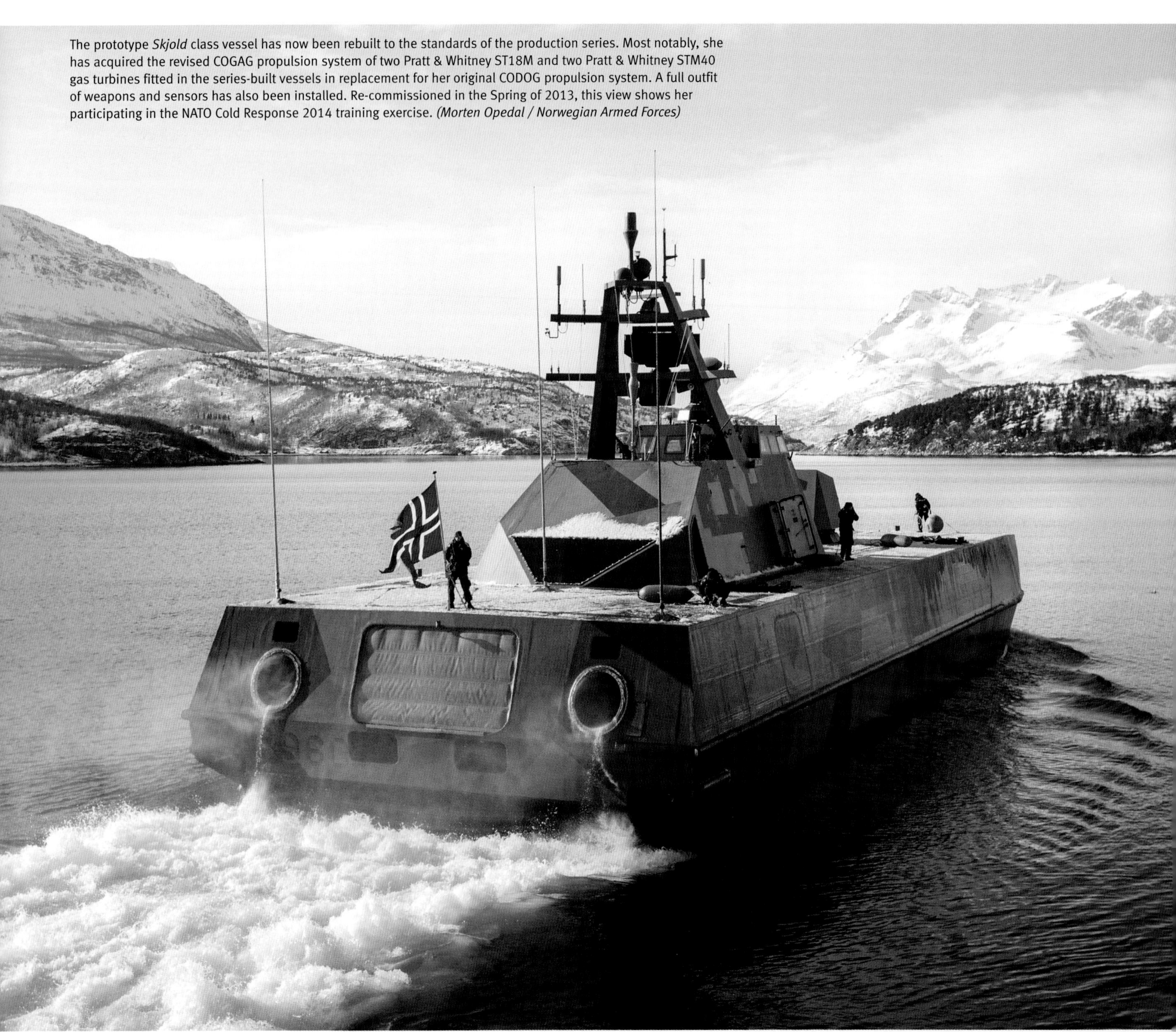

The prototype *Skjold* class vessel has now been rebuilt to the standards of the production series. Most notably, she has acquired the revised COGAG propulsion system of two Pratt & Whitney ST18M and two Pratt & Whitney STM40 gas turbines fitted in the series-built vessels in replacement for her original CODOG propulsion system. A full outfit of weapons and sensors has also been installed. Re-commissioned in the Spring of 2013, this view shows her participating in the NATO Cold Response 2014 training exercise. *(Morten Opedal / Norwegian Armed Forces)*

(ECDIS), radar and electro-optical (EO) data, as well as weapons system functionality.

Damage control is an important issue, with fire a principal concern. The RNN learned a lot of lessons from a catastrophic fire on board the *Oksøy* class minehunter *Orkla* in November 2002 and many of these have been incorporated into the *Skjold* class design. The ship is divided into six gas- and water-tight sections and features two engine rooms, one in each hull. The ship can continue to operate with one engine room out of action. Both are encapsulated with fire-retardant insulation material and incorporate Halotron and Hi-Fog water-mist fire-extinguishing systems. There is both a primary and secondary damage control station, both of which can access the IBDCS embodied in the L-3 MAPPS IPMS. This provides an instant overview of all aspects of the ship's status and provides the opportunity to react in a very tight timeframe.

PROPULSION

The *Skjold* class was originally designed for a combined diesel or gas (CODOG) propulsion system. However, the RNN decided to change this to a combined gas and gas (COGAG) turbine configuration with two Pratt & Whitney ST18M and two Pratt & Whitney ST40M gas turbines driving two Kamewa 80S2 water-jets. Each hull has one propulsion train incorporating two gas turbines, a water-jet and a reduction gearbox. Adapting the ST18 and ST40 aircraft engines for use in a marine environment and the complexities of the associated COGAG layout proved to be a difficult process but was justified by the higher performance and better fuel economy offered across the full spectrum of different speeds and operating profiles. The ships have a range of 800 nautical miles at 40 knots and an endurance of around eight days. The reason for selecting water-jets as the main propulsion system was due to the combination of their favourable acoustic properties, low draught requirements and excellent manoeuvring capabilities.

Operation of the surface-effect air cushion is in the hands of a stabilisation system provided by VT Maritime Dynamics. This includes a ride control system that regulates the pressure of the air cushion between the two hulls that is created by a pair of 800kW lift fans driven by two MTU 12V 183 TE92 diesels in the bow. Flexible rubber 'finger' type seals in the bow and a 'bag' seal in the stern prevent air from leaking out of the cushion formed between the two side hulls. Vent valves and a seal management system in the stern, combined with a variable geometry inlet to the lift fans, control air flow and cushion pressure, improving the ship's sea-keeping by minimising pitch and heave accelerations. The ability to manipulate the air cushion, combined with the water-jet propulsion, make the *Skjolds* both easy to handle and seaworthy. There is the option of choosing between speed and comfort, or a compromise. The class can maintain excellent sea-keeping qualities at 45 knots in Sea State 3 as well as achieving 60 knots in Sea State 1. The installation of a replenishment at sea (RAS) rig was approved following conclusion of a design review in mid-2012, offering the prospect of longer endurance.

COMBAT MANAGEMENT SYSTEM

The *Skjold* class is equipped with a SENIT 2000 combat management system (CMS) and associated

Below: The surface effect air cushion on the *Skjold* class is created by controlling the pressure of an air 'pocket' between the two catamaran hulls that is generated by two lift fans. Flexible rubber seals in the bow and a bag seal in the stern prevent air leaking from the cushion between the twin hulls, whilst vent valves on either side of the stern are used to regulate the air pressure. These images show the 'finger' type rubber seals in the bow, the space between the twin hulls where the air cushion forms and the circular stern valve outlets. *(Guy Toremans)*

KD2000 multi-function consoles. It is a derivative of the SENIT 8 system installed onboard the French aircraft carrier *Charles de Gaulle*. The SENIT 2000 CMS is, however, tailored specifically for coastal warfare, with emphasis on anti-surface weapons, passive detection, tactical data-links and fast response to 'pop-up' air threats.

Jointly developed by DCNS and Kongsberg, SENIT 2000 migrates existing functionality to a new open architecture that is based on PowerPC processors and the Linux operating system. It provides the ships with a processing capability comparable to that of a frigate. The CMS incorporates five consoles that feature a new generation of fully multi-functional LCD flat screen displays. This is claimed to be the first such application of this technology in a warship's combat information centre.

SENIT 2000 performs all usual combat management functions, including the operation of weapons, sensors, data links and navigational equipment. It makes use of an extensive decision support system, capable of mission planning and execution, and of holding intelligence, cartography, Electronic Support Measures (ESM) and Electro-Optical (EO) databases. The system also includes extensive real-time recording and debriefing facilities, and provides comprehensive, on-board simulation and functionality for single operator, multi-operator, command and squadron level training. There is also, a sixth, additional console that has been provided for installation of a specific Norwegian command and control system.

EFFECTORS

Although originally classified as fast attack craft the *Skjolds* are now often referred to as 'littoral combat

Table 3.3.1.

SKJOLD PRINCIPAL PARTICULARS

Building Information:	
Laid Down:	4 August 1997
Launched:	22 September 1998
Commissioned:	17 April 1999/29 April 2013[1]
Builders:	Umoe Mandal at its yard in Mandal, Vest-Agner, Norway.
Dimensions:	
Displacement:	275 tons full load displacement.
Overall Hull Dimensions:	47.5m x 13.5m x 2.3m/0.9m.[2]
Equipment:	
Armament:	2 x quad launchers for Kongsberg NSM Naval Strike Missiles. Mistral portable twin surface-to-air missile launcher. 1 x 76mm/62 Oto Melara Super Rapid gun. 2 x 12.7mm machine guns.
Countermeasures:	Exelis ES-3701 electronic support measures. Rheinmetall MASS decoy launcher.
Principal Sensors:	1 x Thales MRR-3D-NG multi-role radar. Navigation radar. 1 x Saab CEROS 200 fire-control director. 1 x Sagem VIGY-20 electro-optical tracker.
Combat System:	SENIT 2000 combat management system. Integrated communications system includes Links 11 and 16.
Propulsion Systems:	
Machinery:	COGAG. 2 x Pratt & Witney ST40M each rated at 4MW and 2 x Pratt & Witney ST18M gas turbines each rated 2MW drive 2 x 80S2 Kamewa water-jets. 2 x MTU 12V 183 TE92 diesels power 2 x lift fans.
Speed:	Maximum speed is c. 60 knots. Range is 800 nautical miles at 40 knots.
Other Details:	
Complement:	The core crew is c. 20, including 13 officers/petty officers. Accommodation is provided for 21.
Class:	Six *Skjold* class vessels are in service: *Skjold* (P960), *Storm* (P961), *Skudd* (P962), *Steil* (P963), *Glimt* (P964) and *Gnist* (P965).

Notes:

1 Dates refer to initial commissioning for trials and re-commissioning after modification to production standard.

2 Differences in draught are dependent on whether or not the air cushion is in operation.

corvettes', due to their powerful combat suite.[5] This reflects their primary purpose as fast anti-surface warfare platforms. For long-range engagement, the units rely on KDA's Nytt Sjømals Missil (NSM) anti-ship cruise missile.[6] The system consists of two quadruple launchers aft of the deck house, which elevate to fire and then retract to maintain the low RCS. The missile efflux is vented through an opening in the vessel's stern. The missiles are equipped with a programmable intelligent multi-purpose fuze (PIMF) semi-armour piercing warhead of 120kg, GPS-aided mid-course guidance with an advanced dual-band imaging infrared (IIR) seeker for automatic target recognition. Range is c. 185km (100 nautical miles). Their digital flight control computer allows the missile to follow the complex contours of fjords before seeking its target. Their IIR-seeker detects, classifies and selects targets and, in its terminal approach, manoeuvres the missile randomly to defeat close-in defences. The NSM test firing and evaluation programme included a first firing at sea in October 2012 and a successful test against the target vessel *Trondheim* in June 2013.

For engagements in the shorter ranges the RNN's initial intention was to mount a 57mm gun but, later, it was decided to fit Oto Melara's more powerful 76mm/62 Super Rapid. The switch required a stronger and more flexible composite structure to absorb the shock pulses generated by this larger-calibre system. With a rate of fire of 120 rounds per minute, the gun can engage targets at ranges exceeding 16,000m (c. nine nautical miles) in anti-surface mode or up to 5,000m in anti-air mode.

The *Skjolds* also mount a man-portable air-defence systems (MANPADS) launcher for Mistral surface-to-air missiles with a range of up to 2.2

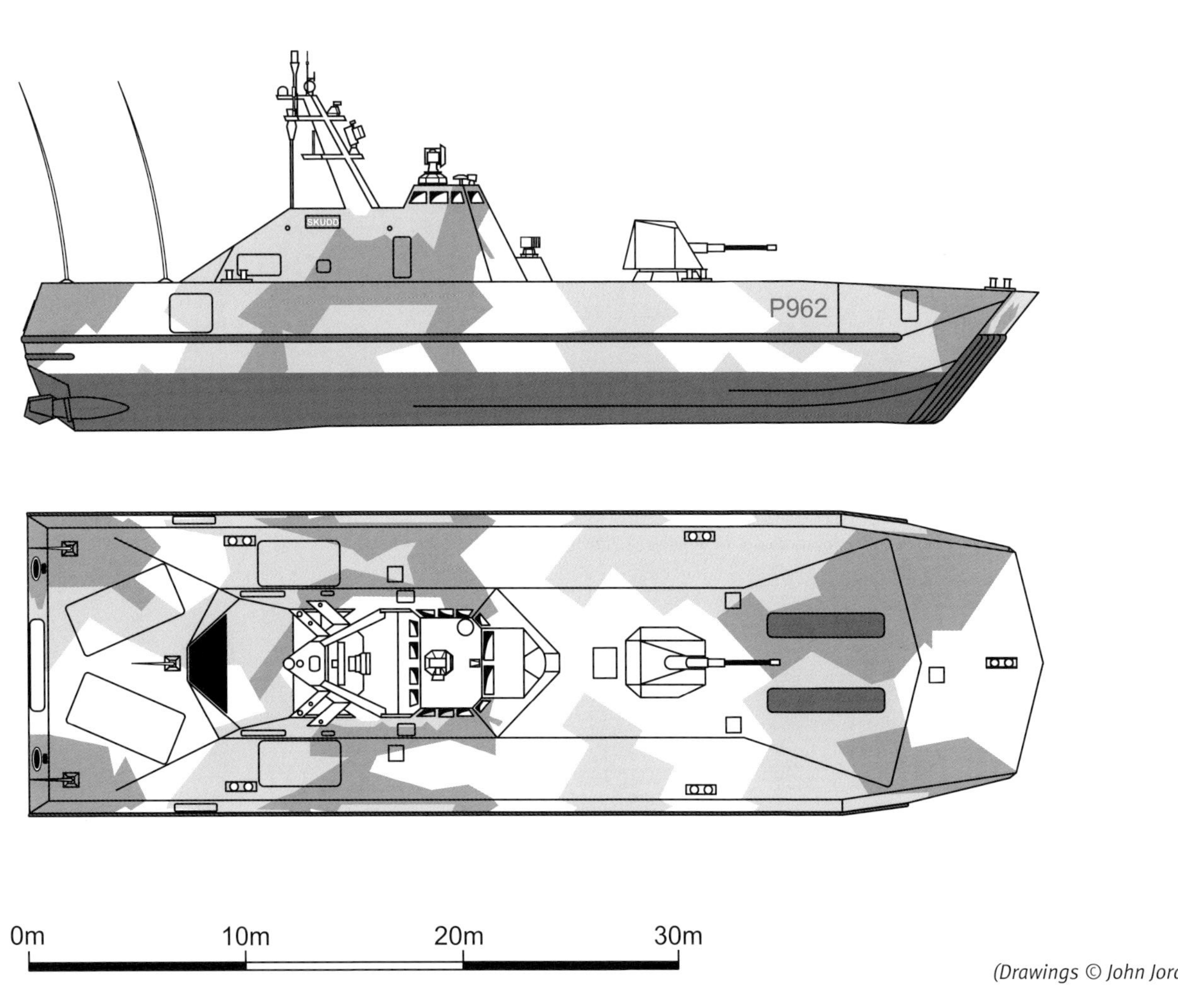

(Drawings © John Jordan, 2014)

In June 2013, *Steil* and *Gnist* participated in firing trials of the NSM Naval Strike Missile in which the decommissioned frigate *Trondheim* was destroyed by a missile launched from *Steil*. These images of the two corvettes give an indication of the class's different profile with their SES air cushion turned off and on, as well as the massive damage the Naval Strike Missile caused to its target. *(Peder Torp Mathisen/ Norwegian Armed Forces)*

A Kongsberg Defence & Aerospace NSM Naval Strike Missile pictured being launched from *Glimt* during the first firing trials of the system from the class at the Andøya Test Centre on 10 October 2012. The *Skjold* class is equipped with two quad launchers that elevate to fire the missile before retracting back into the hull, the missiles' efflux venting from a rectangular opening in the stern. *(Kongsberg Defence & Aerospace)*

nautical miles and a warhead of 3kg; two 12.7mm machine guns and a Rheinmetall Multi Ammunition Soft-kill System (MASS) decoy launcher. The latter can deploy up to thirty-two projectiles from a stealthy, lightweight carbon-fibre directable launcher in a time-staggered process, deflecting enemy anti-ship missiles and guided projectiles from their intended target step by step. The decoys are programmable to provide protection across all relevant wavelengths of the electromagnetic spectrum, including ultra-violet, electro-optical, laser, infrared and radar. The launcher is permanently stabilised in both pitch and roll.

There are plans to install the Kongsberg fully-stabilized remotely-controlled 127mm Sea Protector gun by 2015. This gun incorporates automatic target tracking and comprehensive fire-control solutions. Unique separate servo axes enable the sensors to track the target while the weapon is corrected for ballistics. In the longer term the navy would like to equip the units with more potent air-defence missiles, preferably using the same launchers as those of the NSM-missiles.

The units' sensor package is focused on a Thales MRR-3D-NG G-band (US Navy C-band) three-dimensional multi-role radar. This features a light-weight phased array antenna and associated IFF, with automatic mode switching. The radar provides the *Skjold*-class with long-range 3-D air and surface surveillance, tracking and self-defence, target evaluation and weapon allocation, target classification support, and weapon control capabilities. In surface surveillance mode (scanning at ten rpm) the MRR-3D-NG can detect low and medium-level targets at ranges of up to seventy-five nautical miles and in

A detailed view of *Skudd*'s bridge structure. A MASS decoy launcher is pictured in front of the bridge's face, with the Saab CEROS-200 radar and optronic fire-control director mounted on the bridge roof. The carbon-fibre mast supports the Thales MRR-3D-NG multi-role radar on the lower platform, with a navigation radar above. The top of the mast houses the Sagem VIGY-20 electro-optical fire-control system with a pole for the ES-3701 ESM antenna immediately behind. *(Guy Toremans)*

long-range 3-D air surveillance mode targets up to around 100 nautical miles; in the self-defence mode (scanning at 30 rpm) it can detect and track any threat within a radius of about 30 nautical miles. Other sensors include an Exelis ES-3701 tactical radar surveillance system, featuring a 360° cylindrical interferometer antenna. This is specifically designed to provide electronic support measures (ESM) functions in a littoral environment. Other equipment includes a Saab CEROS-200 fire control director; a Sagem VIGY-20 electro-optical tracker; a navigation radar; and a SOFRESUD Quick Pointing Device allowing rapid line-of-sight target designation in azimuth and bearing.

COMMUNICATIONS

The *Skjolds* mount a state-of-the-art communications system integrated by the German Aeromaritime group. Engineered to give an optimal solution in terms of communication performance and compactness, it includes HF, VHF and UHF radio links, as well as satellite communications, and supports NATO Link 11 and 16 connectivity. From mid-2014 onwards, the class is being equipped with the Thales' SURFSAT-S satellite communication system, which includes connections with the Inmarsat and Iridium civilian networks as well as military satellites. The overall communications system allows class members to have a secure means of sharing an overall operational picture, thereby supporting closely entwined operations.

CREW

Operating the *Skjolds* is personnel-intensive. Although the IMPS and IBS provide a very high level of automation and make the performance of onboard tasks both accurate and easy, the carefully organised employment of every member of the crew is imperative in order to supervise and control the class's systems effectively. Initially the ships were designed for a crew of sixteen but, after the lessons learned from *Skjold*'s deployment to the United States, it was decided to increase this to twenty-one.

As far as the accommodation is concerned there is one single cabin for the commanding officer; four double cabins for the other officers; and four-berth cabins for the petty officers and the ratings. Officers and petty officers share a wardroom while ratings have their own mess. There is a modern galley, two showers and two toilets. As no spare bunks are available, any additional personnel must sleep on improvised bunks in the wardroom or ratings' mess. The RNN is studying possibilities to augment the number of crew because long-lasting high-intensity operations have proved to be very challenging. Commander sg Ståle Kasin – Commander Corvette Squadron Norwegian Navy – said that possible solutions could either be the introduction of 'hot bunking' or an increase the number of bunks: 'Some of the cabins now have two bunks, so we're looking into possibilities to install a third.' During operations the crew can remain inside a nuclear-biological-chemical 'citadel' which encompasses the critical interior spaces, i.e. the crew's quarters, the operations room and the bridge.

Officers and petty officers on the *Skjold* class share a wardroom, pictured here on *Skudd*. Ratings have their own separate mess. *(Guy Toremans)*

The commanding officer's cabin on *Skudd*. Accommodation standards on the *Skjold* class do not reach the high standards seen on larger modern frigates but have been described as spacious and comfortable. The commanding officer is the only member of the crew to have a single cabin. *(Guy Toremans)*

Upon the return from the United States, Commander Rune Andersen – *Skjold*'s commanding officer – confirmed that the living and accommodation standards were quite comfortable: 'The interiors are spacious and comfortable. She has been our home for thirteen months now without problems. The staterooms provide comfort and privacy. We produce enough fresh water to shower and do laundry, the noise level is low and the temperature inside is nice no matter what temperature you find outside. She was just as comfortable in the Arctic waters as she was in the Caribbean.'

OPERATIONAL EXPERIENCE

The *Skjold* class vessels have participated in a variety of exercises and activities. Each year they take part in Exercise Flotex: a Norwegian exercise conducted each November; in Exercise Northern Coasts: an exercise which takes place in Danish, Finnish, German or Swedish waters during September; in the Joint Warrior series off the west coast of Scotland and, every second year, in the NATO Exercise Cold Response. In addition to these manoeuvres the vessels have been taking part in a variety of smaller national exercises and operations, varying from support to the police and customs, to live missile firings and air exercises.

***Skjold* (P960)**: Launched on 22 September 1998, *Skjold* first commissioned into the RNN on 17 April 1999. She immediately started an intensive test period focussing on electromagnetic compatibility, signature reduction, speed and sea-keeping, as well as general arrangement and layout functionality. Just three days after her handover, she joined Exercise Blue Game 1999 alongside other fast attack craft from Denmark, Germany and Norway. Although not yet fitted with her weapons and weapon control system, it was essential for the RNN to try to operate the ship just like any other fast patrol boat. During the exercise *Skjold* crossed the Skagerrak six times, achieving a best average speed of over 50 knots. Upon completion of the exercise, she sailed to Oslo for demonstrations to the Chief of Defence, Minister of Defence and a number of politicians. After this, she sailed to her home base at Haakonsvern for the first time. Although experiencing conditions up to Sea State 5, she was still able to maintain speeds of 40–50 knots.

In August, KDA mounted two SENIT CMS multifunction consoles, after which *Skjold* sailed to Stavanger where an Oto Melara 76mm/62 Super Rapid gun was installed. In this configuration the ship attended to the DSEi-99 Exhibition in London.

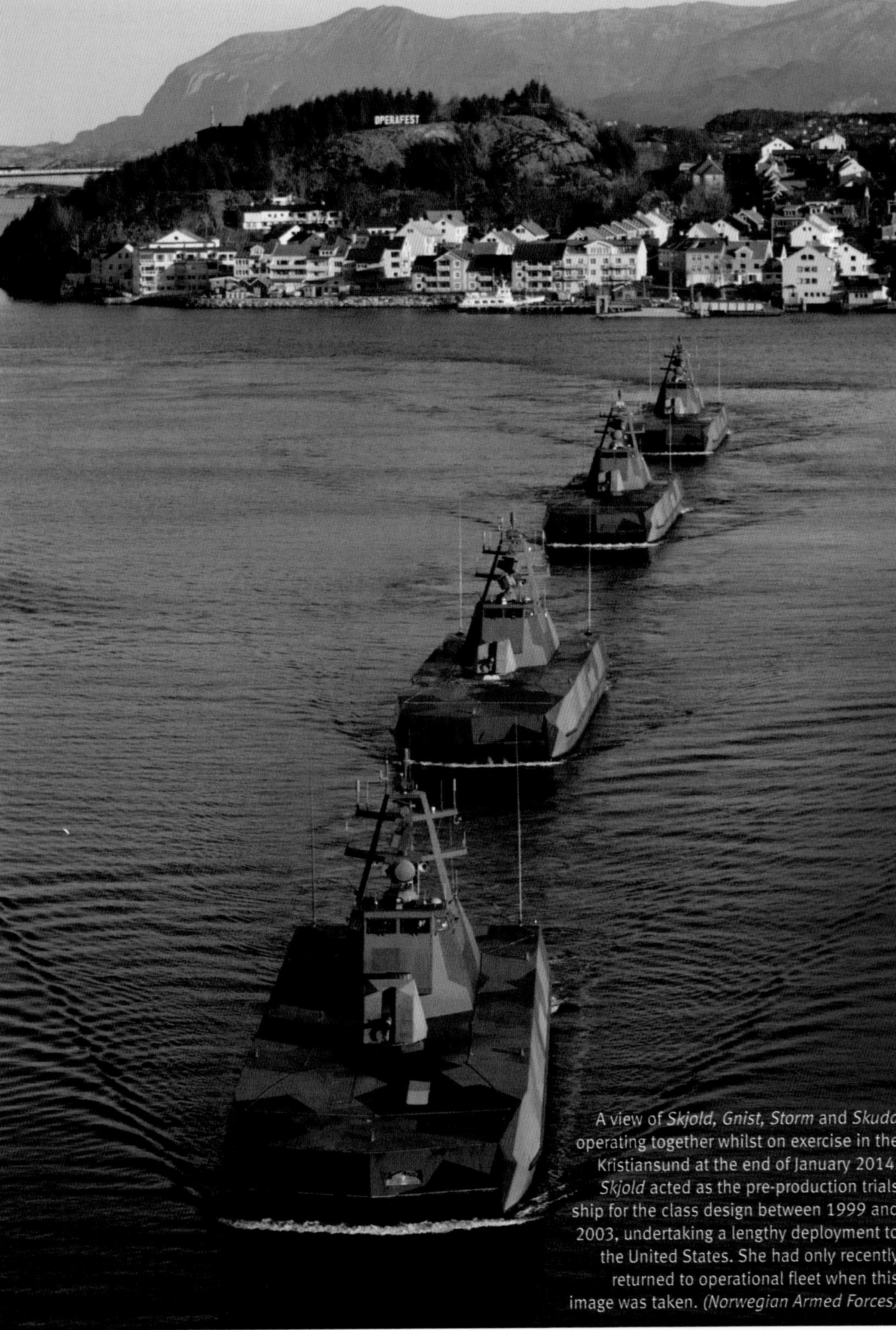

A view of *Skjold, Gnist, Storm* and *Skudd* operating together whilst on exercise in the Kristiansund at the end of January 2014. *Skjold* acted as the pre-production trials ship for the class design between 1999 and 2003, undertaking a lengthy deployment to the United States. She had only recently returned to operational fleet when this image was taken. *(Norwegian Armed Forces)*

This was followed by test firings with the gun towards the end of September. The Millennium-year started with cold weather trials in the Tromsø and Skjervøy area (Finnmark) until end-February. This was followed by further firing tests with the main gun to measure strains on the hull and further extensive trials of all the ship's systems and equipment. During one of these exercises *Skjold* pushed her top speed to 59.8 knots. The gun was removed upon completion of this trial period.

In March 2000 the US Navy Special Warfare Command personnel visited the ship to assess whether the high-speed design had any relevance to developing network-centric warfare concepts, including the Littoral Combat Ship (LCS) programme. This resulted in signature of an agreement between the US and Norwegian governments for the lease of *Skjold* for a twelve-month demonstration and evaluation program with the US Navy research establishments.

Prior to her departure to the United States, *Skjold* received a number of adjustments to her systems, including new navigation, radar, antenna and satellite equipment, as well as a device to handle US Navy type rigid inflatable boats (RIBs). The most obvious change, however, was a new colour scheme. The ship was repainted into lighter shades to reduce the surface temperature on the hull while operating in a warmer climate. Under the command of Commander Rune Andersen, *Skjold* departed Bergen on 4 September 2001. Calling at the Faeroe Islands and Reykjavik, she proceeded along Greenland's eastern coast to the Eskimo village of Ammassalik. She then transited through Prince Christian Sound and called at Nanortalik and Cartwright, prior to reaching Corner Brook at the East Coast of Newfoundland. From here she sailed to Halifax, Newport, Rhode Island, and New York before arriving at the US Navy's Amphibious Base in Little Creek, Virginia – her homeport for the next year – on 25 September. Here she became a fully integrated unit of Special Boat Squadron Two.

Skjold conducted an intensive trials programme whilst in the United States. She was used to assess the extent to which a high-speed platform of the type the ship represented could be used as a front-line 'node' in network-centric warfare and whether enhanced connectivity could enable such ships to undertake roles previously denied to them. The programme included simulated threats from air, surface and sub-surface sources; Special Forces and

unmanned vehicle operations; and a range of instrumented tests encompassing sea-keeping, structural and signature performance. During this time, she was involved in a number of exercises. These included the mine-countermeasures focused GOMEX 02 in the Gulf of Mexico between 29 November and 14 December; and JTFEX 02-1 with the *John F Kennedy* (CV-67) Carrier Battle Group.[7] Assigned to the opposition force, she reportedly managed to stay undetected and attack the aircraft carrier. Upon completion, she made several port calls in the Caribbean, conducting experimental training with the Naval Special Warfare Unit 4 SEALS Platoon at US Naval Station Roosevelt Roads, Puerto Rico. Returning to Little Creek at the end of May 2002, she participated in the Fleet Battle Experiment (FBE-J) and 'Millennium Challenge' exercises, followed by signature testing from airborne sensors and trials with a rig for replenishment-at-sea.

By mid-August preparations were underway for *Skjold*'s return trip to Norway. The homeward voyage saw calls at New York, Halifax, Cape Breton in Newfoundland, Labrador in Greenland, Reykjavik, Vestmannaeyar and the Faeroes. She arrived at Haakonsvern on 27 September 2002. The US deployment demonstrated the ship's ability to be reconfigured quickly for disparate missions, to defend herself in a littoral environment and her suitability for Special Operations. However, the ship's limited 800 nautical mile range was a drawback, in the US Navy's opinion.[8]

A view of the third *Skjold* class vessel, *Steil*, at the Umoe Mandal shipyard on 30 June 2011, the day of her delivery to the RNN. Another four ships can be seen in the course of fitting out or undergoing maintenance in the background. Umoe Mandal completed its work on the construction programme with redelivery of *Skjold* to final production standard in April 2013. *(Magne Åhjem / Norwegian Armed Forces)*

The RNN view was more unequivocally positive. Commander Andersen – *Skjold*'s first commanding officer – said, 'She is extremely manoeuvrable and capable of maintaining high speeds in rough weather. The ship has met all the requirements laid down by the Norwegian Navy prior to her design. Since her commissioning in April 1999 she has impressed us with her high performance and high availability.'

A view of *Storm* undergoing sea trials in July 2007. The first production-series *Skjold* class vessel, *Storm* was only commissioned in September 2010 after a lengthy period of pre-delivery evaluations. *(Umoe Mandal)*

Having served as the pre-production platform test bed for more than four years, during which she sailed some 85,000 nautical miles with high technical availability, *Skjold* was temporarily decommissioned on 24 June 2003. She returned to Umoe Mandal to be upgraded to final production standards and to act as training platform for the other units' crews. She was re-delivered on 29 April 2013 and one of her first foreign visits took her to Rouen, France for the 'Armada de Liberté' in June 2013. This voyage was followed in November by exercise Flotex 2013. Subsequently, in 2014, *Skjold* took part in the Cold Response series and NATO's Exercise Unified Vision 2014.

***Storm* (P961):** *Storm,* the first production *Skjold* class vessel, was launched on 30 October 2006 and commissioned into service on 9 September 2010 after a lengthy and extensive series of pre-delivery trials. In November of that year she took part in the Flotex 2010 exercise. In September 2011 she attended the 2011 DSEi exhibition in London, followed by participation in Flotex in November. Subsequently, she was one of the participants which stood out during the Danish/German exercise Danex/Northern Coasts 2012. Three of the class – *Storm*, *Skudd* and *Steil* – attended the exercise as it was one of the evaluation periods required to certify the units as being fully operational capable. Participation in this and Cold Response 2012 gave the RNN the opportunity to assess the ships' combat capabilities in a wide variety of scenarios and enhance the crews' warfighting skills. In 2013, she took part in Joint Warrior 2013-1 off Scotland and the 2013 edition of Flotex. Early 2014 again saw *Storm* taking part in the Cold Response series, after which she returned to the shipyard to have the NSM missile system installed.

***Skudd* (P962):** Launched on 3 May 2007, *Skudd* joined the fleet on 28 October 2010. Soon after her commissioning, she started an intensive series of sea readiness checks and trials of the integrated weapon and sensor suites to ensure that these met all operational requirements. In February 2011 she conducted cold weather trials in Finnmark, followed by firing tests with the Oto Melara 76mm/62 Super Rapid gun. After summer leave *Skudd* commenced preparations for Danex/Northern Coasts 2011.

This was the first time that the RNN participated in large multi-national manoeuvres with an operational *Skjold*-class unit and many lessons were learned, as the ship's commanding officer, Lieutenant-Commander Beisland attested, 'Danex/ Northern Coasts 2011 was an excellent tool to enhance our warfighting skills and assess the ship's combat capability in a wide variety of areas ranging from damage control to full-scale warfighting. The exercise focuses on what our navy also focuses on, namely anti-surface and anti-air warfare. The air-related exercises, in particular, were quite interesting.' At this time, *Skud*d had yet to be fitted with her satellite communications system, whilst, pending the installation of a replenishment-at-sea rig, fuel consumption remained an issue, 'Currently we remain dependent on replenishments from land and our endurance is approximately eight days'. In spite of the inevitable challenges from this first-time participation, Lieutenant-Commander Beisland was content the exercise had demonstrated that his crew's efforts during a demanding work-up period had paid off, 'We managed to display *Skudd*'s great potential. The SENIT 2000 combat management

Table 3.3.2: *SKJOLD* CLASS LIST

NAME	PENNANT	ORDERED	LAID DOWN	LAUNCHED	COMMISSIONED
Skjold	P960	30 August 1996	4 August 1997	22 September 1998	29 April 2013[1]
Storm	P961	28 November 2003	October 2005	30 October 2006	9 September 2010
Skudd	P962	28 November 2003	March 2006	3 May 2007	28 October 2010
Steil	P963	28 November 2003	October 2006	15 January 2008	30 June 2011
Glimt	P964	28 November 2003	May 2007	15 August 2008	29 March 2012
Gnist	P965	28 November 2003	December 2007	18 May 2009	8 November 2012

Notes

1 *Skjold* first commissioned for prototype trials on 17 April 1999. She was decommissioned on 24 June 2003 before being reconstructed to production standard.

An image of the third *Skjold* class vessel, *Skudd*, taken in September 2010 shortly before her formal commissioning. She was the first of the class to participate in a large international naval exercise as an operational unit, with the need to address the type's limited endurance one important lesson learned. Nevertheless, the class has considerable potential to carry out lengthy, out-of-area deployments, as *Skjold*'s early deployment to the United States demonstrated. *(Guy Toremans)*

system provides us with a processing capability comparable to that of a frigate.'

Skudd has subsequently participated in a wide range of additional training exercises, most recently in Cold Response 2014. Installation of her NSM cruise missiles is scheduled for completion by the summer of 2014, making her the last unit of the class to be fitted with the system.

***Steil* (P963):** *Steil* commissioned on 30 June 2011, in time to take part in Flotex 2011. After her participation in Cold Response 2012 she was fitted with the NSM system. The final trimester of that year saw her taking part in Northern Coasts 2012 and in the Flotex series. In June 2013 she fired a NSM at the Andøya Rocket Range in northern Norway, successfully hitting the target: the decommissioned *Oslo* class frigate *Trondheim*. This was the first vessel-to-vessel firing of the KDA NSM equipped with a live warhead. After joining further training exercises, she also became the first unit to receive a satellite communications system, being scheduled to test it during the Northern Coasts 2014 exercise.

***Glimt* (P964):** *Glimt* commissioned on 29 March 2012. Having passed her sea readiness checks, validation of her combat system and the integration of the weapon and sensor suites, she conducted live-firing tests with her Oto Melara 76mm/62 Super Rapid gun. She was the first of the class to receive the NSM system – in September 2012 – and the first vessel to conduct technical evaluation firing trials. These took place on 10 October at the Andøya Test Centre. In November of that year she participated in the Flotex Silver 2012 exercise, whilst further NSM firings are planned for 2014.

***Gnist* (P965):** *Gnist*, the fifth and final production-standard *Skjold* class vessel, entered the fleet on 8 November 2012. She took part in Joint Warrior 2013:1, together with her sister-ship *Steil* and the supply vessel *Valkyrien*. This was followed by participation in Flotex 2013. In early 2014 she sailed to northern Norway to take part in Exercise Cold Response 2014, the first of several exercises she is scheduled to attend during the course of the year.

CONCLUSION: THE WAY AHEAD

The *Skjold* class is capable of contributing substantially to a wide range of operations in both the littoral and in blue water. Although designed to patrol Norway's littoral waters, the units have already proved to be amongst the most flexible assets in the RNN. In particular, thanks to state-of-the-art communications and sensor suites, they are able to make a significant contribution to international operations. As demonstrated by *Skjold*'s deployment to the United States, even lengthy out-of-area deployments can be sustained and their top speed of 60 knots could prove quite useful to the EU or NATO counter-piracy operations. In short, *Skjold* and her sisters are rapid, powerful and inter-operable general purpose combatants that will be useful for a wide range of tasks.

Notes

1. *Skjold* is actually the prototype vessel, launched in 1998 but now upgraded to bring her to the same standard as the five production ships in the class.

2. NAVMATCOM was merged into the new Norwegian Defence Logistics Organisation (NDLO) when the latter was formed on 1 January 2002.

3. A surface effect ship (SES) combines the flexible air cushion of a hovercraft with the rigid twin hulls of a catamaran. When the air cushion is turned off, the ship is fully supported by the buoyancy of the hulls; when the air cushion is turned on the ship rises and less of the fixed hull area remains in the water.

4. At this time the Mandal yard was part of the Kvaerner group. The facility was acquired by Umoe AS in 2000.

5. The Royal Norwegian Navy has classified the *Skjold* class as corvettes since 2009.

6. Kongsberg Naval Strike Missile in English.

7. GOMEX is undertaken to transform a mine warfare readiness group from training to ready-to-deploy status.

8. A variant of the *Skjold* design proposed by a Raytheon-led consortium was one of three concepts awarded preliminary development contracts for the future US Navy Littoral Combat Ship in July 2003. However, it was competing design teams, then headed by General Dynamics and Lockheed Martin, that were eventually allocated production contracts in May 2004. Concerns over the *Skjold* design's overall size and range may well have played a part in this decision.

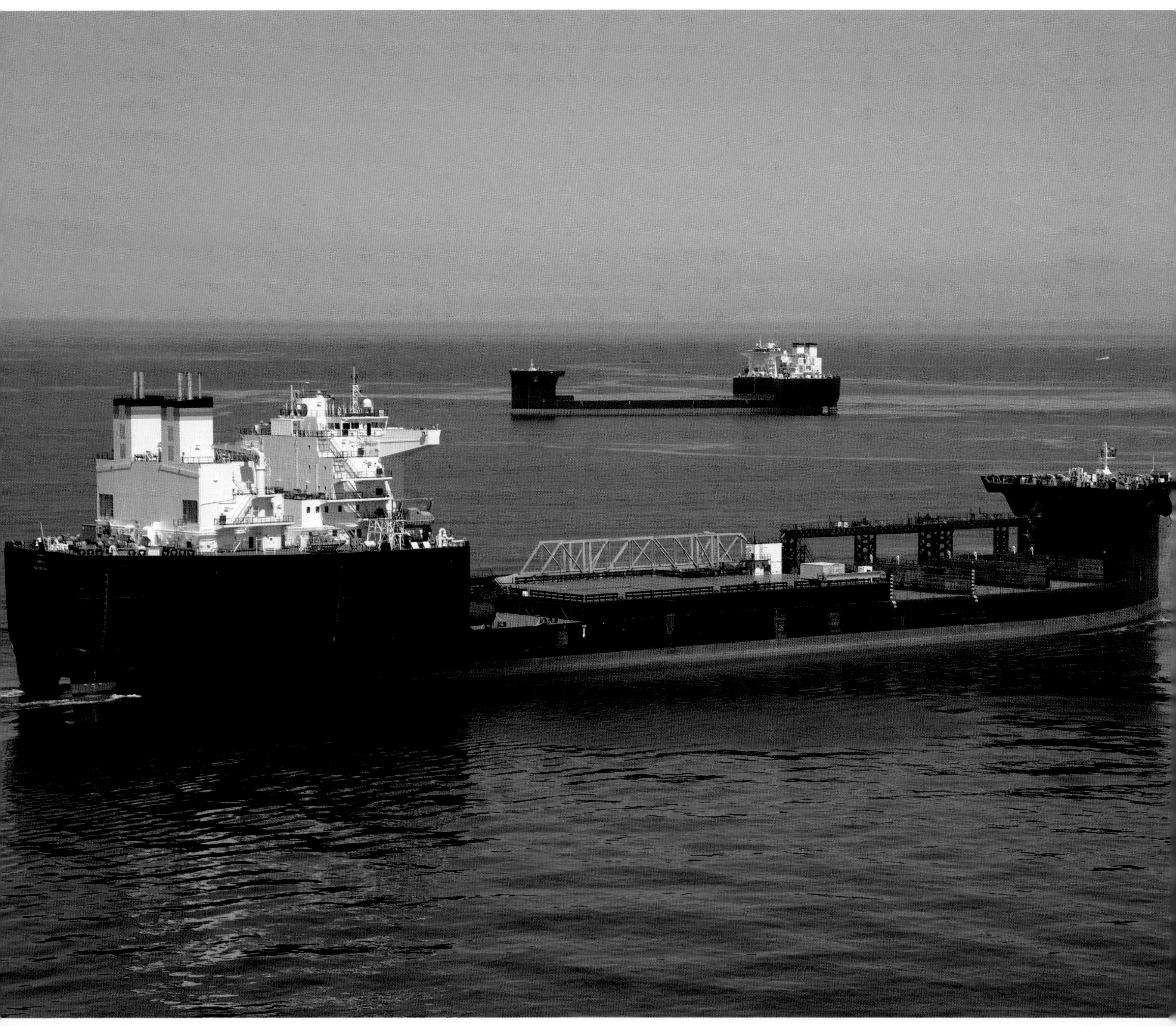

3.4 SIGNIFICANT SHIPS

Author:
Scott C Truver

MONTFORD POINT (MLP-1) CLASS

A 'Sea Base' coming to a Theatre near You

The MOB, or Mobile Offshore Base, was one element of a transformational vision – well before 'transformation' came into vogue – that US Navy Vice Admiral William A Owens, Vice Chairman of the US Joint Chiefs of Staff, sought to infuse during the mid-1990s in a military uncertain about the way ahead after the Berlin Wall came a-tumblin' down and the Soviet Union and Warsaw Pact imploded. Right outside his Pentagon office was a scale model showing how oil platforms could be lashed together to create a floating air base rivalling the size of the US Navy's nuclear-powered aircraft carriers.[1] Although just a gleam in the Admiral's eye, it offered the promise of a broader techno-operational revolution in the American way of war – crucially important as the United States searched for 'peace dividends' supposedly accruing from the end of the Cold War.

Two decades on, no stones are being left unturned as the US Navy, along with the other four US military services, searches for innovative ways to sustain global operations during a period of intense scrutiny, squeaky-tight budgets and increasing threats to national, naval and maritime security.

Just one of numerous innovations is the US Navy's first purpose-built Mobile Landing Platform

Left: A May 2014 image of the first purpose-built US Navy mobile landing platform *Montford Point* (MLP-1). Derived from an oil tanker, her basic design can be configured in a variety of ways. The standard MLP 'sea base' requires integration of a core capabilities set (CCS) that includes a raised vehicle deck, a vehicle transfer ramp and three LCAC lanes; all shown here. Her sister, *John Glenn* (MLP-2), seen in the background, had yet to have her CCS installed when the picture was taken and therefore shows the basic design. *(General Dynamics NASSCO)*

Above: The mobile landing platform *John Glenn* (MLP-2) pictured on sea trials in January 2014. The mobile landing platform is one of numerous innovative vessels the US Navy is introducing as it attempts to sustain global maritime security in an era of intense budget pressures. *(US Navy)*

(MLP) vessel.[2] Constructed at General Dynamics' NASSCO shipyard in San Diego, California, the first-of-class USNS *Montford Point* (MLP-1) was delivered on 14 May 2013 and will be operational in FY2015. Based on NASSCO's commercial BP 'Alaska'-class crude oil carrier, the US Navy's programme of record calls for two 'straight-stick' MLPs and two modified MLPs configured as Afloat Forward Staging Bases (AFSBs). Prospects for a third AFSB are in the offing. The first AFSB, *Lewis B Puller* (AFSB-1), is expected to deliver in September 2015.

Operated by the Military Sealift Command (MSC) in support of the US Navy and Marine Corps, as well as other joint forces and naval partners, the MLPs are manned by thirty-four civilian contract mariners, while forty-four civil-service mariners will compose the AFSB crews. The class is named in honour of African-American Marine Corps recruits who trained at Montford Point Camp, North Carolina, from 1942 to 1949.

'The *Montford Point* is the centrepiece of Twenty-First Century sea-basing, allowing the US Navy to raise forward-operations to a new level,' Rear Admiral Lawrence Jackson, Military Sealift Command Deputy Commander, remarked during a 13 May 2014 interview. 'The AFSBs will help free up more capable and much more expensive warships to do more demanding missions and tasks. Wherever the need, the MLPs and AFSBs are key elements of the Navy's global force for good.'

While not as ambitious – or as expensive – as Admiral Owens' MOB, the MLPs/AFSBs will undergird the sea-basing revolution that dramatically expands the US Navy's legacy Maritime Pre-positioning Forces and Ships (MPF/MPS). 'They all-but sever the umbilical between operating forces and ports or staging bases on land,' Admiral Jackson added, 'and they catalyse experimentation, innovation and discovery of naval and maritime power … from the sea.'

'Look at the MLPs as piers in the oceans,' Captain Henry W Stevens III, US Navy, said during a 2 May 2014 interview. The Navy's Program Manager for Strategic and Theater Sealift (PMS 385), Captain Stevens added the ships would provide important theatre logistics and operational command-and-control capabilities not dependent on host-nation permission, as is the case for land-based solutions. In addition to the two baseline MLP vessels, the modified AFSBs support mine countermeasures (MCM) and special operations missions aimed at defeating adversaries' anti-access/area-denial (A2/AD) strategies.

Montford Point Marines

On 25 June 1941, US President Franklin D Roosevelt issued Executive Order No. 8802 establishing the fair employment practice that began to erase racial discrimination in the Armed Forces. A board led by US Army Brigadier General Keller E Rocher studied the integration of African-Americans being assigned to the Composite Defense Battalion, which included coastal artillery, anti-aircraft artillery, infantry and tanks.

In 1942, President Roosevelt signed a presidential directive giving African-Americans the opportunity to be recruited into the Marine Corps. These recruits, however, were not sent to the traditional boot camps of Parris Island, South Carolina and San Diego, California. Instead, they remained segregated, with basic training at Montford Point Camp, a separate facility at Camp Lejeune, North Carolina. Some barriers stood strong.

On 18 August 1942, the Marine Corps stood up Headquarters and Service Battery of the 51st Composite Defense Battalion. Eight days later, Howard P Perry of Charlotte, North Carolina, was the first African-American recruit to arrive at the camp and was soon joined by 119 other privates, who began recruit training in September. During the next two years, Montford Point would be the training site for the 51st and 52nd Defense Battalions.

Some 20,000 African-American recruits received training at Montford Point (about 10 per cent of the Marine Corps end strength) during the Second World War. The great majority of them proved the worth of their training in the Pacific Theatre, others at the US Navy Depot in McAlister, Oklahoma, and still others at the Philadelphia Supply Depot. Exceptional recruits were singled out to assist in the training of their own platoons. Mortimer A Cox, Arnold R Bostick, Edgar R Davis, Jr., Gilbert H 'Hashmark' Johnson and Edgar R Huff were selected for their leadership and maturity and became the first black drill instructors (DIs). Colonel Samuel A Woods, first commanding officer of the 'special duty units' that were created and trained at Montford Point, was justly proud of his Marines and his association with all black Marines.

African-Americans would train and become Marines, but they would still be kept separate from the white troops at nearby Camp Lejeune. Unless accompanied by a white Marine, they were not allowed to set foot in Camp Lejeune. When they were shipped off to battle zones, they served exclusively in African-American units.

The initial intent of the Marine Corps hierarchy was to discharge these African-American Marines after the War, returning them to civilian life – leaving the Marine Corps an all-white organisation. Attitudes changed and reality took hold as the war progressed. Once given the chance to prove themselves, it became impossible to deny the fact that this 'new breed' of African-American Marines was just as capable as all other Marines regardless of race, colour, creed or national origin.

In July 1948 President Harry S Truman issued Executive Order No. 9981 ending segregation in the military. In September 1949, Montford Marine Camp was deactivated – ending seven years of segregation. On 19 April 1974, the Marine Corps renamed Montford Point Camp Johnson, in honour of Sergeant Major 'Hashmark' Johnson. Johnson was one of the first African-Americans to join the Corps, a distinguished Montford Point DI and a Second World War and Korean War veteran. In 2014, the camp remained the only Marine Corps installation named in honour of an African-American.

General Leonard F Chapman, Jr., who later became Commandant of the Marine Corps, said, 'The footprints of the Montford Point Marines were left on the beaches of Roi-Namur, Saipan, Guam, Peleliu, Iwo Jima and Okinawa. Tides and winds, long ago, washed them out into the seas of history, but, "The Chosen Few," in field shoes and canvas leggings, also left their mark in the firm concrete of Marine Corps History.'

Sources:

Montford Point Marines Association, Quantico, Virginia
General Dynamics, NASSCO, San Diego, California

'We will continue to flow our advanced capabilities forward where they can be used interdependently with other joint forces for best effect,' Admiral Jonathan W. Greenert, U.S. Chief of Naval Operations, wrote in his foreword to the *U.S. Navy Program Guide 2014,* 'and a mix of highly configurable expeditionary support ships like the Mobile Landing Platform, Joint High Speed Vessel, and Afloat Forward Staging Base are already in, or coming to, a theatre near you.'[3]

Two computer-generated images of the MLP concept. The MLP is designed to act as part of a 'sea base' that can provide logistical support irrespective of the availability of port facilities. It acts as a transhipment point for supplies and personnel that are delivered to the MLP by transport ships and then transferred ashore by fast LCAC ship-to-shore connectors or other vessels. *(US Navy)*

SEA BASING

The fundamental idea behind 'sea basing' is that a 'steel bridge' of supply transfer ships can be used to support floating platforms at sea, which, in turn can support forces ashore.[4] This concept enables cargo transfer between ships, or to fast ship-to-shore connectors and slower lighters for transport ashore. Under normal conditions, offload functions are performed in ports, which will always have a higher capacity than 'at-sea' ship-based solutions. That said, ports are not always available when and where they are needed. Port infrastructure might also be attacked and damaged, frustrating the timely flow of materiel.

The US Navy's current approach to sea basing is focused on the Maritime Prepositioning Force within the MSC. This initially comprised three (although, since 2012, only two) Maritime Prepositioning Ship Squadrons (MPSRONs) when it was established in the 1980s. These are forward deployed to the western Pacific (MPSRON-3) and Diego Garcia in the Indian Ocean (MPSRON-2); MPSRON-1, focused on the Mediterranean, stood down in 2012.[5] Each MPSRON carries weapons, munitions, vehicles, equipment and supplies and materiel for a US Marine Corps Marine Expeditionary Brigade, about 16,000 marines and sailors in all. The idea is for US Marine Corps forces

The US Navy's current approach to sea basing is focused on two Maritime Prepositioning Force Squadrons (MPSRONs) within the Military Sealift Command. Comprising a range of supply ships, each MPSRON carries sufficient equipment and supplies for a USMC Marine Expeditionary Brigade. These images show lighters and equipment being offloaded from USNS *1ST LT Jack Lummus* (T-AK-3011), a *2ND LT John P Bobo* class dry cargo ship that forms part of MPSRON-3, during an exercise off Thailand in 2011. *(US Navy)*

The large multi-role, roll-on/roll-off ship *Watkins* (T-AKR-315) seen moored next to the charted heavy lift ship *Mighty Servant I* off San Diego in the autumn of 2005 during trials of the MLP concept. The mobile landing platform is part of US Marine Corps and Navy efforts to strengthen the capability of sea basing to replace reliance on vulnerable port-based logistics. *(US Navy)*

Two images of *John Glenn* (MLP-2), one of two baseline MLPs ordered to strengthen the sea basing concept. Along with the derived AFSB afloat forward staging bases and other ships such as the JHSV joint high speed vessels and LCS littoral combat ships, the MLP forms part of an 'alphabet-soup' of new vessels intended better to align ships with missions. *(US Navy)*

to be airlifted to a region and 'marry up' with prepositioned materiel and equipment. But, the MPF still tied the logistics from the sea to ports or nearby airports. As a result, political and military vulnerabilities remained a concern.

This approach was not new for the US Navy or US Marine Corps. As naval historian Norman Polmar explained, the forward-deployed, prepositioning concept was first introduced by Secretary of Defense Robert S McNamara in the mid-1960s. He proposed that a fleet of thirty Fast Deployment Logistics ships (FDLs) be constructed for the US Navy, along with a complementary force of long-range transport aircraft for the US Air Force. The US Congress refused to fund the FDLs, but did fund the C-5A Galaxy strategic airlift force, which, fifty years on, is still receiving upgrades, modernisations and service life-extensions to the remaining C-5Bs to keep them flying for years to come. Undeterred, McNamara was successful in modifying several existing cargo vessels and tank landing ships to be forward deployed, carrying munitions, supplies and even nuclear weapons.

Moving forward to the present, it is the US Marine Corps that is the driving force for sea basing in the second decade of the twenty-first century.[6] For the US Marines, sea basing is the 'deployment, assembly, command, projection, sustainment, reconstitution and reemployment of joint power from the sea without reliance on land bases within the operational area.' Numerous platforms compose the sea base, including amphibious warfare ships, prepositioning ships, aircraft and surface connectors. 'The overall intent of sea basing is to make use of the flexibility and protection inherent in maneuver at sea while minimising the presence of the Marine Air Ground Task Force … ashore. Sea basing will minimise the need to build up logistics assets ashore, reduce the operational demand for strategic sealift and airlift capabilities, and permit forward positioning of joint forces for immediate employment.' In addition, the sea base will support US Navy and other United States joint forces as well as naval and maritime partners in peacetime, crisis and war.

'Viewing the sea base as a capability,' the US Marine Corps sea-basing concept continues, 'it can be formed by a small group of ships or a larger, more diverse force. The key is capability; the capability will increase as the sea base grows. All components will play a role in sea basing and will compress deployment and employment times to permit power projection within days rather than weeks or months without reliance on easily targeted and often geographically unsuitable ports or airfields ashore.'

The growing demand for naval forces requires an innovative combination of rotational deployments, forward basing, rotational crewing, and the use of partner nation's facilities overseas, the US Navy's 2014 *Program Guide* explains.[7] And in that regard, the US Navy is working better to align ships with missions by fielding an 'alphabet-soup" of MLPs, AFSBs, JHSVs (Joint High-Speed Vessels) and LCSs (Littoral Combat Ships). 'We're looking at this as being adaptive and creative,' said Major General Robert S. Walsh, director of the US Navy's Expeditionary Warfare Division (N95), in December 2013.[8] 'The effort is infused with a mind to how we can use platforms in new ways and increase the mission possibilities for these new ships.'

'It is important to keep in mind, however, that the MLPs and AFSBs are *not* warships,' Admiral Jackson noted, 'but they enable and support US Navy/US Marine Corps operations – from humanitarian assistance and disaster relief to regional crisis and conflict.'

THE MONTFORD POINT SOLUTION

The MLP is a new class of US Navy auxiliary ships manned and operated by the MSC. The MLP's basic mission is to serve as a transfer point between large ships and small landing craft, acting as a floating base in non-anchorage depths for amphibious operations so as to allow equipment and cargo to be delivered from ship to shore when there are no friendly bases available. The ship provides the US Navy and Marine Corps with the ability to conduct selective at-sea offload of equipment and cargo, and to manoeuvre ashore via surface connectors.

The two baseline MLPs will join MPS Squadrons to provide 'piers in the ocean' to support the US Navy and US Marine Corps sea-basing concept. Designed to increase intra-theatre agility, the MLPs are a highly flexible ship class that will allow the Large Medium-Speed Roll-On/Roll-Off (RO/RO) vessels (LMSR/T-AKRs) and *Spearhead* class JHSVs to offload equipment, materiel and people to the MLP for trans-shipment to shore using Landing Craft Air-Cushion vehicles (LCACs) or other vessels, such as lighters.

The MLP is something of a modular ship that emphasises both payloads *and* platforms. While not as modular as the Littoral Combat Ships, with their mine countermeasures, anti-surface and anti-submarine mission modules/packages that can be swapped out/in during the course of a couple of days, the

Table 3.4.1.

MONTFORD POINT (MLP-1) PRINCIPAL PARTICULARS

Building Information:	
Laid Down:	19 January 2012
Launched:	12 November 2012[1]
Delivered:	14 May 2013[2]
Builders:	General Dynamics NASSCO, San Diego, California.
Dimensions:	
Displacement:	78,000 tons (80,000 tons with core capability set installed).
Overall Hull Dimensions:	239m x 50m x 12m (at load line). Length between perpendiculars is 233m.
Equipment:	
Armament:	None. Possibility of installing weapons positions for light machine guns.
Aircraft:	None. Possibility of establishing a capability to operate unmanned aerial vehicles.
Sensors:	Commercial navigation radars. Differential GPS.
Communications:	Commercial communications suite with additional military satellite communications. VHF & UHF radio links.
Cargo Capabilities:	155m x 50m mission deck providing space for 3 x LCAC lanes and a 2,300m^2 vehicle deck.
	Storage for 380,000 gallons of JP-5 fuel and 100,00 gallons of potable water.
Loading Support:	105-ton transfer ramp capable of transporting an M1A2 main battle tank (68 tons) in Sea State 3.
Propulsion Systems:	
Machinery:	Integrated electric propulsion. Four MAN/B&W 6L48/60 diesel engines rated at 25MW total provide power to two 10MW electric motors driving two shafts and to one 2MW azimuth bow thruster.
	Sustained speed is in excess of 15 knots with maximum speed c. 20 knots. Range is 9,500 nautical miles at 15 knots.
Other Details:	
Complement:	Accommodation is provided for 34 crew. These are civilian-contract MSC mariners.
Class:	Three ships have been ordered; *Montford Point* (MLP-1); *John Glenn* (MLP-2) and *Lewis B Puller* (AFSB-1). A second AFSB has been authorised and a third is planned.

Notes:

1 Date of float out. Christening was on 2 March 2013.

2 Refers to delivery from NASSCO. Installation of the core capability set took place between November 2013 and April 2014; the ship is expected to become operational in 2015.

MLP in its basic form comprises a common hull/machinery/propulsion package with add-on modifications that compose the core capability set (CCS).[9] The CCS includes a vehicle staging area, vehicle transfer ramp, large mooring fenders and three LCAC vehicle lanes that enable surface connector interface for manoeuvre of equipment and cargo ashore. The MLP design is based on commercial float-on/float-off technology to provide a surface interface between large supply ships and LCAC surface connectors.[10]

The MLP can typically operate 25 miles (40.2km) or more from shore, in seas up to Sea State 3, to transfer equipment and materiel at sea, depending on the threat risk and operational scenario. With its mission deck removed, it can serve as a semi-submersible platform, offering salvage and point-to-point heavy-lift transfer capabilities. Ship utility services that are linked in to the mission deck provide the flexibility to incorporate potential future platform upgrades that could include additional capabilities such as berthing, medical services, command and control, mission planning, a vehicle transfer system, connected under-way replenishment, a container handling crane and an aviation operating spot.

The MLP-1's programme provenance extends back to the US Navy Maritime Prepositioning Force-Future (MPF-F) initiatives in the early 2000s. The original MLP program envisioned three MLPs for each of the three notional MPF-F squadrons (nine MLPs in all) and included an enhanced surface connector interface capability that would permit the MLP to operate US Navy and US Army craft, for example, the Landing Craft Utility, and future ship-to-shore connectors, up to

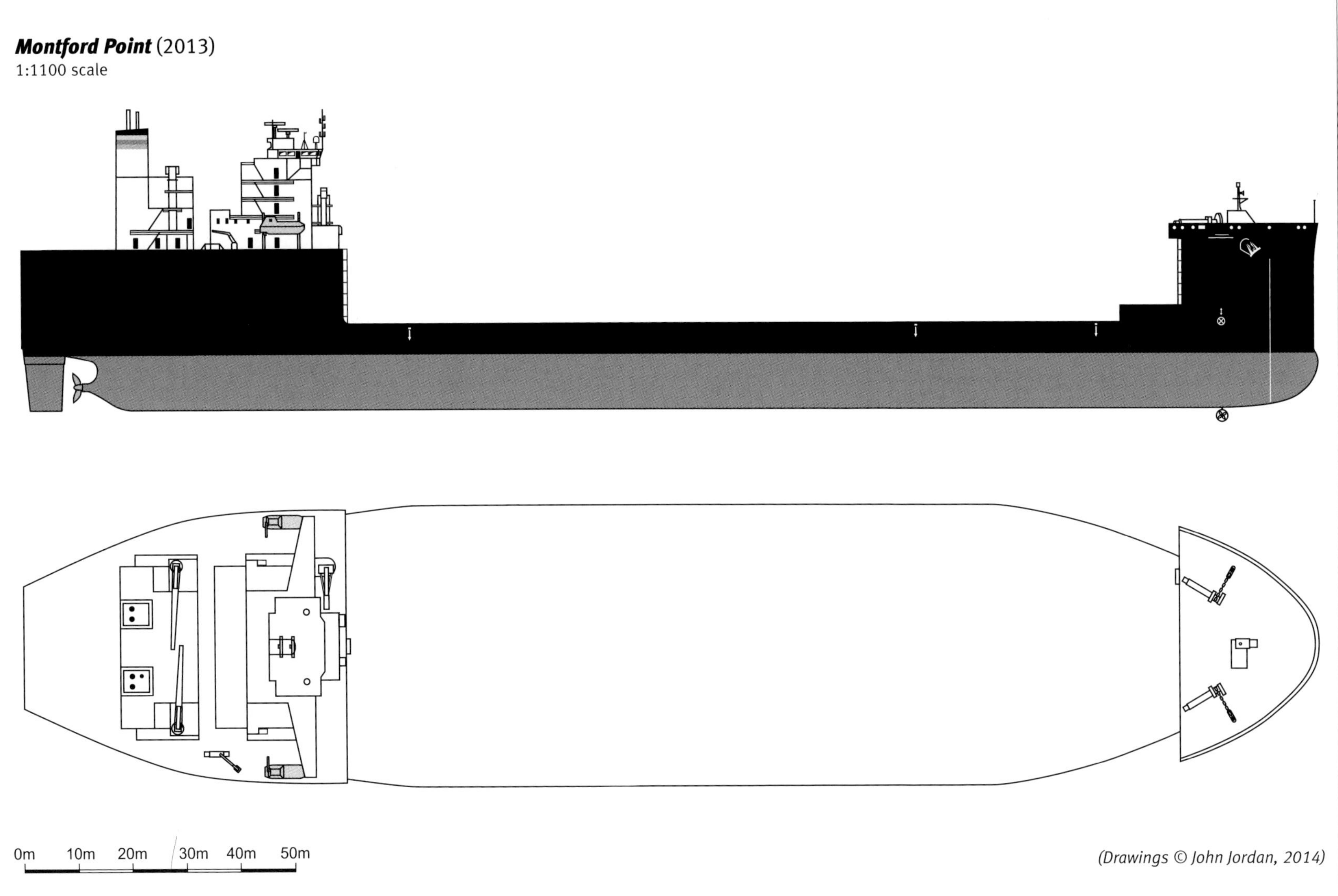

(Drawings © John Jordan, 2014)

Sea State 4. A preliminary design by NASSCO included provision of utility services support to an 80,000ft^2 mission deck for a US Marine Corps brigade-size force, the flexibility to incorporate future platform upgrades, and the capability to accommodate six LCACs. The notional MPF-F squadron was to comprise three MLPs, two LHA-R large-deck amphibious ships, one LHD large-deck amphibious ship, three T-AKE cargo ships, three LMSR cargo ships and two legacy maritime prepositioning ships. The MPF-F ships were to be capable of prepositioning critical equipment and twenty days of supplies for a future Marine Expeditionary Brigade.[11]

As more requirements and capabilities were added to the MPF-F MLP design, however, costs increased to about US$1.3bn for the lead ship. Significant cost reductions had therefore to be achieved to save the programme. NASSCO worked with the US Navy to achieve those cost reductions by leveraging an existing NASSCO product tanker design. In November 2010, NASSCO proposed to the US Navy an MLP concept based on the 'Alaska'-class tankers. 'I took Navy officials with me to visit the BP tankers and to ask them what they liked and didn't about the ships, NASSCO's President Fred Harris remarked.[12] 'And we took their evaluations and our experience in building the tankers as a powerful baseline in which to improve the USN version of this ship.'

The US Navy worked very closely with NASSCO to identify cost savings early in the revamped MLP design work while pursuing a concurrent design and production engineering approach. 'These efforts ensured a high degree of design and production-planning maturity prior to the start of construction

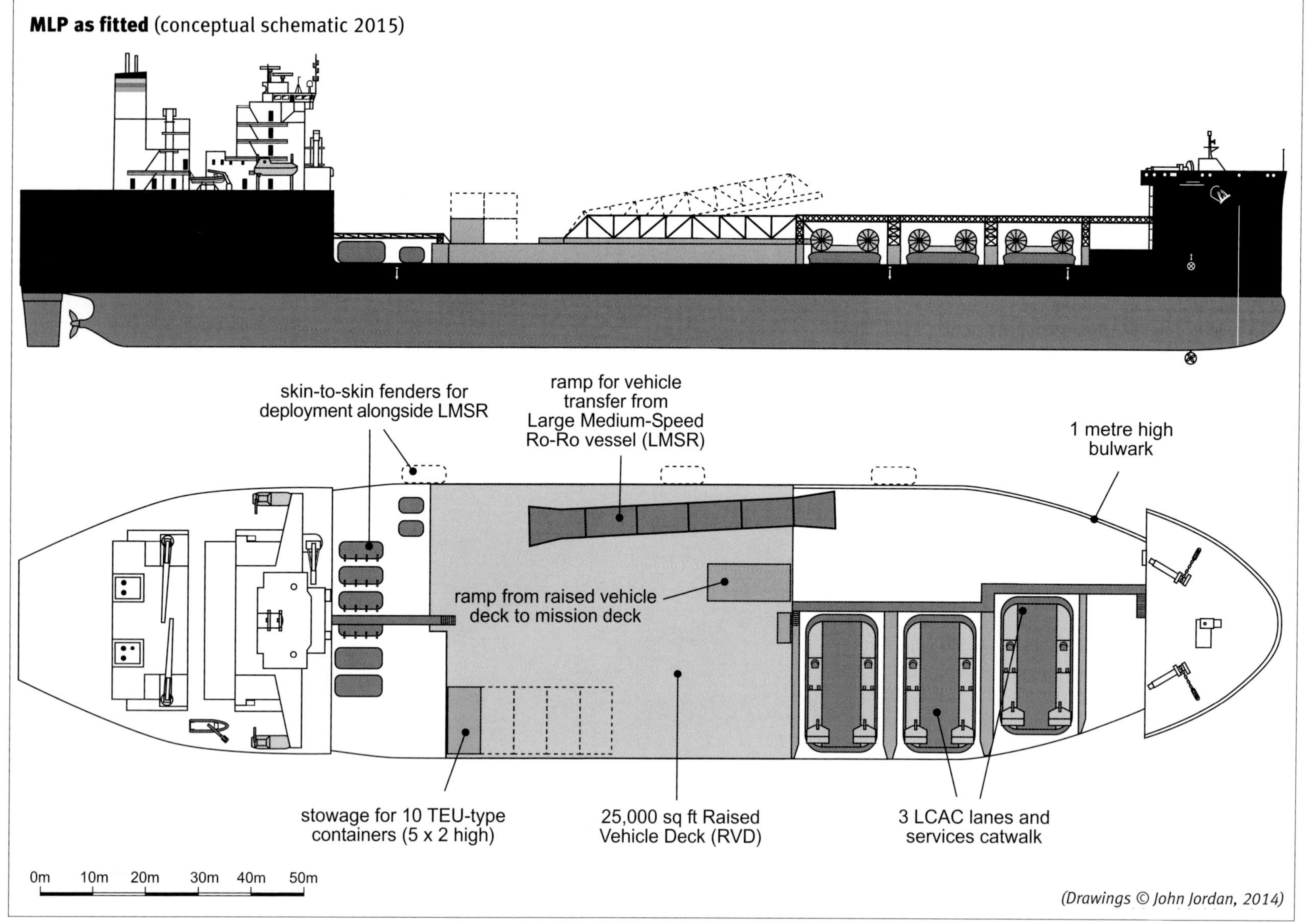

(Drawings © John Jordan, 2014)

to minimize cost and schedule risk,' Captain Stevens said, 'and resulted in a very stable design. In fact, 100 per cent of the MLP-1 design was completed before construction began.' Since then, there has been virtually no 'design churn,' a factor contributing to price and delivery success.

TEST-A-LITTLE...

US Navy Rear Admiral Wayne E Meyer, 'Father of Aegis,' was famous for his dictum – 'Build-a-little, test-a-little, learn-a-lot!' – that helped ensure the Aegis anti-air and ballistic missile-defence systems were among the most successful weapon systems programmes ever – at least in the United States. Taking a cue from Aegis, the US Navy thoroughly tested the MLP concept during a series of at-sea trials that used surrogate MLP ships and RO/RO vessels to demonstrate the ability in a range of sea states, from dead calm to Sea State 4.[13]

For example, in the autumn of 2006, two MSC ships performed a unique at-sea demonstration off Norfolk, Virginia. The USNS *Red Cloud* (T-AKR-313), a 950ft LMSR ship loaded with combat vehicles and trucks, was paired with the MSC-chartered M/V *Mighty Servant III*, a 594ft semi-submersible heavy-lift ship. Both ships were moored together in the seaway and offloaded vehicles from *Red Cloud* onto the *Mighty Servant* surrogate, driving down the *Red Cloud*'s side ramp and onto LCACs that carried them ashore and back from the *Mighty Servant III*'s semi-submersible deck. The demonstration followed a September 2005 experiment involving the LMSR USNS *Watkins* (T-AKR-315) and the MSC-chartered *Mighty Servant I*, which gauged the MLP potential.

In March 2008, the US Navy staged a sea-basing exercise off the coast of Liberia, using Improved Navy Lighterage System (INLS) causeways to transfer supplies from the transport ship *2ND LT John P Bobo* (T-AK-3008) to the chartered high-speed catamaran *Swift* (HSV-2). This further advanced the MLP concept. *(US Navy)*

In March 2008, the US Navy staged a sea-basing exercise off the coast of Liberia as part of the Africa Partnership Station's West Africa Training Cruise '08. This marked the first time the US Navy's Improved Navy Lighterage System (INLS) causeways were used at sea to transport cargo from ship-to-ship and from ship-to-shore. First, the MSC's *LCPL Roy M Wheat* (T-AK-3016) used cranes to assemble the INLS RO/RO discharge facility at sea. Once assembled, MSC sailors transferred trucks, equipment and humanitarian aid supplies from *Wheat*, the MSC's *2ND LT John P Bobo* (T-AK-3008) and the amphibious landing ship *Fort McHenry* (LSD-43) to the MSC-chartered high-speed catamaran *Swift* (HSV-2). *Swift* then ferried these humanitarian aid supplies to the Liberian port of Monrovia, where they made deliveries to schools and clinics.

Further successful trials of MLP technology took place in early 2010. In tests sponsored by the Strategic Theater Sealift Office of the Program Executive Office Ships (POE Ships), a new, self-deploying ramp system deployed on the chartered *Mighty Servant III* was used to transfer vehicles and equipment to a self-deploying platform on the MSC's *Soderman* (T-AKR-317) in conditions up to Sea State 4. *(US Navy)*

Two years later, in February 2010, the US Navy completed an at-sea exercise that confirmed the ability to transfer vehicles between a surrogate MLP ship and an LMSR using a self-deploying ramp system installed on the *Mighty Servant III*, and a new self-deploying side-port platform installed on the MSC's *Soderman* (T-AKR-317). Personnel and

The basic MLP design is a variant of General Dynamics NASSCO's BP 'Alaska'-class oil tanker. This image shows the fourth and final vessel of the class, *Alaskan Legend*, on sea trials in 2006. *(General Dynamics NASSCO)*

vehicles successfully transferred between the ships in high Sea State 3 and low Sea State 4 conditions during several days of testing in the Gulf of Mexico. Later that year, the US Navy's Naval Sea Systems Command explained the MLP concept: 'The platform in its basic form possesses add-on modules that support a vehicle staging area, side-port ramp, large mooring fenders and up to three [LCAC] lanes to support its core requirements. The February 2010 Test Article Vehicle Transfer System (TAVTS) demonstrated a self-deploying ramp system and a new self-deploying side-port platform that successfully transferred vehicles between a surrogate MLP (outfitted with a dynamic positioning system) and a LMSR (T-AKR 317) into Sea State 4. The program of record MLP will still transfer at sea vehicles and equipment with the LMSR but will use a skin-to-skin/fendering – rather than TAVTS – operation that will be capable of operating through Sea State 3.'

COMMERCIAL DESIGN AND CHARACTERISTICS

The *Montford Point* design is based on the BP 'Alaska'-class tanker that was already in the NASSCO portfolio.[14] In September 2000, BP awarded NASSCO a US$630m contract for the construction of three, state-of-the-art, double-hull tankers for transporting crude oil from Valdez, Alaska, to BP's US Pacific coast refineries. BP exercised an option for a fourth ship a year later. The 185,000 deadweight ton, double-hull ships have a length of 941ft (287m) and a beam of 164ft (50m). Capacity is approximately 1.3 million barrels of oil at a design draft of 61.5ft (18.7m). The first ship, *Alaskan Frontier,* was delivered in August 2004; the second ship, *Alaskan Explorer*, in March 2005; the third ship, *Alaskan Navigator,* in November 2005; and the fourth and final ship, the *Alaskan Legend,* in August 2006.

The ships' design emphasises environmental safety and redundancy, shaped by the *Exxon Valdez* disaster of 24 March 1989, when a single-hull tanker ran aground in Prince William Sound, spilling as much as 750,000 barrels of crude oil. In addition to a double hull, the ships have twin diesel-electric propulsion systems in segregated engine rooms, two propellers and twin rudders. Diesel-electric power was chosen because of its low emissions and reliability. Seawater rather than lubricating oil cools the propeller shafts, and cargo piping is installed in the cargo tanks instead of on deck to reduce the chance of accidental oil spills. The ships incorporate leading-edge-of-the-shelf technology in ship navigation and control systems.

'There is significant commonality between BP's Alaska class tankers and the MLP-1 design,' Captain Stevens said. 'When we looked at the design for the MLP, about 65 per cent of it is common with the BP tanker. We redesigned the mid-section of the ship to account for required structural changes and the MLP's core capabilities set.'

The MLP is shorter than the 'Alaska'-class tanker, being 785ft (239m) in length but retaining a beam of 164ft (50m). This is more than a third wider than most ships of similar length, making it an extremely stable platform for sea-base operations. The mobile landing platforms are built to commercial steel-hulled vessel rules rather than warship standards and are not shock-qualified.

The ships displace 78,000 tons without the core capability set (CCS) installed. The CCS adds around 2,000 tons to overall displacement (the AFSB variant displaces about 90,000 tons). They are powered by a commercial twin-screw, diesel-electric propulsion system integrating four MAN/B&W medium-speed diesel generators with two 10MW electric motors and a 2MW azimuth bow thruster as part of an integrated electric propulsion arrangement. The propulsion system operates most economically at a sustained speed of around 15 knots, providing an endurance of more than 9,500 nautical miles. Top speed is about 20 knots.

MLP-1 and MLP-2 are engineered to ballast down and lower into the water, with a 2° list. This allows three LCACs to access lanes for amphibious loading and unloading as well as equipment transport. The baseline MLP has a 25,000ft^2 raised vehicle deck for vehicle and equipment storage. The two ships are also equipped with a 105-ton transfer ramp capable of transporting an M1A2 main battle tank (weighing 68 tons) in Sea State 3.

MLP-3 AFSB VARIANT

The flexibility of the basic MLP concept was demonstrated on 5 November 2013, when NASSCO laid the keel for *Lewis B Puller* (MLP-3/AFSB-1), the US Navy's first specifically-designed afloat forward staging base. The AFSB is an affordable alternative to deploying more-costly forces for peacetime presence and low-intensity operations, avoiding tying up the resources of an asset that costs more to operate. The AFSB mission is to provide C4ISR (command, control, communications, intelligence, surveillance and reconnaissance) support to mine countermeasures and special operations, and to maintain mission-specific aircraft and systems. Consequently, the AFSB variant of the MLP concept is designed around four core components; aviation, berthing, an equipment staging area, and command and control.

The need for the AFSB emerged out of a requirement from Central Command for countermine and

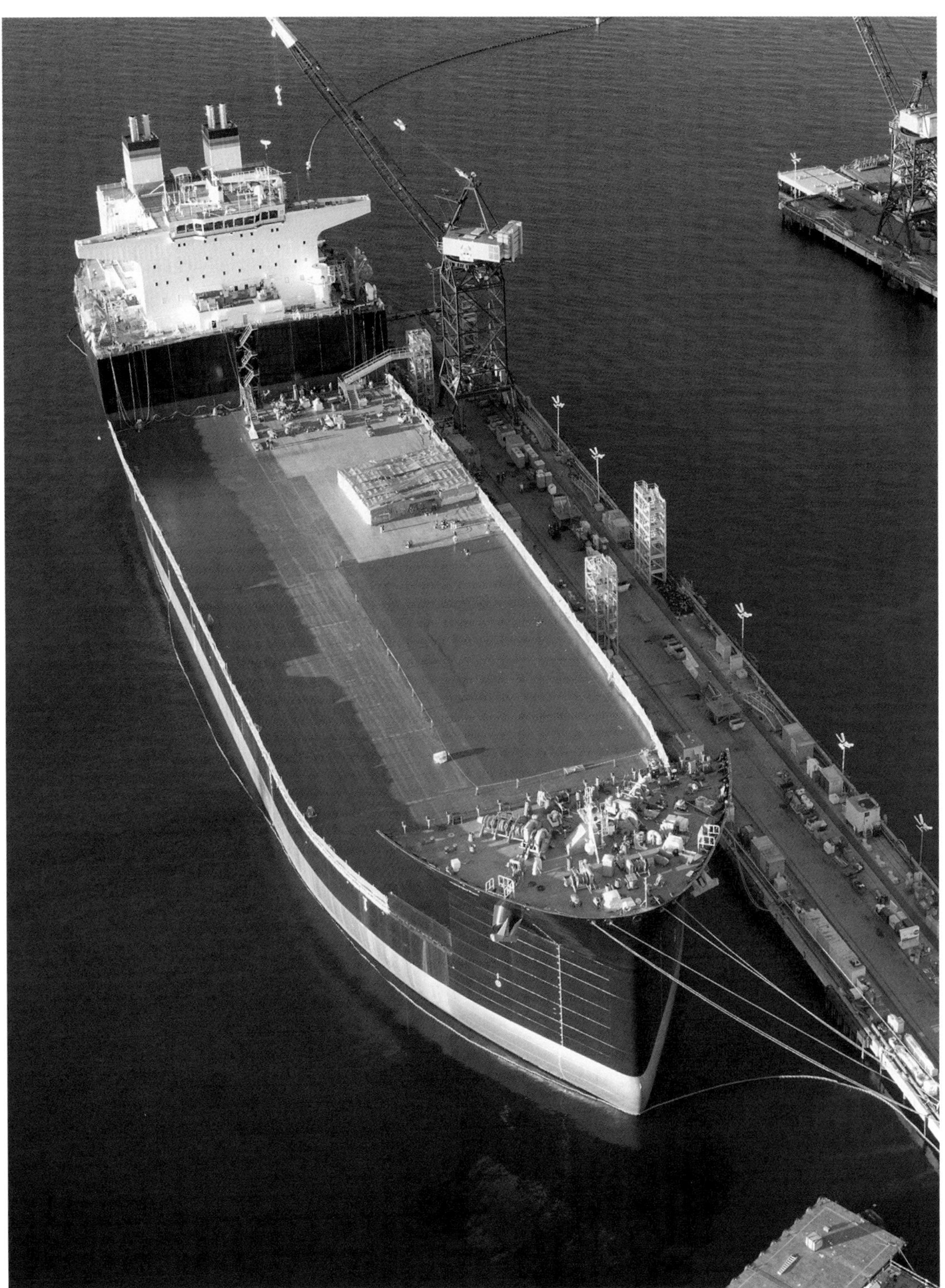

An overhead view of *Montford Point* (MLP-1) in January 2013. The MLP is shorter than the 'Alaska'-class tanker but retains the same 50m beam. This makes them much wider than ships of similar length, providing an extremely stable platform for sea-base operations. *(General Dynamics NASSCO)*

Special Operations forces staging in the Arabian Gulf area. A modified amphibious transport dock, the *Ponce* (AFSB(I)-15) has been performing this mission in the Arabian Gulf since mid-2012 on an interim basis.[15] The US Navy intends to relieve *Ponce* with an AFSB, possibly the initial ship built to this configuration, *Lewis B Puller*. Although some observers have hinted that *Ponce* might remain in the active fleet to support US Southern Command / Fourth Fleet, Admiral Jackson noted that the US Navy's plans for *Ponce* were not settled as of mid-2014.

The two MLP AFSB variants are based on the same basic hull and mechanical and electrical platform of the two initial ships but do not include the MLP core capabilities set. Instead, they are fitted with:

- A forward house (250 military detachment berths) with common spaces to support ready room, command, operations, and logistics functions.
- Operating spots for two MH-53E Sea Dragon mine-countermeasures (MCM) helicopters (or other helicopters or unmanned aerial vehicles) with parking for two more Sea Dragons. There is also a hangar sized for two MH-53Es for O-Level maintenance.
- MCM and Special Operations ordnance magazines.
- Approximately 65,000ft^2 of deck space for MCM or special operations force boats, four Mk-105 minesweeping sleds, unmanned underwater vehicles and equipment.
- Small boat handling equipment.
- An underway replenishment capability.

At the January 2014 Surface Navy Association conference, Captain Stevens noted that the US Navy would evaluate the use of the Osprey MV-22 tiltrotor aircraft from the AFSBs. Although some have called for the AFSB to be something of a VTOL (vertical take-off and landing) air-capable amphibious assault ship, capable of operating the F-35B Lightning II Joint Strike Fighter, Captain Stevens stated in May 2014 that the F-35B was not being considered for AFSB operations. Still, the AFSB/MV-22 combination opens up the mission-task aperture immensely. 'The Marines are already experimenting with MV-22 operations from MSC's T-AKE auxiliary dry cargo ships,' Admiral Jackson noted, 'with good success.'

CONTRACT AND COSTS

The first three ships are funded out of the National Defense Sealift Fund administered by the Secretary of Defense, with programme management and execution under the Assistant Secretary of the Navy, Research, Development and Acquisition and the Program Executive Office Ships. The prime and major contractors are General Dynamics NASSCO, San Diego, California; Lockheed Shipbuilding Seattle, Washington; Raytheon San Diego, California; and Vigor Marine, Portland, Oregon.

On 13 February 2009, the US Navy awarded NASSCO a US$3.5m contract for systems design for the MLP programme that started the procurement process. Various additional awards for further design work and long lead materials followed. On 27 May 2011, these culminated in a US$744m contract with NASSCO for the detail design and construction of *Montford Point* (MLP-1) and *John Glenn* (MLP-2), as well as an option for a third ship, the future *Louis B Puller* (then MLP-3), that brought total programme costs for the three MLPs to US$1.3bn.

The CCS, which includes a raised vehicle deck, a vehicle transfer ramp, LCAC lanes and service (fuel, water and air) connections, was government furnished equipment supplied under a separate contract. On 16 November 2012, the government awarded a US$32.8m competitive contract to Vigor Marine for detail design, construction, and ship integration of the core capability set for *Montford Point* and *John Glenn*. CCS integration for *Montford Point* began in late November 2013 and completed in April 2014.

The USNS *Montford Point* was delivered to the Navy in May 2013 at a cost of US$496m, and will

A stern view of *Montford Point* (MLP-1) in dry dock. Powered by integrated electric propulsion generated by four MAN/B&W medium-speed diesels, *Montford Point* is equipped with twin screws that provide a 9,500 nautical mile radius at a sustained speed of 15 knots. The two AFSB variants of the *Montford Point* design are based on the same hull and mechanical platform but replace the core capabilities set with a different equipment outfit. *(General Dynamics NASSCO)*

Above: In advance of the completion of *Louis B Puller* (AFSB-1), the US Navy has been operating the former amphibious transport dock *Ponce* (LPD-15) as an interim afloat forward staging base under the AFSB(I)-15 designation. She has been operating in the Middle East in support of mine countermeasures and other operations and has been designated as a test bed for the US Navy's trial laser weapon system. This September 2012 view depicts her in the Arabian Gulf during the IMCMEX 2012 international mine-countermeasures exercise; two MH-53E Sea Dragon minesweeping helicopters can be seen on her deck. *(US Navy)*

Below: The flexibility of the baseline MLP design has been demonstrated by its adaptation for use as an afloat forward staging base to support missions such as mine countermeasures and Special Forces operations. This conceptual image of *Louis B Puller* (MLP-3/AFSB-1) demonstrates key differences from the baseline MLP, with the core capabilities set replaced by forward accommodation for up to 250 personnel, a flight deck for helicopter operations and deck space and equipment to handle mine countermeasures or Special Operations force boats. *(General Dynamics NASSCO)*

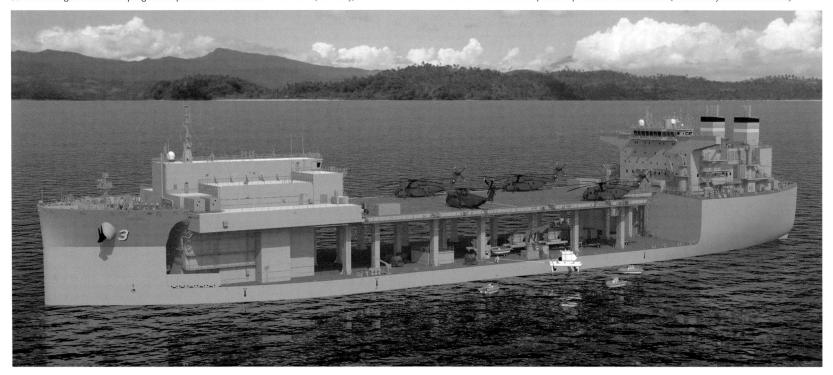

join the Fleet in 2015. NASSCO delivered the USNS *John Glenn* to the Navy in March 2014 and, with its integrated CCS, will cost a total of US$436m.

On 27 February 2012, the USN awarded NASSCO the contract option for the *Lewis B Puller* (MLP-3). MLP-3 construction began on 20 February 2013. The contract was subsequently modified to convert the MLP-3 to an AFSB. The USNS *Lewis Puller* (AFSB-1) is scheduled to be delivered in September 2015 at a cost of US$623m.

The contract took the total value of the three-ship programme for NASSCO to c. US$1.56bn. Interestingly, the original 2008 request for proposals for the MPF-Future MLP program envisioned three ships at a cost of US$3.3bn, with the lead ship alone estimated to cost more than US$1.3bn. Ultimately, therefore, the US Navy was able to procure three ships, including one built to an enhanced configuration, for the price of little more than the first of the originally configured ships. This is, perhaps, one of the best modern examples of the US Navy and a shipbuilder working together to aggressively attack requirements and drive costs down.

The still-unnamed second AFSB is a FY2014 procurement funded out of the Shipbuilding and Conversion, Navy account. Funding will be requested in the FY2017 budget for a third AFSB vessel, which would be delivered in early 2020. There are no ships programmed beyond this fifth ship, although successful trials, exercises and real-world experiences could drive a need for more.

'We deliver what we advertise, in cost and quality,' Captain Stevens underscored. 'For example, builders and acceptance trials conducted by INSURV [Navy Board of Inspection and Survey] went extremely well for the first two MLPs, with no significant issues or "starred cards". MLP-1 final contract trials were completed successfully in September 2013. As of mid-2014, MSC is working up MLP-1, in line with plans to conduct developmental and operational testing in the summer and fall 2014. We expect to do extremely well, there, too.'

'Operational test and evaluation will complete in November 2014', Admiral Jackson confirmed. 'After that, we'll put MLP-1 through her paces, to flesh out what she can and can't do, and then to see how to expand her capabilities. She is already scheduled to participate in three exercises in her first year.'

'MIX AND MATCH' MODULARITY

Some have described the *Montford Point* class MLPs and AFSBs as naval 'Transformers' – vessels that can provide 'mix and match' modularity for support to the US Navy and Marine Corps. The ship can be configured to support humanitarian assistance/disaster relief and regional support crisis-response missions, and sustained at-sea operations, in addition to their baseline missions.

'And they put the *military* back into the Military Sealift Command,' Admiral Jackson said, 'providing war-fighters with capabilities not "standard" to MSC's missions and ops.'

The flexible payload aspect of the MLPs encour-

Two images of *Montford Point* (MLP-1) at various stages of construction at General Dynamics NASSCO's San Diego shipyard. The period from keel-laying to float out was less than eleven months, reflecting the advantages of basing the class on a proven design. This also helped restrict overall costs for the first three ships to just US$1.56bn. *(General Dynamics NASSCO)*

Montford Point (MLP-1) pictured immediately after float-out from General Dynamics NASSCO in November 2012. The flexible payload nature of the design means that it is possible to adapt the basic concept to support a wide range of missions. *(General Dynamics NASSCO)*

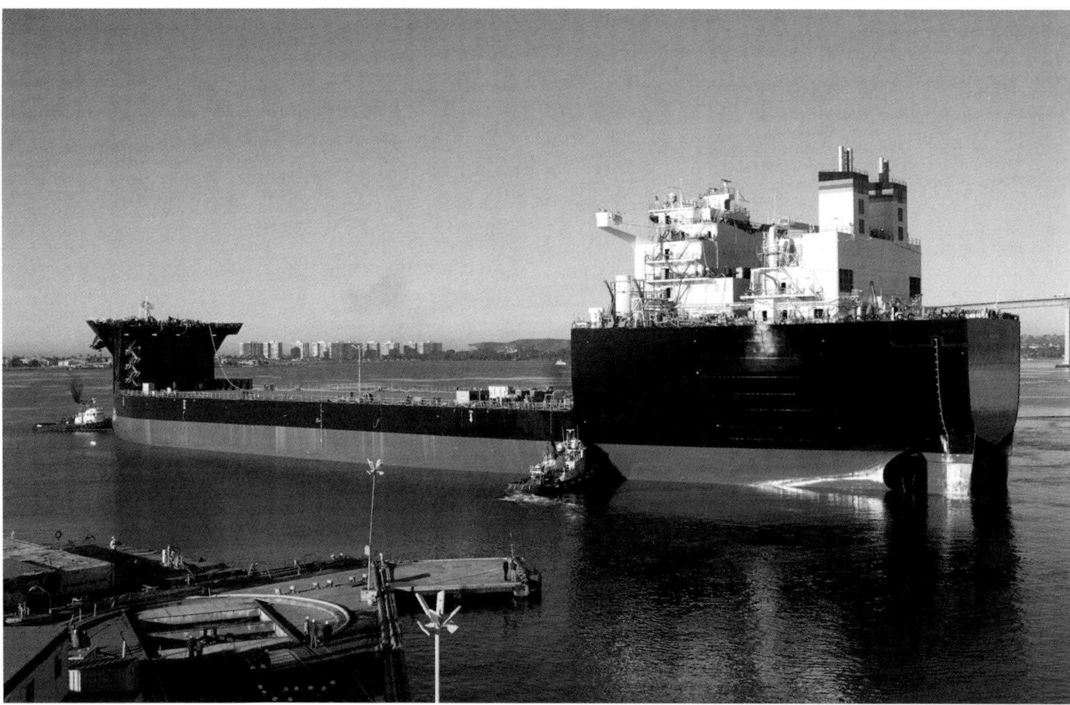

ages this out-of-box thinking. They epitomise Admiral Greenert's focus on payloads versus platforms and, in a sense, 'modularity'. The basic MLP platform, without CCS or AFSB modifications, is a 'truck' that can be configured for a variety of requirements, missions and tasks.

'New modifications to support other missions could be added to support a new generation of sailors and Marines who have yet to be born,' Admiral Jackson said. 'We can easily see this ship serving as a repair ship, a hospital ship, or an aviation depot/support ship, to name just some potential missions.'

Indeed, only lack of imagination (and funding!) can frustrate the experimentation, innovation and discovery that the MLP/AFSB 'connection' brings to the US Navy's fleet.

Notes

1. See Michael R Gordon, 'Admiral with High-Tech Dreams has Pentagon at War with Itself,' *The New York Times* – 12 December 1994 (New York, New York Times, 1994). For further reading, see also William A Owens, *High Seas: The Naval Passage to an Uncharted World* (Annapolis, MD, Naval Institute Press, 1995), pp.163, 165 and William A Owens and Edward Offley, *Lifting the Fog of War* (New York, Farrar Straus Giroux, 2000), pp.175–6, 205. Cited by Sam J Tangredi, 'Sea Basing: Concept, Issues, and Recommendations,' *Naval War College Review* – Autumn 2011 (Newport, RI, US Navy War College, 2011) pp.28–41.

2. *U.S. Navy Program Guide 2014* (Washington, DC, Department of the Navy, Office of the Chief of Naval Operations, 2014), pp.6–7, 99–100. See also the 'Mobile Landing Platform Fact Sheet' on the General Dynamics NASSCO website which can be found by searching http://nassco.com and J F Alexander's 'Mobile Landing Platform: The Future of Navy Sea-Basing,' posted to *Sealift*, the US MSC's official blog on 23 May 2013. This can currently be accessed at: http://mscsealift.dodlive.mil/2013/05/23/mobile-landing-platform-the-future-of-navy-sea-basing/

3. *U.S. Navy Program Guide 2014*, op. cit., p i. See also the author's 'Significant Ships: USNS Spearhead (JHSV-1),' *Seaforth World Naval Review 2014* (Barnsley, UK Seaforth Publishing, 2013), pp.121–35 and 'JHSV-1: 'Spearheading' Joint High-Speed Ops,' *Naval Engineers Journal* – December 2013, (Alexandria, VA, American Society of Naval Engineers, 2013), pp.43–50.

4. 'The US Navy's Mobile Landing Platform Ships (MLP)', accessed at the UTC *Defense Industry Daily's* website at: http://www.defenseindustrydaily.com/the-us-navys-mobile-landing-platform-ships-06525/. See also, Commander Gregory J Parker, USN, *Seabasing Since the Cold War: Maritime Reflections of American Grand Strategy, 21st Century Defense Initiative Policy Paper* (Washington, DC, Brookings Institution, 2010) and Sam J Tangredi, 'Sea Basing: Concept, Issues, and Recommendations,' op. cit.

5. Norman Polmar, *Ships and Aircraft of the U.S. Fleet* – 19th edition (Annapolis, MD, Naval Institute Press, 2013), pp.51–6.

6. *Seabasing Required Capabilities: Annual Report 2013* (Washington, DC, US Marine Corps, 2013). On sea basing in general, see pp.5–6. The report also provides good data on current and future programs in addition to the MLP.

7. *U.S. Navy Program Guide 2014*, op. cit, p.7.

8. Kris Osborne, 'Navy, Marine Corps Build New Sea-Basing Ships,' DoD Buzz website, 10 December 2013, accessed at: http://www.dodbuzz.com/2013/12/10/navy-marine-corps-build-new-sea-basing-ships/

9. The author has previously described the two variants of the Littoral Combat Ship programme in the 2010 and 2011 editions of *Seaforth World Naval Review.*

10. *U.S. Navy Program Guide 2014*, op. cit, pp.99–100.

11. *2006 Concepts + Programs* (Washington, DC, Commandant, US Marine Corps, 2006), pp.50–2.

12. Robbin Laird, '80,000 Tons of Innovation: USNS Montford Point, The Navy's New Mobile Landing Platform,' published on the *Breaking Defense* website on 8 March 2013. This can currently be accessed at: http://breakingdefense.com/2013/03/80-000-tons-of-innovation-usns-montford-point-the-navy-s-new-m/

13. 'The US Navy's Mobile Landing Platform Ships (MLP)', op cit.

14. The following information is taken from NASSCO's BP 'Alaska'-Class Tankers Fact Sheet.

15. This was not new. In the mid-1990s, the US Navy modified and re-designated the amphibious helicopter carrier *Inchon* as an MCM Support Ship, MCS-12, assigned to the Naval Reserve Force.

16. Dr Truver, Director, TeamBlue, National Security Programs, Gryphon Technologies LC, Washington, DC, thanks the Military Sealift Command, Naval Sea Systems Command and General Dynamics NASSCO for their assistance with this chapter.

4.1 TECHNOLOGICAL REVIEW

Author:
David Hobbs

WORLD NAVAL AVIATION
An Overview of Recent Developments

The first 'Ford' class carrier *Gerald R Ford* (CVN-78) took to the water for the first time when her building dock was flooded out during October 2013. The new carrier was subsequently christened by the former President Ford's daughter and ship's sponsor, Susan Ford Bales, on 9 November 2013 prior to being towed down the James River to her fitting out berth some ten days later. *(Huntington Ingalls Industries)*

INTRODUCTION

Current world naval aviation continues to be dominated by developments in the US Navy. Whilst both acquisition and deployment plans for conventional embarked aircraft have been significantly affected by budget cuts, capability gaps and technical delays, ongoing investment in unmanned air vehicles (UAVs) has the potential to revolutionise the way navies use aircraft. Exciting new operational capabilities are evolving in the US Navy that other fleets will have to replicate if their naval aviation capabilities are to remain affordable and effective.

AIRCRAFT CARRIERS AND THEIR AIR WINGS

The future of US Navy carrier operations came closer to realisation when the first 'Ford' class carrier, *Gerald R Ford* (CVN-78), left her building dock in November 2013 to begin a 27-month fitting-out and test period prior to her planned delivery in early 2016. Externally she has a smaller island than the *Nimitz* class, placed further aft, and only three side-lifts; internally she has been designed

Table 4.1.1: US NAVY PLANNED AIRCRAFT PROCUREMENT: FY2014–FY2019

TYPE	MISSION	FY2014[1]	FY2015[2]	FY2016	FY2017	FY2018	FY2019	FYDP 2015–19 [3]
Fixed Wing (Carrier-based)								
F-35B Lightning II JSF	Strike Fighter (STOVL)	6	6 (6)	9 (9)	14 (14)	20 (20)	20	**69 (55)**
F-35C Lightning II JSF	Strike Fighter (CV)	4	2 (6)	2 (9)	6 (14)	10 (20)	16	**36 (53)**
EA-18G Growler	Electronic Warfare	21	0 (0)	0 (0)	0 (0)	0 (0)	0	**0 (21)**
E-2D Advanced Hawkeye	Surveillance/Control	5	4 (5)	5 (6)	6 (8)	5 (8)	5	**25 (32)**
Fixed Wing (Land-based)								
P-8A Poseidon	Maritime Patrol	16	8 (16)	15 (16)	13 (14)	13 (10)	7	**56 (72)**
C-40A Clipper	Transport	0	0 (0)	1 (0)	0 (0)	0 (1)	0	**1 (1)**
KC-130J Hercules	Tanker	1	1 (1)	1 (1)	2 (1)	1 (2)	1	**6 (7)**
UC-12W Huron	Transport	1	0 (0)	0 (0)	0 (0)	0 (0)	0	**0 (1)**
Rotary Wing								
AH-1Z/UH-1Y Viper/Venom	Attack/Utility	21	26 (26)	28 (27)	26 (28)	26 (30)	27	**133 (136)**
VXX (VH-92)	Presidential Transport	0	0 (0)	0 (0)	0 (0)	0 (0)	6	**6 (0)**
CH-53K Super Stallion	Heavy-Lift	0	0 (0)	0 (2)	2 (4)	4 (7)	7	**13 (13)**
MV-22B Osprey	Transport	19	19 (19)	19 (19)	18 (18)	4 (4)	4	**64 (78)**
MH-60R Seahawk	Sea Control	19	29 (29)	0 (29)	0 (0)	0 (0)	0	**29 (77)**
MH-60S Seahawk	Multi-Mission	18	8 (8)	0 (0)	0 (0)	0 (0)	0	**8 (26)**
Unmanned Aerial Vehicles								
MQ-8 Fire Scout/Fire-X	Reconnaissance	2	0 (5)	0 (8)	0 (2)	0 (2)	0	**0 (18)**
MQ-4 BAMS Triton	Maritime Patrol	0	0 (3)	4 (4)	4 (4)	4 (6)	4	**16 (17)**
STUAS[4]	Tactical reconnaissance	0	0 (0)	0 (0)	1 (0)	2 (0)	5	**8 (0)**
Training								
T-6A/B Texan II	Training	29	0 (0)	0 (0)	0 (0)	0 (0)	0	**0 (29)**
Totals:		162	103 (124)	84 (130)	92 (107)	89 (110)	102	470 (636)

Notes:

1 FY2014 base numbers relate to the authorised procurement programme, this varied only marginally from the Presidential budget request.

2 Numbers for 2015 to 2019 relate to base FY2015 budget plans; numbers in brackets reflect purchases for that year previously envisaged in the FY 2014 budget, as adjusted for the authorised 2014 programme.

3 Future Years Defence Programme; numbers in brackets reflect FYDP for 2014–18.

4 Small Tactical Unmanned Aircraft System.

to increase sortie generation by 25 per cent. However, the late delivery of equipment such as the immature electro-magnetic aircraft launch system (EMALS) and advanced arrester gear (AAG) has resulted in the need for structural changes, causing cost increases and delay. AAG has to be installed in sections through holes cut in the flight deck and EMALS may require post-trial changes after the ship is complete.

Meanwhile, previous and planned budget reductions are having a marked impact. For example, the Chief of Naval Operations, Admiral Jonathan Greenert, has stated that five carrier air wings are being limited to the minimum flying hours necessary to maintain proficiency in 2014. From 2015 the US Navy will introduce a new Optimized Fleet Response Plan (O-FRP), to try to alleviate some of the pressure that has built up from maintaining current deployment schedules under fiscal and other constraints. Under the new scheme, carrier strike groups (and ultimately other naval components) will work within a 36-month cycle during which they will be deployed operationally for eight months; the remaining time will be spent on training, maintenance and evaluation activities. O-FRP should provide naval personnel with more time at home and greater stability but comes at the cost of reducing the number of aircraft carriers normally deployed to two, albeit with scope for surge reinforcement in an emergency.

Financial constraints are also having a big impact on orders for new aircraft, with Table 4.1.1 illustrating a further large fall in planned purchases in the FY2015 Presidential Budget Request. Total orders over the five years of the Future Years Defence Programme (FYDP) 2015–19 amount to some 470 aircraft of all types; 25 per cent lower than the equivalent FYDP for 2014–18.

The request was notable in confirming previous controversial plans to halt purchases of F/A-18E/F Super Hornet and EA-18G Growler aircraft; production will cease in 2016 according to Boeing if

An EA-6B Prowler electronic warfare aircraft assigned to the US Navy's Electronic Attack Squadron VAQ-140 (the 'Patriots') pictured whilst operating from the carrier *Dwight D Eisenhower* (CVN-69) during a combat mission in support of Operation 'Enduring Freedom' in May 2013. The US Navy's remaining EA-6B squadrons will transition to the EA-18G Growler by 2015 but the US Marine Corps will continue to operate the type for a while yet. *(US Navy)*

E-2D Advanced Hawkeye aircraft undergoing pre-delivery checks at Northrop Grumman's aircraft integration centre in St Augustine, Florida. The type progressed to full-scale production during 2013. *(Northrop Grumman)*

no further orders are placed. By 2015 there will be thirty-six F/A-18E/F Super Hornet squadrons, nearly double the original plan for twenty. The increase is due, at least in part, to the delays which have prevented the F-35C version of the Lightning II Joint Strike Fighter entering service as planned to replace 'legacy' F/A-18C/D Hornets which have been retired at the end of their fatigue lives. F-35C carrier landing trials are planned for the second half of 2014 and a training squadron, VFA-101 the 'Grim Reapers', has been formed alongside other US Marine Corps and US Air Force training units at Eglin Air Force Base. However, the Presidential Budget Request reveals a marked reduction in future orders compared with the previous plans, leading some commentators to speculate that the US Navy has reservations about introducing a new manned aircraft into service given the potential of UAVs. Meanwhile, the electronic attack community will have completely replaced the EA-6B Prowler with the EA-18G Growler in ten carrier-based squadrons by 2015; the US Navy also operates three expeditionary EA-18G units from land bases. The US Marine Corps, however, continues to utilise the EA-6B and there have been political moves to fund more Growlers as replacements in lieu of some Marine Corps F-35 orders.

The E-2D Advanced Hawkeye has equipped its first operational squadron, VAW-125, the 'Tigertails', and VAW-121 the 'Bluetails', is scheduled to be the next carrier airborne early warning squadron to complete the transition. The new aircraft is due to achieve initial operational capability (IOC), in 2015. Full-scale production of the type began in 2013 following Northrop Grumman's receipt of a US$617m for five aircraft (a further twenty have already been delivered or are in manufacture under previous low rate contracts) and a multi-year purchase of a further twenty-five towards a planned total of seventy-five was confirmed on 30 June 2014. The re-equipment of US Navy air wing helicopters with the MH-60R/S Seahawk is also to be completed in 2014; planned curtailment of further purchases after FY2015 was another controversial element of the FY2015 navy budget.

The British aircraft carrier *Queen Elizabeth* was due to be named by Her Majesty Queen Elizabeth II at Rosyth on 4 July 2014. Completion is due in 2016, and will be followed by an extensive test and work-up programme before fast jet flying trials commence in 2018. By 2015 a significant number of Royal Navy (RN) personnel will have served in US Navy aircraft carriers to gain 'big-deck' experience and qualifications as part of a long-lead specialist skills program (LLSSP), which followed a US/UK agreement signed in 2012 to ensure the generation, training, operation and sustainability of carrier forces with maximum interoperability. The First Sea Lord, Admiral Sir George Zambellas, announced in 2013 that the first Royal Navy Lightning II unit would be commissioned as 809 Naval Air Squadron (NAS). The RN intends the F-35B Lightning II for use primarily as a carrier strike aircraft but the US Marine Corps sees the same short take-off and vertical landing (STOVL) variant principally as a provider of close air support for marines on the ground. The US Marine Corps has already formed its first operational unit, VMFA-121 the 'Green Knights', at Marine Corps Air Station (MCAS) Yuma with a planned IOC in December 2015. This is defined as the capability to deploy a six-aircraft detachment under austere conditions with Block 2B software. However, the US Directorate of Operational Test and Evaluation (DOT&E), has stated that software delays make late 2016 a more realistic date.

The British Royal Navy's new aircraft carrier *Queen Elizabeth* pictured under construction at Rosyth in early January 2014. She was due to be named by Her Majesty Queen Elizabeth on 4 July 2014 prior to float-out. Initial sea trials are scheduled for the second half of 2016. *(Aircraft Carrier Alliance)*

809 NAS will form and work up in the United Sates with the US Marine Corps but Royal Air Force (RAF) Marham in Norfolk has been designated as the UK F-35B base. It is too early to say precisely when it will be ready since there has, as yet, been no announcement about the timing of an initial UK series production order.[1] The three British F-35B pre-production aircraft that have been delivered so far operate alongside the US Marines' VMFAT-501 at Eglin AFB with identical software. The US Navy plans to achieve IOC with the F-35C in February 2019 with improved Block 3F software but the DOT&E considered the autonomic logistics information system (ALIS), to be 'immature and beyond schedule' in mid 2014 and further delays to this system, which is at the core of F-35 operations, maintenance and supply-chain management could have serious consequences. The US Marine Corps is

Two images of United States F-35B STOVL Lightning II variants operating off the amphibious assault ship *Wasp* (LHD-1) during a second phase of development testing in August 2013. The tests saw the RAF Squadron Leader Jim Schofield become the first British pilot to carry out F-35B operations at sea. The US Marine Corps plans to achieve initial operational capability with the type in 2015 but British trials on *Queen Elizabeth* will only happen in 2018. *(Lockheed Martin)*

particularly concerned with the lack of progress with a deployable ALIS which could limit early operations. The UK Ministry of Defence has yet to make a statement about the British relationship with ALIS, or the development of a national alternative. On a more positive note, Lockheed Martin has stated that by the end of 2014 it will have completed 7.4 million out of the required 8.4 million lines of code for Block 2B software, with flight testing due to be completed by mid-2015.

Doubt about the number of Lightnings the UK will ultimately acquire were seemingly dispelled by a senior Lockheed Martin official in 2014 who stated that the UK profile has always been for 138 aircraft, hence the large number of British firms with a major stake in the project. This seems to contradict the 2010 Defence Review, which stated that the UK will 'reduce our planned number of Joint Strike Fighter aircraft'. Asked for comment, the UK Ministry of Defence confirmed the total, blamed any confusion on a misplaced full stop and explained that the temporary decision to switch to the more capable F-35C from the less capable F-35B in 2010 meant that fewer aircraft would have been required to achieve the desired effect. Any reduction in numbers was, therefore, conditional upon changing production to the 'C' variant and fitting the new carriers with catapults and arrester wires, as mentioned in a subsequent sentence. However, this explanation poses further questions. If catapults and arrester wires enabled the procurement of fewer, more capable aircraft, why was this saving not set against the cost of fitting them? Furthermore, when the decision was taken to revert to the 'B' variant in 2012, why was the 'extra' cost of having to buy the original 138 aircraft not mentioned? Of course, any reduction in orders could have an adverse effect on British industrial participation and this is probably the reason why the final number of British orders remains so opaque.[2]

Queen Elizabeth will also operate Merlin HM 2 anti-submarine helicopters and eventually some form of airborne surveillance and control, ASaC, helicopter. Modernised Merlin HM 2s are due to achieve operational capability by 2015 and will, therefore, be available for the new carrier. Meanwhile, Project 'Crowsnest' seeks to fill the ASaC requirement with a version of the Merlin fitted with either the Thales Searchwater/Cerberus system removed from the existing Sea King ASaC 7 or a Lockheed Martin Vigilance system fitted in a pod. Lockheed Martin is also believed to be offering a version with an Israeli Elta radar. After a considerable period of procrastination, the UK MOD are now seemingly getting a grip on the replacement programme and it was announced in February 2014 that the system selected would be operational by 2019, some eighteen months earlier than planned. In addition, it seems that a limited number of the existing Sea King ASaC 7 helicopters will be kept in service when the rest of the Sea King fleet is retired in March 2016 to bridge the gap until the new type is ready.

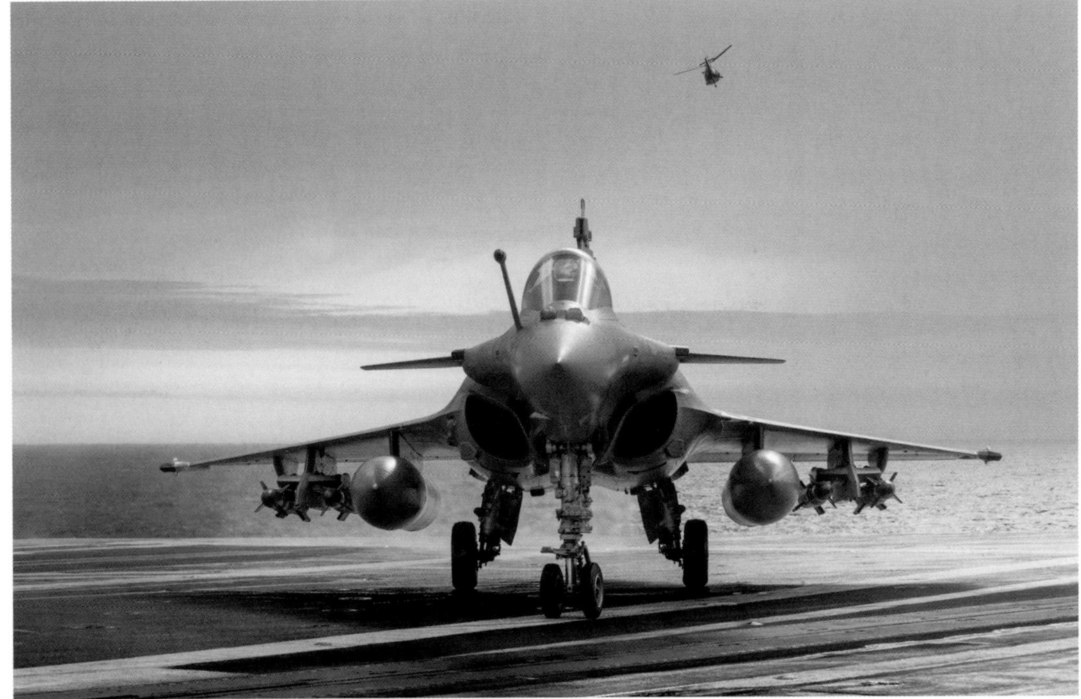

A Rafale M of the French Navy's *Aéronautique navale* onboard the carrier *Charles de Gaulle* in May 2012. The French defence white paper of 2013 has curtailed the number of Rafales that are going to be purchased but a planned upgrade to F3R standard has been confirmed. *(Dassault Aviation – S Randé)*

France's April 2013 defence white paper dropped plans to build a second aircraft carrier, PA2, and reduced the total number of Rafales to be procured for the *Aéronavale* and Air Force from 286 to 225. However, the planned upgrade of the type to F3R standard software, incorporating the Meteor air-to-air missile, HAMMER air-to-ground weapon and other upgrades, has been confirmed. A small number of Super Etendards will be retained by Flotille 17F until 2015/16, after which *Charles de Gaulle*'s air wing will comprise three squadrons of Rafales, with two embarked at any one time and the third ashore at BAN Landivisiau. The remainder of the air wing remains unchanged. A carrier design based on PA2 has been offered for export by DCNS and a model was displayed in Brazil during 2014. The Brazilian Navy has a requirement to replace *São Paulo* by 2025 and the French design might be attractive. However, the possibility of a shared purchase of Rafales with the Brazilian Air Force looks less likely following the latter's selection of the Saab Gripen NG for its FX-2 fighter programme in December 2013. The Brazilian Navy's Skyhawks have undergone an upgrade by Embraer. Re-designated AF-1Bs, they have Israel Aircraft Industries' Elta 2032 electronically-scanned radar which is capable of both air-to-air and air-to-ground modes, new 'glass' cockpits and displays. They are due in service by 2015 to form an air wing with the navy's Sea King helicopters.

Both India and China tested newly-completed aircraft carriers in 2014 and both should reach operational maturity in late 2015. India's *Vikramaditya* suffered a further boiler failure on her delivery voyage, compounding a series of technical problems that delayed her completion and adding to fears about the reliability of her machinery. The elderly *Viraat* was still operating in 2014 with Sea Harriers that have been upgraded with the same radar as the Brazilian Skyhawks and Sea Kings with systems that are showing their age. The ship and her air wing must be regarded as having limited capability but a major refit has allowed *Viraat* to run on until 2018 when the indigenously-constructed *Vikrant*, launched on 12 August 2013, is due to be completed. She will use the STOBAR technique to operate Mig-29K fighters and helicopters but a further carrier is planned to follow her, provisionally named *Vishal*, and it is rumoured that she might have catapults instead of a 'ski-jump'. In May 2013 the Indian Navy commissioned 303 Squadron with Mig-29Ks for service in *Vikramaditya*. It is shore-based at Indian Naval Air Station (INAS) Hansa in Goa, where training facilities for ski-jump take-offs and arrested landings have recently been completed.

The Chinese *Liaoning* continued a programme of embarking aircraft for training and development purposes in 2014. The Shenyang J-15 Flying Shark will form the strike fighter element of her air wing. It has Shenyang developed engines and a Chinese airborne electrically-scanned array, AESA, radar. Reports in Chinese media say that the J-15 has entered full-scale production and recent pictures of aircraft in a fleet grey paint seem to confirm this. The remainder of *Liaoning*'s initial air wing will comprise an interim airborne early warning and control (AEW&C) type, the Z-8YJ Black Bat, based on a derivative of the SA 321 Super Frelon with its search radar mounted on the rear-fuselage ramp. A developed variant, the Z-18YJ, is expected to replace it and another version of the Z-18 is likely to operate in the anti-submarine and sea control roles. The Z-9, a derivative of the Eurocopter AS365 Dauphin, will probably undertake the combat SAR role.

Since completion in 1991, the Russian aircraft carrier *Admiral Kuznetsov* has carried out only five deployments from the Northern Fleet, all to the Mediterranean. The most recent of these took place between November 2013 and May 2014, when the carrier reinforced the increased presence Russia has maintained in the eastern areas of the sea since the outbreak of the civil war in Cyprus.

Italy continues to show *Cavour*'s versatility. She carried out a deployment to the Middle East and around Africa in 2013/14 with an air wing of AV-8B Harriers and Merlins embarked, during which she carried out trade promotion, humanitarian and maritime security operations. During this time, she joined *Charles de Gaulle* and *Harry S Truman* (CVN-

The newly delivered Indian aircraft carrier *Vikramaditya*, the former Russian *Admiral Gorshkov*, sails in company with the elderly *Viraat*, formerly the British Royal Navy's *Hermes*, in January 2014. Her arrival marks the first time since 1997 that the Indian Navy has had two aircraft carriers in commission. *(Indian Navy)*

The British Royal Navy Type 45 destroyer *Dragon* is pictured shadowing the Russian carrier *Admiral Kuznetsov* as she passed through the English Channel in May 2014 after a deployment to the Mediterranean. A major refit of the 24-year-old ship is overdue. *(Crown Copyright 2014)*

75) in the Arabian Sea to carry out exercises and enhance regional maritime security and stability. In the longer term, however, there must be doubts about how many F-35Bs the Italian Navy will receive to replace its aging Harriers. At the start of 2014, Italy planned to acquire sixty F-35As and fifteen F-35Bs for the Air Force and a further fifteen F-35Bs as AV-8B replacements for the Navy. Although these figures are well below the original plan to procure 'at least 131' aircraft, Government plans to save €3bn from the defence budget by the end of 2016 may lead to further cuts to a programme that is not popular domestically. The planned out-of-service date for the AV-8B is 2020.

The most enigmatic ship in the broad carrier category is the Japanese *Izumo* (DDH-183), which was launched on 6 August 2013. Officially rated as a helicopter-carrying destroyer, she is considerably larger than the British *Invincible* class at 24,000 tons full load displacement and is 248m (813ft) long. Her air wing is focused on SH-60K anti-submarine helicopters, which can be augmented or replaced by MCH-101 mine-warfare helicopters. However, it is the ship's potential that intrigues analysts. MV-22 Osprey tilt rotors have already operated from the smaller *Hyuga* (DDH-181) class through-deck 'destroyers' during exercises with the US Navy but *Izumo* is big enough to operate the F-35B Lightning II and, if fitted with a ski-jump, support infrastructure and appropriate magazines, she could do so effectively. Since there appear to be no technical obstacles and Japan already intends to procure the F-35A land based variant of the Joint Strike Fighter, the decision on whether to purchase the 'B' variant for service at sea is essentially a political one.[3]

'BIG-DECK' AMPHIBIOUS WARFARE CARRIERS AND THEIR AIRCRAFT

The first of the US Navy's new generation of amphibious assault ships, *America* (LHA-6), will be carrying out work-up in 2015 following delivery on 10 April 2014 and a commissioning ceremony that is currently scheduled for San Francisco's Fleet Week in October. Designed to mount an airborne assault from greater distances offshore than earlier amphibious assault ships using the capabilities of the MV-22 Osprey and F-35 to the full, her air wing will also comprise CH-53E heavy-lift helicopters, AH-1Z 'gunships' and MH-60S Seahawks. *America* and a second ship, *Tripoli* (LHA-7), ordered in 2012 have an electronically-reconfigurable C4ISR suite that allows them to change seamlessly from amphibious to sea control missions for which an air wing of twenty-two F-35s and twelve MV-22 or SH-60S helicopters would deliver a capability second only to a CVN.

Another significant development in the US Navy's amphibious capabilities occurred on 5 May 2014 when Sikorsky Aircraft Corp officially

The Italian carrier *Cavour* sales in company with the US Navy's *Harry S Truman* (CVN-75) and France's *Charles de Gaulle* on 3 January 2014 in the Gulf of Oman during a deployment around the Middle East and Africa. *Cavour* is proving to be a versatile and effective ship but Italian hesitation over F-35 purchases is casting a shadow over the long-term future of her air group. *(US Navy)*

The first of a new class of amphibious assault ships, *America* (LHA-6), pictured on trials in the Gulf of Mexico in November 2013. Delivered in April 2014, she will undertake a voyage around the coast of South America before a planned commissioning ceremony in San Francisco during October 2014. Unlike previous assault ships, she does not include a well-deck, relying entirely on aviation assets for her amphibious role. *(Huntington Ingalls Industries)*

unveiled the new CH-53K heavy lift helicopter, which will be named the King Stallion. Featuring new, more powerful engines, larger main rotor blades and an airframe built from lightweight, composite materials, the new helicopter will effectively triple the external load carrying ability of the existing CH-53E to more than 12,245kg (27,000lbs) over a range of 110 nautical miles. A first flight is scheduled for the end of 2014, marking the start of a three-year flight test programme. The ultimate plan is to field 200 production variants in one training and eight operational squadrons.

Australia's first new LHD-type amphibious assault ship, *Canberra*, commenced sea trials on 3 March 2014 and a second ship, *Adelaide*, is being completed at Williamstown. Smaller than *America*, these ships still have an excellent amphibious assault capability and are the biggest ever built for the Royal Australian Navy. The *Canberra* class is based on the Spanish *Juan Carlos 1* design, which is capable of operating both helicopters and STOVL strike fighters, even retaining the 'ski-jump' on the forward part of the flight deck.

Prior to 2014 the Australian Government gave too much credence to claims that land-based fighters could support naval or amphibious operations anywhere in the Western Pacific and, consequently, expressed little interest in embarking STOVL fighters like the British, Italian, Spanish and United States fleets, despite their obvious advantages. More sensible counsel now seems to have prevailed. Following an announcement on 23 April 2014 by Australian Defence Minister David Johnston that an extra fifty-eight land-based F-35A Lightning IIs would be procured for the Royal Australian Air Force (to make a total of seventy-two), it emerged that the STOVL F-35B was an option that was 'being considered' for any further purchases. In May Prime Minister Tony Abbot instructed planners working on the next Defence White Paper to examine the possibility of embarking a squadron of twelve F-35B Lightning IIs on an LHD. The ships

United Technologies Corp's Sikorsky subsidiary unveiled the new CH-53K King Stallion helicopter on 5 May 2014. A planned replacement for the existing CH-53E Super Stallion in the maritime heavy lift role, the new type is likely to enter operational service around the end of the decade. *(Sikorsky)*

would need modification, not least to incorporate the autonomous logistics information system, ALIS, but such changes are within the design's scope and would enormously enhance the nation's ability to deploy a credible force when needed. The Australian ships will, in any event, deploy MRH-90 and Chinook transport helicopters and, probably, AS665 Tiger 'gunship' helicopters in the amphibious role. The Royal Australian Navy's 808 NAS was commissioned to operate a small number of MRH-90 helicopters in 2013 but the majority of the embarked helicopters will be provided by the Army Air Corps as part of an amphibious battle group.

Progress has also been made with the Russian *Mistral* class amphibious carriers. The stern of the first, *Vladivostok*, was launched from the St Petersburg yard of Baltiisky Zavod in June 2013, and subsequently taken to St Nazaire to be docked and mated with the bow section prior to launch in October of the same year. Sea trials commenced on 5 March 2014 and delivery is expected around the end of the year. Work on a sister, *Sevastopol*, is also well advanced. They will have an air wing of eight Ka-52K and eight Ka-29 helicopters. Western sanctions imposed against Russia after its take-over of Crimea in early 2014 have not yet affected the project but the matter is clearly sensitive.

Political indecision over replacement options has severely limited what was once an impressive Royal Navy amphibious capability. The final *Invincible* class carrier *Illustrious* was scheduled for final retirement by the end of 2014 after thirty-two years' service, and is to be replaced in the amphibious helicopter carrier (LPH) role by the refitted *Ocean*. When she provided humanitarian relief in the Philippine Islands after Typhoon Haiyan, *Illustrious*' air wing comprised only one Merlin, three Sea King HC 4s and three Army Air Corps Lynx; just enough to keep the art of amphibious operations alive but little more. Five hundred tons of supplies were landed before she resumed her deployment programme.

Training for Sea King HC 4 pilots ceased in December 2013 when 848 NAS decommissioned. 846 NAS had already been withdrawn from service and naval personnel have trained on the Merlin HC 3 with 28 Squadron RAF since 2011. 846 NAS was due to re-commission with Merlin HC 3s at RAF Benson in 2014 and return to RNAS Yeovilton during 2015, when responsibility for the type will be handed to the Fleet Air Arm and the relevant RAF units disbanded. Most Sea King HC 4s have been retired but eleven are to be retained by a flight of 845 NAS until March 2016; the remainder of the unit

The lead unit of two new Royal Australian Navy amphibious assault ships, *Canberra* , is seen entering Sydney Harbour for the first time on 13 March 2014. Based on *Juan Carlos I*, she is fitted with a ski jump in similar fashion to her Spanish sister. Australia is considering operating F-35B Joint Strike Fighter jets from the ship. *(Royal Australian Navy)*

Russia's first French-built *Mistral* class amphibious assault ship, *Vladivostok*, is pictured whilst fitting out at STX Europe's Saint-Nazaire yard in February 2014. Although France has suffered significant pressure to cancel the sale from other NATO countries following the Russian annexation of the Crimea, she is still likely to be delivered as planned at the end of 2014. *(Bruno Huriet)*

will begin to re-equip with Merlin HC 3s from August 2015. To help provide operational capability during the transition period, seven Merlins will be modified to an interim HC 3i standard with a power-folding rotor head, lashing points and naval communications to allow embarked operations. The full upgrade programme to HC 4 standard will install the same 'glass' cockpit as the HM 2, a power-folding rotor head and tail pylon together with other necessary improvements. The first batch will not be delivered until 2018, however, and the last of twenty-five conversions will not be delivered until after 2020, leaving a significant gap in capability and amphibious skills. Meanwhile 847 NAS gave up its Lynx helicopters in 2014, becoming the first unit to operate the new AW159 Wildcat AH 1. Its shore base is Royal Naval Air Station (RNAS) Yeovilton, which is to be the main base for all RN and Army Air Corps (AAC) Wildcats.

SEA CONTROL HELICOPTERS

Naval NFH variants of the NH-90 helicopter are finally being delivered in their intended operational configuration but problems remain and late deliveries are likely to persist into 2015. Norway is particularly unhappy and may yet seek an alternative. The US Navy, on the other hand, is now completing the transition from the legacy Seahawk to the SH-60R/S, which has proved effective and affordable in operation with a planned series of spiral developments to maintain tactical efficiency. The Royal Australian Navy's first two SH-60Rs have been delivered to 725 NAS, temporarily based at NAS Jacksonville in Florida where it will work up as an operational training unit alongside the equivalent US Navy organisation. A total of twenty-four are to be delivered, seven of which will equip 725 NAS in the USA before it moves to its permanent home at RANAS Nowra, New South Wales. The first

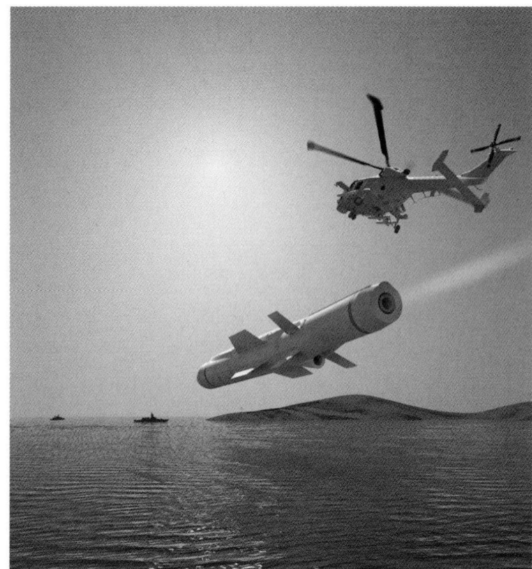

A computer-generated image of the Royal Navy's new Wildcat HMA 2 helicopter firing an MBDA future air-to-surface guided weapon (heavy) – FASGW(H) missile. Although the helicopter will enter operational service in 2015, delays to signing the contract for the missile (an Anglo-French joint venture) mean that it will not be ready before the end of the decade. *(MBDA)*

SH-60R is due to arrive in Australia in late 2014 to prepare for sea trials in 2015. Deployment of the first operational flight is planned for 2016.

The Canadian CH-148 Cyclone project is still far from becoming operational. It originated with a 1992 project to replace the Sea King but successive Canadian governments selected, then cancelled the AW101 Merlin and then selected an undeveloped derivative of the Sikorsky H-92. In 2000 a contract was signed for twenty-eight aircraft to be delivered in 2008 but, as of mid-2014, the project had failed to deliver a single aircraft to meet the specification. Part of the problem is a requirement for the aircraft to float if it ditches and be fitted with a rear loading ramp and cargo handling system so that it can be used in a variety of roles, ruling out obvious alternatives such as the SH-60R.

A more pragmatic approach was demonstrated by New Zealand in 2013 with an agreement to procure the ten Kaman SH-2G(I) Seasprite helicopters originally rejected by the Royal Australian Navy. The contract covers the airframes, spare parts, flight/mission simulators and logistic support, all to be delivered by 2016. The Royal New Zealand Navy has operated an earlier version of the Seasprite since 2001 and describes the new aircraft as an 'advanced, integrated, maritime weapons system capable of multiple missions by day and night in all weathers'. SH-2Gs also serve with the Polish and Egyptian Navies.

The Wildcat HMA 2 is due to enter operational service with the RN in 2015 but the two missiles intended to be its principal air-to-surface armament will not be ready until c. 2020. A development and production contract for the future air-to-surface guided weapon (light) – FASGW (L) – also known as the lightweight multirole missile (LMM) was signed with Thales back in 2011 but arrangements were only concluded in mid-2014 to integrate it into the new helicopter. Meanwhile, contracts for the future air-to-surface guided weapon (heavy) – FASGW(H) – were signed in March 2014 when it was confirmed the programme would be taken ahead as a joint £500m (c. US$825m) project with the French government. In May 2014 the RN announced that 815 NAS will continue to operate Sea-Skua armed Lynx HMA 8 Flights until the type is withdrawn from service on 31 March 2017. A new unit, 825 NAS, is to be formed in September 2014, absorbing 702 and 700W NAS. It will be responsible for Wildcat training, tactical development and, in the short term, administration of the first four operational Wildcat HMA 2 Flights. 815 NAS will begin to convert from the Lynx to the Wildcat during the second half of 2015 and will eventually comprise twelve single-manned Wildcat Flights for embarked operations in destroyers and frigates and two double-manned Flights at very high readiness for the maritime counter terrorism task in the UK The South Korean Navy has also ordered the Wildcat but selected the proven Israeli Rafael Spike missile as its primary armament.

SHORE-BASED NAVAL AVIATION

Fast jet flying resumed in the Royal Navy when 736 NAS was re-commissioned at RNAS Culdrose on 6 June 2013 with fourteen Hawk T1 fast-jet trainers, assuming the roles of the former civilian-manned fleet requirements and air direction training unit used to simulate airborne threats in training exercises. Some civilian pilots will remain but a growing number of RN fixed-wing pilots will be able to maintain flying currency in the unit once they return from flying US Navy and French fighters until they move on to Lightning II training.

The P-8A Poseidon entered operational service with the USN as planned in 2013 but the conversion of squadrons to the new type was slowed for a while to allow aircraft production to catch up with demand. Thirteen aircraft had been delivered by mid-2014, whilst a US$2.4bn contract for the first full rate production batch of twenty-two (taking total orders to fifty-three out of total planned production of 117 US Navy aircraft) was signed on 26 February 2014. By 2014 three P-8A units had become operational with more undergoing conversion at NAS Jacksonville. The US Navy has awarded a contract to Boeing to supply precision wing kits for Mark 54 torpedoes to enable their release from high altitude. The high altitude anti-submarine weapon uses technology developed for the joint direct attack munition and small diameter bomb wing kits and allows aircraft to remain high where they have maximum fuel economy rather than having to descend to low level. The first Indian Navy P-8I arrived at NAS Rajali in mid 2013, having completed testing in the United States, to be used for crew training before joining an operational unit. A contract for a further four P-8Is is planned; the type is known as the Neptune in Indian Navy service. In February 2014, Australia's Prime Minister Tony Abbott announced that eight new P-8A Poseidons are to be procured for the Royal Australian Air Force as Orion replacements, with an option to procure a further four subject to the outcome of the next defence review. The first aircraft is to be delivered in 2017 and the last in 2021.

Turning to shore-based maritime UAV aviation, the Northrop Grumman MQ-4C Triton flew for the first time in May 2013. Intended to complement the P-8A in the broad area maritime surveillance, BAMS, mission by flying long, autonomous missions at over 50,000 feet in 'orbits' over designated areas of ocean, this UAV can examine over 2,000 square miles of sea surface at any one time using radar and EO/IR cameras, sending real-time digital images to fleet units and command centres in the USA using CEC software. It uses its own 'intelligent' systems to fly the mission but changes can be ordered via secure data-links. The first MQ-4C unit, VUP-19, was formed at NAS Jacksonville in Florida in late 2013. IOC is planned for around 2016 when it will deploy its first aircraft to a forward operating base from which orbits will be maintained. A second unit, VUP-11, is to be formed at NAS Whidbey Island. The forward operating bases will launch and recover the MQ-4Cs but their direction while on task will be exercised from the main bases in the United States. In March 2014, Australia confirmed its intention to order the type to operate in conjunction with its own P-8A Poseidons.

UNMANNED AIRCRAFT – A RAPIDLY DEVELOPING FUTURE

After the Northrop Grumman X-47B, call sign 'Salty Dog 2', landed on the USS *George H W Bush* on 10 July 2013, Secretary of the Navy Ray Mabus said 'it isn't very often you get a glimpse of the future. Today those of us aboard the *George Bush* got that chance'. The ability to operate unmanned aircraft as integral components of carrier air wings will have a profound effect on naval aviation over the coming decades and further trials are scheduled to evaluate deck handling and the X-47's air-to-air refuelling capability, both as a tanker and a receiver.

Even without refuelling, the X-47B is reported to have a radius of action of 1,600 nautical miles or the ability to loiter for two hours 1,000 miles from the parent carrier. It has radar, electro-optical and infrared cameras and two internal bays capable of carrying a combined total of 2,040 kg (4,500lb) of weapons or extra fuel tanks. Information from the sensors can be transmitted in real time to shore headquarters in the United States or to any warship with co-operative engagement capability, CEC. The X-47B has all-aspect, low-observable, stealth characteristics superior to those of the F-35 and, unlike earlier unmanned aircraft, it is not 'flown' by a remote pilot but carries out an autonomous mission using its own 'artificial intelligence', monitored by a controller who can, if necessary, make changes via a secure communications link and authorise the use of weapons. On deck the X-47 is given standard signals by marshallers but is taxied by a controller with a remote-control unit strapped to his arm. Once airborne it is co-ordinated within the carrier control zone by ship's staff but long-range mission co-ordination is handed to a shore HQ in the USA. The air vehicle navigates using GPS technology and returns to a designated 'wait' position near the carrier where it orbits, conserving fuel, until given the command to enter the approach pattern. In multiple UAV recoveries, their 'artificial intelligences' exchange position data to maintain safe separation.

The US Navy's next step is to identify the airborne component of the unmanned carrier-launched airborne surveillance and strike system (UCLASS), which it hopes to deploy from 2020.

The US Navy intends to operate the unmanned MQ-4C Triton surveillance aircraft in conjunction with the B737-based P-8A Poseidon. The Poseidon has now entered operational service, whilst the Triton is making good progress in development testing. Australia has agreed to buy eight P-8As and also plans to order Triton drones. *(US Navy / Northrop Grumman)*

Table 4.1.2: CURRENT MARITIME UNMANNED AERIAL VEHICLES

AIRCRAFT[1]	X-47B UCAS	MQ-8B FIRE SCOUT	MQ-8C FIRE SCOUT	SCAN EAGLE	RQ-21A BLACKJACK	K-MAX
Manufacturer:	Northrop Grumman	Northrop Grumman	Northrop Grumman	Boeing Insitu	Boeing Insitu	Kaman
Role:	Carrier UAV jet trials	ISR & Fire Support	ISR & Fire Support	Tactical ISR	Tactical ISR	Heavy Lift
Type:	Fixed Wing Jet	Helicopter	Helicopter	Fixed Wing	Fixed Wing	Helicopter
Length:[2]	11.6m	7.3m	12.6m	1.7m	2.5m	15.8m
Wing/Rotor span:	18.9m	8.4m	10.7m	3.1m	4.8m	14.7m
Maximum Take-off Weight:	20,000kg	1,400kg	2,700kg	22kg	61kg	5,400kg
Engine:	1 x PW F100-PW-220U	1 x RR 250-C20W	1 x RR 250-C47B	1 x piston engine	1 x piston engine	1 x Honeywell T53-17
Maximum Speed:	460 knots (850km/h)	115 knots (210km/h)	140 knots (260km/h)	80 knots	90+ knots	100 knots (180km/h)
Altitude:	40,000ft (12,200m)	20,000ft (6,100m)	17,000ft (5,200m)	20,000ft (6,100m)	20,000ft (6,100m)	16,000ft (4,900m)
Range:	›2,100 nautical miles[3]	110nm radius + 6H	140nm radius + 11H	n/a	n/a	270 nautical miles
Endurance:	9 hours on internal fuel	8+ hours	14 hours	24+ hours	16 hours	3 hours
Weapons/Load:	Twin weapons bays 2,000kg designed load	270kg internal	450kg internal 1,200kg slung load	3.5kg	17kg	2,700kg external

Notes:

1 Data has been compiled from manufacturers' documentation and other publicly available information. Due to considerable variations in published information, data should be regarded as indicative only.

2 Fuselage length.

3 Some reports suggest figures considerably in excess of this.

UCLASS is intended to deliver a persistent intelligence-gathering, surveillance, reconnaissance and strike capability at considerable distances from the carrier. With longer sorties and no requirement for human pilots to maintain proficiency, UCLASS will be significantly less expensive to operate than manned aircraft. The air vehicles would not even need to return to the United States at the end of a carrier deployment but could be passed on to replacement ships, reducing the total number of airframes required. Reinforcements or loss replacements could be flown direct to the carrier from the United States and there will be no requirement for pilot training ashore.

The US Navy is understandably enthusiastic and funding for UCLASS has continued despite budget cuts in other areas. A development of the X-47B would have obvious advantages and Northrop Grumman was one of four companies awarded US$15m contracts to develop airframe designs on 14 August 2013. Boeing, possibly offering a devel-

An image of Northrop Grumman's X-47B unmanned combat air system (UCAS) demonstrator undergoing carrier testing. RFPs for a follow-on operational unmanned carrier-launched airborne surveillance and strike system (UCLASS) were issued in April 2014. *(Northrop Grumman)*

opment of the Phantom Ray; General Atomics, offering the Sea Avenger; and Lockheed Martin, offering the Sea Ghost, are the other three contenders. A draft request for proposal, RFP, to design and manufacture the UCLASS aircraft was subsequently released to the four companies in April 2014 prior to a final selection planned for 2015. Although classified, it seems that the RFP emphasises intelligence-gathering and surveillance capabilities over strike and survivability considerations, albeit sufficient margin will be incorporated into the design to allow these to be added at a later date.

On a much smaller scale, the US Navy is deploying the lightweight Boeing Insitu ScanEagle system from an increasing number of warships. The air vehicle has a maximum take-off weight of 22kg (48lb) and is powered by a 1.5hp two-stroke engine that weighs 2.27kg (5lb). It carries trainable electro-optical or infra-red cameras and is launched into wind by a rotatable catapult and recovered by being flown into a vertical cable rigged above the launcher unit which engages with hooks in the aircraft wingtips. The system gives small deck warships and auxiliaries a surface surveillance capability that can persist longer than manned helicopter sorties at considerably less cost. Boeing Insitu is also developing the follow-on RQ-21A Blackjack, a larger vehicle with a much greater take-off weight to meet the small tactical unmanned air system (STUAS), requirement.

The Royal Navy is one of a number of navies that has also tested the type, deploying two ScanEagle systems during maritime security operations in the Arabian Sea and Indian Ocean during 2014. They flew from the frigate *Somerset* and the royal fleet auxiliary *Cardigan Bay*, the latter highlighting a trend towards using unsophisticated platforms rather than conventional warships as a base for helicopters, detachments of Royal Marines and UAVs. The RN contracted for 600 flying hours per month under a contractor-owned, contractor-operated agreement with Boeing Defence UK but plans to use rotary-wing UAVs in the longer-term. AgustaWestland has been contracted to provide a concept capability demonstration using an unmanned PZL: SW-4 light helicopter. Trials ashore in 2014 are to be followed by embarkation in a Type 23 frigate in 2015.

Meanwhile the broadly equivalent MQ-8B Fire Scout has already been deployed operationally on a number of US Navy frigates and commenced trials

The Boeing Insitu ScanEagle is one of a number of ultra-lightweight UAVs that can provide tactical intelligence, surveillance and reconnaissance functions. Developed from a commercial system, it has been used in both land-based and maritime environments. *(Boeing)*

The RQ-21A Blackjack UAV has been selected for the US Navy's small tactical unmanned air system (STUAS) programme. It uses a larger aircraft to provide greater capability than the previous ScanEagle. The system underwent 'at sea' trials on the amphibious transport dock *Mesa Verde* (LPD-19) in 2013. *(US Navy)*

Two views of a MQ-8B Fire Scout UAV operating from the first Littoral Combat Ship *Freedom* (LCS-1) during search and boarding training off southern California in May 2014. The training combined the capabilities of the unmanned Fire Scout with those of a more conventional SH-60R Sea Hawk helicopter, the Littoral Combat Ship being designed to embark both types. *(US Navy)*

on the new Littoral Combat Ships. A larger version of the MQ-8, the MQ-8C, using the airframe of the Bell 407 helicopter continued development trials during 2014 after a first flight on 31 October 2013 which are scheduled to culminate in sea trials on *Jason Dunham* (DDG-109). The 'C' has the same avionics as the 'B' but the larger airframe allows a greater radius of action or time on task. Up to thirty may be ordered, with nineteen currently contracted following an order for a further five in April 2014.

Elsewhere, the Italian Navy has evaluated the diminutive Schiebel Camcopter S-100 unmanned helicopter and procured a single unit for embarkation in ships employed on anti-piracy missions in the Indian Ocean. It has an endurance of six hours and images from its Wescam MX-10 can be data-linked back to the parent vessel. The French Navy is one of a number of fleets that have also trialed the type but, like its United States and British equivalents, is also looking at a larger rotary capability. To this end it embarked a Boeing H-6U 'Little Bird' unmanned helicopter for trials on the frigate *Guépratt* in the autumn of 2012.

UAVs have also been tested ashore in the logistic support role by the US Marine Corps. Two Kaman K-Max unmanned cargo-lifting helicopters were deployed to Afghanistan from November 2011 as an experiment. Each is capable of lifting 2,720kg (6,000lb) of cargo as an underslung load. They were operated by Kaman under USMC control and proved so successful that the Corps decided to retain the two aircraft indefinitely, although one subsequently crashed in June 2013. In 2014 the USMC planned to evaluate the K-Max against other types to identify the best vehicle for a long-term load-carrying UAV capability.

Notes

1. Whilst there have been many reports that an initial series production order for fourteen British F-35Bs will be placed imminently, there has been no official confirmation of this order to date, nor of that for a planned fourth pre series-production aircraft. The first British operational F-35B unit will be the Royal Air Force's 617 'Dambusters' Squadron, with 809 NAS the second operational squadron to be formed.

2. Government statements have indicated that there is an initial commitment to forty-eight F-35Bs, with the number of additional aircraft ordered to be determined by the 2015 Strategic Defence and Security Review (SDSR) prior to contract award in 2017. In the meantime, the official programme remains for 138 F-35s. The SDSR will also determine whether both *Queen Elizabeth* class carriers will enter operational service.

3. Article 9 of the Japanese constitution outlaws war as a sovereign right and prohibits the maintenance of forces with war potential. In practice, this has been interpreted as prohibiting the acquisition of offensive weapons, such as aircraft carriers. Whilst Japan's current administration is considering ways to loosen the interpretation of Article 9, this has limited public support. As such, the acquisition of F-35Bs for maritime use would be a significant and highly controversial decision.

4. This chapter has been compiled from a wide range of periodicals, of which *Air International*, *Flight*, *Jane's Defence Weekly*, *Warship World* and *The Navy* (the journal of the Navy League of Australia) provide particularly good sources of further reading. Reference should also be made to the following publications, as well as to the websites of relevant aircraft manufacturers and navies:

- Gunter Endres and Michael J Gething, *Jane's Aircraft Recognition Guide- Fifth Edition* (London, Collins-Jane's, 2007)
- Norman Friedman, *The Naval Institute Guide to World Naval Weapon Systems – Fifth Edition* (Annapolis, MD, Naval Institute Press, 2006)
- *Jane's Fighting Ships* – Various Editions (Coulsdon, Surrey, IHS Jane's)

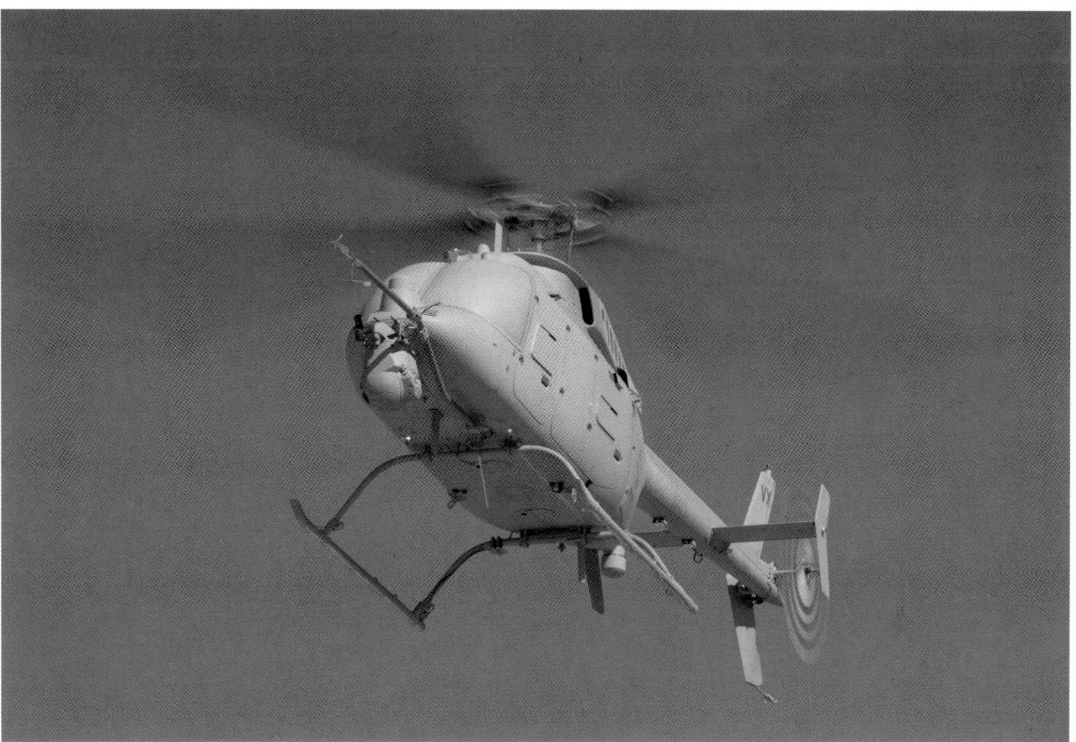

The MQ-8B Fire Scout is being superseded by the larger MQ-8C version, which uses a Bell 407 helicopter airframe to provide greater radius and carrying capacity. *(Northrop Grumman)*

An unmanned version of the Kaman K-Max transport helicopter has been operated by the US Marine Corps to support operations in Afghanistan. The design uses intermeshing rotors for additional efficiency and stability and is specifically designed to handle large external loads. *(Lockheed Martin)*

4.2 TECHNOLOGICAL REVIEW

MINE WARFARE

Author:
Norman Friedman

The history of the two World Wars shows that even moored contact mines – mines which exploded only when a ship touched them – were effective enough to have enormous results.[1] Influence mines do not need contact. The first were magnetic; deployed as early as 1918 in the form of the British 'M Sinker'. The British also developed an acoustic mine just too late to see service during the First World War. Both magnetic and acoustic mines were used in quantity during the Second World War. They were joined by pressure ('Oyster') mines which reacted to the suction generated by a ship passing over them. Magnetic and acoustic mines could be swept by something simulating a ship's acoustic or magnetic fields (signatures), but it proved impossible to create a realistic pressure signature with anything short of a ship-sized object (the US Navy developed an explosion-resistant device for this purpose, but it was too unwieldy to use). There are also UEP mines which respond to the electric field created by the corrosion current between a ship's hull and her propeller. During the Second World War, mine designers learned to set ship counters, so that their weapons would not be set off by the first few ships in a group (which would likely be sweepers). With the advent of microprocessors, it became possible to set a mine for the signatures of specific ships. Some manufacturers offer dummy mines which collect signatures in peacetime so that they can be inserted as desired. That is why some sweep manufacturers offer elaborate sweeps which distribute their magnetic fields to simulate real ships.

Most influence mines lie on the seabed. Their targets have to be close enough to them to suffer damage when they explode, so they are generally useless in water more than about 200ft (61m) deep. However, moored mines can have acoustic, magnetic and UEP sensors, so they can be laid in much deeper water.

The British Royal Navy battleship *Audacious* sinking after hitting a German contact mine in October 1914; she was the only British dreadnought-type battleship lost to enemy action in the First World War. Simple contact mines were effective enough to have a significant impact on both the Russo-Japanese War of 1904–5 and the subsequent First World War; much more sophisticated varieties have been developed and deployed subsequently. *(Editor's collection)*

In the 1950s, the Soviets developed a new kind of mine: a rising mine. The initial version fired a rocket directly up when a target passed overhead. The mine listened for a target, then pinged to obtain target depth (it was a dual-purpose anti-submarine/anti-ship mine). The Chinese received the design before the Sino-Soviet split, and they currently market this weapon; the Iranians are said to have bought it. Later Soviet rising mines used homing torpedo payloads. The most exotic rising mine advertised, although possibly not made, used a manoeuvring rocket that could hit a target to one side of the mine.

Yet another development is remote control (RECO). Minefields can be defensive or offensive. A defensive field normally leaves a gap so that friendly ships can pass through. With RECO, the minefield can be turned on and off using an acoustic signal. The Chinese currently offer RECO mines for export and, presumably, use such mines themselves. However, 'Western' navies have been reluctant to adopt RECO because prolonged immersion may ruin the sensor and even internal circuitry.

As in any other form of naval warfare, mine warfare involves ploys by the miner and the attacker. It is often said that a cheap mine can disable or sink a rather expensive ship, but that cheap mine covers only a minute area of sea. The expensive ship is dealt with by a *minefield*, which typically involves hundreds of mines. Moreover, the mines are hardly recoverable. Mine inventories are not published, but some years ago it was reported that a typical Third World inventory was about 8,000. Inventories are typically limited because mines carry a life cycle cost (stowage and maintenance) but do not contribute to peacetime naval presence or power. Against this, for decades there have been mines converted from standard aerial bombs, which exist in far larger quantities. Storing special fins and sensors is far cheaper than storing complete mines. The Russians produced bomb-mines as early as the Second World War. However, the modern type seems to have originated in the United States during the early 1960s as the Destructor (the current United States type is called Quickstrike). Argentina and Chile advertise their own versions, and presumably there are others. These mine-bombs are limited to use in shallow water.

Then there is really shallow water, which amphibious vehicles may have to cross *en route* to a beach. The weapons involved are likely to be anti-tank mines, which can withstand water pressure down to about 40ft (12m). They are available in huge numbers, and special vehicles can strew them automatically over a beach at low tide. They use both magnetic and pressure sensors on land (pressure in the sense that the target vehicle presses down on them), but in the water only the short-range magnetic sensor is likely to be effective.

A view of the Iranian minelayer *Iran Ajr* after her capture by US Navy forces in September 1987; a number of mines – believed to be Russian-designed M-08 types – can be seen on her deck. Mines, often considered to be a cheap way of sinking an expensive ship, are potentially a key means by which weaker powers can conduct asymmetrical warfare but need to be used in quantity to be effective and carry a not-immaterial life cycle cost. Nevertheless, they continue to offer considerable potential as both offensive and defensive weapons, including as a means to control strategic straits. In particular, they have had considerable influence on operations in the Persian Gulf, where use of extemporised vessels such as *Iran Ajr* has made it more difficult to identify minelaying activities. *(US Navy)*

THE CONTEXT OF MINE COUNTERMEASURES

The meaning of mine countermeasures depends very much on context. During the Second World War, for example, Axis forces laid mines offensively in enemy home waters such as those around the United Kingdom. They also mined potential invasion areas such as the French coast as a defensive measure. Some strategic straits, for example in the Mediterranean, were also mined. Allied navies, particularly the British Royal Navy, had to deal with all three types of threat. For home waters, the need was for thorough and repeated mine clearance. Cleared paths had to be identified to merchant ships and, if possible, not to the enemy, so that he did not know that the paths had to be re-mined.[2] Clearance was vital, but some delays were acceptable. The mine-clearance effort included a systematic attempt to ascertain where the Germans were laying mines. Most mines in British home waters were laid by air, and special mine-watching radars were developed. In this sense British air defence had important mine countermeasures implications. The later Cold War view of the mine threat to home waters varied as the view of a possible war changed.[3]

The situation with respect to an invasion beach was very different. Clearance had to be rapid, not least because a sustained clearance effort would identify the beach to be used, giving an enemy time to mass troops and other defences.[4] It was also necessary to clear a wide area, because a mass of invasion shipping had to approach the enemy beach. The requirement in a strategic strait was more for ships to be able to evade or individually neutralise mines. The need for submarines attempting to penetrate enemy waters to confront defensive minefields was a related issue.

All of these possibilities are still important. Although the threat to British home waters receded with the end of the Cold War, NATO navies are still very much involved in guaranteeing the security of some foreign waters, for example in the Gulf. The Iranians periodically threaten to close the Gulf to vital tanker traffic using, among other weapons, simple mines. In 1987 they tried to do so. Western ability to deal with this kind of offensive is a major deterrent to any Iranian attempt to close the Gulf.

Nor is support of an invasion a distant possibility. In 2003 British and US Marines landed in Iraq in the face of Iraqi threats to mine the coast. These threats had to be taken seriously because mines had featured prominently in the 1991 Gulf War; the US

Navy's missile cruiser *Princeton* (CG-59) and its helicopter carrier *Tripoli* (LPH-10) being damaged. Perhaps ironically, *Tripoli* was serving as mine-countermeasures flagship at the time. The United States currently gains enormously from the US Marine Corps' ability to use the sea as a manoeuvre space off an enemy's coast, and it is investing heavily in the sea basing assets that this requires. However, offshore manoeuvre becomes rather difficult if the waters involved are not cleared of mines. Amphibious operations also require an ability to move heavy stores and vehicles across a beach – which may be mined. Thus the invasion requirement includes the ability to deal with extemporised beach defence mines, which will most likely be the mechanically-strewn anti-tank mines previously mentioned.

Finally, the bulk of the world's shipping continues to move through a few strategic straits. As such, threats such as those issues by the Iranians to close the Straits of Hormuz (at the mouth of the Gulf) emphasise that the need to protect strategic waterways is still a real issue. In short, effective mine countermeasures have thus become a necessary requirement to exercise many forms of sea power.

FIGHTING MINES

Mine countermeasures can be broken down into sweeping, hunting and self-defence. Originally sweeping meant finding mine mooring cables and, typically, cutting them. The mine released from its cable floated to the surface, where it could be sunk by rifle fire. With the advent of influence mines, sweeping came to include triggering mines remotely by creating false signatures, with pressure mines being the most difficult case.[5]

The advent of pressure mines led to a different approach to mine countermeasures: hunting. The minehunter is intended to detect mine-like objects one by one. When it finds one, it examines the object and then deploys an explosive charge to neutralize it. This approach seems to have originated with the US Navy immediately after the Second World War. Many pressure mines had been dropped in Japanese coastal waters late in the war, and they had to be cleared (it was probably assumed, too, that the Japanese had either copied this mechanism or had obtained it from the Germans, so their mines, too, had to be dealt with). To this end the US Navy developed a series of Underwater Object Locators (UOL), ultimately adopting a high-frequency sonar. US Navy landing craft were converted into minehunters, the sonar being coupled with a minedestruction mortar.

It was soon apparent that coastal waters were strewn with mine-like objects which were not mines. Marine growth did not help. This problem has only worsened. Some mines, such as the Italian Manta, were designed specifically to blend into the sea bottom, so that a hunter needed more time to seek them out. It is not difficult to imagine mines made out of (or made to resemble) oil drums and other detritus common off the shores of industrialising countries. On the other hand, hunting could deal

The US Navy helicopter carrier *Tripoli* (LPH-10) in dry dock after striking a mine laid by Iraq during the 1991 Gulf War. The war demonstrated that the threat of mine warfare still has a considerable role to play when planning amphibious operations. *(US Navy)*

A mine is detonated during mine countermeasures training in the BALTOPS 2013 exercise. The ability to conduct effective mine countermeasures is essential to the exercise of many forms of naval power. *(US Navy)*

The Royal Norwegian Navy's support vessel *Valkyrien* leads the minehunter *Måløy* (M342) and the minesweeper *Rauma* (M352) during Exercise Cold Response 10. Mine countermeasures can be broken down into sweeping, hunting and self-defence; in contrast to some other fleets the Royal Norwegian Navy continues to maintain ships specialised for both hunting and more traditional sweeping tasks. Norway has been one of the leaders in mine warfare technology, using air-cushioned hulls to make its mine countermeasures vessels more mobile and being in the forefront of unmanned vehicles operations with its Hugin unmanned vehicle and associated Minesniper anti-mine weapon. *(Norwegian Armed Forces – Torbjørn Kjosvold)*

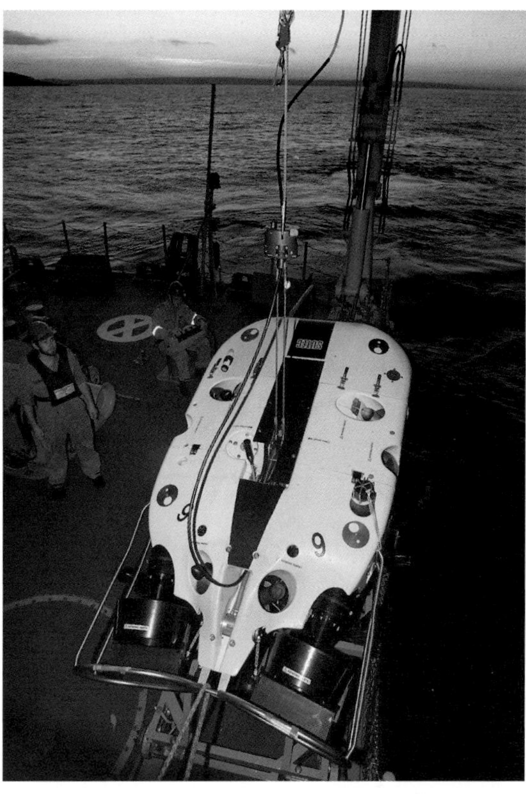

Two images of minehunting training operations onboard the Royal Australian Navy's mine countermeasures vessel *Gascoyne.* Suspicious objects are typically spotted by the ship's sonar and then investigated by a Saab Double Eagle remotely-operated vehicle (ROV), which is equipped with an extendable manipulator arm to plant a charge on any confirmed mines. This allows the vehicle to maintain a safe distance if the mine detonates. *(Royal Australian Navy)*

with any mine, no matter how it was triggered, whereas sweeping influence mines required some knowledge of their mechanisms.

Hunting began with high-frequency sonars and divers to investigate what the sonars saw. Later the divers were largely replaced by submersibles. Mines were neutralised by charges deployed by the submersibles, exploded after the submersibles had been recovered. This is still the current technique.

In theory hunting guarantees that all mines are found. In reality no one is ever sure that an area has been completely cleared. In 1984, for example, a Libyan Ro-Ro ship laid a string of mines in the Red Sea along the route taken by pilgrims sailing for Mecca. The object was to embarrass the Saudis, who are the protectors of that most holy Muslim place. An international force cleared the relevant part of the Red Sea – or thought it had. After the area had been declared mine-free, the captain of a pilgrim ship reported an explosion. The search was resumed – no one was very sure that it had succeeded. It turned out that the captain was seeking insurance money, and that no mines were involved. What seems significant is that, after very considerable effort had been expended, no one was willing to bet that he was lying.

Sweeping and hunting are ways of clearing areas, but ships sometimes have to pass through areas which may have been mined. The first self-protection device, introduced during the First World War, was the paravane, a submerged float whose wire would catch the mooring cable of a mine. It might cut the mooring cable, but at the least it would hold the mine away from the ship. During both World Wars surface warships typically streamed paravanes while passing through potentially-mined areas, and merchant ships were fitted with them. With the large-scale advent of influence mines, paravanes no longer offered full protection, and they were generally discarded.

The alternative to something like a paravane is mine evasion. Although it is difficult to detect a ground mine, a mine floating in deep water is a very different proposition. The earliest example of a mine evasion sonar seems to have been the United States FM sonar fitted to some submarines so that they could penetrate the minefields protecting Japanese waters. Many submarines have mine-evasion sonars, and in recent years they have spread to surface ships. That has probably been possible due to the declining cost of the electronics involved.

PRECISION MINEHUNTING

It seems that the most important mine countermeasures technology development in recent decades has been pervasive precision navigation, due mostly to GPS. Precision navigation makes for a new style of warfare, which might be called precision warfare, in which the act of finding a target (in this case a mine) can be separated from the act of attacking it. In many areas of warfare, the consequence of this is that attacks are usually surprises, because the victim is never warned by the attacker's search for him. In mine countermeasures, where the object of attack is a mine, the consequence is rather different. For the first time, it is possible to separate the sensor (usually

The Lockheed Martin built AN/WLD-1 Remote Minehunting System (RMS) depicted undergoing trials from the Littoral Combat Ship *Independence* (LCS-2) in early 2012. The development of precision navigation will increasingly allow the task of hunting mines to be separated from their destruction, with unmanned autonomous vehicles being used to carry out the hunting function. RMS, combining a Remote Multi-Mission Vehicle (RMMV) with an AQS-20A VDS sonar, can operate at considerable distance from its mother ship and has an endurance of twenty-four hours. Data collected by the system is transmitted back to littoral combat ship by radio link. *(US Navy)*

a high-definition sonar) from the device intended to destroy the mine. In the past, minehunters had to proceed through a supposed minefield mine by mine, because whatever they missed might sink them. It took time to examine a mine, and time to neutralise it using an explosive. To further complicate the process, the explosion was generally at a distance, and the mine often was not visibly affected (even though it might be disabled). Many mines are filled with insensitive explosives specifically to protect them from nearby explosions. The minehunter had to register the location of each underwater object it dealt with, so that neither it nor any cooperating minehunter would go back to that object. The entire process was slow. That was particularly unfortunate if the minefield in question was just off an invasion beach. The longer the mine clearance effort took, the more time an enemy would have to fill the beach with troops and armour.

A precision approach to mine clearance is very different. Unmanned vehicles can be sent into the minefield to detect and to image mine-like objects. They or those on board a command ship can decide which objects are likely to be mines. With enough computing power, it may be possible for the unmanned vehicle to decide that an object probably is or is not a mine. Claims that this has been done date back about a decade, but there are still many sceptics.

Given precise locations of the supposed mines, unmanned anti-mine torpedoes can neutralise the minefield. The most important part of this new way of mine countermeasures is that the anti-mine weapons can be sent to the locations indicated by the unmanned sensors. In the past, such precision was inconceivable. The idea of the anti-mine torpedo is hardly new, but typically it is associated with a minehunter which would command it to attack a mine the hunter could see on its own sonar. Typically the hunter's high-frequency sonar spots a

A Seafox mine disposal system being operated by the British Royal Navy. Although such disposable anti-mine torpedoes have been used for some time to give greater certainty of destruction than simply detonating explosives near a mine, their potential increases if they can be sent to minefield locations that have been previously identified by autonomous vehicles. *(Crown Copyright 2011)*

The British 'Hunt' class mine countermeasures vessel *Hurworth* in May 2013. The 'Hunt' class were amongst the most expensive ships in the Royal Navy on a 'ton-for-ton' basis when first commissioned. Whilst precision minehunting has yet to take over from classical hunting, the high cost of specialist mine countermeasures vessels suggests they will be increasingly replaced by modular systems deployed on more general-purpose vessels as the current generation of ships falls due for replacement. *(Conrad Waters)*

The US Navy *Avenger* class mine countermeasures ships *Pioneer* (MCM-9) and *Warrior* (MCM-10) onboard a heavy lift vessel in February 2013 prior to long distance transportation to a new location. Lack of strategic mobility is a major limitation of traditional mine countermeasures vessels; precision minehunting offers one potential solution to this problem as autonomous vehicles can be shipped in general-purpose vessels. *(US Navy)*

mine-like object and sends down a submersible to investigate it. The submersible carries a higher-frequency imaging sonar and, often, an underwater spotlight and camera. It is connected to the minehunter by an umbilical which carries both power and data. Those on board the minehunter examine the object. If they decide it is a mine, typically they order the submersible to drop a charge nearby. The submersible cannot go right up to the mine because it may trigger the mine; submersibles are not carried in numbers. How effective a nearby charge may be depends on how rugged the mine is. Anti-mine torpedoes were conceived as a better way of using the same technique: the torpedo goes right to the mine. If it sets the mine off, so much the better.

Nearly all navies use this technique. Its drawbacks include the sheer number of minehunters required to clear even a small minefield. Minehunters are expensive. They have to be built (and maintained, at considerable cost) so that none of their signatures are likely to set off mines within the range set by the onboard minehunting sonar. After the Second World War mines, particularly magnetic mines, became far more sensitive, presumably specifically to destroy sweepers. It was not enough to use wooden or plastic hulls. Sweepers needed special forms of construction and special means of degaussing, ultimately with sensors and feedback, because a ship's magnetic field varies according to where she is on the earth, and even her heading. The next step up in cost was the advent of minehunting, which demanded imaging sonar and means of dealing with mines one by one. By the late Cold War, a minehunter probably cost about as much as a frigate. Even before minehunting, the need for special construction made minesweepers at least as expensive, ton for ton, as submarines. Yet increased cost did not increase the rate at which a hunter could explore and clear a potential minefield.

Since mines are likely to be set off nearby, minehunters have to be shock-hardened. Minehunting sonars and the associated target analysis electronics are not inexpensive, either. Small minehunter size generally means low transit speed (the Norwegians use SWATH hulls to overcome this problem). At present the only way to give nearly all minehunters strategic mobility is to transport them by float on-float off ship — and those ships are not very fast, either.

One simple way out is the 'dog on a leash', in which the submersible carries not only a close-in

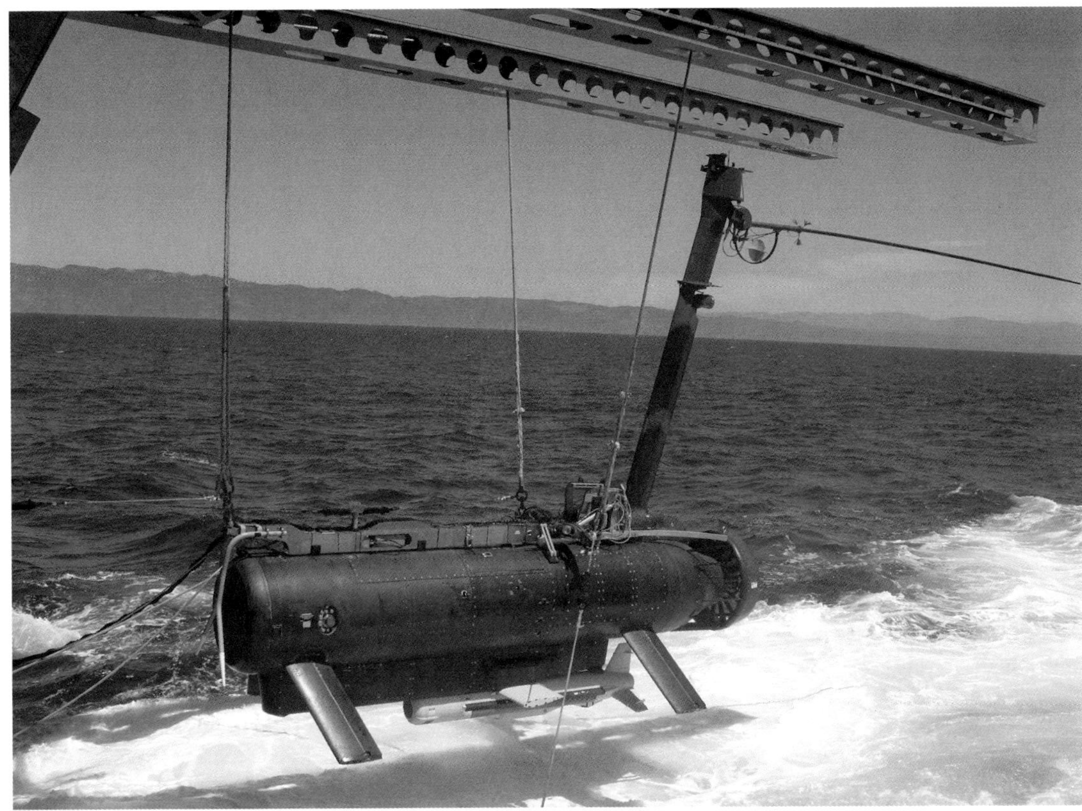

The Littoral Combat Ship *Independence* (LCS-2) seen deploying a Remote Multi-Mission Vehicle (RMMV) whilst testing the LCS mine countermeasures module. A low-observable, semi-submerged vehicle, the RMMV can be navigated by GPS and is easy to recover. It is designed to remain in radio contact with its command ship. *(US Navy)*

imaging sonar but also the minehunting sonar. The minehunter need not come nearly so close to a possible mine, so it need not be so elaborately silenced. However, it is still examining mines one by one, and the dogs on the leash are not inexpensive.

What if an unmanned vehicle could collect enough data, perhaps including optical, for a decision as to whether an object was or was not a mine? Several such vehicles could be sent into a potential minefield. They would not have to embody enough intelligence to decide whether something was a mine; they would only have to provide a mother ship with the basis for such decisions. The mother ship (or perhaps a helicopter) could then attack the minefield with a sudden burst of anti-mine torpedoes or other weapons. One advantage of this approach would be that whoever had laid the minefield would have little warning of the attempt to deal with it. That might be particularly important in an assault situation.

The first to develop this approach was the Royal Norwegian Navy, using the Hugin unmanned vehicle. It was associated with the Norwegian Minesniper anti-mine weapon. The current US Navy remote minesweeping system, a module to be on board Littoral Combat Ships (LCS), represents a similar approach. The most important difference is that Hugin collects data and has to be recovered before its data can be processed. In the United States' case, the system embodies a semi-submersible in radio contact with its command ship.

Even an unmanned vehicle collecting cruder data may be useful. An enemy typically mines only a limited area. It is immensely useful to know which areas definitely have *not* been mined. A covert unmanned underwater vehicle can be sent into an area which may or may not have been mined. If it detects numerous mine-like objects, the area can be considered dangerous. Otherwise ships may be able to operate freely in it. Such mine reconnaissance is an alternative to slow mine clearance in a possible fleet operating area. Of course mine reconnaissance fails if the miner can watch it being done; all he has to do is mine the areas declared safe. In 1991, during the build-up to the first Gulf War, the US Navy conducted what it thought amounted to mine reconnaissance by observing Iraqi minelaying activities. The Iraqis had two ex-Soviet minesweeper/minelayers, which were both dutifully tracked. Unfortunately most Iraqi mines were laid by small craft, which seem to have been disregarded on the theory that they were carrying loot from Kuwait. The two US Navy warships were said to have been mined in apparently cleared waters. In fact they were mined in places which were thought to be mine-free, but had never been explored for mines: it seemed (incorrectly) that the Iraqis had never mined those places at all.

The US Navy's solution was to develop a submarine-launched unmanned underwater vehicle (BLQ-11) which would explore an area covertly, then return to the mother submarine with what amounted to a map of safe and possibly unsafe areas. Thanks to GPS and satellite communication, this chart could be sent to and used by an approaching fleet. This project was terminated in favour of general-purpose unmanned underwater vehicles (UUVs), which presumably can be fitted for mine reconnaissance. The current stand-off mine countermeasures module for the US Navy's LCS employs a low-observable semi-submerged vehicle. This vehicle has the considerable advantage of simpler precise navigation via GPS, and it is easier to recover.

COST AND MODULARITY

Precision minehunting certainly has not yet taken over from classical hunting or, for that matter, sweeping, but it seems to be the only way to deal with the single greatest fact of modern naval life: the number of ships is shrinking because unit cost is rising. Classical forms of mine countermeasures demand large numbers of specialist ships because they have to cover the entire area of a possible minefield, and because they tend to do so slowly. The more sophisticated the mines, moreover, the slower the clearance process. Yet a mine countermeasures force does not contribute to many important naval missions, particularly those executed in peacetime or in periods of tension. For example, minehunters are hardly the ideal instruments of naval presence. It is difficult to imagine how navies will afford to buy the next generation of such ships. Even 'dog on a leash', which minimises the need for signature control,

An MH-53E Sea Dragon airborne mine countermeasures helicopter trains with a Mk. 105 sled in the Persian Gulf. The US Navy has long-operated minesweeping helicopters – perhaps the forerunners of modular mine countermeasures – but precision minehunting might further extend their usefulness. Developments in technology should also allow lighter helicopters such as the MH-60 to be used in the mine-countermeasures role. *(US Navy)*

demands large numbers of ships. That is difficult enough to arrange on a sustained basis in a benign environment. What happens when an enemy realises that mine countermeasures craft are high-value units, the destruction of which ends his problem?

The obvious solution to the numbers problem is to develop modular systems which can be brought aboard ships intended for other purposes. The US Navy has long operated minesweeping helicopters, which might be considered the original modular mine countermeasures system. Precision mine countermeasures makes these sweepers into potential minehunters. The helicopters are normally operated by large-deck amphibious ships with minimal modification.[6] The alternative is a minehunting module added to a surface ship. The original example was the Danish Stanflex corvette; the US Navy's LCS is a current one. In both cases, the question is whether the ship's crew is flexible enough to execute radically different missions. In the Danish case, ships which were in theory modular actually specialised in only one mission. The LCS takes on board some specialised crew members for whatever module it carries but it is not yet clear whether there are enough of them.

The Littoral Combat Ship *Freedom* (LCS-1) seen undergoing pre-deployment work-up off the coast of San Diego in early 2013 before undertaking the type's first voyage to South East Asia. The US Navy sees the use of minehunting modules on its LCSs – one of three sets of mission-specific modules being developed for the design – as key to its future mine countermeasures capability. *(Lockheed Martin)*

AMPHIBIOUS MINE COUNTERMEASURES

Clearance of beach mines demands a different approach. In the ideal case, the amphibious attackers can land anywhere along a broad beach. The enemy may have thousands of anti-tank mines, but these will not be enough to cover the whole area. Probably the key question is whether he has time to prepare a particular stretch of beach. If he has time, the beach is likely to look like that at Normandy on D-Day, and obstacles will have to be destroyed one by one. Anti-tank (which become anti-landing craft) mines will be buried carefully; hence they may become difficult or impossible to detect before they destroy valuable craft and their cargoes. Given less time, the defender can and will strew mines over a beach, typically using vehicles with automated systems. The attacker's advantage is that the mines will remain visible and hence can be attacked one by one.

Time also decides how much enemy defence there is inland from the beach. The Second World War provides an apt analogy. After the slaughter at Gallipoli during the First World War, the British resolved never to attack a narrow beach, because the narrowness of the beach gave the defender a clear idea of where to place defences. In North Africa, Sicily and in Italy, that was possible. It is why the histories of these assaults do not generally include much or any fire support from the sea, at least at the outset. Fire support was generally a means of dealing with enemy counter-attacks. Probably the most important issue was to achieve surprise, so that the enemy would not be waiting on the beach with a superior force. To that end, landings were typically made at night, with no preparatory bombardment.

The US Navy, however, had very different experiences in the Central Pacific, where it landed Marines on small islands. Their defenders could often be fairly sure of where the attack would be mounted, and they prepared extensively. There was no point in seeking surprise, so the navy opted for daylight landings (to avoid confusion) and heavy shore bombardment (not to mention large-scale mine countermeasures). What had worked well in Italy nearly failed at Normandy, particularly at Omaha Beach, because the Germans had enough time to build beach defences at all possible landing places in France. It did not much matter that there was no bombardment to give away the landing place, because the Germans had guns and other fixed defences already in place. They also had plenty of mines and beach obstructions. After the problems encountered in Normandy, the US Army acceded to naval arguments, so the invasion of the South of France was run much more like a landing on a Pacific island. During the build-up to the planned assault on Japan, United States planners tried to deceive the Japanese as to where they planned to land, but the beach adopted had such obvious advantages that the Japanese successfully predicted that it would be used.

In this sense current US amphibious technology has important mine countermeasures implications. Although the Marines have retained amphibious troop-carriers, they rely much more heavily on helicopter troop-carriers and the new Osprey tilt-rotor. These aircraft can disregard details of the beach. Their drawback is that once landed the Marines lack mobility. The Marines tried but failed to develop a fast amphibious protected fighting vehicle, which would have solved the problem. Without such transportation, they must rely on vehicles brought across the beach to link up with Marines landed by helicopter or Osprey. The reason for adopting air-cushion landing craft (which carry the vehicles) is twofold. First, because of their speed, they can approach from beyond the horizon, making it much more difficult for a defender to use the positions of amphibious ships offshore to indicate where they will come ashore. Second, they can cross a far wider variety of beaches than a conventional landing craft. In the past, the US Navy maintained data on all world beaches suited to its landing craft, and defenders could do the same thing. Now no such database is worth compiling.

Air-cushion vehicles and helicopters or Ospreys do not solve all problems. Defenders of a small island or a small stretch of beach would still be able to guess what was coming, and they might still be able to mine their beach sufficiently to wipe out the air cushion vehicles. The death of major warships has eliminated classical forms of fire support, though the new 155mm gun and the newer rail gun may make up for some of that. However, most of the places in the world the Marines may land are broad areas in which precise landing points are difficult to predict. Beach mining is therefore more and more likely to be a last-minute affair using visible mines projecting from the surface of the beach.

After numerous false starts, such as massed crab-like robots and explosive nets projected from landing craft, the US Navy adopted a precision attack approach to the beach problem. Its Assault Breaching System (ABS) combines a sensor/analysis system which locates mines and beach obstacles with a separate precision attack exploiting the fact that the analysis system precisely registers the locations of obstacles and mines. These are destroyed by submunitions (such as darts) released by Joint Direct Attack Munition (JDAMS) bomb casings. JDAMS fits this system well because JDAMS bombs are directed to GPS locations. Its COBRA (Coastal Battlefield Reconnaissance and Analysis) sensor is carried on board an unmanned Fire Scout helicopter. The sensor is designated DVS-1, the V indicating optics. No description has been published, but a photograph shows a typical optical turret carrying cameras and one or more lasers. COBRA is said to be capable of detecting buried beach mines as well as mines in the water down to 40ft (12m). Detection is not done onboard the helicopter

Technological innovations such as the Boeing MV-22 Osprey tilt-rotor and the LCAC have had important implications for US Navy mine countermeasures, as they make it much less obvious to an attacker where a landing might take place, making beach mining more and more likely to be a last-minute affair. *(Boeing)*

but on the ship receiving the helicopter's data.

During the war in Iraq the United States acquired considerable expertise in detecting buried improvised explosives, based on the appearance of disturbed soil at various wavelengths. Presumably DVS-1 builds on that experience. Given the precise location of a buried explosive, it can be attacked by the inexpensive guided bomb, which is called JABS (Joint Assault Breaching System). The in-water part of the system probably builds on previous attempts to develop a blue-green water-penetrating laser. In the past, the laser (AES-1) was paired with a gun firing supercavitating bullets. Presumably the submunitions replace them.

One advantage of this approach is that the airborne sensor will also reveal obstacles which can be attacked by precision bombs. The official description refers to patterns of obstacles and mines, which would be created by a vehicle strewing mines.

These two new approaches to mine countermeasures are only examples of a larger trend towards precision warfare in which sensors and weapons are separated. This is the approach which makes UAVs and other remote sensors so much more important. This type of warfare is sometimes called network-centric, but the separation aspect is at least as important as the networking element.

US Marines working to dislodge a mine from a beach during a training exercise. The US Navy has now also adopted a precision attack approach to the beach mining problem, developing an Assault Breaching System that combines sensors which precisely locate and record mines that are then destroyed by sub-munitions directed to their locations by GPS. *(US Navy)*

Notes

1. All opinions expressed are the author's, and are not necessarily those of the US Navy or of any other organisation with which he has been associated.

2. During the First World War, the Royal Navy developed Leader Cable, which could be laid on the bottom in shallow water. A merchant ship could detect and follow the cable, which identified a safe (cleared) path. Leader cable was also used during the Second World War and after. Descriptions appear in released documents in the PRO; Leader Cable was probably declassified in the 1950s. GPS and electronic charts now make it possible to specify a cleared path without a physical indication like Leader Cable.

3. Changing views explain the shift from the mass minesweeper programmes of the early 1950s to much more limited programmes later on. Initially it was assumed that a hot war arising out of the Cold War would resemble the Second World War. NATO relied heavily on United States supplies, so enormous effort went into building up sweeping forces. War-built sweepers had been made almost completely obsolete by the advent of sensitive magnetic mines. The advent of thermonuclear weapons convinced many that no such central war would break out. The British Government in particular abandoned many home waters forces (including coastal forces) after a 1957 defence review which announced that future wars would probably be limited and fought in the Third World. The United States counterpart of this decision was to abandon harbour defences and to focus on mine countermeasures in the context of amphibious and expeditionary operations. In the 1980s, however, there was a general fear that the Soviets might fight a non-nuclear war, secure in the knowledge that NATO would not escalate to nuclear warfare. British home waters were again a focus (the Royal Navy also became vitally interested in minelaying, using ferries). The US Navy became interested in defending its harbours against mines which Soviet submarines might lay. It ordered a new generation of mine countermeasures craft. Also at this time the US Navy became aware of Soviet rising mines, which it considered a direct threat to strategic submarines. The current US Navy minehunting submersible (SLQ-48) was given unusually great diving depth specifically to deal with this threat.

4. Typically specific lanes were cleared and mine clearance proceeded during the assault. For example, during the Normandy operation clearance of German pressure mines continued after troops were ashore. This discussion omits physical obstacles such as anti-landing craft obstructions strewn across the D-Day beach. They were cleared by engineers, using explosives placed by hand.

5. Pressure-mine sensors can be fooled by the turn of the tide, so most such mines incorporate additional magnetic or acoustic sensors. The US Navy incorporated a pressure sensor in its helicopter-drawn sweep sled. The Soviets tried to use a pressure pulse projected by a fast ship suddenly turning (it is not clear how well this worked).

6. Before the helicopters there were minesweeping boats (MSBs), which could go abroad in the well decks of amphibious ships, and minesweeping launches (MSLs) which could be carried in the davits of amphibious ships. Neither was completely satisfactory. Until they were given hunting sonars, the helicopters were limited to towing influence-sweep sleds with magnetic and acoustic generators on board. They were not considered sufficient to clear an area. However, they could generate a signature stronger than that of a minehunter, so they were sent in first to detonate mines intended to destroy the hunters.

4.3 TECHNOLOGICAL REVIEW

Author: Ian Buxton

WARSHIP RECYCLING

Redundant warships have always had a potential value. Even in the days of wooden walls, breaking up (or scrapping or demolition or recycling – all essentially synonyms for the same process) yielded some re-usable timber, as well as copper fastenings and sheathing. But demolition of such vessels was something of a cottage industry with ships bought, then beached, somewhere convenient for hordes of labourers to strip the hulks. Better organised was Henry Castle on the River Thames, who bought many vessels from the British Admiralty from the 1860s. The Royal Dockyards would occasionally break up a ship in dry dock to help counter a downturn in workload.

THE FIRST CENTURY OF WARSHIP BREAKING

When iron, later steel, hulls and steam-propelled vessels came to the end of their lives towards the end of the nineteenth century, there was greater potential value in recycling their materials, so a more industrialised process was needed. A deep-water wharf or quay was desirable, steam cranes were needed to lift the heavier components, a rail connection was useful to transport scrap metal to steelworks for re-melting in open hearth furnaces, and space was required to store and sort the greater variety of materials that made up their hulls and machinery. Land based scrap companies began to invest in shipbreaking, notably T W Ward of Sheffield who started shipbreaking at Preston in 1894. However, their first warship was not purchased until 1899; the 1866 turret ship *Prince Albert.*

In the early twentieth century, the Admiralty regularly held auctions of redundant naval vessels at dockyards like Portsmouth, Chatham and Devonport. The pace of disposals quickened after 'Jacky' Fisher, who cleared out dozens of obsolete ships, became First Sea Lord in 1904. Elaborate

Many in the United Kingdom were saddened when *Ark Royal* was decommissioned in 2011 under the SDSR 2010 defence cuts. She was sold to Leyal in Turkey in 2013. She arrived at Aliaga on 10 June from Portsmouth. She is seen on 10 July with her hangar and forward lift mechanism already opened up; she was out of the water by November. Redundant warships have always had a potential value from recycling of the materials they contain – the sale of *Ark Royal* reportedly raised £2.9m for the British taxpayer. *(Selim San)*

brochures would be printed by auctioneers Fuller, Horsey, Sons & Cassell, with dates advertised. After the sale, *The Times* would print a list of ships sold, buyers and prices. This process encouraged new yards to set up at places like Felixstowe, Briton Ferry in South Wales and Boness on the Forth. Sometimes the bidders were from Holland, so ships would be towed across to Rotterdam *en route* to their final grave at places like Hendrik-ido-Ambacht.

Shipbreaking virtually ceased during the First World War apart from a few useless wrecks and hulks, but expanded rapidly from 1919 as hundreds of redundant warships were sold off, some barely four years old. The Admiralty invited bids from many newly formed companies, favouring those employing ex-servicemen. If their bid was successful, they had to put down a 25 per cent deposit, the balance being paid over a year or more. Existing companies established new yards, especially Ward at Inverkeithing, Grays in Essex, Rainham (Essex), New Holland on the Humber, Milford Haven, and Hayle in Cornwall. To clear the dockyards crammed with redundant ships, the Admiralty sold warships *en bloc*; thirty-four to Stanlee in November 1921 and 113 to Ward in May 1921 at a fixed price of £2.50 per ton displacement. Seeing the unprofessionalism of most of the new breakers, engineer Robert McCrone set up Alloa Shipbreaking in 1923. Starting at Charlestown on the Forth, it soon expanded into Rosyth Dockyard after that had been put on care & maintenance. Using more advanced techniques, especially gas cutting, and sorting the materials to maximise scrap values, his company, later renamed Metal Industries (MI), came to rival Ward in size.

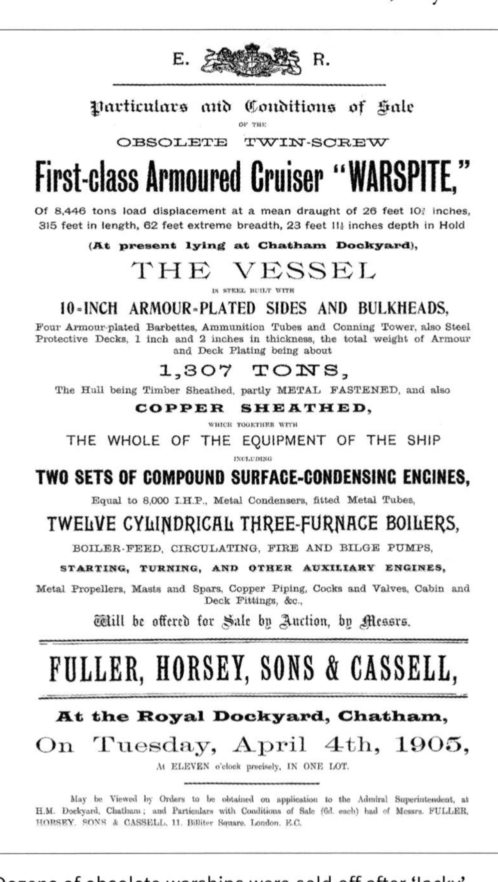

E. R.

Particulars and Conditions of Sale

OF THE

OBSOLETE TWIN-SCREW

First-class Armoured Cruiser "WARSPITE,"

Of 8,446 tons load displacement at a mean draught of 26 feet 10½ inches, 315 feet in length, 62 feet extreme breadth, 23 feet 11½ inches depth in Hold

(At present lying at Chatham Dockyard),

THE VESSEL

IS STEEL BUILT WITH

10-INCH ARMOUR-PLATED SIDES AND BULKHEADS,

Four Armour-plated Barbettes, Ammunition Tubes and Conning Tower, also Steel Protective Decks, 1 inch and 2 inches in thickness, the total weight of Armour and Deck Plating being about

1,307 TONS,

The Hull being Timber Sheathed, partly METAL FASTENED, and also

COPPER SHEATHED,

WHICH TOGETHER WITH

THE WHOLE OF THE EQUIPMENT OF THE SHIP

INCLUDING

TWO SETS OF COMPOUND SURFACE-CONDENSING ENGINES,

Equal to 8,000 I.H.P., Metal Condensers, fitted Metal Tubes,

TWELVE CYLINDRICAL THREE-FURNACE BOILERS,

BOILER-FEED, CIRCULATING, FIRE AND BILGE PUMPS,

STARTING, TURNING, AND OTHER AUXILIARY ENGINES,

Metal Propellers, Masts and Spars, Copper Piping, Cocks and Valves, Cabin and Deck Fittings, &c.,

Will be offered for Sale by Auction, by Messrs.

FULLER, HORSEY, SONS & CASSELL,

At the Royal Dockyard, Chatham,

On Tuesday, April 4th, 1905,

At ELEVEN o'clock precisely, IN ONE LOT.

May be Viewed by Orders to be obtained on application to the Admiral Superintendent, at H.M. Dockyard, Chatham; and Particulars with Conditions of Sale (6d. each) had of Messrs. FULLER, HORSEY, SONS & CASSELL, 11, Billiter Square, London, E.C.

Dozens of obsolete warships were sold off after 'Jacky' Fisher became First Sea Lord. Regular auctions were held at naval dockyards. Fuller, Horsey, Sons & Cassell of London prepared detailed catalogues for the major ships. The 1888 armoured cruiser *Warspite* was sold at Chatham to T W Ward of Sheffield on 4 April 1905 for £18,150. *(Newcastle University Marine Technology Special Collection)*

Shortly after the end of the Second World War, Britain disposed of all its battleships except the five newest. *Nelson* had been used in bombing trials in the Forth before scrapping. She departed Rosyth Dockyard on 15 March 1949 for the short tow to Ward's yard at Inverkeithing. To reduce her draft aft, her six twin 6in turrets had been removed. *(Newcastle University Marine Technology Special Collection)*

The Washington Treaty of 1922 speeded the process of shipbreaking, limiting the number of capital ships that the major navies could build or retain. The British Royal Navy scrapped eighteen battleships and battlecruisers over the next ten years. By the 1930s the plucky amateur breakers had all disappeared from the scene, with the remaining companies surviving largely on merchant ships and fishing vessels. But they faced increasing competition from Germany, Holland, Italy and Japan. However, the Admiralty would only sell redundant warships to British breakers, albeit in modest numbers. MI was able to supplement those by buying the salvage rights to German warships scuttled at Scapa Flow in 1919. After raising them, the hulks were towed, usually upside down, to Rosyth for demolition in a leased Admiralty dry dock, which was a hugely profitable operation.[1] The US Navy also used dry docks to break up five battleships at Philadelphia in the mid-1920s.

After the Second World War there was a similar mass disposal programme of warships, both in the United Kingdom and United States. With high demand for steel for reconstructing its post-war economy, the United Kingdom used a centralised system for scrapping ships. The British Iron & Steel Corporation (Salvage) Ltd – normally known as BISCO – handled the supply of raw materials to the British steel industry, including ships for scrap. Warships, unlike merchant ships, were not 'sold' to shipbreakers as erroneously stated in many reference books, but 'handed over' to BISCO by the Admiralty. BISCO would then allocate a ship to a suitable breaker; for example, all the battleships were broken up in deep-water Scottish yards. After breaking up, demolition costs would be deducted from the sale proceeds and the net amount returned to the relevant Government department. Typical amounts were £450,000 for a battleship and £30,000 for a destroyer.

This system produced about 500,000 tons of steel scrap a year to the British steel industry, about 3 per cent of its annual output. This system remained in place until 1962, when the Admiralty, soon to become the Ministry of Defence (MOD), reverted to the former system of inviting bids for redundant warships. There were then about a dozen major breakers in the United Kingdom, who would send staff to inspect ships, usually laid up at one of the dockyards. They would calculate the net value based upon their estimate of the quantity of each type of material on board, the likely scrap prices of each, and the demolition and delivery costs; although the Admiralty would often arrange for towage to the vicinity of the yard, where local tugs would take over. The whole process between invitation to bid and delivery to the yard typically took only two to three months.

Such contracts were valuable to the industry, which was facing increased competition for merchant ships from countries like Belgium, Spain and Italy, and then in the 1970s from Taiwan. But the MOD soon began to invite tenders from foreign yards, with oiler *Tidesurge* being sold to Spain in 1976. The British Steel Corporation (BSC) usually offered higher prices for ship scrap compared with land scrap, but even so many of the smaller breakers had closed in the 1960s. Eventually even Ward closed all but their largest yards at Inverkeithing and Briton Ferry, both of which had broken up many Royal Navy ships from battleships downwards. In 1980 BSC withdrew its price support for ship scrap, which prompted nearly all the major British shipbreakers to close down, unable to offer competitive prices compared with Spanish or Asian yards. These included Shipbreaking Industries' Faslane yard, which as Metal Industries (Salvage) had taken over the wartime emergency port on the Clyde in 1946. It broke up seven capital ships in the next fifteen years. Its facilities were incorporated into extending the Clyde Submarine Base, home to the Royal Navy's Polaris submarines from 1967.

The American shipbreaking industry went through a similar process. In the years immediately following the Second World War, large numbers of US Navy warships were scrapped at places like Baltimore, San Francisco Bay, Kearny New Jersey, Portsmouth Virginia and later Brownsville Texas. A few, such as escort carriers were sold to Japan, while large numbers were retained in lay-up including the four *Iowa* class battleships – Britain's last, *Vanguard*, had been scrapped in 1960 at Faslane. A score or more of Second World War warships were preserved, as well as the First World War battleship *Texas*. At that time, scrap prices and wage levels were such that warships could be sold, i.e. their value exceeded the costs. European navies generally scrapped their warships in their home country, including France, Germany, Belgium and Italy. Countries without a shipbreaking industry like Australia or South America sold their warships, initially to Japan until that country could no longer offer competitive prices, then Taiwan and India. In the 1980s Turkey entered the market, breaking up warships from European navies as well as the smaller merchant ships.

After the break-up of the Soviet Union, Russia sold redundant warships to European breakers as they could bring in hard currency. Dozens of conventional submarines were delivered under tow or on barges, eight arriving at Blyth in north-east England in February 1990 followed by some

The long-established shipbreaking yard of Van Heyghen Freres (now part of the Galloo group) is located at Ghent in Belgium. The 1979-built 2,000-ton Belgian frigate *Westhinder* is seen here awaiting dismantling on 7 September 2001. Belgium is one of a number of European countries that have traditionally broken up warships at domestic facilities. *(Ian Buxton)*

destroyers and escorts. But they were in poor condition, full of asbestos and with comparatively little in the way of valuable non-ferrous metals, so breakers usually made a loss on them.

But during the 1990s increasing concerns about environmental issues were being raised in Western countries, as many of these elderly vessels had significant quantities of asbestos, lead-based products, PCBs (polychlorinated biphenyls) and heavy fuel oil on board; all potentially hazardous if simply released or piled up as waste, rather than handled and disposed of in an approved manner. The health and safety of shipbreaking workers in countries like India also caused concern, due to lack of personal protective equipment, lax standards of operating techniques and high accident and death rates. Developed countries became reluctant to sell warships for breaking under such conditions, and pressed for higher standards through international agreement. The emphasis was now on 'recycling', i.e. re-using the maximum amount of material from ships. By 2000, major navies like the US, British and European would only agree to their ships being recycled in approved yards which worked to high standards.

THE OPTIONS AND ECONOMICS OF DISPOSING OF WARSHIPS

There have always been several options available for disposing of obsolete warships. If still in reasonable condition, they may be sold by a larger navy like the US Navy or Royal Navy, to a smaller navy with less demanding requirements. Auxiliary types may be sold for conversion to civilian roles. A few may be of sufficient interest to be sold or donated to preservation groups as memorials. Simply scuttling (sinking) off the coast has been used in the past, particularly where the vessel was far from a scrapping location. Such a technique has been used more recently where the vessel may be suitable as an artificial reef to stimulate sea life or as a recreational dive site. But preparing a ship for scuttling nowadays requires the removal of hazardous material, so there is a significant cost, as with the US Navy aircraft carrier *Oriskany* (CV-43) off Florida in 2006. Some have been sunk as targets to test new weapon systems – popular with Royal Navy ships, with about fifteen frigates being so used from 1984 onwards. But the great majority have gone for recycling, which offers the prospect of a modest return for the taxpayer.

The basic financial equation is:

Recycling Sale Price = Value of Recovered Materials – Demolition Costs – Preparation, Delivery and Commission costs.

For this sum to be positive requires the value to be high, whether from scrap steel or re-usable materials and equipment, and/or the labour and delivery costs to be low. The value is highest in areas where steel can be re-rolled, typically as reinforcing bars for concrete construction rather than just melted down, and where there is a ready market for re-usables such as accommodation and galley fittings, electrical equipment such as generators, and mechanical equipment such as pumps. Those conditions tend to occur in low wage countries like India and Bangladesh, which now, with China, dominate commercial shipbreaking.

But if a government has access to funds for ship recycling, as in the United States or France, a negative price may be acceptable if the ship will be recycled to the highest standards. That means that the shipbreaker is paid to recycle the ship, the actual amount depending on current prices in the equation above. This was the situation with the French aircraft carrier *Clemenceau*, which was broken up by Able UK in dry dock at Hartlepool in 2009. But before actual demolition work could start, 'remediation' was required, i.e. several weeks' work to remove hazardous materials. The contract appears to have been that the French Government paid for the delivery and demolition work but received the value of the recovered materials, although the latter would have been less than the former.

So far the British MOD has not had to resort to paying for its warships to be recycled, as it has been able to find shipbreakers within OECD countries operating with acceptable standards. A recent example was the aircraft carrier *Ark Royal* being sold to Leyal, which has its main yard at Aliaga in Turkey, some 60km north-west of Izmir. The reported sum was £2.9m, with the ship towed at the breaker's expense from Portsmouth in May 2013, a voyage of three weeks. Former Royal Navy frigates are reportedly sold for prices around £350,000. In the case of

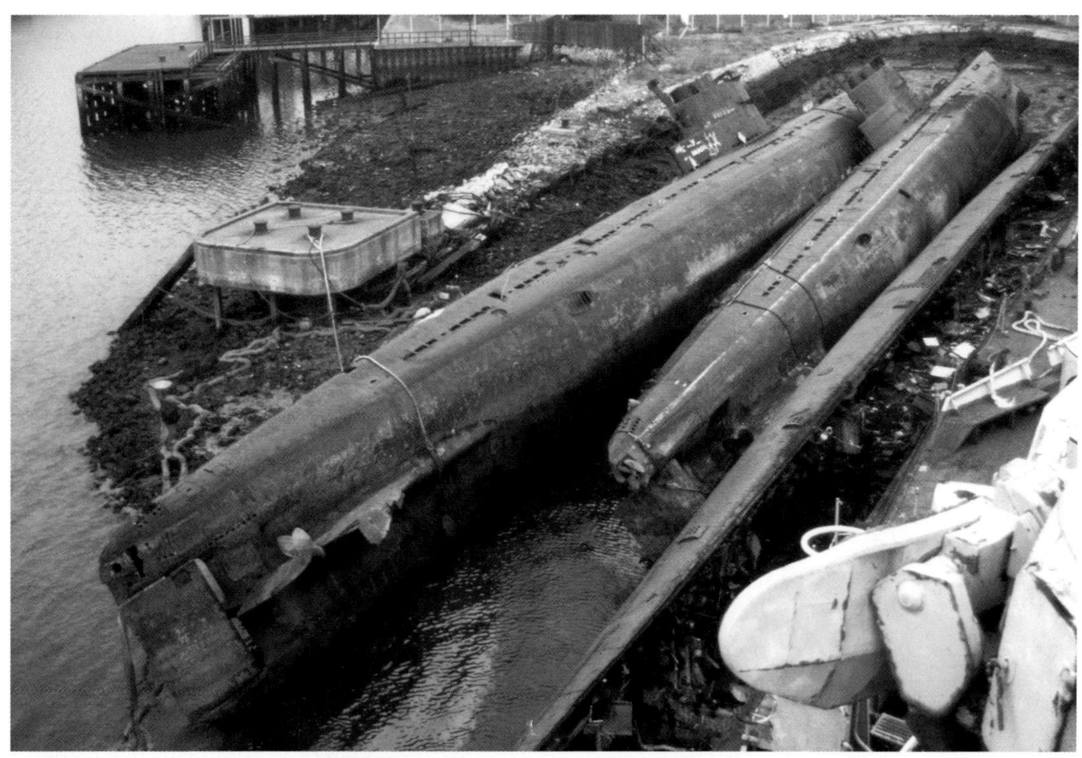

Under a complicated deal, former Soviet submarines and escorts were broken up at Blyth in 1990–2 at the site of the former Hughes Bolckow shipbreaking yard, which had closed in 1980. 'W' class sub *357* and another lie over at angle, outboard of the British *Sealion*, already opened up to remove equipment. The floating hoses are designed to contain any oil spills. The view was taken from the mast of corvette *SKR 63* on 11 August 1990. *(Ian Buxton)*

the former US Navy aircraft carrier *Forrestal* (CV-59), the breaker paid a mere one cent, in effect given the ship for free. She was towed from Philadelphia to All Star Metals in Brownsville in February 2014. A similar contract was made in May 2014 with ESCO Marine of Brownsville for *Saratoga* (CV-60), laid up at Newport, Rhode Island, while *Constellation* (CV-64) is planned to go to ISL also at Brownsville.

Such recycling yards are inspected before bids are invited – known as pre-qualification – and regularly checked during the demolition process. The standards demanded are at least as high as the International Maritime Organisation's 2009 Hong Kong International Convention for the Safe and Environmentally Sound Recycling of Ships. This sets out acceptable standards both from an environmental and health and safety point of view, supported by guidelines on best practice, including a 'green passport' listing all the hazardous materials on board. When fully ratified, this will apply to merchant ships, although not warships. However, yards in many countries are already working to these standards, which encourages responsible ship owners to place work with them. Thus, the British MOD will only consider bids from approved yards. In its turn, its Disposal Reserve Ship Organisation based at Portsmouth prepares the ships for sale, removing classified equipment and items of potential use as spares for sister-ships, cleans out tanks, makes the ship watertight regarding hull openings, doors etc., and prepares an inventory of hazardous material remaining on board. The ships have to be made suitable for towing, having no working propulsion, electrical or piping systems. The United Kingdom's Disposals Services Authority (DSA) advertises the ships for sale on its website, and reviews bids, whether for conversion or breaking up. In recent years Royal Navy warships have been broken up in the United Kingdom, Belgium and Turkey, mostly in the latter.

Finding a suitable recycling yard for the aircraft carrier *Clemenceau* took the French Government six years. She finally arrived to break up on 8 February 2009 at Able UK's yard at Hartlepool. The large dry dock was drained and remediation work began to remove hazardous materials. By 23 April 2010, dismantling is well under way, with the bows cut back to just ahead of the hangar. A section of the aviation fuel tanks is exposed. To the left is the former US Navy submarine depot ship *Canopus* (AS-34). *(Ian Buxton)*

Four Royal Navy Type 22 Batch 3 frigates were sold by the Disposals Services Authority in July 2013 after advertising on its website. Three were sold to Leyal at Aliaga in Turkey and *Cornwall* to Swansea Drydocks. The first to be towed from Portsmouth was *Chatham* on 9 October. Astern are (left to right) *Cornwall*, *Campbeltown* and *Cumberland* awaiting their tugs. *(David Byrne)*

In some cases, a navy may have limited options. When the Royal Australian Navy acquired destroyers and tank landing ships from the United States, a condition was made that the ships be returned to the United States at the end of their lives, or scuttled as reefs/dive sites. Hence bids were invited from US shipbreakers in 2013 for the old tank landing ships *Kanimbla* and *Manoora.* Given the high demolition costs in the United States and the long tow from Sydney, it is unlikely that they were sold for other than a modest sum. They arrived as a paired tow at Southern Recycling's yard in New Orleans in October 2013 – part of the worldwide EMR Group.

For decades, old US government-owned cargo ships in the National Defense Reserve Fleet have been moored at three sites managed by the

Department of Transportation's Maritime Administration (MARAD), theoretically awaiting re-activation in an emergency. The sites are at Suisun Bay near San Francisco, Beaumont, Texas, and on the James River, Virginia. Some of these ships are former US Navy warships or auxiliaries, although most decommissioned front-line warships are laid up at the Naval Inactive Ship Maintenance Facilities (NISMFs) at Bremerton, Washington (home to most of the US Navy's former conventionally-powered carriers), Philadelphia, Pennsylvania and Pearl Harbor, Hawaii. Many of the MARAD-controlled ships are totally obsolete, with recycling the most realistic option. It is now a requirement that MARAD ships be cleaned underwater before delivery to the shipbreaking yard to prevent the transfer of invasive species from, say, the Pacific to the Gulf of Mexico. BAE Systems' floating dock at San Francisco is often used, although in-water cleaning by divers is also possible. This cost, plus towage expenses of US$1m or more to Brownsville plus Panama Canal transit costs of around US$250k, significantly reduces the sums that shipbreakers can offer. Over recent years, this figure has fluctuated between positive and negative. When steel scrap prices were high as in 2012 sums in the region of US$1–2m were offered for larger naval auxiliaries like oilers, but at other times the breaker has had to be paid US$1m or more to undertake the process.

For many years, redundant French warships have been laid up near Brest or used as floating wave breaks (*brise-lames*), e.g. near Toulon. The French government has now established a procedure for disposing of these lingering hulks to required environmental and security standards, at as low a cost as possible. A floating dock was acquired and berthed at La Seyne near Toulon, where recycling started with oiler *Saone* in 2013. Galloo's Van Heyghen Recycling yard at Ghent has also been contracted to dismantle the 50-year old destroyer *La Galissonière* and several escorts over the 2014–17 period. The estimated costs per vessel range from a few hundred thousand Euros to several million, depending on size and type and scrap prices, paid for by the French government.

RECYCLING TECHNIQUES

Traditionally, warships berthed alongside a shipbreaking yard would be demolished from the superstructure downwards, and then horizontally deck by deck, until machinery spaces were reached. The highest superstructure decks would be cut off first, and if within reach of a crane, lifted ashore for further cutting, if not simply allowed to fall ashore or on to a lower deck. Usually equipment, timber fittings and furniture would be stripped out first, leaving little more than a steel shell. Masts would be felled after attaching a wire to the top, and then cutting through most of the base, when it would be pulled over by a winch, falling along the deck.

In the early days cutting gases were expensive, usually oxygen and acetylene compressed in cylinders transported from a manufacturing site, but labour was comparatively cheap. It was then economic to 'unbutton' riveted structures by cutting off the head of each rivet by hammer and cold chisel. With plates and stiffeners so separated, they could be lifted ashore. If gases could be made on site, or oxygen cooled and stored as a liquid, they became cheaper and it was then much quicker to use gas cutting with hand-held torches. Larger sections could be cut off the ship, lifted ashore and there cut by shore burners to open hearth furnace size, typically 5ft x 2ft (1.5m x 0.6m). The pieces would be lifted into rail wagons each carrying about 15 tons before being sent to the local steelworks. Gas cutting was readily able to cut through thick steel, whether gun bodies or armour plate. These usually had a significant nickel content, adding to the scrap value compared with mild steel.

As decks were opened up, re-usable equipment could be more easily removed, including accommodation fittings, especially if there was demand locally for furniture or sanitary ware in good condition. Sometimes items had to be returned to naval stores depots as spares, e.g. electrical equipment or smaller guns. Some yards had fixed derrick cranes up to about ten tons capacity with an outreach of about 60ft (18m), positioned to cover much of the hulk. A few of the better equipped yards had travelling cranes up to about thirty tons capacity, sometimes on sites which had been previously used for shipbuilding, e.g. the former Beardmore shipyard on the Clyde. Occasionally a yard might have the use of a floating crane, owned as at Faslane (60 tons) or hired from a local port authority, to lift particularly heavy

A creek at Landévennec on the south side of Brest harbour has long been used to lay up redundant French warships. On 27 July 2011 the 52-year-old cruiser *Colbert* is flanked by destroyers *Duperré* (left) and *La Galissonière* (right), the latter due to be scrapped at Ghent. *Colbert* and the former helicopter-carrying cruiser *Jeanne d'Arc* will be dismantled in dry dock at Bordeaux by the Veolia group companies during 2015. *(Conrad Waters)*

items or those beyond the reach of shore cranes, such as belt armour plates. As machinery spaces opened up, it was easier to remove items like turbines and condensers – the latter full of valuable non-ferrous metals. If there were sister-ships of the vessels, complete units might be removed for sale – the uncompleted aircraft carrier *Leviathan* had her steam turbines, condensers and gearing removed at Faslane in 1968 to replace those in the Argentinian *Veinticinco de Mayo* (the former Royal Navy *Venerable*). Smaller items like pumps, fans, purifiers or diesel generators could be lifted out complete if in good condition, refurbished and sold. Otherwise they were stripped down in workshops ashore to extract non-ferrous metals. If separated into different grades to sell to metal merchants, higher prices were obtained. However, they had to be stored in lockable sheds to deter local thieves. Timber decks in good condition could be removed plank by plank, especially teak, which lent itself to making garden furniture; otherwise simply sold as firewood. Anchors, cables, ropes, shafts and boiler tubes could often be sold for further use, rather than as scrap.

By now the hulk was at a much lighter draft, typically no more than 10ft (3m), so could be moved to a nearby beaching ground which dried out at low tide for finishing off. If the tidal range was small, as in the Mediterranean, hulks could be dragged progressively up a beach by shore based winches and cables. Very occasionally a dry dock was used, although they were usually too expensive to rent on a regular basis. Metal Industries needed to use the 850ft x 110ft (259m x 33.5m) dry docks at Rosyth to dismantle the German battleships salvaged at Scapa Flow, as they arrived upside down floating on a cushion of compressed air, with no inherent hull buoyancy to allow cutting up afloat.

The yard would then take stock of all the materials recovered, their weight and value to give a total sales value. After deducting costs of wages, gases, transport, and overheads plus any delivery costs, the profit (or loss) would be determined.

Depending on yard facilities and the scrap market, a small warship like a destroyer would take around three to four months to get 'out of the water', while a large warship could take as much as two years. During that time, a mix of ship and shore burners, riggers, crane-men, sorters, weighers, and labourers would be working on one or more of the ships alongside as well as ashore, supported by a small office and maintenance staff. A smaller yard might employ around thirty, a larger yard 200. There would usually be a core of well-paid experienced men, supplemented by more casual labour paid modest wages – although good burners could earn high bonuses.

Recycling sometimes provides the opportunity to acquire equipment that can be used on sister-ships that are still operational. When the six Australian *Oberon* class submarines began to reach the end of their lives, the first to go was *Oxley*, which was carefully dismantled to provide equipment and spare parts for her sisters. She was slipped at Henderson near Fremantle, and the parts removed and stored in a nearby shed in a very tidy operation. She is seen on 31 August 1992, viewed from her port side. *(Ian Buxton)*

This basic technique was used in European yards until the 1970s, and is still used in some Asian yards. A few new yards invested in purpose-built facilities with new concrete jetties and travelling cranes, which could handle several ships at once. But yards in countries new to shipbreaking such as Taiwan used beaching techniques with minimal facilities. Ships, usually merchant ships still capable of steaming, would be run up bows-first onto a gently sloping beach. The modest lifting equipment might be a few derricks and winches removed from cargo ships. The bow would be cut off first, usually in one large section which would be dragged up the beach for further cutting. Then work would progress aft, as the lightened hull was dragged further up the beach, until the last section was out of the water.

A broadly similar technique has been used in Turkey, which became a significant shipbreaking country in the 1980s. A mile-long length of beach at Aliaga has been divided into plots and leased out to some twenty shipbreakers. Some yards purchased crawler cranes and built concrete roadways. Reusable items could be separated from the sections and moved to storage. Non-ferrous items are sold to specialist companies who can extract the various metals. The hull steel is cut to smaller sizes and loaded into trucks for transport to nearby steelworks, with their electric arc furnaces. Asbestos and other hazardous materials are removed by specialist squads. By these means, a shipbreaker can finish a modest-sized cargo ship in a few weeks, although warships take longer as a result of their more complex compartmentalisation and on board equipment. However, demolition of *Invincible* by Leyal Gemi Sokum took only nine months, using about sixty men.[2]

In the United States, shipbreaking is now concentrated in Gulf of Mexico ports, particularly Brownsville near the Mexican border and, to a lesser extent, the New Orleans area. Brownsville is a man-made port with a 17-mile (27.3km) long entrance channel, on the sides of which commercial wharves and shipbreaking yards have been established. The latter have excavated 'slips' at an angle to the main channel, into which hulks can be placed, and progressively demolished from the bows aft. The yards are subject to demanding standards and frequent visits from regulatory bodies such as US Environmental Protection Agency to minimise the extent of any release of potentially hazardous materials and accidents to the workers – many of whom are new arrivals from Mexico. Until the health hazards of exposing men to asbestos dust and fibres was fully understood, asbestos insulation in engine and boiler rooms and in accommodation would be stripped by hand before being taken away for burying. Nowadays, compartments containing such material have to be sealed-off and asbestos removed (by specially trained workers wearing breathing apparatus), bagged, sealed and taken to approved landfill disposal sites.

Brownsville in Texas is the location of most of the United States shipbreaking yards. Yards have been laid out on each side of the long entrance channel from the Gulf of Mexico, with slips excavated to allow lightened hulks to be pulled up. On the north side (right) on 8 April 2014 is All Star Metals with the newly-arrived carrier *Forrestal* (CV-59) alongside. Further up that side is ESCO Marine, who will dismantle *Saratoga* (CV-60). Across the channel is Marine Metal, then International Shipbreaking Ltd with Baybridge (nearest). *(Bob Berry)*

Heavy oil fuel can still be found in tanks on board ships, which can spill into the water or soak into the beach if not carefully removed and processed. Today it is more common for such fuel to be removed from warships by the naval authorities before sale. United States yards are also more likely to employ special equipment like shredding or shearing machines to reduce the steel to smaller sizes than yards with lower wage costs.

Great efforts are made to recycle as much material as possible, with detailed returns made by the shipbreaker to the naval authority. Usually over 95 per cent of a ship's final displacement is recycled. But some material is unsaleable – working fluids in machinery systems, cement and tiles from sanitary facilities, plastic, concrete ballast and some insulating materials such as foam. Thus the 'outturn' is always less than the light displacement (empty ship). The British DSA publishes reports of recycling some of its warships, including *Fearless*, *Invincible* and Type 42 destroyers – the latter's outturn summarised in Table 4.3.1.

DISPOSING OF NUCLEAR SUBMARINES

As might be expected, much more elaborate methods are required in disposing of nuclear powered submarines. The US Navy has remained in total charge of the inactivation, disposal and recycling process of both nuclear reactors and hulls. The work is done at Puget Sound Naval Shipyard, Bremerton. The reactor core is first removed in dry dock by a process similar to that when cores are renewed. The submarine is then placed in a (larger) dry dock, often with three others. Batteries, lead ballast and re-usable

Table 4.3.1: RECYCLING TYPE 42 DESTROYERS *SOUTHAMPTON*, *EXETER* AND *NOTTINGHAM* AT LEYAL, ALIAGA 2011–12

MATERIAL	AVERAGE TONNES
Steel	2,288
Non-ferrous metals	128
Other saleable products	34
Waste	70
Total	**2,520**

Notes:

1 79 tonnes was pig iron and lead ballast.

2 This information was taken from *Recycling of Type 42 Destroyers Exeter D89, Southampton D90, Nottingham D91* (Bicester, DE&S, UK MOD, 2013) at https://www.gov.uk/government/publications/type-42-destroyers-exeter-southampton-and-nottingham-recycling.

As well as overhauling US Navy warships, Puget Sound Naval Shipyard at Bremerton near Seattle is also used to berth inactivated warships including aircraft carriers and submarines. It is the only site in the US where redundant nuclear-propelled vessels can be dismantled. Submarines are first defueled, then their reactor compartments are cut out of the hull in dry dock for burial in a trench at Hanford, Washington State. Seen at Bremerton on 12 September 1995 awaiting recycling are (left of the pier) the guided-missile cruiser *Texas* (CGN-39) with *Triton* (SSN-586) outboard, right of pier *Sculpin* (SSN-590), *George Washington* (SSBN-598), *Dace* (SSN-607), *Skipjack* (SSN-585), *Snook* (SSN-592) and *Patrick Henry* (SSBN-559). The last five already had their reactor and missile compartments removed but were not finally demolished until 1998. *(Ian Buxton)*

equipment are removed. The reactor compartment is cut out of the hull still within its surrounding pressure hull and its ends sealed with additional bulkheads. The cylindrical section is transferred onto a barge alongside in the dry dock. The refloated barge is then towed up the Columbia River to be buried in a deep trench at Hanford, Washington State. For early ballistic missile submarines (SSBN), the missile compartment was also removed, and the forward and after halves of the truncated boat re-joined for storage afloat until the time for final disposal. Today the whole process is done in one operation. The remaining parts of the hull, now with no nuclear contamination, are recycled in the conventional way. The yield from a typical nuclear attack submarine is set out in Table 4.3.2:

Table 4.3.2: US NAVY NUCLEAR-POWERED ATTACK SUBMARINE (SSN) RECYCLING

MATERIAL	WEIGHT '000lb
HY-80 pressure hull steel	2,500
Other steel	738
Aluminium	85
Non-ferrous metals	497
Lead ballast, up to	1,800
Total (2,550 tonnes)	**5,620**

Notes:

1 This information was taken from *US Naval Nuclear Powered Ship Inactivation, Disposal and Recycling* (Washington DC, United States Department of the Navy, April 2008)

Between 1991 and 2007, 103 submarines had been handled in this way at Bremerton. A broadly similar process has been used for nuclear-propelled guided-missile cruisers (CGNs). These have two reactors within the hull, which have to be transferred into newly-built steel containment compartments before transfer to Hanford. Seven CGNs had been so handled up to 2007.

The French Navy has developed its own process. Redundant nuclear submarines are inactivated at Cherbourg, where the reactor core is removed. The hull is then drawn up on land, where the reactor compartment, 7m long and weighing 700 tonnes, is cut out. It is then moved on trailers to earthquake proof land storage at nearby Homet. The two remaining parts of the hull are re-joined and put back into the water. They will be recycled in France, using conventional techniques, at a future date. The *Redoubtable* class SSBNs are the first to undergo this process and will be followed by the *Rubis* class attack submarines as the latter decommission.[3]

The United Kingdom has yet to implement a final disposal strategy for its redundant nuclear-powered submarines. Reactor cores have already been removed, but the otherwise complete vessels remain laid up at Rosyth and Devonport.

The former Soviet Union appears to have had a less responsible strategy for its submarines. Many have been hulked in the Murmansk area, and two have sunk at sea nearby. Some dismantling has been done at the Nerpa shipyard. The neighbouring Norwegians are concerned about the potential hazards and have made funds available to help dispose of such vessels in a safer manner.

Notes:

1. See the author's *Metal Industries: Shipbreaking at Rosyth and Charlestown* (Kendal, World Ship Society, 1992).

2. The overall recycling process was described in *Recycling of ex-HMS Invincible* (Bicester, DE&S, UK MOD, 2013). An online copy can currently be accessed at the following web link: https://www.gov.uk/government/publications/recycling-of-hms-invincible

3. For further reading, please refer to the ever-informative *Mer et Marine* website at http://www.meretmarine.com/fr/content/ou-en-est-le-demantelement-des-anciens-snle-francias

Contributors

Ian L Buxton, BSc, PhD, CEng, FRINA is a naval architect who was Reader in Marine Transport in the School of Marine Science and Technology at the University of Newcastle upon Tyne from 1974–2002. He continues to lecture, and is President of the World Ship Society. He graduated in naval architecture from Glasgow University, concurrently serving his apprenticeship with Denny of Dumbarton. Following work on computer applications in shipbuilding, he moved to the British Ship Research Association in London and Wallsend, concerned with computer-aided design and techno-economic analysis of commercial ships. Interests include warships, shipping, shipbuilding and shipbreaking, resulting in many journal articles. *Big Gun Monitors* was published in 1978 with a second edition in 2008. *The Battleship Builders* was published in 2013 with Ian Johnston. The British Shipbuilding Database has been a focus of research in recent years. He continues to devote time to the Marine Technology Special Collection at Newcastle University.

Norman Friedman is one of the best-known naval analysts and historians in the US and the author of over thirty-five books. He has written on broad issues of modern military interest, including an award-winning history of the Cold War, whilst in the field of warship development his greatest sustained achievement is probably an eight-volume series on the design of different US warship types. A specialist in the intersection of technology and national strategy, his acclaimed *Network-Centric Warfare* was published in 2009 by the US Naval Institute Press. The holder of a PhD in theoretical physics from Columbia, Dr Friedman is a regular guest commentator on television and lectures widely on professional defence issues. He is a resident of New York.

David Hobbs is a well-known author and naval historian. He has written sixteen books and co-authored eight more. He writes for several journals and magazines and in 2005 won the Aerospace Journalist of the Year, Best Defence Submission. He lectures on naval subjects worldwide and has been on radio and TV in several countries. He served in the Royal Navy from 1964 until 1997, retiring with the rank of Commander. He qualified as both a fixed and rotary wing pilot. His log book contains 2,300 hours with over 800 carrier landings, 150 of which were at night.

John Jordan is a former languages teacher. He wrote about the post-war Soviet Navy in the late 1970s and authored two major books on the subject. He subsequently turned his attention to the inter-war *Marine Nationale*, producing a series of articles for *Warship*, taking over from Antony Preston as editor in 2005. His first major book for Seaforth was *French Battleships 1922–1956*, which was co-authored with Robert Dumas and published in 2009; a sequel, *French Cruisers 1922–1956*, with Jean Moulin, followed in 2013. John Jordan also contributed the chapter on the French Navy to *On Seas Contested* (USNIP, 2010), and a book about the impact of the Washington Treaty of 1922 on the major fleets, *Warships After Washington*, was published by Seaforth in late 2011.

Mrityunjoy Mazumdar, whose father served in the Indian Navy, has been writing on naval matters since 1999. His words and pictures have appeared in many naval and aircraft publications including several of the *Jane's* family, *Ships of the World* and the Royal Institute of Naval Architects' *Warship Technology*. He is also a regular contributor to several naval annuals including *Combat Fleets of the World, Flotes des Combat, Jane's Fighting Ships, Seaforth World Naval Review* and *Weyers Flotten Taschenbuch*. Besides his writing, he maintains a comprehensive website on the Indian Navy at www.bharat-rakshak.com. Mr. Mazumdar lives in Alameda, California with his wife.

Jean Moulin did his national service in the *Marine Nationale*, and worked as an IT technician until his retirement in 2000. He has written widely on the French Navy, and is the author of monographs on the light cruisers of the *La Galissonnière* class (Marines éditions, 1995) and the treaty cruiser *Algérie* (Marines, 1999). Books on the *contre-torpilleurs* of the *Guépard* and *Aigle* classes, also published by Marines éditions, followed in 2010 and 2012 respectively. Jean was the co-author, with John Jordan, of *French Cruisers 1922–1956* (Seaforth, 2013). He has contributed articles to the French-language periodical *Marines et Forces Navales*, and wrote the chapter on the French Navy for *To Crown the Waves* (USNIP, 2013).

Guy Toremans is a Belgian-based, maritime freelance correspondent and a member of the Association of Belgian & Foreign Journalists, an association accredited by NATO and the UN. His reports, ship profiles and interviews are published in the English-language naval magazines *Jane's Navy International*, *Naval Forces* and *Warships IFR*, as well as in the French *Marines & Forces Navales* and the Japanese *J-Ships*. Since 1990, he has regularly embarked on NATO, Asian, South African and Pacific-based warships, including aircraft carriers, destroyers, frigates, mine-countermeasures vessels and support ships.

Dr Scott C Truver is Director, Team Blue, at Gryphon Technologies LC, specialising in national and homeland security, and naval and maritime strategies, programmes and operations. Since 1972 Dr Truver has participated in numerous studies and assessments – most notably supporting the inter-agency task force drafting the US *National Strategy for Maritime Security* (2005) – and has also written extensively for US and foreign publications. He has lectured at the US Naval Academy, Naval War College and Naval Postgraduate School, among other venues. His further qualifications include a Doctor of Philosophy degree in Marine Policy Studies and a MA in Political Science/International Relations from the University of Delaware.

Conrad Waters is a lawyer by training but a banker by profession. Educated at Liverpool University prior to being called to the bar at Gray's Inn in 1989, his interest in maritime affairs was stimulated by a long family history of officers in merchant navy service. He has been writing articles on historical and current naval affairs for over twenty years. This included six years producing the 'World Navies in Review' chapter of the influential annual *Warship* before assuming responsibility for *Seaforth World Naval Review* as founding editor. Managing Director for Credit Sanctioning at the European arm of one of the world's largest banks, he lives with wife and family in Haslemere, Surrey.

A,